Collins

Cambridge IGCSE™

Design & Technology

Also for Cambridge IGCSE™ (9-1)

Student's Book

Dawne Irving-Bell
Gary England
Sarah Finnigan
Matt McLain
Stewart Ross
David Wooff

Series editor: Stewart Ross

William Collins' dream of knowledge for all began with the publication of his first book in 1819.

A self-educated mill worker, he not only enriched millions of lives, but also founded a flourishing publishing house. Today, staying true to this spirit, Collins books are packed with inspiration, innovation and practical expertise.

They place you at the centre of a world of possibility and give you exactly what you need to explore it.

Published by Collins
An imprint of HarperCollins*Publishers*
The News Building, 1 London Bridge Street, London,
SE1 9GF, UK

HarperCollins*Publishers*
Macken House, 39/40 Mayor Street Upper, Dublin 1,
D01 C9W8, Ireland

Browse the complete Collins catalogue at
collins.co.uk

10 9 8 7 6 5 4 3 2 1

ISBN 978-0-00-878087-6

British Library Cataloguing-in-Publication Data

A catalogue record for this publication is available from the British Library.

Authors: Dawne Irving-Bell, Gary England, Sarah Finnigan, Matt McLain, Stewart Ross, David Wooff; with thanks to Justin Harris and Chris Hughes for their work on previous editions
Series editor: Stewart Ross
Publisher: Catherine Martin
Product manager: Saaleh Patel
Development editor: Lucy Hyde
Copyeditor: Carolyn Anderson
Proofreaders: Haremi LTD
Cover designer: Kevin Robbins and James Hunter
Cover pattern: James Hunter
Typesetter and illustrator: York Publishing Solutions Limited
Production controller: Alhady Ali
Printed and bound in the UK by Martins the Printers

MIX
Paper | Supporting responsible forestry
FSC www.fsc.org FSC™ C013254

Endorsement indicates that a resource has passed Cambridge International Education's rigorous quality-assurance process and is suitable to support the delivery of their syllabus. However, endorsed resources are not the only suitable materials available to support teaching and learning, and are not essential to achieve the qualification. For the full list of endorsed resources to support this syllabus,
visit www.cambridgeinternational.org/endorsed-resources

Any example answers to questions taken from past question papers, practice questions, accompanying marks and mark schemes included in this resource have been written by the authors and are for guidance only. They do not replicate examination papers. In examinations the way marks are awarded may be different. Any references to assessment and/or assessment preparation are the publisher's interpretation of the syllabus requirements. Examiners will not use endorsed resources as a source of material for any assessment set by Cambridge International Education.

While the publishers have made every attempt to ensure that advice on the qualification and its assessment is accurate, the official syllabus, specimen assessment materials and any associated assessment guidance materials produced by the awarding body are the only authoritative source of information and should always be referred to for definitive guidance.

Our approach is to provide teachers with access to a wide range of high-quality resources that suit different styles and types of teaching and learning.

For more information about the endorsement process, please visit www.cambridgeinternational.org/endorsed-resources

Contents

Introduction

Your Cambridge IGCSE™ Design & Technology course

Design & Technology has many applications for everyday life. For example, the design process requires problem solving skills that can be applied to any problem you encounter. Design & Technology is a very 'real world' subject – everything made around you has been designed, from the chairs you sit on to the pens and pencils you write with. As you learn about the topics in this book, try to relate them to the products, materials and systems you see and use on a daily basis. Looking closely at familiar, everyday products in this way will not only help you to develop your Design & Technology skills, but will also make the course more interesting and enjoyable.

After working through the contents of this book, you will have a good understanding of the principles of Product Design, which is a core part of this course. You will also study either the Materials option or the Graphic Products option in more depth as a specialism.

The book is organised into the following sections:

Section 1: Product Design	This section examines the role of the designer and how to develop designs that consider influences such as user needs, society and different cultures, sustainability and the impact of design on markets. You will learn about designing and making principles, and how to effectively communicate your design ideas. You will also learn about structures, mechanisms and electronics, and how these technological areas can be linked together to design controllable systems.
Section 2: Materials	This section looks at a broad range of materials, techniques, tools, equipment, methods and processes. Studying this section will help you to develop your understanding of both the physical and working properties of a range of woods, metals and polymers, as well as smart, modern and alternative materials. You will analyse real-world products and learn about different manufacturing methods.
Section 3: Graphic Products	This section focuses on graphic products, including how to communicate your ideas effectively. Studying this section will help you develop a number of techniques, from improving your formal drawing skills and understanding the importance of modelling prototypes, to using technology to develop and present ideas quickly and easily.
Section 4: The Project	This section gives advice on how to go about project work during your course. Project work allows you to explore materials, be creative, apply critical thinking, analyse and produce an outcome to solve a problem. You will learn about different project management techniques and how to produce a portfolio of work to demonstrate the design process you have followed.

Your assessment

The information in this section is based on the Cambridge International Education syllabus. You should always refer to the appropriate syllabus document for the year of examination to confirm the details and for more information. The syllabus document is available on the website: www.cambridgeinternational.org.

Throughout the course you will be required to demonstrate **knowledge and understanding** of the theories and techniques, facts, terms and concepts included in common content (Product Design) as well as your chosen option (Materials or Graphic Products). You will also need to demonstrate a wider **application** of Design & Technology strategies **and design** communication skills. You should be able to show **development and realisation** of design proposals and solutions, as well as **analysis and evaluation** of products in terms of their design and production.

Assessment objective	You should be able to:
AO1 Knowledge and understanding	• demonstrate knowledge and understanding of: o iterative design principles o a range of materials, processes, tools and equipment used in design and technology o methods of communication used in design and technology o the interaction between design and society.
AO2 Application and design communication	• apply knowledge and understanding to a variety of design problems • use research skills to develop a design brief and design specification • use different design strategies to generate design proposals • apply design communication skills to explore and communicate ideas.
AO3 Development and realisation	• use modelling to make and test design proposals • develop design proposals, taking responsible design into consideration • develop design solutions, using working knowledge of materials • realise design solutions, using appropriate materials and practical processes • use safe working practices when making models and products.
AO4 Analysis and evaluation	• analyse, test and evaluate products made by yourself and others • identify and propose how to improve or modify products • analyse and evaluate the needs of the user in relation to the design problem and justify design decisions • assess the impact of design and products in relation to design responsibility.

∆ **Table 1** Assessment objectives

You will take two written examination papers and will complete an individual project.

Assessment component	Marks available	Proportion of overall grade	Length of examination
Paper 1 (Product Design)	50	25%	1 hour
Component 2 (Project)	100	50%	n/a
Paper 3 (Materials) OR Paper 4 (Graphic Products)	50	25%	1 hour

△ **Table 2** Assessment components

Your individual project forms a significant part of the course. You will decide on the project area you want to focus on with advice from your teacher. You will produce both a portfolio of work and a final product. The made product itself is not submitted.

How to use this book

This book has useful features that have been designed to help you understand all the aspects of Design & Technology that you will need to know for this syllabus.

We hope you enjoy the course and that you find this book a useful and valuable companion on your Design & Technology journey of discovery. Good luck!

A brief introduction gives context to the design and technology area covered in the section.

Starting points will help you to revise previous learning and see what you already know about the ideas in the section.

Section contents shows the topics of the syllabus covered in the section.

Learning aims cover what you need to learn in each unit.

Top tips include practical advice on how to develop key skills.

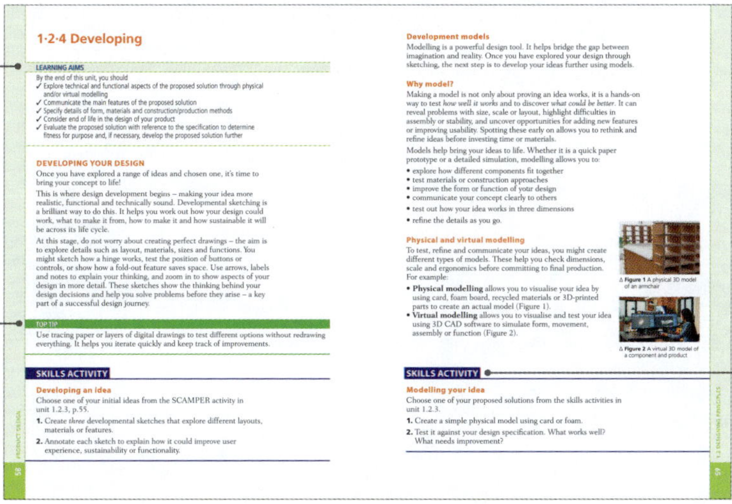

You can develop the skills you need to succeed by doing the **Skills activity** tasks.

Each unit concludes with **Knowledge check** questions that test your understanding of the main concepts you have learned.

Key terms boxes explain technical or difficult terms. These words are in bold in the main text when first used, are listed at the end of each subsection and are also found in the Glossary at the back of the book. Definitions marked with an asterisk (*) are also listed in the Glossary section of the syllabus.

Design in action case studies provide inspiring real-life examples of Design & Technology in action. In some cases, these case studies may extend beyond the requirements of the syllabus.

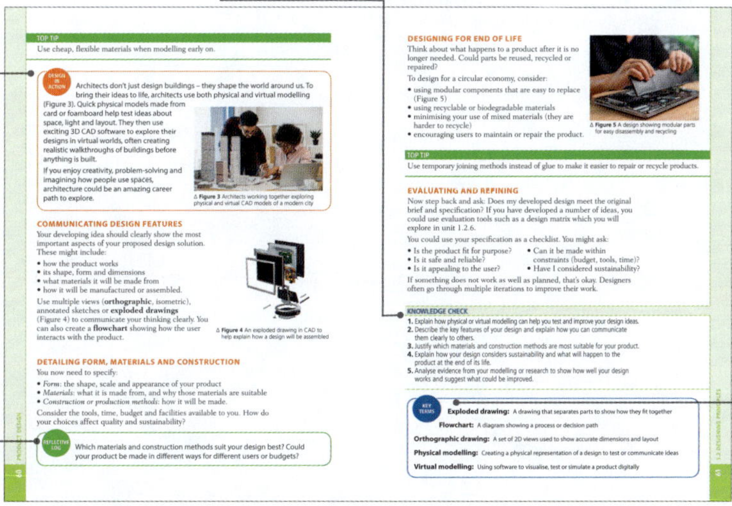

Reflective logs encourage you to look back over what you have learned and consider whether there is anything you could do differently or should re-visit.

Practice questions provide a checkpoint for your learning and help you prepare for your exams.

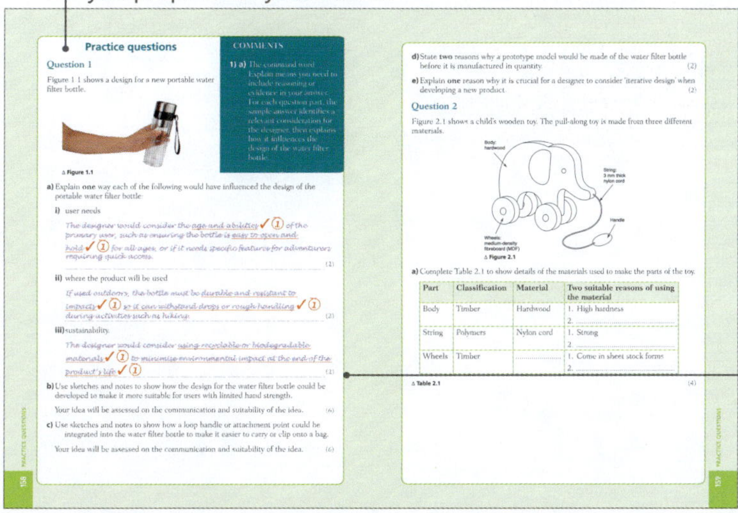

Sample answers and comments have been written by the authors to illustrate a possible response and show where it answers the question with the level of detail required or how it could be improved. Practice questions and sample answers have been written by the authors. In examinations, the way marks are awarded may be different.

Look around you. Every product you see – from your phone to the chair you are sitting on – started as an idea. Product design is the process of turning those ideas into real, useful products. It is not only about appearance; it combines science, art, engineering, systems and control, and technology to solve problems and improve everyday life.

So, how do designers turn a spark of an idea into a real product? They follow a systematic journey: *identifying* the problem or challenge; *defining* what users, society and the environment really need; then *developing* imaginative solutions. This is followed by careful *planning* to consider every detail before *testing and evaluating* to ensure the product is ready for use.

Good design also considers impact: how products affect users, communities and the environment. Along the way, designers communicate ideas through sketches, models and digital tools, before moving into practical making – measuring, shaping, joining and finishing materials with accuracy. Understanding materials and how they behave is just as important as planning how the product's systems and control elements will function.

This section is a core element of your Cambridge IGCSE™ Design & Technology course. Get ready to delve into the fascinating world of product design, uncovering the systematic steps and vital skills you need to find problems and create solutions.

STARTING POINTS

- How does a design affect the user experience?
- What are the societal impacts of new products?
- How can designers make sure their products are environmentally friendly?
- What market trends make a product successful?
- How do designers identify and solve design problems?
- What methods do designers use to develop and plan their solutions?
- How can designers use systems and control to make their products smarter?
- Why is testing and evaluating designs so important?

SECTION CONTENTS

1 Product design

1·1 Influences on designing

Designers need to think about many different factors when creating a new product.

A successful design does not just look good – it meets **user needs**, works safely and reliably, and considers its impact on the environment and society.

There are many reasons why new products are designed and manufactured. Design and Technology can play an important role as a **STEAM** subject to help develop solutions to global problems. A successful product can also help companies make money. Designers develop new **design solutions** and improve existing products to make people's lives better.

In this section, you will learn about the key influences on designing.

KEY TERMS

Design solution: A design idea or development of an idea that meets the required needs. This can be a drawn design, a prototype or an existing product*

Needs: The problems or opportunities that drive a design

STEAM: Science, Technology, Engineering, Arts and Mathematics, working together in design

User: The person who will use the product

1·1·1 Influences on designing – the user

LEARNING AIMS

By the end of this unit, you should:

- ✓ Understand how user needs influence the design of a product
- ✓ Understand how the environment where a product is used affects its design
- ✓ Understand how anthropometrics and ergonomics help create comfortable and suitable products
- ✓ Understand the importance of designing inclusive products that suit a wide range of users

USER NEEDS

Every product that is designed and manufactured must solve a real problem. These problems could be difficulties faced by a specific user or part of a larger global issue. Identifying a suitable problem is the first step to creating a **sustainable design** solution.

Understanding the needs of other people is crucial. It will help you develop potential solutions to their problem(s).

Before you start sketching, think about:

- Who will use the product?
- What do they need?
- Is this a new or evolving problem?
- Are there products already on the market that do not solve the user's problem(s)?
- Who will buy it? (The **client** might be different from the user.)

Products for children, adults, athletes, or people with disabilities all need different features (Figure 1).

△ **Figure 1** Lego® figures representing a range of ages, cultures and physical abilities

Things you could consider include:

- age, size, abilities and interests
- daily activities and challenges
- special requirements, such as wheelchair access or limited hand strength.

In some industries, large companies use data to create new products based on what they know about people's buying habits, online activity and lifestyle. They can gather this information by tracking phone or computer usage. For example, by looking at what you buy, the websites you visit and your interests, companies can design products that appeal to you specifically. While this helps companies create products that people want, it also raises important questions about privacy and how much information should be shared.

When working on your own projects, designing products for real clients you know can make a big difference. You will be able to get regular feedback from them, which helps you adjust and improve your design as you go along. This process means your final product will be much better and more suited to the client's needs.

Designing and developing ideas by constantly checking and improving them with feedback from a client is called the **iterative design** process. You might have heard of '**iterations**' – these are the different versions or changes you make to your design as you go. It is all about working in stages and improving your design each time based on feedback.

WHERE THE PRODUCT WILL BE USED

Imagine designing a product for use in the depths of the ocean. You would need to consider water resistance, pressure and user functionality in extreme conditions. Compare that to a product designed for use in a busy office where comfort and quietness are essential, such as an office chair. These are two very different environments that need very different design considerations.

The 'physical environment' refers to where the product will be used. Different environments require different properties in the final product. This directly affects its design. A product's location or intended use also influence the choice of materials and how the product is constructed. For example:

- A swimming pool ladder must be rust-resistant, strong enough to support weight and safe to use in wet conditions.
- A trolley suitcase for travel needs to be durable, lightweight and have smooth wheels for easy transport.
- A backpack for a mountain hiker must be waterproof, durable and able to handle rough conditions (Figure 2).

△ **Figure 2** A mountain hiker wears a modern, waterproof backpack.

When designing a product, always ask yourself:

- Is it for indoor or outdoor use? Or both?
- Is it likely to get wet?
- Does it need to be portable?
- Will it face extreme weather, chemicals or rough handling?

Asking yourself questions like these will help you decide what features your design must have to perform well in the intended environment.

SKILLS ACTIVITY

Mind map: Identifying environments and their implications

Create a mind map to explore different environments where products might be used – for example, outdoors, kitchen, hospital, office.

1. Place 'Environment' in the middle of the mind map. Use **one colour for the primary branches**, which represent different **environments** (for example, garden, underwater, kitchen, space).
2. Then, use a **separate colour** for the **design implications** that come from each environment, such as what materials or features are needed for the product to work well in that environment. For example, if the product is used outdoors, branch out to ideas such as 'must be waterproof', 'must withstand heat/cold' and 'durable for rough handling'.

This activity will help you understand how to adapt your designs to suit different environments and their specific challenges.

TOP TIP

Consider the specific conditions a product will face (for example, extreme temperatures, humidity, outdoor exposure) to select appropriate materials and finishes for durability.

ANTHROPOMETRICS AND ERGONOMICS

When designers create new products, they need to think about how people will actually use them. This means considering how products fit and work for different users. There are two key factors that help make a product comfortable and efficient: **ergonomics** and **anthropometrics**.

Ergonomics

Ergonomics is the study of how people interact with products and systems. It focuses on making things comfortable to hold, wear or use, and helping people avoid strain or injury. For example, holding a badly designed phone for too long might make your hand ache.

Designers use ergonomics to make sure products suit real people. Because users come in all shapes and sizes, there are a few different strategies designers can use:

- Different sizes – for example, small, medium and large bike helmets.
- Anthropometric data to find measurements that work for most users.
- Adjustable features such as office chairs or car seats that can be moved and tilted (Figure 3).

By thinking about ergonomics from the start, designers can create products that are safe, comfortable and enjoyable to use.

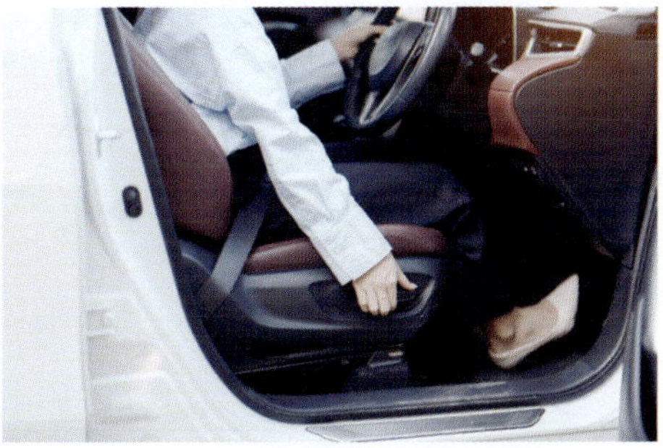

△ **Figure 3** A driver adjusts the seating configuration to allow correct posture and reach.

Anthropometrics

Anthropometrics is the study of human sizes and measurements and how they relate to products. It is about understanding how to create designs that fit most users. You have probably sat at a desk where the chair was too small or too big, and it made working uncomfortable (Figure 4). That is because the design did not fit your body size properly.

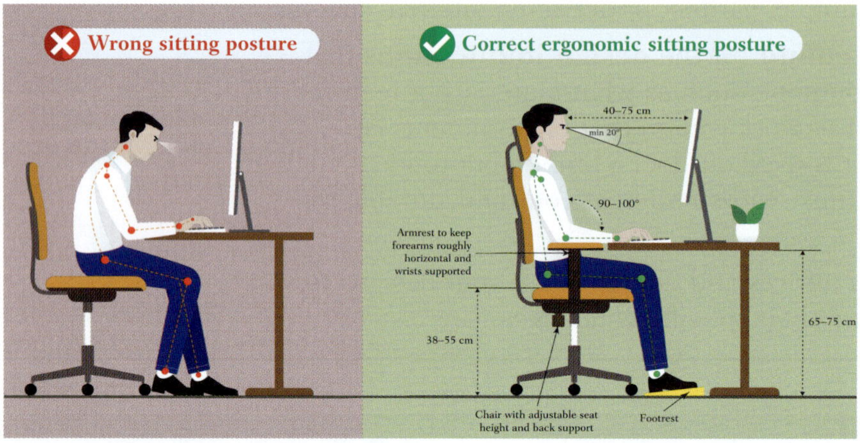

△ **Figure 4** An example of using anthropometric data to set up an office chair correctly

Now, imagine being part of the crew on a submarine. Imagine there is an emergency – and it's time to use the escape hatch. The hatch has been designed with the 50th percentile (average-sized) person in mind. When you try to get through, you struggle. You are either too tall or too short for the average size. If you are taller, you might find your shoulders or head hitting the sides. If you are shorter, you might have to stretch to reach the hatch handle.

When products are designed only for the average person (the 50th percentile), they will not fit everyone well. There are people smaller, and larger, than the average. If you design only for the middle group, other people could be left out or face discomfort.

To ensure that a product is comfortable and usable for as many people as possible, designers aim to design for the 5th to 95th percentile (Figure 5). This approach helps create products that can accommodate a wide range of users, from the shortest to the tallest, and from the narrowest to the broadest.

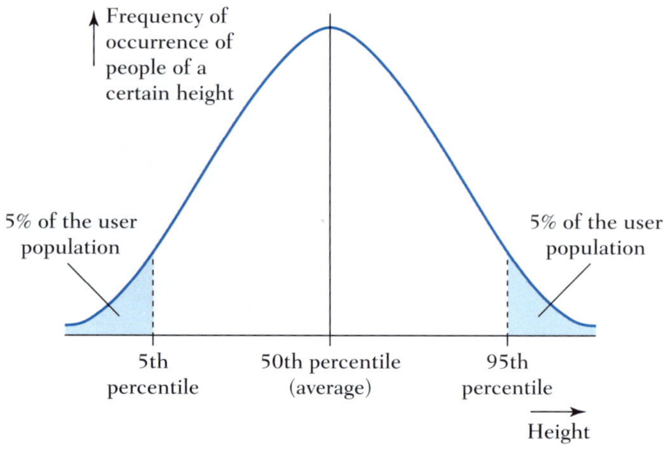

◁ **Figure 5** A normal distribution graph highlighting the 5th and 95th percentile range

TOP TIP

When designing, use anthropometric data for the 5th to 95th percentile of your target users (not the average), to ensure maximum comfort and usability for a diverse group.

SKILLS ACTIVITY

Create your own ergonomics chart

Choose an everyday product, such as a chair, desk or backpack. Use a simple chart to map out the typical height, width or size of users who might use that product. Think about whether the product would fit most people, or if it needs adjustments for different body sizes. Then consider if your design would be comfortable for both the smaller and larger end of the user population.

INCLUSIVITY

Inclusive design ensures that products are made to be accessible and usable by as many people as possible, regardless of their age, size or ability. This **inclusivity** is especially important in making sure that people with disabilities, the elderly and children can all interact with products in everyday situations. Designing inclusively means considering the needs of a wide range of users to ensure that products are practical, functional and enjoyable for everyone.

What makes a design inclusive?

The focus is on making products accessible to a broad group of users. An inclusive design targets usability for people with disabilities, older adults, children and anyone with different physical or cognitive abilities. For example, a can opener can be designed to be easier to use by people with limited hand strength, such as those suffering from arthritis.

Key features of inclusive design

- *Ergonomics:* Making sure the product is comfortable and easy to use for a wide range of people.
- *Adjustability:* Allowing users to modify the product to fit their needs, such as adjustable grips or handles.
- *Easy operation:* Ensuring that the product can be operated without excessive strength or dexterity.
- *Consideration for different needs:* Factoring in the needs of people with physical, cognitive or sensory limitations.

Why inclusive design matters

- Inclusive design helps ensure products are usable by everyone, making them accessible to a larger group of people.
- It creates a better overall user experience by reducing frustration for those with diverse needs.
- It increases market reach by designing for a wider audience, making products more appealing and practical for various users.

User testing

Engaging real users, especially those from diverse backgrounds and with different needs, is essential to improving the design. More inclusive feedback leads to a better and more accessible final product.

SKILLS ACTIVITY

Design a game controller for inclusivity

Imagine you have been asked to design a game controller that can be comfortably used by all players, including those with limited hand strength or mobility.

Think about the following:

- How could you adjust the controller's shape and buttons for smaller hands or for users with physical limitations?
- Could customisable features such as button remapping or different grip options improve usability?
- What could you do to ensure the controller is accessible and easy to use by everyone?

Sketch your design. Explain how each choice you made helps make the controller more inclusive for all players.

KEY TERMS

Anthropometrics: The study of measurements and data of the human body that is used in designing products and systems*

Client: The person who has asked for the product or is paying for it. Sometimes the user and the client are the same, but not always

Ergonomics: The study of people and their working conditions to improve user experience with a product or system*

Inclusivity: Producing designs, or modified designs, that are suitable for all users*

Iteration: A cyclic process of prototyping, testing, analysing, and refining a product or process, where each version is improved based on feedback and evaluation*

Iterative design: A way of designing where you test, improve and repeat changes based on feedback

Sustainable design: Creating products that solve real problems while considering long-term impacts on people and the planet

KNOWLEDGE CHECK

1. Explain how inclusive design can improve both a product and the user experience.
2. Suggest features that could be added to a kitchen tool, such as a can opener, to support users with limited hand strength.

1·1·2 Influences on designing – society

LEARNING AIMS

By the end of this unit, you should:

✓ Understand why safety must always be considered when designing
✓ Understand why legal requirements must be followed when creating products
✓ Understand how society and different cultures influence design decisions

SAFETY

Safety is one of the most important aspects of designing any product. The goal is for products to be useful and effective, while also keeping users safe. A product that is dangerous to use defeats its purpose.

Designing for safety means identifying potential **risks** early on and removing them before the product is made. There are some key considerations when it comes to safety in design.

Sharp edges

Sharp edges can cause cuts or scrapes, making a product uncomfortable or unsafe to use. Designers must ensure that any edges are smooth and rounded. For example, think about a kitchen knife – while it has a sharp blade, the handle and other parts of the design are rounded to make it safe to grip. When designing a product, always ask yourself: 'Could this edge harm someone?'

Toxic materials

Some materials can be harmful if touched or inhaled, especially when they are used in products that people use daily. It is important to make sure the materials you use are safe for people, especially in children's toys and food containers. Toxic materials might include certain plastics or metals that can release harmful substances. For example, if you designed a water bottle using a plastic that releases dangerous chemicals when heated, that would create a safety issue. Always make sure your materials are non-toxic and safe for their intended use.

Moving parts

Products with moving parts, such as a fan or a toy with wheels, can be great, but they also come with safety risks. Moving parts need to be designed so they cannot hurt people. For example, a toy with small moving parts that a child could get their finger stuck in is a **hazard**. Moving parts should be shielded or out of reach to avoid injury (Figure 1).

Electrical hazards

When working with electrical products, safety is even more critical. Exposed wires or faulty connections can cause electric shocks or even fires. To avoid these risks, designers make sure all wiring is properly insulated, and all electrical components are securely enclosed. For example, a hairdryer charger might have a design that protects the plug from water damage and ensures the wires are shielded, reducing the risk of electrical hazards.

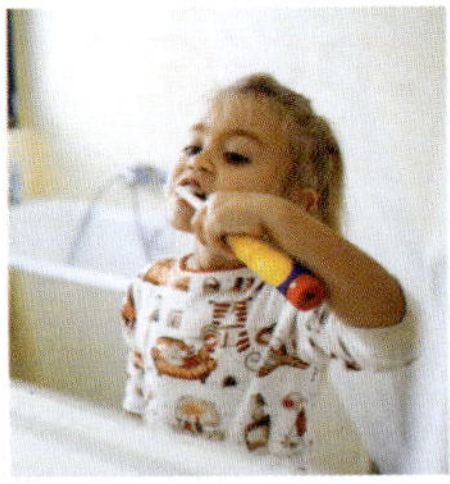

◁ **Figure 1** In an electric toothbrush, the rotating brush head is safely enclosed to avoid harm.

Designing for safety: Identifying risks

In a good design, the designer has identified risks before the product is even made. A designer is a problem-solver: they look for potential hazards – such as sharp edges or exposed electrical wires – and fix them in the design phase. This is why **testing** is so important: it helps you identify any overlooked safety issues that might not be obvious at first. For example:

- In an electric toothbrush, the rotating brush head is designed to be safe for use, with no exposed moving parts that could cause injury. The charger is designed to keep electrical components safe from water, ensuring no electrical hazards.
- A well-designed baby car seat ensures the safety of infants during travel by providing secure straps, impact protection and side shields to absorb force (Figure 2). These features protect babies from injury in the event of an accident.
- The blades in a food blender are hidden inside the device to prevent anyone from accidentally touching them. The motor is also protected to prevent electrical hazards.

△ **Figure 2** A young child being safely fastened into a well-fitting car safety seat

Many safety features link back to choosing the right **dimensions** (see 1.1.1 on anthropometrics). Designers use body measurements to make sure products not only feel right but are also safe to use. As a student designer, you can do the same.

Imagine designing a virtual reality (VR) headset – if the straps are too tight or the padding is in the wrong place, it could be uncomfortable or even cause injury. Or think about a bike helmet – if it does not fit properly, it will not protect your head in an accident. Getting the size and shape right is not just about comfort – it helps keep people safe while they use your product.

DESIGN IN ACTION

Childproof safety caps

Childproof medicine bottles are designed with special caps that are hard for children to open, but easy for adults.

In the 1960s, Dr Henri Breault saw a serious problem – young children were accidentally opening medicine bottles and getting poisoned. As a paediatrician, he was often treating emergencies where children had swallowed pills such as aspirin. Even though health warnings were given, accidents kept happening.

Dr Breault realised something needed to change. Instead of just telling people to be careful, he worked on a design solution: a special bottle cap that young children could not easily open. In 1967, he teamed up with an engineer to invent the 'Palm-N'-Turn' safety cap. To open it, you have to push down and twist at the same time (Figure 3) – something that small children cannot do.

The design worked brilliantly. In Dr Breault's local area, child-poisoning cases dropped by over 90 per cent. By 1974, this clever safety cap became a legal requirement on medicine bottles in Ontario, Canada, and eventually across North America. It is now a standard feature on all medicine bottles that has saved countless lives.

This is a powerful example of how thoughtful design can solve real-life problems and protect people – especially those most at risk.

△ **Figure 3** A Palm-N'-Turn childproof cap on a medicine bottle

LEGAL REQUIREMENTS

When you are designing products, it is not just about creativity – you also have to abide by the rules. There are many laws and standards that affect what you can (and cannot) do as a designer. These rules help make sure that products are safe, of good quality and are kind to the environment.

Ignoring the legal requirements can cause big problems for companies – and put users in danger. So, it is very important to understand how the law influences designing.

Safety first!

Have you noticed the tiny 'CE' mark on a phone charger, toy or even a pair of headphones (Figure 4a)? That small symbol stands for *Conformité Européenne,* which means 'European Conformity'. It shows that the product meets essential health, safety and environmental protection standards for sale in the European Economic Area (EEA).

In other parts of the world, products may carry different marks to show they meet local rules. For example, in China, products often carry the 'CCC' mark (China Compulsory Certificate) to show they meet Chinese **safety standards** (Figure 4b).

a b

△ **Figure 4** Safety and quality logos for products manufactured or sold in **a** the EEA and **b** China

TOP TIP

If a product is not safe, it is not just badly designed – it is illegal.

Protecting the planet

There are also laws to protect the environment. For example, recycling symbols and labelling laws tell people how to dispose of products responsibly. Designers need to make sure materials are labelled clearly and that products are made in ways that are energy-efficient and sustainable. Not following these rules can mean huge fines for companies – and it can seriously damage a brand's reputation.

Respecting original ideas

In design, ideas are valuable. That is why there are copyright, patent and **intellectual property (IP)** laws. These protect original designs, logos, inventions and creative work. If someone copies a design without permission, it is called **infringement**, which can lead to expensive legal battles.

Good designers always check that they are not accidentally copying someone else's work. They also register their own designs to protect them (Figure 5).

Table 1 shows some of the ways designers can protect their designs or ideas (IP).

△ **Figure 5** A designer considers ways to protect their ideas.

IP method	What it protects	Legal cover	Requires registration
Patent	New inventions, including machines, products or processes that are novel and useful.	Prevents others from making, using, selling or copying the invention for a set number of years (usually 20).	Must be officially applied for and granted.
Copyright	Original artistic or creative works, such as drawings, books, music, films, software and logos.	Stops others from copying, using or publishing the work without permission.	Copyright is automatic when the work is created – no registration is required in many countries.
Trademark	Brand identity – such as names, logos, slogans and product – shapes linked to a business.	Stops others from using your brand to sell their own goods or mislead customers.	Although the ™ symbol can be used without registration, the ® symbol shows a registered trademark.
Registered design	The look of a product – its appearance, shape, decoration and style.	Gives stronger legal protection than unregistered design rights and lasts longer (up to 25 years).	Requires an application and approval process.

△ **Table 1** Ways to legally protect designs

Why it matters for you as a designer

- Breaking the rules is a big risk, potentially leading to fines, product recalls or being banned from selling your product.
- Poor design could put users in danger. Imagine the consequences if a faulty toy or a broken phone charger caused harm.
- Good design builds trust. Customers are more likely to buy from brands they trust to be safe, ethical and responsible.

Understanding legal requirements is not just about ticking boxes – it is about making products that are safe, sustainable and original. It is about being the kind of designer who protects people, the planet and your own brilliant ideas!

SOCIETY AND DIFFERENT CULTURES

A good design respects and responds to different cultures, lifestyles and societal needs. Designers have a responsibility to ensure their products are suitable, accessible and appropriate for a wide range of users, without causing offence or harm.

Colours, patterns and the way products are used can carry very different meanings across the world. For example, white symbolises purity at weddings in many Western countries; but in some Asian cultures, it is associated with mourning. A product that uses colour insensitively could therefore upset potential users.

△ **Figure 6** Ways of eating varies between cultures.

Everyday rituals, like eating, involve customs and tools that vary significantly across the globe. Some cultures predominantly use tools like knives and forks; others rely on tools such as chopsticks; and in many parts of the world, people traditionally eat using their hands. Designers must be sensitive to this spectrum of cultural practices to ensure their products are functional, respectful, and widely accepted.

Ethical and sustainable design goes further than just the appearance or function of a product. It also involves:

- avoiding the exploitation of workers and communities
- sourcing materials locally, when possible, to reduce environmental impact and support local economies
- ensuring safe, fair working conditions for all people involved in production
- applying **Fairtrade** principles where appropriate (Figure 7).

△ **Figure 7** The Fairtrade logo

With global **trends** pushing for greater ethical and sustainable practices, designers today are increasingly expected to think about the whole **life cycle** of their products – from **raw material** sourcing to end-of-life recycling.

Designing for society and culture is also about embracing diversity and inclusion. Products that are designed to be adaptable, repairable and long-lasting not only reduce waste, but also show respect for the people and places they are intended for. In a world where different cultures and societies are more connected than ever, understanding and celebrating these differences is key to creating thoughtful, successful designs.

SKILLS ACTIVITY

Redesign a childproof cap on a medicine bottle

Your task is to redesign the medicine bottle cap (Figure 3, p.19). While ensuring it remains fully childproof and secure from young children, your new design must make it significantly easier for adults with limited hand strength or dexterity to open. Consider how your design will achieve this balance between accessibility and safety.

This activity will challenge you to apply your design skills to a real-world safety product, as Dr Henri Breault did.

KNOWLEDGE CHECK

1. Explain what the CE mark on a product shows.
2. State whether an original drawing is automatically protected by copyright.
3. Identify which type of intellectual property protects a brand's name, logo or slogan.
4. Describe what is meant by 'infringement' in design.
5. Give the typical length of time patents last.
6. Identify what each of the following protection type covers:
- Patent
- Copyright
- Trademark
- Registered design

7. Explain why it is important for designers to understand legal requirements.

KEY TERMS

Dimensions: The measurements of an object

Fairtrade: A certification that ensures producers in developing countries are paid fairly and work in safe conditions

Hazard: A potential source of harm or damage

Infringement: When someone uses or copies protected work, designs or inventions without permission

Intellectual property (IP): Creations of the mind – including inventions, designs and creative work – that can be legally protected

Life cycle: The journey of a product from raw material to disposal or recycling

Raw material: Unprocessed material; it has not yet been manufactured

Risk: How likely it is that harm will happen from a hazard, and how serious the harm could be

Safety standards: Legal rules that make sure products do not harm users and are safe to use

Testing: Carrying out experiments or trials to check if something works

Trend: A general direction in which something is developing or changing, especially in fashion, technology or culture

1·1·3 Influences on designing – the environment

LEARNING AIMS

By the end of this unit, you should:
✓ Understand how sustainable thinking and the 6Rs can be applied in design
✓ Understand how the availability of materials and technologies affects design choices

SUSTAINABILITY

Every product has an impact – from the materials it is made from to how it is used and eventually thrown away. **Sustainability** is about protecting the planet for future generations; sustainable design is about designing in a way that solves real problems while considering long-term impacts on people and the planet.

As a designer, you have the power to make choices that reduce waste, use less energy and create products that last longer or can be reused. Whether it's choosing eco-friendly materials, designing for repair or reducing packaging, thinking sustainably is now a vital part of good design. In this section, you will explore how to make smart, responsible design decisions that are better for people and the planet.

Energy sources: Why they matter for designers

Energy is all around us – it powers everything we design, from smart devices and transport to homes and entire cities. For a long time, most of this energy has been generated from burning fossil fuels, such as oil, gas and coal. However, these resources are **finite**, meaning they will eventually run out. In addition, their use is harming the planet through pollution and climate change. This is where you come in!

As a future designer, engineer or innovator, you have the power to create products and solutions that are part of the move toward a more sustainable world. Thinking about energy use, material choices and designing for the environment will be important for many of your projects.

Conventional energy sources: Fossil fuels and nuclear

Fossil fuels such as coal, oil and gas took millions of years to form – but we are burning them fast (Figure 1). They release harmful gases, including carbon dioxide, which contribute to a greenhouse effect that is causing global warming.

∆ **Figure 1** A coal power plant creating pollution

Nuclear energy does not produce carbon emissions when generating electricity and is capable of generating high volumes of energy. However, it involves very high set-up costs and does create dangerous waste that remains radioactive for thousands of years.

Both fossil fuel and nuclear energy sources are finite and come with big problems for the environment. That is why **renewable energy** is so important – and why future designers need to think differently.

Renewable energy sources: Designing a better future

Renewables are sources of energy that will not run out. They are key components in the fight against climate change. Smart design can make them even better, more efficient and easier to use.

Table 1 describes the main types of renewable energy and ideas for design **opportunities**.

Renewable energy	How it works	Real-world impact	Design opportunity
Solar photovoltaic (solar panels) 	Special panels (usually placed on roofs or open land) capture sunlight and turn it directly into electricity using semiconductors.	Solar panels can power homes, schools and even whole towns. Designers are working on solar-powered products such as chargers, backpacks and cars.	How could solar energy be built into everyday products?
Wind power 	Giant turbines with blades are turned by the wind. The spinning motion drives a generator that creates electricity.	Large wind farms are now common across Europe, America and offshore at sea.	Can you design a small turbine for home or school, or think of new ways to harness wind energy for transport?
Hydroelectric 	Water stored in a reservoir flows downhill through turbines, spinning them to generate electricity.	Some countries get a huge part of their electricity from hydro schemes (for example, Norway and Canada).	How could small-scale hydroelectric power be used in rural or off-grid communities?

Renewable energy	How it works	Real-world impact	Design opportunity
Tidal energy	Underwater turbines are placed where the tide flows powerfully in and out each day, turning generators and creating electricity.	Tidal energy is predictable (unlike wind and solar), making it a reliable energy source. The largest tidal power plants are in South Korea, France and the UK.	Could tidal turbines be adapted for smaller rivers and estuaries?
Biomass	Organic waste materials (wood, plants or food scraps) are burned or fermented to create fuel and electricity.	Biomass can recycle waste into energy and lower landfill use.	Could you design a product that turns waste into energy locally?

△ **Table 1** The main types of renewable energy

Why this matters for your future

- Sustainable design is the future. Companies everywhere are demanding greener products.
- Energy-efficient products use less power and help slow climate change.
- Renewable-energy driven **innovations** are changing transport, homes, fashion and technology.

When you are developing ideas, think about:

- How will my product use or save energy?
- Could it be powered by renewable energy?
- Can I use sustainable materials and processes?

Design is not just about making things look good – it is about making the world a better place.

How designers can reduce energy consumption

A good designer is well-informed, environmentally responsible and thoughtful throughout the process of creating new products. To effectively reduce a product's energy consumption, designers must consider the energy requirements at every stage of its life cycle:

- When choosing materials:
  - Is a large amount of energy needed to extract the raw materials?
  - Could recycled or more sustainable materials be used instead?

- During manufacturing:
  - Can simpler, more energy-efficient methods be used?
- When disposing of products:
  - Can the product be easily recycled at the end of its life?
- During transportation:
  - Can the distance the product travels be reduced?
  - Are there more energy-efficient ways of delivering the product?

The six Rs

The original three environmental Rs were: *Reduce*, *Reuse* and *Recycle*. However, today's designers consider a wider framework known as the **six Rs**, which supports the creation of more sustainable products:

- *Reduce* the amount of electricity, materials and resources used in the design, manufacture and use of a product.
- *Reuse* components, packaging or materials wherever possible, extending their life and reducing waste.
- *Recycle* materials so they can be used again in different applications rather than ending up in landfill.
- *Rethink* how products are designed and how consumer choices and behaviours affect the environment.
- *Repair* rather than throw away. Designers can make this easier by creating products with replaceable parts.
- *Refuse* to buy or design unnecessary or harmful products that contribute to environmental damage.

Designers are in a strong position to influence the sustainability of a product. By applying the six Rs, they can make products that are more eco-friendly, longer-lasting and easier to reuse or recycle. For example, food packaging is one of the biggest contributors to household waste. It is often made from **polymers**, which are derived from oil – a non-renewable, polluting resource. Switching to more sustainable packaging is vital for reducing environmental impact. One solution is the use of **biopolymers** – plant-based materials that break down naturally after disposal. These materials help reduce pollution and the amount of waste sent to landfill.

By considering the six Rs throughout the design process, you can create products that are responsible and sustainable.

TOP TIP

Design products with longevity and easy repair in mind, allowing components to be replaced or the product to be disassembled for reuse or recycling at the end of its life.

DESIGN IN ACTION

Plastic power at Jerudong International School

At Jerudong International School (JIS) in Brunei, students are actively engaged in transforming plastic waste within their Design and Technology department. This initiative showcases sustainability in action.

JIS utilises machines to recycle plastic waste, such as bottle tops and food packaging, collected from students, teachers and the local community. This process involves **upcycling**, where materials are given a higher value than their previous use, extending their lifespan.

Polymers such as **HDPE**, **LDPE** and **PP** (recycling symbols 2, 4 and 5 – see Figure 5, p.27) are safely shredded (Figure 2c). Using an injection moulding machine (Figure 2d), these shredded plastics are then formed into products like medals for school events, rulers, coasters and tiles (Figure 2e). These items are designed for durability, aiming to increase the life cycle of the material.

Additionally, JIS operates an extrusion machine, which produces beams from recycled plastic. Students can then use these beams to design and construct larger items, including benches, bleachers and seating.

The school-wide initiative emphasises preventing and reducing waste, only recycling materials when necessary. This allows students to gain direct experience in sustainability efforts and observe the impact of the six Rs firsthand. This programme demonstrates how design and technology can address real-world challenges and foster a more sustainable future.

Figure 2 Recycling ▷ plastic waste: **a** collecting the waste, **b** shredding machine, **c** shredded waste, **d** injection moulding machine and **e** product

Designing for a circular economy

How do all these ideas about sustainable design come together?

The answer lies in something called the **circular economy**.

The circular economy is about designing products that keep materials and energy in use for as long as possible. Instead of the old 'take–make–dispose' model, designers now focus on preventing or reducing waste, reusing materials and thinking ahead to the recovery phase of a product, seeing the materials not as waste, but as a valuable resource for the future.

Everything you have explored in this unit connects to that goal:

- *Energy systems:* By designing products that use less energy, or can be powered by renewable sources, you reduce the environmental impact of using the product over time.
- *Materials:* Choosing sustainable, recycled or recyclable materials helps reduce the energy used in production and reduces waste.
- *Waste and disposal:* **Designing for disassembly**, repair or recycling means your product stays in use for longer and becomes part of a circular system.

- *Transport:* If you can design products that are smaller, lighter or locally sourced, you help reduce the **carbon footprint** linked to delivery and distribution.

As a designer, you are not just solving problems – you are helping shape a more sustainable future. Whether you are sketching an idea, making a **prototype** model or manufacturing a product, keep asking yourself:

- Could this be made to last longer?
- Is there a better material that creates less waste?
- How will this product be reused or recycled?
- How does this design reduce harm to the planet?

Designing for a circular economy is positive, creative and powerful. It is about designing smarter – not just for now, but for the future (Figure 3).

△ **Figure 3** Ways to design for a circular economy

Recycling

Recycling, much like reusing, plays a critical role in reducing waste and minimising environmental damage. By repurposing existing products and materials, we reduce the need to extract new raw materials from Earth – a process that often causes pollution and habitat loss.

However, despite growing awareness and effort, we are still consuming more than we recycle. This means the overall amount of waste continues to rise. More individuals and companies are embracing recycling, but there is still a long way to go (Figure 4).

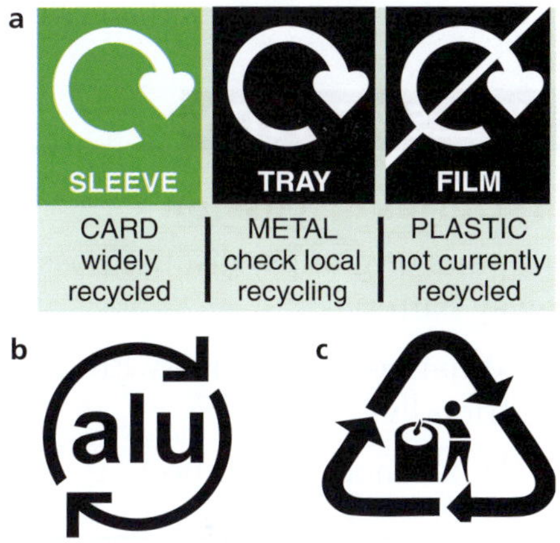

△ **Figure 4** Recycling symbols: **a** packaging, **b** aluminium and **c** glass

Commonly recycled items include:

- aluminium cans
- certain glass drink bottles
- clothing and textiles
- paper and card.

Many materials, such as polymers, can be recycled when properly processed. Polymers are categorised into two groups: **thermosetting polymers** and **thermo polymers**. Thermo polymers can be recycled, while thermosetting polymers cannot. Many products made from thermo polymers are marked with a recycling triangle containing a number (Figure 5). This number indicates the type of plastic, helping to sort materials more efficiently for recycling.

Composite materials, are much harder to recycle. These include substances like concrete, drinks cartons, MDF board and printed circuit boards (PCBs). When these materials are combined in manufacturing, they become difficult to separate and reuse in their original form, creating additional challenges for recycling efforts.

△ **Figure 5** The system of plastic recycling symbols

By designing products with recyclability in mind and using materials that are easier to disassemble and recycle, designers have the power to make a significant positive impact on the environment. Reducing waste through recycling and designing for sustainability is key to creating a greener future for all.

The battery problem

Many of you will use electronic devices every day – phones, tablets, laptops – and these rely on **rechargeable batteries**. While these are convenient and reduce the number of disposable batteries, they still pose environmental challenges as they are difficult to recycle responsibly. Batteries contain **hazardous chemicals** that can leak into soil or water if not disposed of properly. This contamination can harm wildlife, pollute drinking water and damage ecosystems.

The problem remains: How can we manage and recycle batteries in a way that truly protects the environment?

SKILLS ACTIVITY

Batteries discussion

In pairs or groups, discuss possible solutions to the issue of throwing away batteries.

1. What could be done with them that is more environmentally friendly?
2. What modern methods are being developed to dispose of batteries?

AVAILABILITY OF MATERIALS AND TECHNOLOGIES

You could come up with the most incredible product idea in the world. However, if the materials are not available, or the technology does not exist yet (or is far too expensive), your idea might stay just that: an idea.

When designing, you always have to balance creativity with reality. A brilliant design must be achievable using the materials and technologies that are available – and it should be as sustainable as possible.

The key thing to think about is: What materials are available locally? Using materials from nearby sources helps to cut down transport costs and pollution, and it supports local industries. For example, using locally grown bamboo for furniture design instead of imported **hardwoods** (Figure 6) reduces the carbon footprint and supports sustainability.

Δ **Figure 6** Hardwood being loaded onto a cargo ship for export

The cost and environmental impact of different choices

Some materials may be available, but they might be too expensive or damaging to the environment. Polymers, for example, can be cheaper than other material options – but unless they are recycled or **bio-based**, they might not be a great choice for the planet.

As a designer, you need to ask:

- Can I use recycled or repurposed materials?
- Can I design the product to be easily recycled at the end of its life?
- What is the carbon footprint of the materials I am choosing?

Developing sustainable designs that fully consider these questions shows skill – and it makes a real difference to the future of our planet.

New technologies that might improve the product

Technology moves forward very quickly. New manufacturing techniques such as 3D printing, advanced robotics or smart textiles can offer exciting opportunities. Staying aware of new technologies means you can design smarter, more efficient and more innovative products. For example, a shoe designer might look at using **biodegradable** foams or self-healing materials to make footwear that lasts longer and creates less waste.

Good design is about creativity – but it is also about being practical, responsible and sustainable. Thinking carefully about what materials and technologies you can actually use is a huge part of influencing your final design decisions.

KNOWLEDGE CHECK

1. Explain what is meant by the term 'fast fashion' and why it is a concern for sustainability.
2. Give **two** examples of how consumer trends can result in increased waste.
3. Describe the term 'circular economy' and explain how it applies to fashion and technology products.
4. Suggest questions a designer should ask to ensure their material choices are environmentally responsible.
5. Give an example of a new or emerging technology that could improve how a product functions or is made.
6. Suggest reasons why a designer might choose recycled or repurposed materials instead of using new ones.

KEY TERMS

Bio-based materials: Materials made from renewable biological sources, such as plants or natural fibres

Biodegradable: Breaks down naturally in the environment

Biopolymer: A polymer derived from renewable biomass sources

Carbon footprint: The total greenhouse gases produced during the life of a product or activity, usually measured in carbon dioxide equivalents

Circular economy: A system where products are designed to last, be repaired, reused or recycled, keeping resources in use for as long as possible

Composite: A material made by combining two or more different materials to create a new material that has improved properties

Design for disassembly: Designing products so they can be taken apart easily for recycling or repair

Finite: Having a limit or an end; a finite resource will eventually run out

Hardwood: Wood that comes from broad-leaved trees, such as oak, beech and ash

Hazardous chemical: A substance or mixture that can cause harm to humans and the environment

HDPE: High-density polyethylene – a thermo polymer with good chemical resistance

Innovation: The use of new methods or ideas to generate or develop design proposal*

LDPE: Low-density polyethylene – a thermo polymer with good chemical resistance

Opportunity: A chance to solve a problem with design

Polymer: A large molecule built from smaller molecules, called 'monomers'

PP: Polypropylene – a very common thermo polymer found in food packaging

Prototype: An early model or sample of a product used to test a concept*

Rechargeable battery: An electrical battery that can be charged, discharge and recharged multiple times

Renewable energy: Using power from natural sources, such as sunlight, wind and water

Six Rs: Six things a designer must consider when designing a product for sustainability: reduce, reuse, recycle, rethink, repair, refuse.

Sustainability: The use of resources and energy in a way that meets the need of the present generation without compromising the ability of future generations to meet their own needs*

Thermo polymer: A polymer that softens when heated and can be repeatedly reshaped upon cooling

Thermosetting polymer: A polymer material that can't be remoulded or reshaped by heating or melting

Upcycling: Transforming old or unwanted materials or artefacts into more desirable products

1·1·4 Influences on designing – the market

LEARNING AIMS

By the end of this unit, you should:

✓ Understand the role of aesthetics in making products appealing and successful
✓ Understand how existing products can inspire and improve new designs
✓ Understand how fashion and trends can shape the success of a product

AESTHETICS

Aesthetics is all about how a product looks and feels – it is what makes something visually appealing. We all have different ideas about what is beautiful. But, despite our differences, understanding the basics of aesthetics is crucial for creating products that people will want to buy and enjoy using.

When you pick up a product, whether it's your phone, a chair or a gaming controller, one of the first things you notice is how it looks and feels. Aesthetics is behind that first impression – it's the visual and tactile qualities that make something appealing and comfortable to use. The best designs grab your attention, but they also make you want to keep using the product. There are several key aspects that make products aesthetically pleasing.

Colour

Colour is one of the most powerful tools designers use to communicate. It can make a product pop, set the tone or even tell you how to use it.

Think of a red stop sign or green for go – colour is often used functionally as well as for style. Brands like Coca-Cola® have embraced bold, signature colours that are instantly recognisable. But colour also has emotional power – blue, for instance, creates a calm, cool feeling, which is why hospitals often use it in their rooms. By understanding how colour affects mood, designers can create products that not only look good but feel right for the user.

Shape

A product's shape – its outline or silhouette – plays a huge role in defining its character. Shapes can make a product look sleek, chunky, elegant or bold. For example, the smooth, rounded shape of a smartphone makes it feel modern and comfortable to hold; while a gaming controller might have more angular, sharp lines to give it a high-tech, powerful look. Shapes can be organic, inspired by nature, like the curves of a leaf, or geometric, such as the clean edges of a triangle or square (Figure 1). The right shape can transform a simple object into something that feels iconic.

△ **Figure 1** Geometric shapes are used to inspire a fun character.

Form

While shape is about the outline, **form** refers to the three-dimensional structure of a product. Think of it as the difference between looking at a drawing of a cube (shape) and holding the actual cube (form). Forms can be spheres, cylinders and prisms, and the way they are put together creates a product's personality. For example, the smooth, aerodynamic form of a modern car makes it look futuristic and sleek (Figure 2), while the form of a water bottle is designed for practicality – easy to hold, store and carry.

△ **Figure 2** Futuristic car concept with sweeping curves and streamline form

Proportion

Proportion is how the different parts of a product relate to each other in size. Imagine a chair that is too high for your desk, or a remote control with buttons that are too small to press easily. A product that is poorly proportioned can feel awkward or uncomfortable to use. But when the proportions are just right – like a compact handheld console, which fits perfectly in your hands – everything feels balanced and natural. Proportion is not just about measurements; it is about how things look and feel together. Designers often use the Vitruvian Man by Leonardo da Vinci as a guide, showing how proportion and symmetry are key to creating products that feel just right (Figure 3).

△ **Figure 3** A thrilling experience based on the design of Leonardo da Vinci's Vitruvian Man

Balance

Balance is about ensuring all the elements of a product work together harmoniously. For example, think about a car dashboard – if all the buttons were on one side, it would feel chaotic and unbalanced. But if the design is balanced, with controls evenly distributed, it creates a sense of ease and comfort for the user. Symmetry (where both sides are the same) is often used to create harmony, but sometimes asymmetry – when things are deliberately off-centre – can make a design feel more dynamic and exciting.

Pattern

Pattern is used to add visual interest and texture to a product. Without it, surfaces can look plain or unexciting. By adding repeating shapes, lines or motifs, designers can make a product feel livelier and engaging. For example, a pencil case might have a repeating geometric design, or a reusable water bottle might feature natural patterns inspired by leaves or waves. Whether it is a grid, stripes or flowing shapes from nature, pattern adds personality to a product and helps catch the user's eye (Figure 4).

△ **Figure 4** A modern table inspired by repeat patterns and symmetry

Texture

Texture is how a product feels when you touch it. It adds depth and interest beyond just what you see. Texture can be functional, such as adding grip to a pen so it does not slip in your hand (Figure 5), or decorative, such as a patterned surface on a phone case.

△ **Figure 5** A pen with an elastomer sheath to add a soft textured grip

Textures can be natural, such as the rough surface of concrete used in outdoor furniture, or human-made, such as the smooth, self-finishing feel of a polymer used in a school project or the plastic casing of a remote control. Designers often choose textures carefully to make sure the product is both enjoyable to use and suitable for its purpose.

TOP TIP

Remember that aesthetics go beyond just looks; consider how colour, texture and form can also enhance a product's functionality and user experience.

SKILLS ACTIVITY

Contrasting aesthetics

Sketch two different versions of a solar-powered portable charger:

1. One focusing on a sleek, modern design with a smooth, compact shape and neutral colours, ideal for tech-savvy users.
2. Another with bright, playful colours and geometric patterns, designed to appeal to a younger audience or those with a more vibrant style.

FASHION AND TRENDS

From the vibrant colours of smartphones to the ever-changing shapes of trainers and new-season sportswear, staying aware of trends is vital for keeping designs fresh and appealing. Fashion and trends play a powerful role in shaping consumer preferences and influencing what people want to buy. However, while trends can boost a product's popularity, they also bring sustainability challenges that designers must consider carefully.

Negative influences

One of the most significant sustainability concerns linked to fashion and trends is the overconsumption of resources. **Fast fashion**, for example, drives a constant cycle of new collections and designs, encouraging consumers to purchase clothes and accessories on a regular basis. This demand often leads to the use of cheap, low-quality materials that are not durable and contribute to significant waste. The rapid turnover of trends also leads to more clothing ending up in landfills, contributing to the growing global textile waste crisis (Figure 6).

△ **Figure 6** A mountain of textiles waste polluting South East Asia

Fashion trends can also lead to **planned obsolescence** in clothing and accessories. Just as with electronic devices, certain items are designed to be 'trendy' for a limited time, after which they lose their appeal. This creates a cycle where products are discarded not because they are no longer functional, but simply because they are no longer 'in style'. This phenomenon drives an increase in textile waste, with perfectly usable items being thrown away simply because they are not on trend anymore.

E-waste is another major issue tied to fashion trends, especially in the growing market for tech and fashion crossovers. Smartwatches, fashion-forward phone cases and 'designer' electronics are subject to rapid obsolescence. The desire for the latest tech or style pushes consumers to discard older devices, contributing to the e-waste problem (Figure 7). Many of these devices contain hazardous materials, including heavy metals and plastics, which can pollute the environment if not disposed of properly.

△ **Figure 7** A pile of e-waste

Positive influences

An awareness of trends can present an opportunity for designers to incorporate sustainability into their work. As consumers become more conscious of the environmental impact of their choices, there is growing demand for products that are designed with longevity and ethical production in mind (**ethical consumerism**). This shift is influencing not just fashion, but a wide range of industries – from technology and furniture to packaging and personal accessories.

Designers are increasingly choosing recycled or responsibly sourced materials, and are finding creative ways to design products that are built to last, easier to repair or **modular** so that parts can be updated rather than the entire product being replaced. For example, modular smartphones, furniture made from reclaimed wood, and repairable consumer electronics are all on the rise.

The trend for upcycling and repurposing is also gaining ground. Many consumers now value products that have a story, are one of a kind or have been creatively reimagined from existing materials. Vintage and second-hand products are becoming increasingly desirable across different sectors, driven by a mix of environmental concern, affordability and individuality.

By staying alert to these more sustainable trends, designers have the opportunity to create products that not only appeal to modern consumers, but also help tackle some of the pressing environmental issues facing the world today.

Influence on design

As trends and consumer preferences continue to evolve, designers must navigate both the positive and negative influences fashion and trends bring to product development. Keeping products stylish, on-trend and relevant is essential, but designers must also be mindful of the broader environmental impact of following fleeting trends. By staying aware of these issues and considering sustainability in every stage of design – from material choice to product lifespan – designers can contribute to a more responsible and eco-conscious approach to fashion, tech and beyond.

Fashion and trends significantly influence the designs of products across many industries. While the constant churn of new styles can lead to overproduction, waste and short-lived products, designers have an opportunity to shape these trends in a way that promotes sustainability. By embracing eco-friendly materials, supporting circular design and focusing on durability, designers can play an essential role in creating a more sustainable future.

DESIGN IN ACTION

Trend forecasters predict changes in fashion, technology and culture to help companies design for the future.

EXISTING DESIGNS

Good research leads to great designs! Before creating a new product, it is essential to take a good look at what already exists. Research helps you avoid repeating old mistakes, find out what users really want and spark fresh ideas.

Why is research important?

- It helps you understand what works – and why it works.
- It shows you where existing products fall short, giving you a chance to do better.
- It reveals different ways designers have solved similar problems.
- It can inspire new ideas by showing a variety of styles, functions and materials.

Primary and secondary research

When exploring existing designs, you can carry out:

- **Primary research**: This means investigating products yourself. You could physically disassemble a product to see how it is made (Figure 8), or explore a virtual disassembly online. Hands-on experience can show you hidden details you might not notice otherwise. Primary research gives you first-hand, detailed knowledge about how products are put together, how they feel to use and how well they are made.
- **Secondary research**: This means using information that already exists. You might look at websites, reviews, videos, case studies or magazines to find out how products work, what users think of them and where improvements are needed. Secondary research is quicker than primary, gives access to a variety of different opinions and helps you spot patterns across many products.

△ **Figure 8** A disassembled bike used as primary research to understand assembly of components

When studying existing designs, always consider:

- What works well?
- What could be improved?
- How do different designers solve the same problem?
- What features or materials make the product better (or worse)?
- How could the product be more sustainable, inclusive or user-friendly?

By carefully researching and analysing existing designs, you will make better decisions, avoid common mistakes and create products that are smarter, stronger and more successful.

REFLECTIVE LOG

Find a product you use every day. What do you like about its design? What could be better?

Disassembly

Many products are designed in ways that make them difficult to take apart once they have been assembled. This often leads to people discarding items instead of attempting to repair them. Consequently, these products end up in landfill sites, contributing to environmental harm. However, a more sustainable approach is to design products that can be disassembled easily, using common tools or basic equipment. This makes it simpler to replace or repair parts when they break, extending the product's life and reducing the need for new raw materials. By designing for disassembly, you can reduce waste, save resources and create a more sustainable future.

Unfortunately, some manufacturers resist this idea, as their goal is to sell more products when older ones fail. This leads to unnecessary consumption of raw materials, more waste and, ultimately, a negative environmental impact. It also raises ethical concerns, as this approach prioritises profit over sustainability. Designing for easy repair and disassembly is not just better for the planet – it also promotes a more responsible consumer culture.

Moreover, designing products that can be disassembled at the end of their life allows certain parts or subassemblies to be more easily recycled. For example, many tech devices, such as smartphones and laptops, could benefit from designs that allow easier access to individual components for recycling at the end of their life cycle.

Planned obsolescence

Planned obsolescence refers to the practice of designing products with a deliberately limited lifespan. Manufacturers may intentionally design products to become obsolete after a certain period, often through factors such as:

- material or component failure
- software upgrades
- compatibility issues.

For example, a desktop printer is often designed with a specific lifespan. Users frequently observe that key components begin to fail after a set number of pages are printed or once the warranty period has passed. This common scenario forces customers to decide between purchasing expensive replacement parts or simply buying a whole new printer.

In many cases, the cost of repairs and specialised tools can make replacing the product more cost-effective. This can drive customers to purchase the latest version, feeding into a cycle of consumption.

On the other hand, planned obsolescence can have some positive applications, such as in food products with sell-by dates. These are intended to ensure that products are used before they spoil, helping to protect consumer health. Similarly, some biodegradable materials, such as polylactide (**PLA**) which is often used for 3D printing, are designed to break down quickly to prevent unnecessary waste in the environment.

IMPACT OF DESIGN ON SOCIETY AND MARKETS

Designers have the power to influence society and markets in huge ways. A well-designed product can improve people's quality of life, create new trends and even change how industries operate. That is why, when developing sustainable designs, it is essential to fully consider their wider impacts.

Products affect the way people live, work and interact. They must respect cultural differences and lifestyles (see unit 1.1.2). Simple things – such as colours, patterns, materials and functions – can have different meanings in different places. Designers need to ensure their work is inclusive and sensitive, enhancing lives rather than causing offence or harm.

Sustainability plays a major role. Good design looks beyond the immediate sale. It thinks about the full life of the product:

- Where the materials come from.
- How much energy is used to manufacture it.
- How easily it can be maintained, repaired, reused or recycled.
- How it will eventually be disposed of.

Poorly considered designs can encourage waste, exploitation of resources and unethical working practices. For example, products designed to break easily (planned obsolescence) create unnecessary waste and pressure on raw materials, adding to environmental problems.

Designers also have a responsibility to think about the economic and **social impacts** of their choices. Sourcing materials locally and using Fairtrade principles can help support communities and reduce transport emissions. Choosing ethical suppliers ensures that the workers making the products have safe, fair working conditions.

At the same time, design can have positive influences on markets. Growing consumer demand for sustainable and ethical products is pushing companies to innovate and do better. The rise of upcycling, modular design and 'buy less, buy better' movements show how design can lead change in society.

Technology and material innovations also impact the market by opening up new possibilities – from biodegradable materials to smart fabrics. Designers need to stay informed about new developments and think creatively about how to use them sustainably.

Your designs must not only meet the needs of users but must also consider their impact on society and the environment. Good designs can drive positive change – and that is an influence worth having.

KNOWLEDGE CHECK

1. What is the difference between shape and form in product design?
2. Why is proportion important in designing handheld products?
3. How can texture be both decorative and functional?
4. Explain how poor design choices can negatively affect the environment and society.
5. Give **two** examples of how a product can be made more sustainable throughout its life cycle.
6. Describe how a designer might use pattern to make a water bottle more appealing.

KEY TERMS

Aesthetics: Concerned with the appearance or look of a product*

Ethical consumerism: Choosing to buy products that are made responsibly, considering environmental and social impacts

E-waste: Discarded electrical or electronic devices, often containing harmful substances if not recycled properly

Fast fashion: The rapid production of inexpensive clothing that follows current fashion trends but often results in poor-quality items and high environmental waste

Form: The three-dimensional structure of a product, including volume and depth

Modular design: A design approach that allows individual parts of a product to be replaced or upgraded without discarding the whole item

PLA: Polylactic acid (polylactide) – a biopolymer made from natural materials such as corn starch

Planned obsolescence: Deliberately designing the life cycle of a product to be short, forcing the user to update their products quickly*

Primary research: New information collected directly from users or tests

Proportion: The relationship between different parts of a product in terms of size and scale

Secondary research: Existing information from books, websites, reports or studies

Social impact: The effect a design or product has on communities and people's day-to-day lives

1·2 Designing principles

1·2·1 Identifying

LEARNING AIMS

By the end of this unit, you should;
✓ Identify needs and wants for designing and making
✓ Identify opportunities for designing and making
✓ Analyse products and data
✓ Describe needs and opportunities for designing and making

IDENTIFYING NEEDS AND OPPORTUNITIES

Every product starts with a purpose. It might be designed to fix a small, everyday problem or to tackle a global issue. Some designers work with large companies to make products that will sell and make a profit. Others are driven by a desire to make life better – for users, society or the environment.

Think about the practical problems you or others have or see in your day-to-day lives. Maybe it is the tangled charging cables in your bag, or how difficult it is to carry shopping on a bike; or perhaps you have noticed how much single-use plastic is still being used at your school or local café.

Designers spot everyday problems and imagine how things could work better. This process – identifying a design need – is where great ideas begin.

Identifying a design need is the first of six designing principles (Figure 1) that you will explore in this topic:

- Identifying
- Defining
- Proposing
- Developing
- Planning
- Testing and evaluation.

Note that you do not need to follow these six principles in a linear order in your own design work.

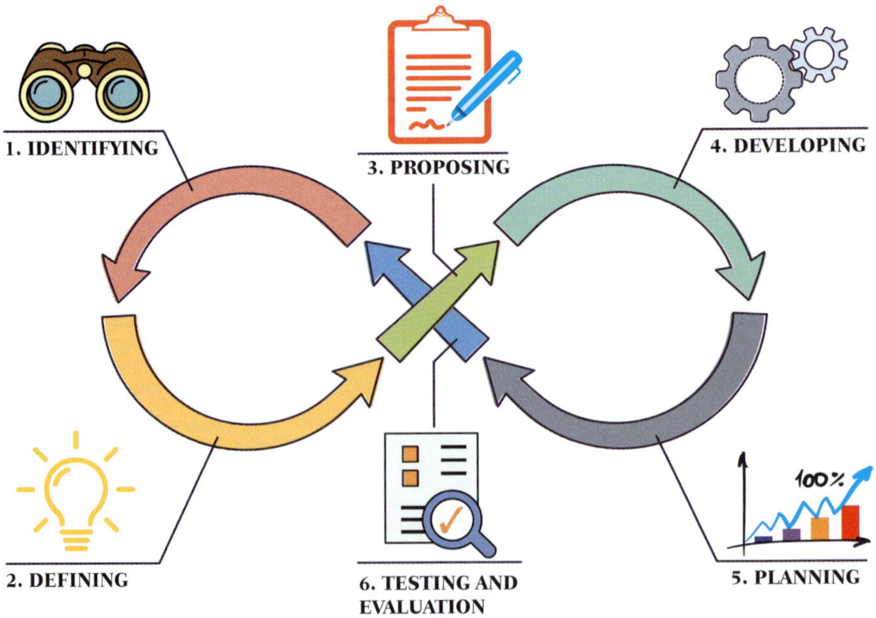

∆ **Figure 1** The six designing principles

Some ideas come from **observing** how people use (or struggle with) existing products. Other ideas come from:

- listening to what others complain about or wish they had
- researching new materials or technologies
- responding to environmental or social challenges.

Modern examples of real design needs

Design needs are everywhere. Table 1 shows examples of problems and opportunities that could inspire your own work.

Problem	Opportunity
Odour from bins in small kitchens in urban apartments is unpleasant.	Design an odour-free compost bin for small urban kitchens.
Online learners often struggle to position their phones comfortably using sustainable tools.	Design a modular phone stand made from recycled plastic for online learning.
Single-use deodorant packaging contributes to bathroom waste.	Design a refillable deodorant stick to reduce bathroom waste.
Commuters who struggle with long journeys have nowhere to rest while waiting or travelling.	Design a foldable commuter seat for those needing rest during long journeys.
Users with limited fine motor skills find standard bottle openers hard to use.	Design a one-handed bottle opener for people with reduced fine motor skills.
Pet owners worry about losing their pets, but lack eco-friendly tracking solutions.	Design a clip-on, solar-powered pet tracker that links to a smartphone app.

△ **Table 1** Some design problems and opportunities

You do not have to invent something completely new. Often, the most effective solutions come from improving what already exists – making it easier to use, more sustainable, more affordable or simply more enjoyable. This is called product evolution. **Product analysis** can also lead to design innovation.

THE ROLE OF THE CLIENT AND USER

While it is often tempting to design a solution for yourself, successful design is about solving problems for others. Designers must understand the needs and **wants** of real people. Most products are developed for a client – the person, organisation or business who sets the task – and a user – the person who will actually use the product. These are not always the same, so good designers take time to understand both perspectives.

Designers usually begin by creating a design **brief** in collaboration with the client. This outlines what the client wants, the problem that needs solving and any specific requirements. However, to create a product that works well in the real world, designers must also study the user carefully. How old are they? What are their habits or routines? Do they have any physical, social or environmental needs that the design must consider?

Designers might not start with sketching ideas – first, they might carry out research to understand what users need. This might involve watching how people use (or struggle with) current products, asking thoughtful questions through interviews or surveys, and even testing out early ideas. This kind of research-led, user-centred approach leads to smarter, more inclusive design decisions. You will learn more about how to carry out this kind of research in unit 1.2.2.

Examples of different clients and users

- A school (client) commissions a product to help students (users) revise better.
- A parent (client) asks for a safe, easy-to-access storage solution for their toddler (user).
- A café (client) requests low-waste takeaway packaging for their customers (users).

Understanding both the client's aims and the user's needs helps shape more thoughtful, impactful design solutions.

DESIGN IN ACTION

A group of students noticed that their school canteen had problems with food waste and long queues. After observing students and talking to the catering staff, they designed a digital pre-ordering system with a smart display for food collection. Not only did it cut waiting times, but it also helped the kitchen prepare more accurate portions, reducing food waste and saving money.

This kind of project links to areas such as technology, engineering, business and sustainability.

TOP TIP

Start with curiosity. Notice the little frustrations people have every day – that is where great design opportunities hide.

Build with empathy. The better you understand your client and users, the stronger your ideas will be. Ask questions, listen closely and imagine yourself in their situation.

SKILLS ACTIVITY

Choose a space, such as a classroom, canteen or school corridor. Observe how people interact with it. What annoys them? What slows them down? Interview one or two classmates.

Now write a sentence describing:

- What the problem is.
- Who has the problem.
- What kind of product might help.

DESIGN IN ACTION

Identifying problems and products

User experience (UX) designers are very interested in how people feel when they use a product. These designers run interviews, test prototypes and ask lots of questions. Their role is all about making things easy, helpful and maybe even fun to use.

△ **Figure 2** A UX designer analysing design elements and colour palettes for a project with a client.

KNOWLEDGE CHECK

1. Describe how a sketch can be a useful starting point in the design process.
2. Compare the differences in designing for yourself and designing for a wider user group.
3. Explain how interviews or observations help you understand what a user really needs.
4. Suggest the ways user 'needs' are different from user 'wants', and why that matters in design.
5. Explain how analysing existing products helps generate stronger and more creative design ideas.

KEY TERMS

Brief: A short, clear statement outlining what the design needs to achieve*

Observation: Watching people use things in real life

Product analysis: Studying how existing products work (and what could be better)

Wants: The things people would like to have

1·2·2 Defining

LEARNING AIMS

By the end of this unit, you should:

✓ Solve problems, such as resource availability, that influence proposed designs
✓ Gather information to solve design problems
✓ Interpret and present data
✓ Analyse data and research to produce specifications

DEFINING THE PROBLEM

Now that you have identified a design opportunity or challenge, it's time to dig deeper. This stage is all about defining – understanding exactly what the problem is, who it affects and what might stand in your way when trying to solve it. That means going beyond guesswork. You need to collect facts, gather feedback and carry out focused research to build a clear picture of what your design needs to achieve.

The insights you discover from your research are key to writing a clear, focused **specification** – the criteria your final design aims to meet. The better your research, the easier it becomes to design a solution that truly works.

THE IMPORTANCE OF RESEARCH IN DESIGN

Research is a vital early step in the design process. Designers explore how people experience similar products, what users need and any technical or environmental considerations that might affect the outcome. This helps you make informed choices and avoid assumptions.

Designers often begin by mind mapping their ideas and exploring the context of the problem. Professional companies might use market research agencies to gather information through interviews, surveys and user testing groups (Figure 1). The data they gather may be:

- **Quantitative**: Measurable information, including statistics, test results or usage patterns.
- **Qualitative**: Opinions, feelings and personal experiences shared by users.

These findings help designers understand the needs and wants of their users. Just like professional designers, you will use this research to create your own design specifications – to shape products that genuinely meets users' needs.

△ **Figure 1** Examples of **a** quantitative and **b** qualitative data research

Primary and secondary research

Designers use primary and secondary research (as described in unit 1.1.4) in the defining stage.

Creating a **research plan** can help define what you need to find out, how you will do it and where you will get your information. This helps ensure your work is focused and efficient.

TOP TIP

Remember that research should continue throughout the entire design process, not just at the start.

Organising your research

When you organise the research you have collected, you need to:

- keep it relevant to your design brief
- discard irrelevant or outdated information
- present the **key findings** clearly and use these in your specification.

TOP TIP

In your research plan, add 'key findings' boxes after each research task to write short summaries of what you discovered and how it will influence your design.

Turning research into action

Once you've gathered enough information, present your key findings. Ensure you use clear formats, such as:

- diagrams, graphs or charts
- bullet point summaries of product comparisons
- notes or quotes from user interviews
- tables of material tests or survey results.

Existing product analysis

A key part of research is studying existing products. You will explore this in units 2.4.1 and 3.4.1.

When you are analysing an existing product, ask yourself or users the following questions:

- What works well in this design?
- What could be improved?
- How is it made and assembled?
- How does it compare to alternatives?
- Does it meet the needs of its users?

Looking at the work of past and present designers – from product designers to architects and engineers – can also be a great source of inspiration. But remember to always avoid copying – use existing ideas as a springboard, not a shortcut.

THE SPECIFICATION

After your initial research, you need to create a design specification. This is a list of requirements for your product, based on your insights. It allows you to set clear design goals and acts as success criteria, guiding your ideas, prototyping and decisions. It also allows you to evaluate your final product to determine whether it meets user needs.

Think of it as your success checklist – clear and measurable points to check if your design achieves its goals. Each point in your specification should be:

- *Justified* (linked to evidence from your research)
- *Measurable* (so it can be tested later)
- *Focused* (not vague or general)
- *Useful* (relevant to solving the design problem).

Use a table format to present your specification. This will help you stay organised and show the link between your research and your design decisions clearly.

Factors to consider when writing a design specification

It is important to be able to transform your research into clear, focused specification points. A great starting point is to use the acronym **ACCESSFM**, which encourages you to consider eight key factors (Table 2).

A	C	C	E	S	S	F	M
Aesthetics	Cost	Customer/ Client	Environment	Size	Safety	Function	Material properties

△ **Table 1** Key factors to consider when writing your product specification

As you consider each factor, back up your responses with evidence from your research findings, ensuring that your considerations are both specific and measurable.

Additional questions to strengthen your specification

You may want to explore additional factors that are relevant to your design. For example:

- *Inclusivity:*
  - o Is the design accessible to users with disabilities or additional needs?
  - o Does the product work equally well for people of different sizes, strengths or cultures?
- *Technology:*
  - o Will digital technologies, sensors or smart features be used?
  - o Can the product be prototyped using **computer-aided design (CAD)**, **computer-aided manufacture (CAM)** or **simulations**?

- *Maintenance and repair:*
    - How easy is the product to clean, maintain or replace parts?
    - Could it be designed to reduce waste over time?
- *Social and ethical impact:*
    - Does the product support fair labour, local production or **ethical sourcing**?
    - Will it positively impact users or the wider community?

SKILLS ACTIVITY

Investigating user needs: Water-efficient handwashing station

Imagine you are designing a water-efficient handwashing station for school settings such as outdoor classrooms or canteens, or near playgrounds (Figure 2). Your task is to gather useful research that helps you understand the problem and develop a strong design specification.

Δ **Figure 2**. Students need to wash their hands during messy play

Step 1: Conduct research:

- Interview students, teachers or cleaning staff to find out common issues (for example, water waste, accessibility).
- Observe how students use handwashing facilities during busy times, such as during breaks or at lunchtime. How do they use the taps? Is water being wasted?
- Research school hygiene and sanitation guidelines for safe and effective handwashing.
- Compare different types of taps and materials (for example, sensor-activated vs. manual taps).
- Explore eco-friendly design solutions in schools or colleges for inspiration.

Step 2: Organise your findings:

- Write a short user needs summary.
- Create a bar chart comparing water usage, accessibility and waste of different tap types.

Step 3: Develop *three* specification points based on your research. For example:

- *Must use less than 1 litre of water per use.*
- *Must be easy for children aged 4–10 years to operate*
- *Should be made from weather-resistant, recyclable materials.*

TOP TIP

Always plan your research tasks. Ask yourself:

- What do I need to know?
- Why do I need to know it?
- Where can I find it?

SKILLS ACTIVITY

Creating a research plan

1. Choose a theme – for example, personal storage, outdoor learning, improving school environments.
2. Create a mini research plan with three or four key tasks.
3. Complete at least one of the tasks and record your findings in a visual format – for example, a table, image analysis or graph.
4. Add a short reflection explaining how the information might shape your design.

KNOWLEDGE CHECK

1. Explain the purpose of carrying out research at the start of a design project.
2. Explain the difference between quantitative and qualitative data, and give one example of each.
3. Describe how interviews or observations can help you understand user needs.
4. Justify why it is important to write a design specification based on research rather than assumptions.
5. Give **one** example of a technical, environmental or user-based consideration that could influence your design.
6. Explain the difference between primary and secondary research, and give one example of each.

KEY TERMS

Computer-aided design (CAD): Using specialist computer programs to help create or test designs

Computer-aided manufacture (CAM): Using machines like 3D printers or computer numerical control (CNC) routers to make models

Ethical sourcing: Ensuring materials and labour are obtained in a responsible way

Key findings: Important information or conclusions discovered during research that help guide your design decisions.

Qualitative data: Descriptive information based on opinions or observations.

Quantitative data: Measurable information such as numbers or percentages.

Research plan: A document detailing what you need to find out, how you will do it and where you will get your information

Simulation: A virtual test, such as stress or airflow analysis, used in digital modelling

Specification: A detailed list of the functions and features that a design must have*

1·2·3 Proposing

LEARNING AIMS

By the end of this unit, you should:
✓ Sketch and annotate a range of distinct, imaginative and innovative designs
✓ Evaluate and explore each design and propose a solution

GENERATING INITIAL IDEAS

Before starting your detailed designs, this is your chance to use your imagination. At this stage, it is all about sketching lots of different ideas – the more unexpected, the better. Do not worry about making the sketches perfect. Think fast, draw freely and explore as many creative directions as you can.

It can feel daunting at first, so try mixing up different techniques to help spark original and exciting ideas. The aim is to break away from the obvious and surprise yourself!

You can use various strategies to trigger creative thinking.

Biomimicry

Biomimicry means using clever ideas from nature to solve human design problems. From the shape of a bird's wing to the way a cactus stores water, nature has already solved many tricky challenges – so why not learn from it? Here are some presentation tips:

- Study natural organisms or systems relevant to your design problem.
- Sketch elements that mimic these natural inspirations.
- **Annotate** to explain the biological principles applied.

Figures 1 and 2 show some examples of biomimicry.

△ **Figure 1** A building ventilation system inspired by termite mounds, which naturally regulate temperature

△ **Figure 2** Japan's bullet trains are designed to be aerodynamic, inspired by the kingfisher bird.

SKILLS ACTIVITY

Biomimicry mind map challenge

Nature is packed with design secrets — now it's your turn to uncover them!

Step 1: Pick a natural example from the following list:

- A gecko's sticky feet
- An owl's silent flight
- A butterfly's shiny, colourful wings
- A choice of your own

Step 2: Research or observe how it works. Use the internet, books or a nature video to learn how your chosen example functions. What is special about it? What problem does it solve?

Step 3: Design something new using this idea. Sketch a quick **concept** for a product that is inspired by the natural feature. Think about how it answers the following questions:

- What problem does my product solve?
- How is it inspired by the natural idea?
- Who might use it?

Step 4: Add a pop-out annotation bubble in your drawing, explaining: *'This idea was inspired by [insert nature example] because...'*

Optional challenge: Present your idea in a 'Nature's Invention Fair' poster format with a catchy product name.

Mood boards

Mood boards are a powerful tool. They explore and communicate your design project's style, atmosphere and personality – particularly for visual elements. They can also include textures, colours, patterns and keywords. A strong mood board sparks creativity, aligns with client preferences and connects to real-world inspiration.

TOP TIP

Complete a mood board with your client or ask for their feedback on it.

Broaden your inspiration. Your mood board should go beyond images of existing products. You could also include material samples. Try to include references from:

- *Architecture:* Is your client drawn to clean lines, organic shapes or bold contemporary structures?
- *Design movements:* Use visual references from styles from the past.
- *Key designers and brands:* Use products designed by influential designers.
- *Cultural and environmental context:* Consider the environment – where will the product be used?

TOP TIP

These presentation tips may be helpful:

- Collect images, colour palettes and textures that reflect the desired aesthetic (Figure 3).
- Arrange them on a board or digitally to establish a visual theme.
- Include annotations to explain the relevance of each element.

◁ **Figure 3** A mood board for a sustainable furniture line includes samples of natural wood textures, earthy colour palettes and minimalist designs.

Use annotations to explain why you have included each image or material swatch. For example, *'This textured wood reflects the client's interest in natural materials and links to sustainable design principles.'*

SCAMPER

SCAMPER is a creative thinking technique. It prompts designers to explore ideas by applying the seven strategies given in Table 1.

S	C	A	M	P	E	R
Substitute	Combine	Adapt	Modify	Put to another use	Eliminate	Reverse

△ **Table 1** The seven strategies of SCAMPER

Use these presentation tips to apply this technique:

- Create a matrix with each SCAMPER prompt and brainstorm corresponding ideas.
- Use quick sketches to visualise each concept.
- Annotate your sketches to explain how each prompt alters the original idea (Figure 4).

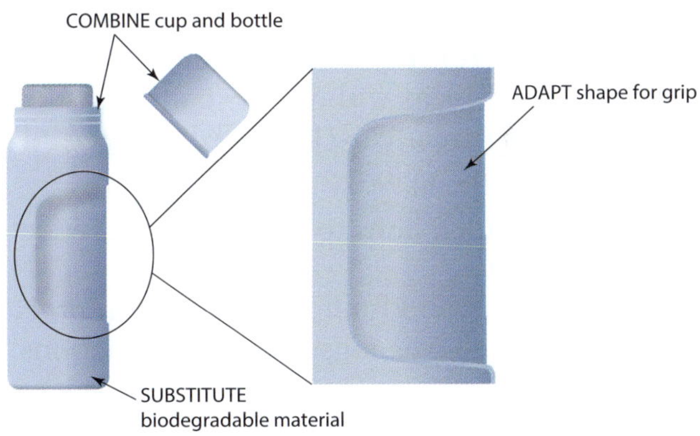

△ **Figure 4** A designer reimagines a standard water bottle by substituting plastic with biodegradable materials, combining it with a cup and adapting its shape for better grip.

Geometric shapes

Using basic geometric forms, such as cubes and cylinders, as the foundation for design can lead to innovative and structured concepts. Try these presentation tips:

- Start with basic shapes, such as circles, squares and triangles, to form the base of your design.
- Explore variations by combining or modifying these shapes.
- Sketch multiple iterations to explore different configurations (Figure 5).

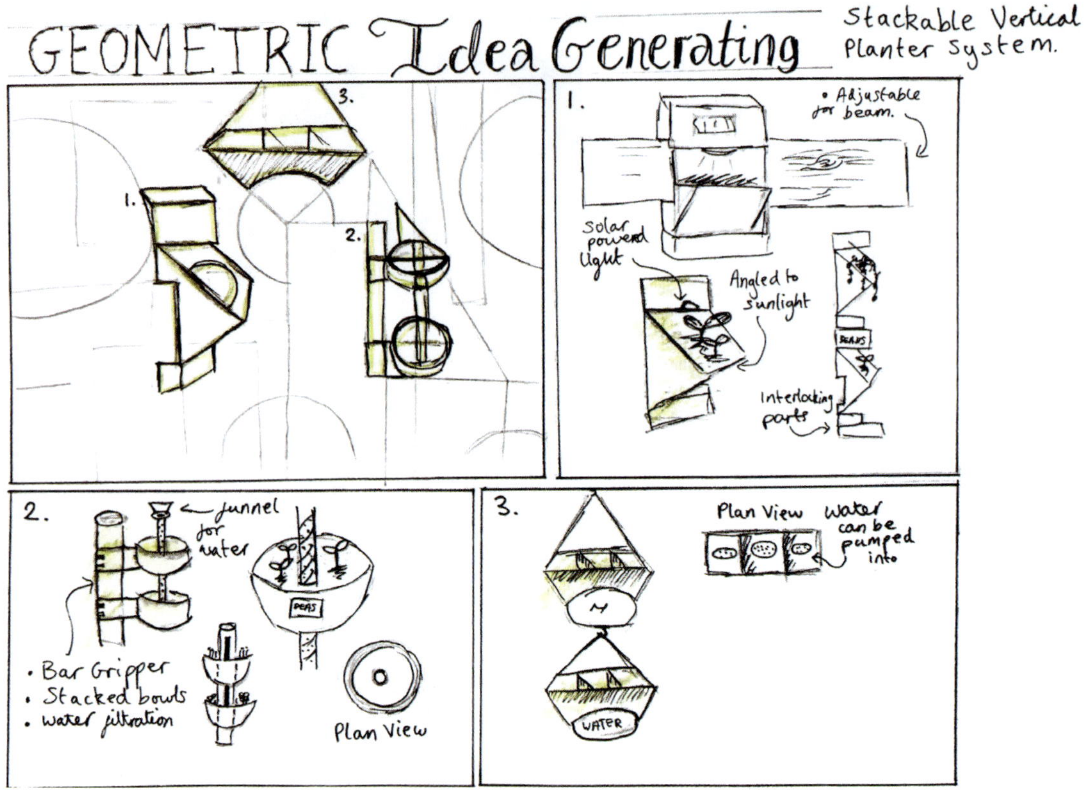

△ **Figure 5** A student example of an initial design exploration using the geometric shapes technique to produce concepts for a stackable vertical planter system for a balcony

Freehand sketches

Freehand sketching allows for rapid visualisation of ideas without the constraints of tools, fostering creativity (Figure 6). Suggested presentation tips include:

- Use loose, quick lines to capture the essence of your concept.
- Focus on form and function rather than precision.
- Iterate multiple versions to explore variations.

△ **Figure 6** Concept sketches of ergonomic chair designs emphasising fluid lines and user comfort

Jackstraws and scruffiti

This technique involves creating random, overlapping lines or shapes and interpreting them into design concepts, encouraging abstract thinking (Figure 7). Use these presentation tips:

- Scribble random lines across the page.
- Identify shapes or patterns that emerge.
- Develop these into coherent design ideas.

△ **Figure 7** Transforming a random scribble into the conceptual design of a futuristic vehicle

MEDIA AND FORMATS FOR EARLY SKETCHES

Use a variety of drawing techniques to communicate your thoughts:

- 2D sketches – front, side and plan/top views – to understand proportion
- 3D sketches – **isometric** or perspective drawings – to visualise depth
- Collages – combining images and materials – to convey mood or a theme

Aim for variety, not perfection. You will learn more about drawing techniques in unit 1.3.1.

Recommended tools include:

- *pencils* for initial sketches and shading
- *markers* for highlighting and adding colour
- *coloured pencils* for adding detail
- *ballpoint pens* for annotations and fine lines
- *chalk/pastels* for adding texture and depth
- *coloured paper* for cut-out models or background enhancements.

TOP TIP

Set a timer for 10 minutes and challenge yourself to create as many ideas as possible in that time. This will help you break any creative mental blocks.

SKILLS ACTIVITY

Use the SCAMPER method

Use the SCAMPER method to develop five quick product ideas for a common object, such as a chair or lunchbox. Present your ideas using different drawing styles and at least two types of media.

USING THE SPECIFICATION TO GUIDE IDEAS

Refer back to your design specification throughout. You should be able to explain how each idea meets the most important criteria. Use the questions in Table 2 to guide you.

Criteria	Explanation
• Who is the product for? • What must it do? • What size, materials or safety limits are required? • What are the sustainability or cost expectations?	As you propose ideas, explain: • How does this idea meet the key requirements? • What makes this solution different or better? • How practical is it to make, using available resources?

△ **Table 2** How does each idea meet the criteria set out in your design specification?

PRESENTING YOUR IDEAS

It is good practice to sketch a minimum of *three* distinct ideas, each clearly annotated. The focus of your design work may vary, but it is often a good idea to include features relating to:

- functionality
- materials and finishes
- target user and context
- aesthetic style and inspiration.

Sketches can be hand-drawn or digital. Annotate important features and explain any decisions that meet the specification (Figure 8).

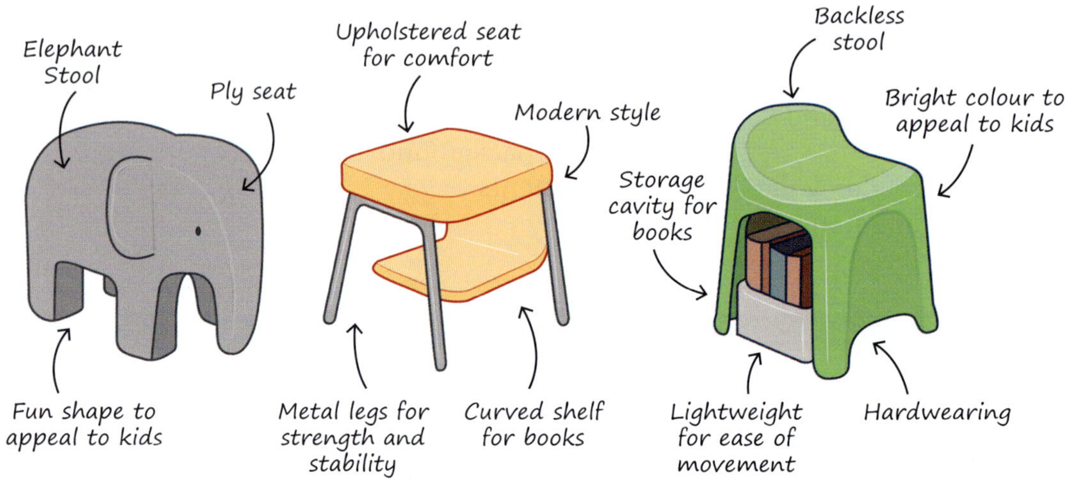

∆ **Figure 8** Annotated sketches: Different approaches to a design problem, creating a child's stool with storage for a junior school library

EVALUATING AND REFINING IDEAS

Once you have several ideas, you need to **evaluate** them. Use your design specification to compare each idea. Then, decide which has the most potential. You could use a comparison table to rate each idea against the most important criteria (Table 3).

Criteria	Idea 1	Idea 2	Idea 3
Easy to use	✓✓	✓	✓✓✓
Eco-friendly	✓	✓✓✓	✓✓
Cost-effective	✓✓	✓	✓✓✓
Meets all user needs	✓✓	✓✓✓	✓

∆ **Table 3** A comparison table

TOP TIP

You may choose to combine aspects from two or more concepts to create a new, improved solution.

DESIGN IN ACTION

Using sketching and evaluating

Product designers, architects, engineers and fashion designers all use sketching and evaluation techniques to test their ideas before committing to one (Figures 9 and 10). These skills are essential in any design career.

Δ **Figure 9** Architects evaluating designs and models

Δ **Figure 10** A fashion designer exploring materials against design specifications

KNOWLEDGE CHECK QUESTIONS

1. State **two** different ways to generate a range of creative ideas for your design.
2. Describe how annotation can help others understand the features or function of your design.
3. Identify the key aspects of your design that annotations should focus on.

KEY TERMS

Annotate: Written explanation of a features or design decisions – more than a label

Biomimicry: An approach to design that takes inspiration from how nature solves problems

Concept: A vision that defines the essential character, purpose, and approach of a design solution

Evaluate: Judging how well a design meets its specification and wider goals

Freehand sketch: A quick drawing to visualise an idea

Isometric drawing: A 3D drawing method using 30° angles to give a realistic sense of shape

1·2·4 Developing

LEARNING AIMS

By the end of this unit, you should

✓ Explore technical and functional aspects of the proposed solution through physical and/or virtual modelling
✓ Communicate the main features of the proposed solution
✓ Specify details of form, materials and construction/production methods
✓ Consider end of life in the design of your product
✓ Evaluate the proposed solution with reference to the specification to determine fitness for purpose and, if necessary, develop the proposed solution further

DEVELOPING YOUR DESIGN

Once you have explored a range of ideas and chosen one, it's time to bring your concept to life!

This is where design development begins – making your idea more realistic, functional and technically sound. Developmental sketching is a brilliant way to do this. It helps you work out how your design could work, what to make it from, how to make it and how sustainable it will be across its life cycle.

At this stage, do not worry about creating perfect drawings – the aim is to explore details such as layout, materials, sizes and functions. You might sketch how a hinge works, test the position of buttons or controls, or show how a fold-out feature saves space. Use arrows, labels and notes to explain your thinking, and zoom in to show aspects of your design in more detail. These sketches show the thinking behind your design decisions and help you solve problems before they arise – a key part of a successful design journey.

TOP TIP

Use tracing paper or layers of digital drawings to test different options without redrawing everything. It helps you iterate quickly and keep track of improvements.

SKILLS ACTIVITY

Developing an idea

Choose one of your initial ideas from the SCAMPER activity in unit 1.2.3, p.55.

1. Create *three* developmental sketches that explore different layouts, materials or features.
2. Annotate each sketch to explain how it could improve user experience, sustainability or functionality.

Development models

Modelling is a powerful design tool. It helps bridge the gap between imagination and reality. Once you have explored your design through sketching, the next step is to develop your ideas further using models.

Why model?

Making a model is not only about proving an idea works, it is a hands-on way to test *how well it works* and to discover *what could be better*. It can reveal problems with size, scale or layout, highlight difficulties in assembly or stability, and uncover opportunities for adding new features or improving usability. Spotting these early on allows you to rethink and refine ideas before investing time or materials.

Models help bring your ideas to life. Whether it is a quick paper prototype or a detailed simulation, modelling allows you to:

- explore how different components fit together
- test materials or construction approaches
- improve the form or function of your design
- communicate your concept clearly to others
- test out how your idea works in three dimensions
- refine the details as you go.

Physical and virtual modelling

To test, refine and communicate your ideas, you might create different types of models. These help you check dimensions, scale and ergonomics before committing to final production. For example:

- **Physical modelling** allows you to visualise your idea by using card, foam board, recycled materials or 3D-printed parts to create an actual model (Figure 1).
- **Virtual modelling** allows you to visualise and test your idea using 3D CAD software to simulate form, movement, assembly or function (Figure 2).

△ **Figure 1** A physical 3D model of an armchair

△ **Figure 2** A virtual 3D model of a component and product

SKILLS ACTIVITY

Modelling your idea

Choose one of your proposed solutions from the skills activities in unit 1.2.3.

1. Create a simple physical model using card or foam.
2. Test it against your design specification. What works well? What needs improvement?

TOP TIP

Use cheap, flexible materials when modelling early on.

DESIGN IN ACTION

Architects don't just design buildings – they shape the world around us. To bring their ideas to life, architects use both physical and virtual modelling (Figure 3). Quick physical models made from card or foamboard help test ideas about space, light and layout. They then use exciting 3D CAD software to explore their designs in virtual worlds, often creating realistic walkthroughs of buildings before anything is built.

If you enjoy creativity, problem-solving and imagining how people use spaces, architecture could be an amazing career path to explore.

△ **Figure 3** Architects working together exploring physical and virtual CAD models of a modern city

COMMUNICATING DESIGN FEATURES

Your developing idea should clearly show the most important aspects of your proposed design solution. These might include:

- how the product works
- its shape, form and dimensions
- what materials it will be made from
- how it will be manufactured or assembled.

Use multiple views (**orthographic**, isometric), annotated sketches or **exploded drawings** (Figure 4) to communicate your thinking clearly. You can also create a **flowchart** showing how the user interacts with the product.

△ **Figure 4** An exploded drawing in CAD to help explain how a design will be assembled

DETAILING FORM, MATERIALS AND CONSTRUCTION

You now need to specify:

- *Form*: the shape, scale and appearance of your product
- *Materials*: what it is made from, and why those materials are suitable
- *Construction or production methods*: how it will be made.

Consider the tools, time, budget and facilities available to you. How do your choices affect quality and sustainability?

REFLECTIVE LOG

Which materials and construction methods suit your design best? Could your product be made in different ways for different users or budgets?

DESIGNING FOR END OF LIFE

Think about what happens to a product after it is no longer needed. Could parts be reused, recycled or repaired?

To design for a circular economy, consider:

- using modular components that are easy to replace (Figure 5)
- using recyclable or biodegradable materials
- minimising your use of mixed materials (they are harder to recycle)
- encouraging users to maintain or repair the product.

△ **Figure 5** A design showing modular parts for easy disassembly and recycling

TOP TIP

Use temporary joining methods instead of glue to make it easier to repair or recycle products.

EVALUATING AND REFINING

Now step back and ask: Does my developed design meet the original brief and specification? If you have developed a number of ideas, you could use evaluation tools such as a design matrix which you will explore in unit 1.2.6.

You could use your specification as a checklist. You might ask:

- Is the product fit for purpose?
- Is it safe and reliable?
- Is it appealing to the user?
- Can it be made within constraints (budget, tools, time)?
- Have I considered sustainability?

If something does not work as well as planned, that's okay. Designers often go through multiple iterations to improve their work.

KNOWLEDGE CHECK

1. Explain how physical or virtual modelling can help you test and improve your design ideas.
2. Describe the key features of your design and explain how you can communicate them clearly to others.
3. Justify which materials and construction methods are most suitable for your product.
4. Explain how your design considers sustainability and what will happen to the product at the end of its life.
5. Analyse evidence from your modelling or research to show how well your design works and suggest what could be improved.

KEY TERMS

Exploded drawing: A drawing that separates parts to show how they fit together

Flowchart: A diagram showing a process or decision path

Orthographic drawing: A set of 2D views used to show accurate dimensions and layout

Physical modelling: Creating a physical representation of a design to test or communicate ideas

Virtual modelling: Using software to visualise, test or simulate a product digitally

1·2·5 Planning

LEARNING AIMS

By the end of this unit, you should:

✓ Produce clear and accurate working drawings with the details needed to make the product
✓ Produce a production plan which includes the stages of making
✓ Specify and justify materials, components and finishes required to make the product
✓ Show a knowledge of available stock forms, types and sizes of materials
✓ Show awareness of social, ethical and environmental factors in planning for production

WORKING DRAWINGS

Working drawings guide the making process. They are essential for communicating your design clearly to others.

Once a proposed solution has been selected and developed, the next step is to prepare detailed working drawings. These should include:

- accurate dimensions
- front, side and top views (known as orthographic drawings)
- **sectional views** to show internal features
- assembly drawings if the product has multiple parts
- notes on materials, fixings, finishes and **tolerances**.

Working drawings can be created by hand or using CAD software. The most important thing is that they are clear, **to scale** and easy to understand (Figure 1).

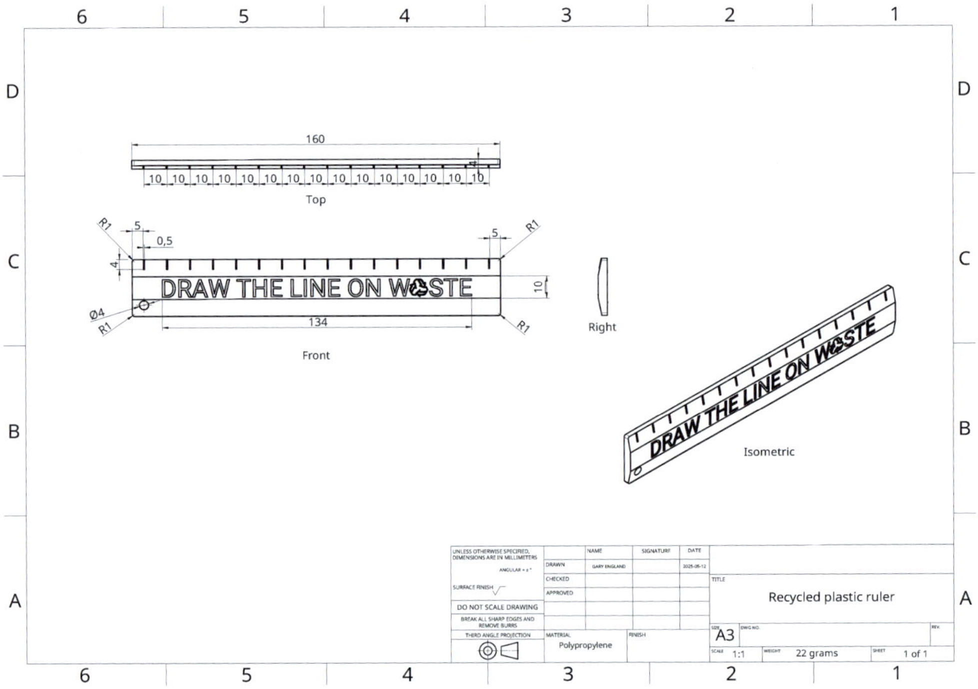

△ **Figure 1** An example of a 3rd angle orthographic projection showing dimensions and scale

TOP TIP

Include a title block on your drawing sheet with your name, the date, scale and drawing title. It looks professional and helps others understand your work.

COMMUNICATING PRODUCTION DETAILS

Once your final design is decided, you need to plan exactly how it will be made. That includes materials, tools and production stages. You also need to clearly explain each aspect.

Exploded views

Imagine your product 'popped apart' in mid-air, with each component hovering in its place – that's your exploded view.

Exploded drawings show how each part of your product fits together (Figure 2). They are especially useful for communicating assembly order and part relationships. Exploded drawings help you, and others, see how to build products and spot any design issues before the making process begins.

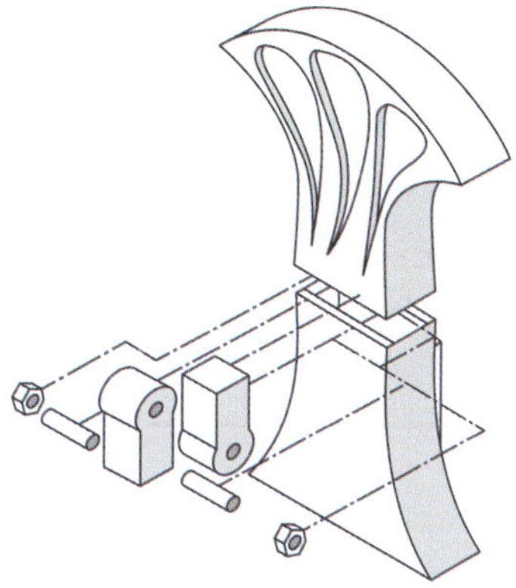

△ **Figure 2** An exploded view of a hinge for a component

Materials list

A materials list is like a shopping list for your design (Table 1). By creating a list of materials, you can save time, reduce waste and ensure that you have not forgotten anything when production of your product begins. It includes:

- what materials or components are needed
- the quantity of each item sizes or dimensions.

Component	Material	Width (mm)	Length (mm)	Depth (mm)	Quantity	Image
Top base	Timber	168	627.8	20	1	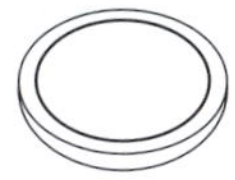
Acrylic tube	PLA	144	452.4	146	1	
Disc stability for tube	Laser plywood	142	447	4	1	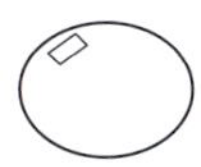
Bottom base	Laser plywood	160	602.7	6	2	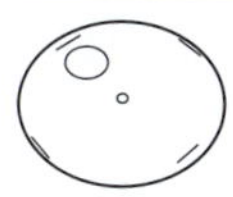
Finger joint	Laser plywood	15	10	3	4	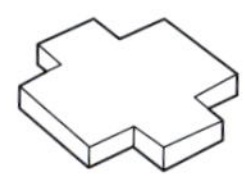

△ **Table 1** An example of a materials list

CREATING A PRODUCTION PLAN

A **production plan** breaks down the stages of making your product in the correct order. It helps you to stay organised, to allocate your time and resources effectively, and to reduce mistakes and waste.

Your plan should include:

- a list of tasks in a logical sequence
- tools and materials required for each stage
- an estimated time for each task
- health and safety considerations
- **quality control** (**QC**) checks.

SKILLS ACTIVITY

Production planning

Create a production plan for a simple wooden desk organiser. Include at least five stages. For each stage, list the tools and materials needed and identify *one* potential risk or challenge.

DESIGN IN ACTION

In architecture and construction, a **Gantt chart** is often used to plan out all the phases of a building project (Figure 3), from foundation pouring to electrical wiring and interior finishes. You can adapt this style to visualise your own production schedule.

△ **Figure 3** Project planning using a Gantt chart to track progress

SELECTING MATERIALS, COMPONENTS AND FINISHES

You must select appropriate materials and components that suit your product's function, appearance and user needs. It is important to explain your reasoning. Think about:

- properties (for example, strength, flexibility, thermal insulation)
- aesthetics (for example, colour, texture, transparency)
- cost and availability
- environmental impact.

Finishes such as paint, varnish or powder coating may improve appearance or protect materials.

REFLECTIVE LOG

Which materials have you selected for the desk organiser in the earlier 'Production planning' activity? Write down **two** reasons for each choice and consider whether they are the most sustainable option available.

UNDERSTANDING STOCK FORMS, TYPES AND SIZES

When planning production, you must know how materials are supplied. For example:

- Timber is often sold as planks, dowels, sheets or mouldings.
- Metals may come in rods, sheets, tubes or bars.
- Polymers are available as sheets, films, rolls and filaments.

Choosing the right **stock form** reduces waste and makes processing easier. You will find more information on stock forms, types and sizes in Topics 2.1 and 3.1.

ETHICAL AND ENVIRONMENTAL PLANNING

Designers have a responsibility to reduce harm and increase fairness in how products are made. When planning production, consider the following questions:

- Can offcuts be reused or recycled?
- Are your materials sourced from sustainable or ethical suppliers?
- Have you reduced transport distances?
- Can you design out unnecessary waste or energy use?

In inclusive design, also ask:

- Can this product be assembled or repaired easily by its user?
- Does the design avoid bias or exclusion (for example left-handed use, physical limitations)?

Some fashion designers use zero-waste pattern cutting techniques, where every part of the fabric is carefully planned and used to avoid waste. This saves money and reduces the amount of leftover textile. In product design, a similar approach is called **nesting** – arranging shapes or parts on a material sheet in the most efficient way to minimise waste (Figure 4).

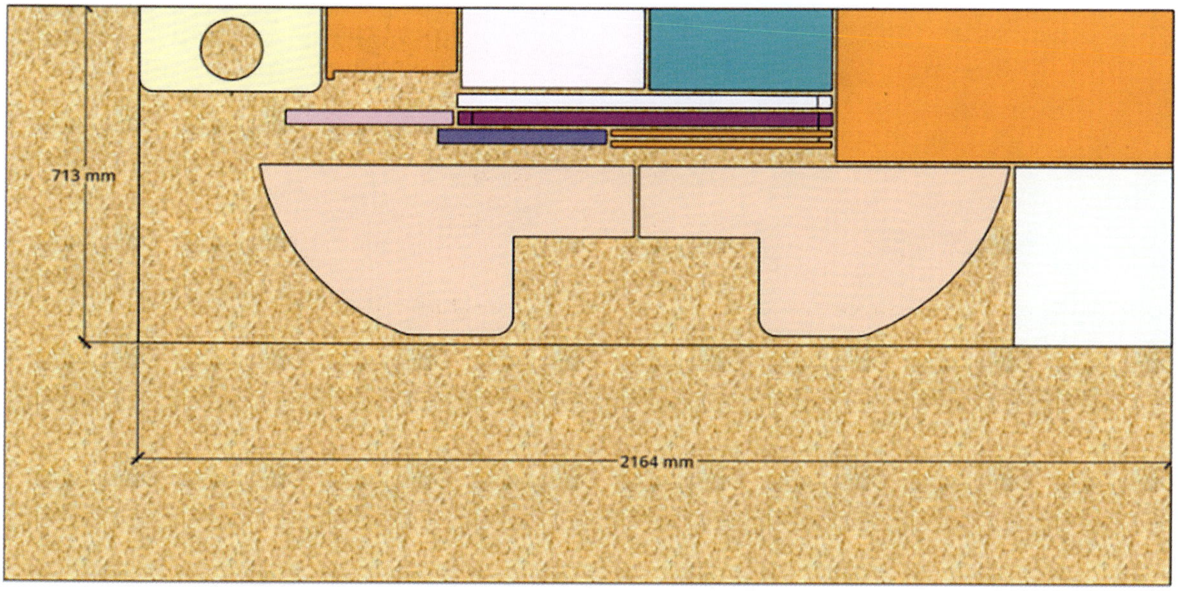

△ **Figure 4** A student's layout plan showing material cuts on a plywood sheet to minimise waste

KNOWLEDGE CHECK

1. Identify the common stock forms of the materials you plan to use.
2. Justify why these stock forms are suitable for your design, and the tools or processes available in school.

KEY TERMS

Gantt chart: A chart that shows a project schedule, showing the start dates and durations of different tasks in the project*

Nesting: Arranging shapes or parts on a material sheet in the most efficient way to minimise waste

Production plan: A step-by-step guide for how a product will be made

Quality control (QC): Checking products at stages during manufacture to find faults

Sectional view: A view of a face of an object as if it has been cut through

Stock forms: The standard shapes, sizes and forms that a material can be bought in*

Tolerance: The amount of variation in a physical dimension or measurement that is allowed in a part or component

To scale: A ratio that shows the relationship between the size of a drawing and the actual size of the object

Working drawing: A detailed drawing that shows dimensions, views and notes for making a product

1·2·6 Testing and evaluating

LEARNING AIMS

By the end of this unit, you should:

✓ Understand the importance of testing and evaluating throughout the design process
✓ Evaluate a product with reference to the specification, and its social, ethical and environmental impact throughout its life cycle
✓ Make concluding comments about the successes and limitations of the design
✓ Identify proposals for further development of a product

WHY TESTING AND EVALUATING MATTERS

Testing and evaluating should take place at different stages of the design process – not just at the end. Whether you are checking the stability of a cardboard model or comparing material durability, regular testing helps ensure your final product meets the needs of users and the expectations set out in your design specification.

Evaluation allows you to reflect on how well your solution works, how it could be improved and how it fits into the world around it. A good designer is never fully finished – they continually refine their ideas through iteration, using each round of testing and feedback to improve their design.

TESTING AT DIFFERENT STAGES

Designers use a variety of testing methods to check performance, gather feedback and make improvements. These tests help ensure that the product is functional, safe and meets user needs. You should be testing your ideas from the very beginning (Table 1).

Stage	Questions to answer
Early modelling	Does an exploratory cardboard or CAD model show that your idea could work? What does not work yet?
Material testing	Which finish is most durable? Which material bends or flexes best? What is safest?
User feedback	Ask your target users to trial an early exploratory model or prototype. What do they like? What confuses them?

△ **Table 1** Stages of testing and the questions to answer

You might carry out:

- *Simulations:* Digital or physical models testing how a product might behave in real-world conditions.
- *User feedback:* Asking people to comment on your ideas, prototypes or models to highlight strengths and areas for improvement.
- *Product analysis:* Examining existing products to identify what works well and what could be better.

- *Expert appraisal:* Getting feedback from a specialist or technician to check quality or suitability.
- *Field tests:* Trying out your product in the environment for which it is designed.

These methods support iterative design by helping you test, evaluate and improve your product at every stage.

SKILLS ACTIVITY

Testing materials

Design and carry out a simple test to compare two different materials based on a specific property.

Choose a property that is important for your product.

For example:

- strength (for example, how much weight it can hold)
- flexibility (for example, how far it can bend without breaking)
- water resistance (for example, how well it repels water)
- thermal insulation (for example, how well it keeps heat in or out)
- surface finish (for example, how smooth or suitable it is for your design).

Record:

1. your testing method

2. the results for each material

3. what you learned about which material is most suitable, and why.

Final check

When your prototype model or final product is complete, you need to check it against your original design specification. This helps you judge how well your design meets its intended purpose and highlights areas for improvement.

Go through each specification point and ask:

- Has it been fully met?
- Has it been partially met?
- Has it not been met at all?

Be specific.

For example:

- If your product was supposed to be lightweight, weigh it and compare it to similar products.
- If it needs to be waterproof, carry out a water-resistance test.
- If it should be intuitive to use, observe someone interacting with it without instructions.

Recording and evidencing your testing

Good designers don't just test their products – they record the results clearly and back up their evaluations with evidence. By doing this, you can validate your design and help others understand the thinking behind your conclusions. You can record your data using different methods, such as:

- tables or checklists to compare your product to your specification points
- photographs or videos showing the product being tested
- graphs or charts for weight, strength or time-based comparisons
- user feedback forms, quotes or interviews
- annotated images showing test results, issues or suggested improvements.

What is RAG rating?

RAG rating is a simple colour-coded system to show how well your product meets each requirement (Table 2).

RAG stands for Red, Amber, Green.

Colour	Meaning	Outcome	For example: your product must hold 1 kg
Red	Does *not meet* the requirement	Your product failed the test or missed the design goal completely	It held only 500 g
Amber	*Partially meets* the requirement	Your product meets part of the requirement but needs improvement	It held more than 1 kg for a short amount of time before collapsing
Green	*Fully meets* the requirement	Your product clearly meets or exceeds the requirement	It held more than 1 kg

Δ **Table 2** How to read RAG ratings

Tips for synthesising your findings

- Summarise your results clearly for each specification point.
- Use RAG rating or scoring systems to make judgements visual and easy to follow.
- Link your evidence directly to your specification. For example, *'Water leaked through the base seam after testing, so this point is rated Amber.'*

Testing and evaluation are key parts of the iterative design process. Your recorded evidence helps justify decisions, guide improvements and show how your design performs in real use.

USING A DESIGN MATRIX TO COMPARE AND IMPROVE IDEAS

When you have several design ideas, it can be difficult to choose which one to develop further. A design matrix enables you to compare each idea against your specification (Table 3). This structured approach makes it easier to identify the strongest concept, areas for improvement and how well your idea solves the problem compared to existing products.

Specification point	Design A: Backpack	Design B: Tote bag	Design C: Messenger bag
Capacity	4	3	5
Comfort	5	2	4
Durability	4	4	4
Style	3	5	4
Sustainability	2	3	3
Total score	**18**	**17**	**20**

△ **Table 3** A design matrix for a new bag design. Design C (messenger bag) is chosen for further development because it scores highest overall, particularly well in capacity and comfort.

REFLECTIVE LOG

Use a design matrix to evaluate some design ideas you have produced for a project. Would you change anything about your initial designs now?

SUCCESS AND LIMITATIONS

Once you have tested and compared your design against the specification and considered wider impacts, you can draw your final conclusions.

Ask yourself:

- What works really well?
- What could have been done better?
- If you had more time or resources, what would you change?

IDEAS FOR FURTHER DEVELOPMENT

Even a good design can be improved. For example, a folding bike design might be improved by using lighter materials, adjusting the folding mechanism or changing the wheel size for better stability. Identify changes or next steps, such as:

- redesigning a component for better strength or sustainability
- changing a material for ethical sourcing
- adding features based on user feedback
- simplifying the construction process.

TOP TIP

One of the most effective ways to communicate your improvements is visually. This can help both you and others understand how your product is developing and why changes are needed.

You could:

- sketch improved versions of parts that need fixing or refining
- create new CAD models showing changes in materials, layout or dimensions
- modify your prototype or model to show how problems have been addressed
- annotate your visuals to explain exactly what has been changed, and why.

THINKING BEYOND THE PRODUCT

A good evaluation does not stop at how well the product functions – it also considers the wider impact of the design (Table 4). Thinking about these broader factors helps you design more responsibly – and prepares you to explain how your product fits into the real world.

Social	**Marketing**
Who benefits from your design? Have you considered inclusivity, accessibility or how different users might interact with it?	How will the product be presented to users? Have you considered the logo, branding or promotional materials that would appeal to your target audience?
Ethical	**Environmental**
Were the materials sourced responsibly? Are workers treated fairly during manufacturing?	What is the product's carbon footprint? Can it be recycled, reused or designed for disassembly?

Δ **Table 4** Questions to consider beyond the product

DESIGN IN ACTION

The Eden Project biodomes

In architectural design, the Eden Project biodomes were evaluated for both function and environmental impact (Figure 1). Designers considered energy use, local biodiversity and visitor accessibility.

Δ **Figure 1** The Eden Project in England, UK

KNOWLEDGE CHECK

1. Explain why is it important to test and evaluate your design throughout the design process.
2. Give **one** method you can use to evaluate a product against the original design specification.
3. Explain the possible social, ethical or environmental impacts your product could have.
4. Give **one** example of an improvement or further development you can make to your product.

KEY TERMS

RAG rating: A simple colour-coded system (Red, Amber, Green) used to evaluate how well something meets certain criteria

1.3 Communicating designs

1.3.1 Drawing techniques

LEARNING AIMS

By the end of this unit, you should:

✓ Use freehand sketching and annotations to communicate design ideas
✓ Understand the use of orthographic, isometric, exploded drawings and developments (nets)
✓ Understand the use of flowcharts, Gantt charts and materials lists in planning for making
✓ Understand the use of computer-aided design (CAD) where appropriate

DRAWING TO EXPLORE AND COMMUNICATE

Design drawings help you to explore ideas, refine your thinking and communicate clearly with others, whether they are team members, users or manufacturers. A good designer selects the most suitable type of drawing or planning tool to match the design stage and audience. For more in-depth guidance on drawing techniques, see Topic 3.2.

ANNOTATING YOUR DRAWINGS

Adding smart, purposeful annotations to your sketches helps explain your thinking and justify your design choices. Annotations are not just labels – they show how and why your idea works. Think of them as your design voice on the page, helping others understand the features, materials, components or construction methods you have chosen.

Use arrows to direct your notes to specific parts of your drawing, and aim to move beyond simple tags such as 'screen' or 'handle'. Use the PEL method: **P**oint, **E**xplanation, **L**ink. This is a powerful way to show that you are designing with purpose. For example:

Point	Explanation	Link to client need/specification
Made from ABS, a strong, impact-resistant thermo polymer	*because it is tough and impact-resistant,*	*so it will not easily break if the user drops it.*

If you are unsure what to write, check your specification. Ask yourself:

- Does this part meet a specification point?
- Why have I chosen this material, feature or shape?
- How does it help solve the user's problem?

TOP TIP

For great annotations:

- *Be efficient:* Write neatly in pen from the start – skip the pencil rewrite.
- *Colour it clever:* Use colour-coding. For example, **green for sustainability**, **blue for client needs** and **red for performance or safety**.
- *All CAPS help:* If handwriting is tricky, PRINT in capitals or scan and add typed annotations.

FREEHAND SKETCHES

Freehand sketching is a fast, expressive way to capture your design ideas before they disappear. It is not about being perfect; it is about communicating what's in your head.

How to improve your sketching skills:

- *Start with simple geometric shapes* – boxes, cylinders, spheres – and turn them into objects.
- *Use light construction lines* to plan proportions before adding detail.
- *Practise sketching everyday items* around you quickly and loosely.
- *Show movement or function* with arrows and annotation.

TOP TIP

You can scan or photograph your sketches and use them as underlays in 2D CAD software to trace, refine and develop accurate models.

ISOMETRIC DRAWING

Isometric drawings show 3D objects clearly, using 30° angles to help represent form without distortion (Figure 1). These are useful for showing how different features and parts fit together. Refer to unit 3.2.1 to see more examples of isometric drawings.

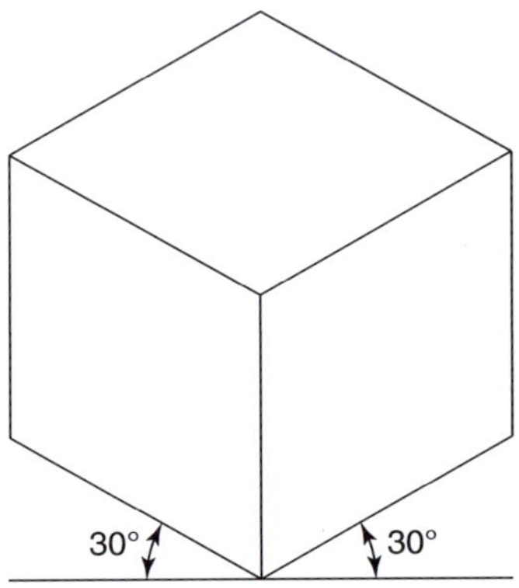

△ **Figure 1** An isometric drawing of a cube

How to draw isometrically:

- Use isometric grid paper or mark 30° angles from a horizontal base line.
- Start by **crating** the overall dimensions to define your product's size – use a box in which you can draw shapes.
- Build up features from the crate: add curves, cut-outs or handles.
- Use parallel lines only – no perspective or vanishing points.
- Keep edges consistent and use darker lines for outlines.

TOP TIP

Most 3D CAD software can automatically generate isometric views from your model. Use this to create polished, annotated views for presenting your idea.

ORTHOGRAPHIC PROJECTION

Orthographic drawings show your product from different views – typically front, side and plan (top) – to give accurate information about size and shape (Figure 2). Refer to unit 3.2.1 to see more examples of orthographic drawings.

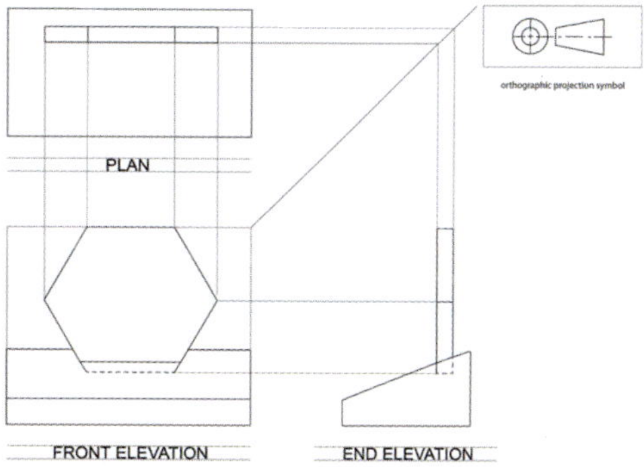

Δ **Figure 2** An orthographic projection of a trophy

How to practise orthographic drawings:

- Draw each view to the same scale on squared or plain paper.
- Use a ruler and sharp pencil for precision.
- Align views vertically and horizontally so they match up.
- Add key dimensions with arrows and measurements.
- Label each view clearly and include a title block.

TOP TIP

CAD software can produce precise orthographic drawings with dimensions from a 3D model. This is particularly useful when preparing technical or working drawings.

EXPLODED DRAWINGS

Exploded views show how a product fits together by pulling apart the components in a logical, spaced-out arrangement (Figure 3). They are excellent for showing assembly.

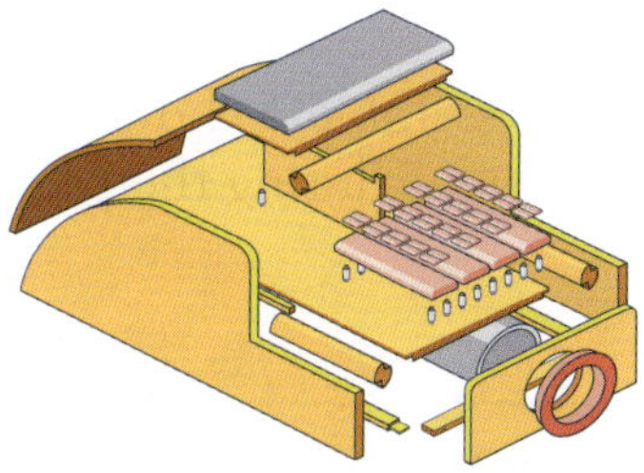

Δ **Figure 3** An exploded view of a component

How to create an exploded view:

- Start with an isometric or 3D base drawing of the full product.
- Gently separate each part while keeping them in line with their positions.
- Use faint lines to show how parts connect (called guide or ghost lines).
- Label each part clearly – this is often combined with a parts list or cutting list.
- Keep the spacing even and logical – too much can be confusing.

TOP TIP

CAD models can be exploded with a click and viewed from any angle. You can also animate the assembly process and generate an exploded view drawing.

DEVELOPMENTS (NETS)

A **development** or **net** is a 2D pattern that folds up to create a 3D shape (Figure 4). Developments are essential for packaging design and any product made from sheet materials. Refer to unit 3.2.1 to see more examples of developments/nets.

Δ **Figure 4** An example of a development/net folded, ready to be made into a 3D package

How to create a net:

- Sketch your product as a box or shape that can unfold.
- Use construction lines to build each face in proportion.
- Add tabs for gluing or slots for glue-less assembly.
- Label each panel and fold line – use dashed lines for folds.
- Test it by cutting and folding a prototype in card or paper.

TOP TIP

Some CAD software can unfold 3D models into flat patterns. This is great for designing packaging or laser-cut components with precision.

FLOWCHARTS

Flowcharts can show processes such as user interactions or making stages (Figure 5). Use clear boxes and arrows to show step-by-step decisions.

A flowchart shows a process in a sequential manner. It is often used in design to give information on how to make something. A flowchart always runs from top to bottom and consists of a series of shapes with connector arrows. Table 1 shows the shapes for different functions during the product design process.

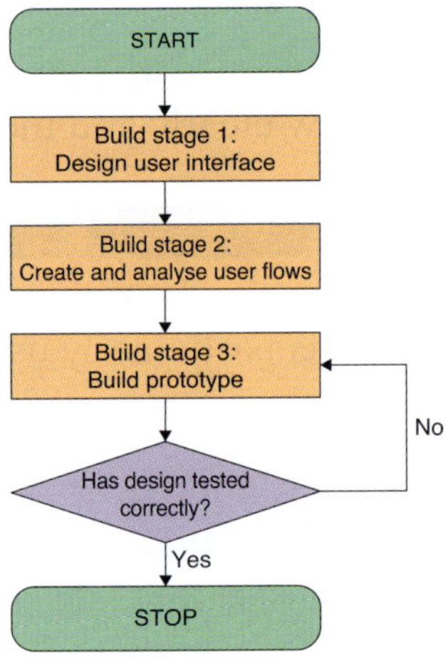

△ **Figure 5** An example of a product design flowchart

Shape	Name	Function
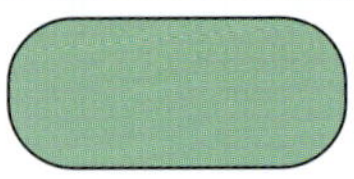	Start/End	An oval shape is called a 'terminator', and is used at the start and end of the process.
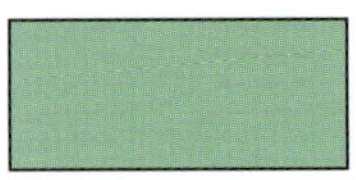	Process	A rectangle is used to show a stage in the process.
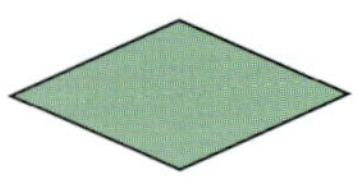	Decision	A diamond shape is used for a decision or quality check. There should be two arrows leading from this box to other parts of the process. This is called a feedback loop.
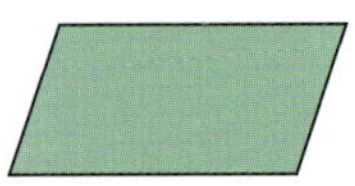	Input/Output	A parallelogram is used for input/output. This stage indicates something which is added or removed from the process.
	Arrow	An arrow is a connector that shows relationships between the different stages.

△ **Table 1** Flowchart shapes for different functions during the product design process

SKILLS ACTIVITY

Create a flowchart

Create a flowchart showing the user journey for a hand-drying station.

Your flowchart should include:

- The step-by-step actions a user takes (for example, approaching the station, placing hands under the sensor).
- Sensor detection and how it activates the dryer.
- Decision points to show what happens if something goes wrong (for example, hands are not detected or held too far away from the sensor).
- Clear symbols for actions, processes and decisions (refer to Table 1 above).

You can draw your flowchart by hand or by using a digital tool.

TOP TIP

Think: What does the user expect to happen at each stage? What if the design fails?

GANTT CHARTS

A Gantt chart is a simple – but effective – way to plan your project (Figure 6). It helps you stay organised and make the most of your time. It shows what tasks need doing, how long each one will take and whether any tasks can be done at the same time. For example, if you are 3D printing a part and it takes a few hours, you could plan another task, such as developing your model or testing materials, while it prints. That way, you are not wasting time by just waiting.

Using a Gantt chart helps you keep your project on track.

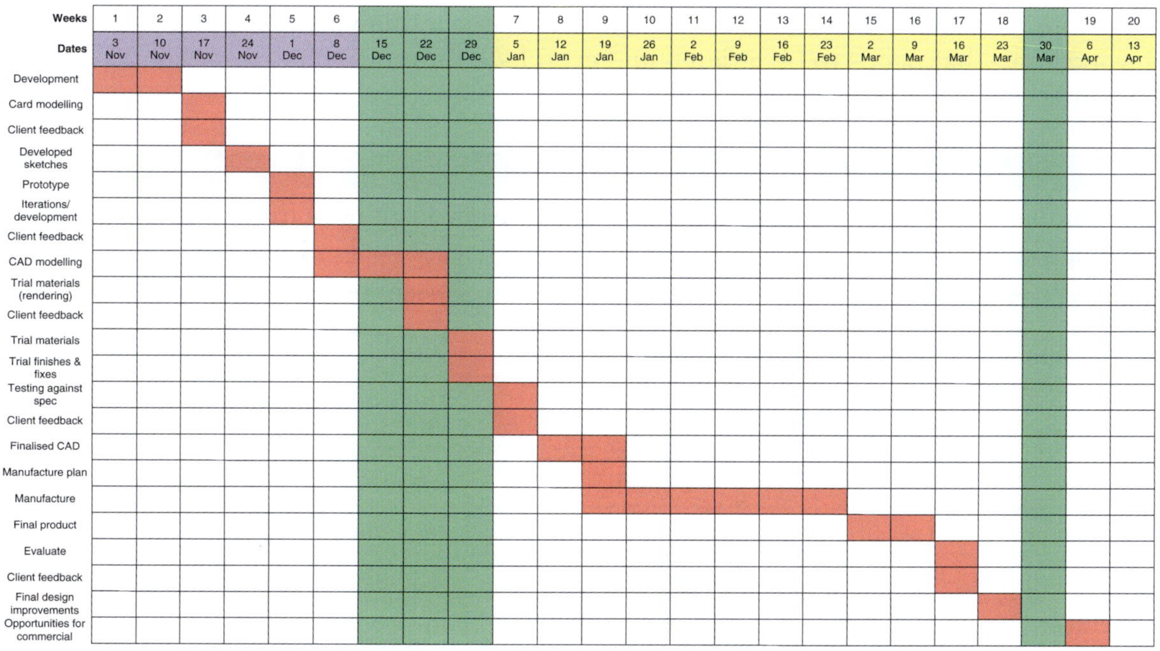

Δ **Figure 6** An example of a Gantt chart

TOP TIP

Try colour-coding your chart to show tasks that need tools, computers, or teamwork – it makes it easier to follow and plan ahead.

SKILLS ACTIVITY

Interpreting a Gantt chart: Project planning and time management

Study the Gantt chart in Figure 6. Then answer the following questions:

1. Identify *two* tasks that took place over the longest period of time. What does this suggest about their importance or complexity?
2. Which *three* stages involved 'Client feedback'? How were these moments spaced throughout the project, and why might this be useful?
3. Which tasks overlapped, and what are the benefits or challenges of overlapping tasks in a project?
4. Suggest *one* way the timing or order of tasks could be improved to make the project run more smoothly. Use evidence from the chart to support your suggestion.

MATERIALS LISTS

A materials list includes everything you will need to make your product – from main materials to fasteners, finishes and components (Table 2). It helps you stay organised, make sure nothing is forgotten and estimate the total cost of your project.

Create your list early. This means you can check what is available in the workshop, what needs to be ordered and even look for more sustainable or affordable alternatives.

TOP TIP

Group similar items together (for example, all finishes or fasteners) to make it easier to find things later.

Item/component	Size/dimensions	Quantity	Purpose/notes
Plywood (A4 sheet)	6 mm A4 sheet	1	Main structure of phone stand
Sandpaper	medium + fine	2 sheets	Smoothing edges and surfaces
Wood glue		1 tube	For joining parts
Clear varnish		Small pot	To protect and finish the surface
Rubber feet	12 mm	4	To stop the stand slipping on smooth surfaces

△ **Table 2** A materials list

TOP TIP

Some CAD software can automatically generate a materials list from your orthographic projection. This is especially useful for planning manufacturing and ordering materials accurately. It also saves time and reduces waste.

USING CAD

Computer-aided design (CAD) is useful for refining and testing your ideas. It can speed up prototyping and reduce errors in manufacturing.

CAREER FOCUS

Architecture, furniture design and manufacturing

Product designers and engineers use CAD software daily. Proficiency in 2D and 3D tools such as AutoCAD, Fusion 360 or SolidWorks can lead to careers in architecture, furniture design and manufacturing.

KNOWLEDGE CHECK

1. Identify which stage of the design process orthographic drawings are used.
2. Explain how exploded views help communicate construction or assembly.
3. Justify the usefulness of Gantt charts when managing a design project timeline.
4. Explain how a flowchart helps plan manufacturing steps or decision-making processes.
5. Describe what should be included in a materials list and explain how it can help with costing and preparation.
6. Give **three** examples of how CAD can be used in the design process.

KEY TERMS

Crating: Drawing a simple 3D shape first (e.g. a box or cylinder), or combination of regular 3D shapes, inside which you can draw a more detailed design

Development/Net: A 2D shape that folds into a 3D object

1·3·2 Modelling

LEARNING AIMS

By the end of this unit, you should:

✓ Understand the reasons for modelling
✓ Understand different types of models, including exploratory and prototype
✓ Produce models and use them to draw conclusions that influence design development

WHY IS MODELLING IMPORTANT?

Modelling turns your ideas into something real. Whether it is a rough cardboard mock-up, a digital simulation or a working prototype, modelling allows you to:

- visualise your idea
- test the design and materials
- explore ergonomics and scale
- identify problems before manufacture
- gather feedback from clients or users.

It is the only way to physically interact with your concept, experiencing how it looks, feels and functions.

DESIGN IN ACTION

Prototyping engineer: Bridging ideas and reality

Prototyping engineers turn creative concepts into testable physical or virtual models; they turn ideas into real innovations.

This is a key role in industries such as product design, consumer technology, architecture, medical engineering and automotive development.

You could be working on anything from testing a new smartphone grip to developing life-saving surgical tools. Prototyping engineers use a wide range of tools and techniques, from hand-building models out of foam, clay or **polymorph**, to running computer simulations or printing complex shapes using 3D printers. Key skills include:

- a strong understanding of materials and their properties
- CAD (computer-aided design)/CAM expertise (computer-aided manufacture)
- creative problem-solving and precision
- the ability to give and respond to constructive feedback
- good communication skills to work closely with designers and engineers.

Pathways

Most prototyping engineers have qualifications in product design, engineering, industrial design or model-making. Some begin with an apprenticeship and build experience in workshops or research and development (R & D) departments.

Did you know?

James Dyson made over 5000 prototypes before launching his first bagless vacuum cleaner. Many companies rely on skilled prototyping teams to test ideas quickly and efficiently.

If you enjoy designing, making and improving things, this could be the perfect role for you.

TYPES OF MODELS

Exploratory models

Exploratory modelling is quick and simple. It involves making a physical or virtual model early in the design process to explore shape, size or layout. The model is not meant to be perfect, just helpful. For example, a designer might make:

- a folded card prototype of a flat-pack bookshelf for tight student living spaces
- a **foamboard** model of a wearable medical device to test fit and comfort
- an exploratory model of an inclusive classroom desk with space for wheelchair users.

SKILLS ACTIVITY

Making an exploratory model

Make an exploratory model of an everyday product using only card, masking tape and scissors. Focus on shape, size and how it fits into its surroundings.

Prototype models

Prototype models are more detailed and functional. They are used to test how well something works and may be used to gather user feedback. For example, a designer might make:

- a working cardboard and plastic model of a solar-powered window fan
- a full-size 3D-printed reusable water bottle with ergonomic grip.

DESIGN IN ACTION

Engineers at Rolls-Royce use detailed 3D models of jet engine parts to test airflow, safety and material behaviour before manufacturing anything at full-scale (Figure 1).

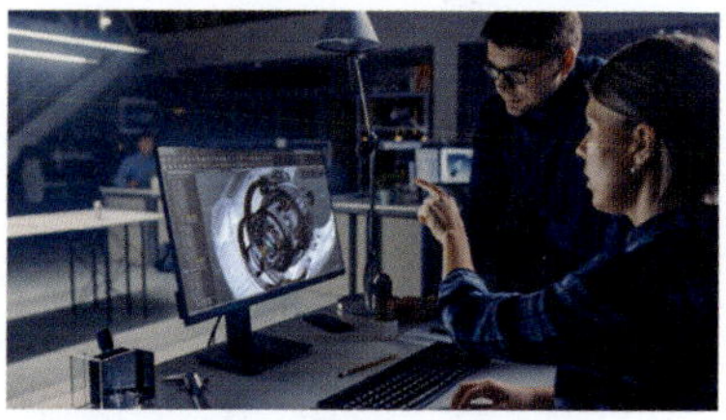

Δ **Figure 1** Engineers using CAD to run simulations on an engine.

MATERIALS FOR MODELLING

You can use a wide range of materials for making models. Some materials are easy to shape or cut, while others are more durable and suited for testing (Table 1).

Material	Best for
Cardboard	Rough exploratory models
Foamboard	Lightweight models for buildings/furniture
Clay/modelling foam	Organic shapes and quick forms
3D printing filament	Accurate functional prototype models
Polymorph	Using a smart material to allow easy remodelling of ideas to test ergonomics or functions
Recycled plastic or scrap materials	Testing sustainable product ideas

△ **Table 1** Materials you can use for modelling

TOP TIP

Use scrap and recycled materials whenever possible to build exploratory models (Figure 2). It saves money and reduces waste. Label your model with sticky notes to explain parts or record things you want to improve later.

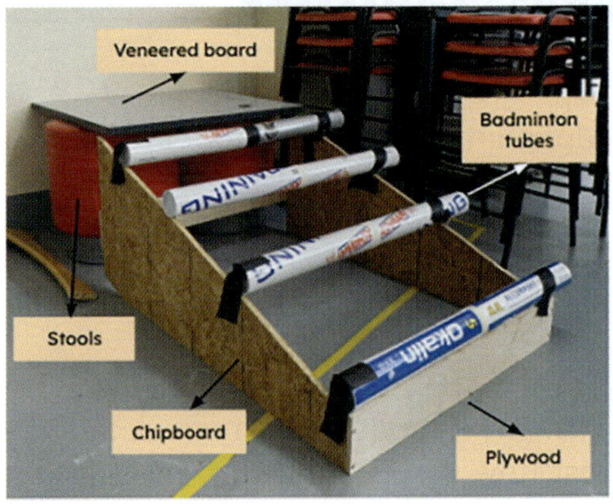

△ **Figure 2** A student's model made with scrap material and workshop furniture

DIGITAL MODELLING WITH CAD

CAD allows you to make detailed virtual models. Many CAD programs enable virtual simulations, such as stress testing or airflow (Figure 3).

CAD modelling has several advantages, including:

- CAD can be shared and edited easily.
- CAD can produce photo-realistic **renderings**.
- CAD can be tested in different environments (wind, pressure, heat).
- CAD can be exported for 3D printing or computer numerical control (CNC) manufacture.

△ **Figure 3** A mechanical engineer testing fluid dynamics using CAD simulation

MODELLING WITH CAM AND RAPID PROTOTYPING

Computer-aided manufacture (CAM) includes 3D printing, CNC cutting and laser cutting. Once your virtual model is ready, you can create precise parts or full models using machines.

DESIGN IN ACTION

Engineers developing earthquake-proof buildings use scaled models placed on a shake table to simulate seismic activity (Figure 4). These models help them understand how their design performs under stress.

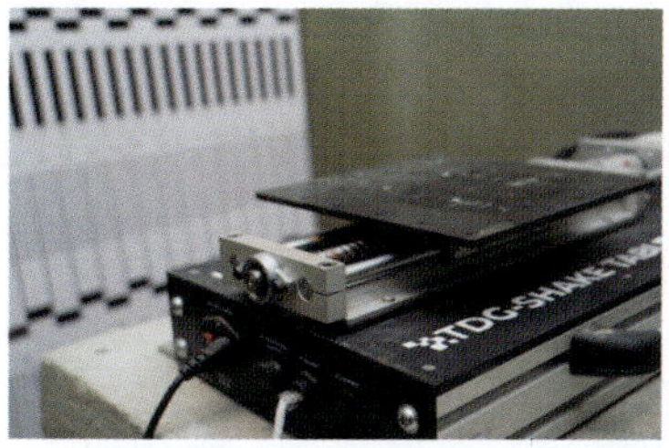

△ **Figure 4** An architect testing a model building using a shake table

USING MODELS TO IMPROVE DESIGN

As you test models, you will notice problems or ideas for improvement. Modelling helps you answer questions such as:

- Is it the right size?
- Can it be assembled easily?
- Does it look as intended?
- Does it function properly?

Using exploratory and prototype models in your design process helps turn ideas into better solutions. Many of the most successful products have been through hundreds of design changes through modelling.

REFLECTIVE LOG

What did you learn from the last model you made? What would you change about your idea? Write what you discovered from building or testing it.

KNOWLEDGE CHECK

1. Explain why designers use different types of model during the development process.
2. Compare an exploratory model and a prototype model.
3. Describe the types of materials commonly used for physical modelling, and explain why each is used.
4. Explain how CAD can help improve a design before physical modelling begins.
5. Analyse the advantages of using CAM tools like 3D printing or laser cutting to create prototype models.
6. Explain how feedback from a client about a model can help you improve your final product.
7. Analyse the ways in which modelling can help with ergonomics, scale or assembly during the design process.
8. Explain how digital simulations in CAD save time and resources when testing ideas.

KEY TERMS

Exploratory modelling: A physical or virtual representation of a design idea, used to test initial concepts, explore different forms and basic proportions

Foamboard: Lightweight, rigid 'sandwich' of foam core between stiff outer layers available in sheets

Polymorph: A polymer that can be easily shaped when heated

Rendering: The process of shading a drawing using light and dark tones

1·4 Making principles

1·4·1 Making principles: tools and materials

LEARNING AIMS

By the end of this unit, you should:

✓ Show knowledge of accurately measuring and marking out using appropriate tools and equipment for papers and boards, timber, metals, polymers, composites and smart materials

✓ Show knowledge of cutting, shaping and forming using appropriate tools and equipment for these materials

✓ Show knowledge of temporary and permanent methods for these materials

✓ Show knowledge of a range of finishes for these materials

MEASURING AND MARKING OUT

What happens once a design solution has been agreed upon and approved by the client and users? The next step is to prepare for production. This stage builds on the drawings, research and exploratory prototypes completed earlier in the design process.

Marking out

Marking out involves transferring measurements from technical drawings onto raw materials in preparation for cutting, shaping or machining.

Before marking out, it is important to ensure that the material has been prepared according to the cutting list and that all dimensions are accurate – this is a key part of quality control.

A crucial step in marking out is establishing a **datum** – a precise reference line or point from which all measurements are taken (Figure 1). This ensures consistency and accuracy throughout the manufacturing process. Once the datum is set, the material can be accurately marked using appropriate tools, ready for the next stages of production.

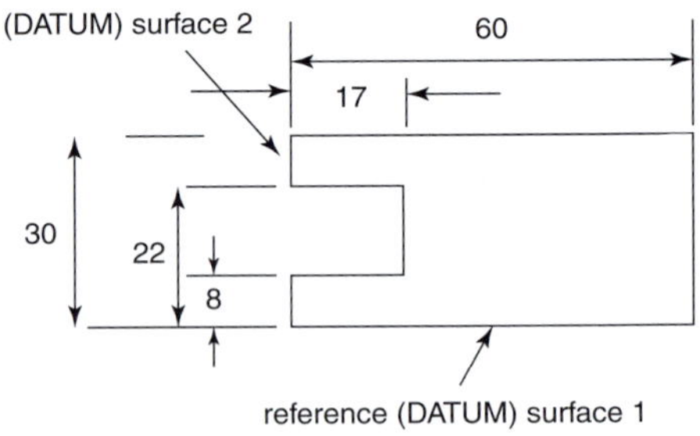

△ **Figure 1** An example of datum lines on an orthographic drawing

Tools for marking out

Table 1 lists common marking out tools used in a basic workshop setting. Accurate marking out is a critical step in the manufacturing process. Mistakes at this stage can lead to wasted materials, lost time and increased costs. To ensure precision and efficiency, always follow these key guidelines:

- Use sharp and well-maintained marking out tools to achieve clean, accurate lines.
- Position marking guides carefully and securely on the material before making any marks.
- Continuously check your measurements and markings against your orthographic drawings to confirm accuracy.

Take your time and work methodically during marking out. This will help ensure a successful and high-quality outcome in the later stages of production.

Tool	Paper/board	Timber	Metals	Polymers	Composite
Pencil	✓	✓	×	×	✓
Marking knife	✓	✓	×	✓	×
Scriber	×	×	✓	✓	×
Marking gauge	×	✓	×	×	×
Odd leg callipers	×	×	✓	×	×
Crayon	✓	×	×	✓	✓
Tri-square	✓	✓	×	✓	✓
Engineer's square	×	×	✓	✓	✓
Compass	✓	✓	×	✓	✓
Templates	✓	✓	✓	✓	✓
Engineer's ruler	✓	✓	✓	✓	✓
Sliding bevel	✓	✓	✓	✓	✓

△ **Table 1** Tools for marking out

TOP TIP

When marking out, follow the saying: 'check twice, cut once.' Mark out your work, double check it against the drawing – perhaps even ask someone else to check it – and then cut.

CUTTING, SHAPING AND FORMING

The products we use every day are made from a wide range of materials, each requiring specific processes to cut, shape, form, join, assemble, finish and test. We use a variety of tools, machines and equipment. While many industrial techniques may not be available in a school workshop, it is important to develop an understanding of commercial manufacturing methods. This knowledge helps you appreciate how products are made efficiently and cost-effectively on a larger scale.

If a product is successful and moves into mass production, it must be manufactured quickly, consistently and at a low cost. Understanding which machines and processes are used in industry is essential for designing products that are suitable for commercial manufacture. Table 2 provides a general overview of materials, and the industrial processes commonly used with them.

Shaping		Paper/board	Timber	Metals	Polymers	Composites
Cutting	Laser cutting	✓	✓	✓	✓	✓
	Planing	×	✓	×	×	×
	Laser cutting	✓	✓	✓	✓	✓
	Die cutting	✓	×	×	×	×
	Sawing	×	✓	✓	✓	✓
Wasting	Turning	×	✓	✓	✓	×
	Milling	×	✓	✓	✓	×
	Routing	×	✓	✓	✓	✓
	Drilling	×	✓	✓	✓	✓
Finishing	Laminating	✓	✓	✓	✓	×
	Painting – oil based	✓	✓	✓	×	×
	– solvent based	×	✓	✓	×	×
	– water	×	✓	✓	×	×
	Polishing	×	✓	✓	✓	✓
	Powder coating	×	×	✓	×	×
Forming	Vacuum forming	×	×	×	✓	×
	Line bending	×	×	×	✓	×
Moulding	Injection moulding	×	×	×	✓	×
	Blow moulding	×	×	×	✓	×
	Rotational moulding	×	×	×	✓	×
	Extrusion	×	×	✓	✓	×
	Compression moulding	×	×	×	✓	×
Joining	Adhesive – solvent	×	×	×	✓	×
	– superglue	✓	✓	✓	✓	✓
	– PVA	×	✓	×	×	×
	– hot melt glue	✓	×	×	×	×
	– epoxy	✓	✓	✓	✓	✓
	– contact	✓	×	×	✓	✓
	Welding	×	×	✓	×	×
Fitting	Rivets	✓	×	✓	✓	✓
	Nuts and bolts	✓	✓	✓	✓	✓
	Screws	×	✓	✓	✓	×
	Nails	×	✓	×	×	×
	Knock-down (KD) fitting	×	✓	×	×	×
	Staples	✓	✓	×	×	×
Casting	Sand casting	×	×	✓	×	×
	Pressure die casting	×	×	✓	×	×
	Lost wax casting	×	×	✓	×	×
Printing	Sublimation	✓	✓	✓	✓	×
	Lithographic	✓	×	×	×	×
	Laser	✓	×	×	×	×
	Screen	✓	×	×	✓	✓
	Etching	✓	✓	✓	✓	✓

△ **Table 2** Overview of the industrial processes commonly used on materials

FIXING AND JOINING METHODS

When manufacturing a product, different parts or subassemblies must be joined together. These connections are made using **permanent joining** or **temporary joining** methods, depending on the product's design and function (Figure 2). The choice of fixing or joining method depends on several key factors:

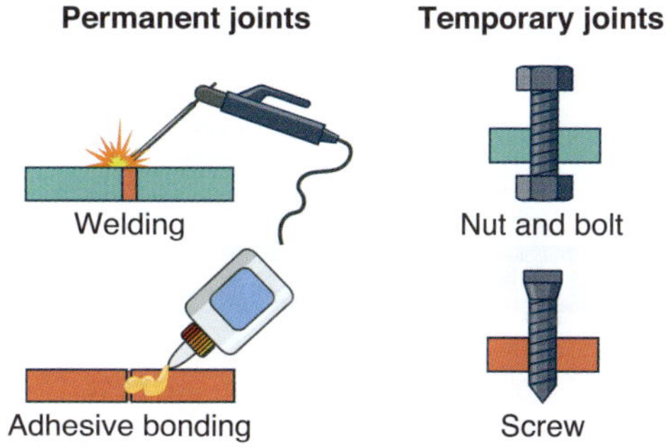

△ **Figure 2** Different joining methods

- Are the materials being joined the same material or different materials?
- Will the product need to be disassembled for maintenance, repair or recycling?
- How strong and durable does the joint need to be?
- Should the joint be visible or hidden for aesthetic reasons?

Based on these considerations, an appropriate joining method must be selected. For example, if you need to join a piece of acrylic to a sheet of metal and require a permanent bond, an adhesive like epoxy resin may be suitable. If the joint needs to be removable, a nut and bolt – made from steel or nylon – might be a better option. There are many possible solutions, and the final decision should be based on the specific requirements of the product and the tools or materials available.

Pre-manufactured components and fasteners (standard components)

Pre-manufactured components and **fasteners** are commonly used in a wide range of products. They include screws, nuts, bolts, staples, paper fasteners, hinges and batteries (Figure 3). Manufacturers do not typically produce these components themselves. Instead, they design their products to accommodate them. For example, a battery-powered torch is designed to fit standard-sized batteries, which are mass-produced by specialist companies.

△ **Figure 3** Nuts and bolts are standard manufacturing components.

Using **standard components** helps manufacturers save time and reduce costs, as these parts are readily available, reliable and produced in large quantities. In the electronics industry, most components – such as resistors, capacitors and microchips – are also standardised, allowing designers to create a variety of circuits by combining them in different ways.

Knock-down fittings

Knock-down (KD) fittings are pre-manufactured components used to join materials together, either temporarily or permanently (Figure 4). They are commonly found in modern flat-pack furniture, allowing consumers to assemble products at home with minimal tools. These fittings offer advantages for both manufacturers and consumers:

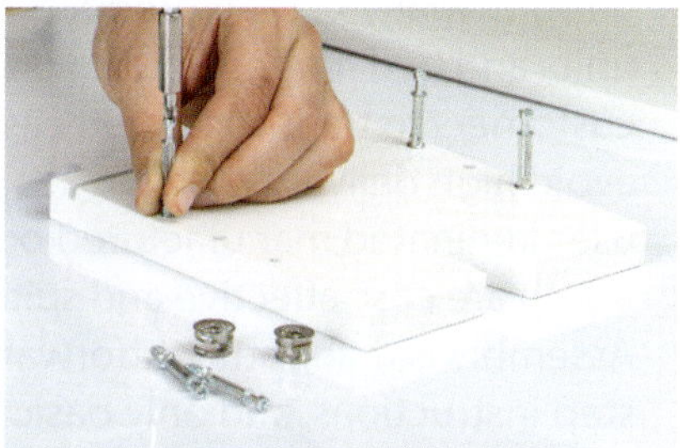
△ **Figure 4** A knock-down fitting

- For manufacturers, they reduce production and assembly costs by shifting part of the construction process to the end user.
- For consumers, they make transportation easier and lower the overall cost of the product, as items can be flat-packed and assembled on-site.

SKILLS ACTIVITY

Researching knock-down fittings

Research and identify as many types of KD fittings as you can. You can use the internet, books from the library or classroom resources to help with your search. For each fitting you find, list its name and describe a typical application where it is commonly used. For example:

- KD fitting: Plastic corner block
- Typical use: Used in kitchen cabinet carcasses

Try to find a variety of fittings and think about where you have seen them used – in flat-pack furniture, shelving units or storage systems. Different fittings are chosen based on function and ease of assembly.

FINISHING

A finish refers to the final treatment applied to a product or material, either to complete its manufacture or to enhance its appearance. Finishes serve two main purposes:

- *Protective*: Finishes help protect the underlying material from damage caused by environmental factors such as heat, moisture and wear. For example, a finish may make a surface resistant to fire, water, corrosion, rust, staining, and mould. Finishes and also improve the material's strength and durability, helping the product last longer.
- *Decorative*: Finishes can significantly improve the visual appeal of a product. They enhance colour, texture and overall appearance, making the item more attractive and suitable for its intended use.

Choosing the right finish is essential to ensure both functional performance and visual quality in the final product. See unit 2.2.4.

DESIGN IN ACTION

KD fittings in furniture design

IKEA makes extensive use of KD fittings in its furniture designs. Many of their products – such as wardrobes, shelving units and bed frames – are sold as flat-pack kits, allowing customers to transport them easily in their own vehicles and avoid high delivery costs. To keep prices affordable, IKEA often uses laminated manufactured boards like MDF and chipboard, which are cost-effective and suitable for mass production. Assembly is made straightforward with clear, illustrated step-by-step instructions, and only basic tools are needed, making the process accessible for most consumers (Figure 5).

△ **Figure 5** An example of knock-down (KD) fittings used in furniture design

TOLERANCE

In manufacturing, tolerances are the acceptable range of variation in the dimensions of a material or component. Every part is designed with a specific size, but slight deviations are allowed to ensure practicality during production. For example, if a steel rod for a lamp is specified to be 1000 mm long with a tolerance of ±1%, it would be considered acceptable if its length falls between 990 mm and 1010 mm.

Tolerances are critical for ensuring that parts fit together correctly. If a component falls outside its tolerance range, it may not assemble properly. In precision applications, such as fitting electronic components into a casing, small inaccuracies can cause loose fittings or misalignment.

SKILLS ACTIVITY

Making a desk organiser

Look at these stationery desk organisers.

What tools could have been used to mark and cut out the parts? Describe how you would cut the body shapes. What fixing methods could be used to hold the different materials together? Name two finishes that could be applied to the main body of the organisers.

△ **Figure 6** Various desk organisers

KNOWLEDGE CHECK

1. Explain the benefits of using standard components and knock-down (KD) fittings for both manufacturers and consumers.
2. Describe material tolerance.
3. Explain why accurate marking out is important during manufacturing.

KEY TERMS

Datum: A reference line or point for all measurements when marking out material

Fastener: A component that mechanically joins two or more objects together

Knock-down (KD) fitting: Pre-manufactured components used to join materials together, either temporarily or permanently

Marking out: The process of transferring measurements in the form of lines or shapes onto a material in advance of cutting, shaping, bending or forming

Permanent joining: A join that is not required to be separated and cannot be taken apart

Pre-manufactured components: Parts or components that are manufactured elsewhere and bought in to produce products*

Standard component: A pre-prepared part that is used in the production of many products

Temporary joining: A join designed so that it can be easily taken apart

1·5 Materials classification

1·5·1 Classification of materials

LEARNING AIMS

By the end of this unit, you should:

- Understand the classification, properties and working characteristics of the following materials:
  - papers and boards
  - hardwoods, softwoods and manufactured boards
  - ferrous, non-ferrous metals and alloys
  - thermo polymers and thermosetting polymers
  - composites and smart materials

WHY DO I NEED TO KNOW ABOUT THE PROPERTIES OF MATERIALS?

Understanding the properties of materials is essential for designers, technologists and engineers. It directly influences the success of a product. When developing a product, you must select materials that meet the functional, aesthetic and manufacturing requirements outlined in the design specification. In order to do this, you need to know how materials are classified, as well as their properties.

Material classification

Knowing how materials are classified (for example, as metals, polymers or composites) gives you access to a broad range of options and helps you understand their functionality and applications. This helps you think beyond the materials you have previously used and encourages innovative and informed choices in your designs.

Material properties

Understanding the properties of materials allows you to:

- choose materials that perform well under specific conditions (for example, strength, flexibility, thermal resistance)
- enhance the look and feel of a product to appeal to users
- determine how materials can be shaped, joined or finished during manufacturing.

CATEGORIES OF MATERIALS

You need a clear understanding of material categories to select the most suitable materials for your design needs. This base-level knowledge allows you to take a systematic and informed approach to selecting materials – especially when working with materials databases or developing product specifications.

The most commonly used material categories are shown in Figure 1. **Smart materials** are engineered substances with unique properties that often respond to environmental conditions. For a range of modern and alternative materials with specific properties tailored for different uses, see unit 2.1.5.

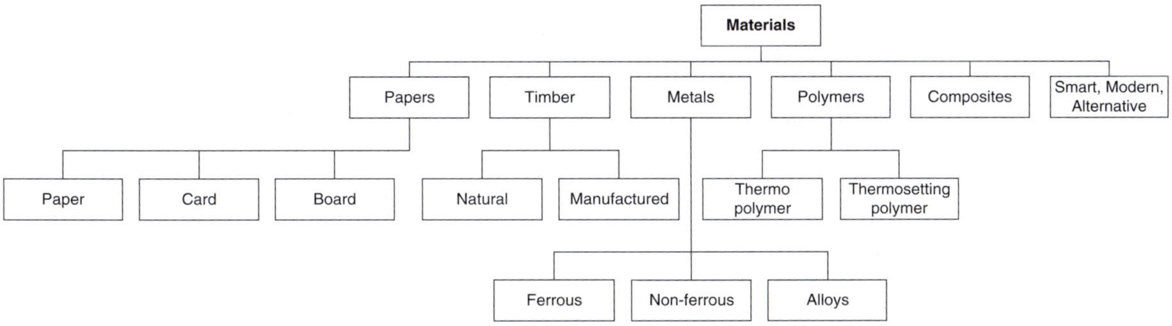

△ **Figure 1** Categories of materials

Textiles form a distinct category of materials. Some materials – such as nylon – can exist in both textile (fabric) and solid forms. Nylon is used in garments as well as in mechanical components.

PHYSICAL PROPERTIES OF MATERIALS

You need to understand the **physical properties** of materials to select the right material for a specific user, purpose or environment. Each property describes how a material behaves under certain **environmental conditions**, helping designers and engineers make informed decisions. Table 1 describes some key physical properties.

Physical property	Description	Example
Mechanical	Describes how a material responds to physical **forces**.	Some materials become brittle when repeatedly bent or flexed.
Electrical	Refers to a material's ability to conduct or resist electricity.	The polymer handle of a screwdriver acts as an insulator, protecting the user from electric shocks through the metal tip.
Chemical	Indicates how a material reacts with other substances.	**Ferrous metals** oxidise and rust in moisture and air.
Thermal	Describes how a material behaves at different temperatures, including melting and boiling points.	Thermo polymers can be reshaped within specific temperature ranges.
Magnetic	Most ferrous materials are magnetic or can be magnetised.	This is used in magnetic catches for cabinet doors.
Permeability	Refers to how easily liquids or gases can pass through a material.	Varnished wood has low permeability, making it more resistant to water.
Aesthetic	Relates to the sensory appeal of a material's surface or form.	It includes aspects like colour, gloss, opacity and finish.
Tactile	Concerns the texture and feel of a material.	Whether it is smooth, rough, soft or hard to the touch.
Absorbency	Refers to a material's ability to take in and retain liquids or moisture.	Cotton fabrics have high absorbency, ideal for towels, whereas plastics repel water and are non-absorbent.

△ **Table 1** Physical properties of materials

WORKING PROPERTIES OF MATERIALS

Working properties describe how a material behaves when it is being shaped, formed or manipulated – an essential consideration during the design and manufacturing process (refer to unit 2.3.1 for more detail). Understanding these properties helps ensure that materials are selected not only for their appearance or performance, but also for how well they can be worked with.

Table 2 describes the most common working properties.

Physical property	Description
Strength	The ability of a material to withstand a constant external force without breaking or deforming.
Hardness	The resistance of a material to surface wear, scratching or indentation. This is particularly important for surfaces that experience frequent contact or abrasion.
Toughness	The ability to absorb sudden impacts or shocks without fracturing. Tough materials can withstand dynamic or 'live' forces.
Durability	The capacity of a material to resist wear and degradation over time, including exposure to weather, moisture or repeated use.
Elasticity	The ability of a material to bend or stretch and then return to its original shape and size once the **force** is removed.
Plasticity	The ability of a material to undergo permanent deformation without breaking. This property applies to a wide range of materials, not just polymers.
Malleability	The ability of a material to be permanently deformed in all directions under compressive forces (for example, hammering or rolling) without cracking.
Ductility	The ability of a material to be stretched or drawn out into a wire or elongated shape without snapping.
Stiffness	A material's resistance to bending or flexing when a force is applied. A stiff material, such as steel, requires a large force to produce even a small deformation, making it ideal for structural applications where rigidity is essential.
Stress and strain	Stress is the internal force per unit area within a material when an external force is applied. It is measured in pascals (Pa) and helps determine how much load a material can bear. Strain measures the change in shape or deformation that occurs as a result of stress. It is a ratio and has no units. Together, stress and strain describe how materials respond to forces, such as stretching, compressing or twisting.

△ **Table 2** Working properties of materials

SKILLS ACTIVITY

Exploring materials in everyday products

Choose a product you use often. Sketch it or take a photo. List the materials you can see. If you are unsure, refer to units 2.1.1–2.1.5 in this book or look online – manufacturer websites often list the materials used.

Pick *one* material and describe why you think it was chosen. Consider:

- Function. How does it perform?
- Appearance. How does it look or feel?

- Cost: Is it affordable?
- Manufacturing. Is it easy to make or shape?

Write a short explanation linking the material's properties to the product's purpose.

SELECTING MATERIALS

Choosing the right materials for a product begins with a well-defined design specification. This specification should clearly outline the needs of the user, the intended function of the product and the conditions it will be exposed to during use. Once the specification is established, it becomes easier to identify the necessary physical and working properties required for the material.

These criteria can then be used to guide a targeted search through materials databases or selection tables. For example, a design specification for a garden chair might state that the product must be durable enough to withstand year-round outdoor conditions and require minimal maintenance. This would lead the designer to consider materials with high durability, weather resistance and low permeability.

SKILLS ACTIVITY

Design a compact, multi-compartment desk organiser

Design a compact, multi-compartment desk organiser that a child could use to keep their school supplies tidy and accessible at home or in the classroom.

- Your design should include clearly labelled sections for items such as pens, pencils, scissors, glue sticks and a small notepad. Consider features such as stackability or flat-pack assembly for easy storage.
- Create an annotated sketch showing how the organiser functions. List all the materials used in your design.
- For each material, explain the specific physical and working properties that make it suitable. For example, corrugated cardboard for its light weight and strength, acrylic for its rigidity and cleanable surface, or foamboard for its ease of shaping and soft texture.

TOP TIP

A common mistake in design is relying only on familiar materials. Expanding your understanding of how materials are classified, what their properties are and how to select them effectively can lead to more functional, innovative and visually appealing products.

The materials chosen for full-scale production should be carefully reconsidered. When developing a specification, selecting alternative materials can improve the product's commercial viability – enhancing cost-efficiency, market appeal and overall functionality.

REFLECTIVE LOG

Evaluating your product through materials

Think about a product you have made recently. Write a short evaluation focusing on the materials you used and their properties. Use the following prompts:

- What materials did you choose for your product?
- Why were these materials suitable for your design? Consider their physical and working properties.

If you were to produce this product in batches or on a larger scale, would different materials be more appropriate? Explain your reasoning, referring to factors such as durability, cost, ease of manufacture and appearance.

KNOWLEDGE CHECK

1. Identify the material classification for the materials listed below.
Categories: Thermo polymer | Non-ferrous metal | Composite | Manufactured board
a. MDF **b.** Acrylic **c.** Copper **d.** Carbon fibre

2. Choose **one** of the following materials: beech (hardwood), polypropylene (thermo polymer), stainless steel (alloy).
For your chosen material, describe **three** properties that make it suitable for a specific product. Include at least **one** physical and **one** working property.

3. What is a smart material? Give **one** example of a smart material and explain how it responds to changes in its environment.

KEY TERMS

Environmental conditions: Physical factors (such as temperature, light, moisture)

Ferrous metal: A metal that contains iron

Force: Push or pull that can change the shape of a material; there are five main types of force that can act on materials: compression, tension, torsion, shear and bending

Physical property: An observable or measurable characteristic of a material, for instance strength

Smart materials: Materials that change their properties in response to external conditions like heat, light, pressure, or electricity.

Stiffness: Resistance to deformation under any applied force

Stress or strain: A force created by pressure on an object or material, that has the potential to damage it by changing its shape

Working property: How a material behaves when it is being shaped

1·6 Structures

1·6·1 Basic concepts of structures

LEARNING AIMS

By the end of this unit, you should:

✓ Understand the classification and characteristics of natural and manufactured, shell, frame and mass structures

WHAT IS A STRUCTURE?

Structures are an essential part of the world around us: designed to provide support, stability and functionality. They range from large-scale constructions, such as buildings, bridges and vehicles, to smaller everyday items, such as food packaging and mobile phone casings. Some structures – for example, sports stadiums – are complex and made up of multiple interconnected components. Others, such as egg boxes, have a much simpler design. Regardless of complexity, each structure is carefully designed to serve a specific purpose.

TYPES OF STRUCTURES

Structures can generally be classified into three main types (Figure 1):

Mass structure Frame structure Shell structures

∆ **Figure 1** Types of structure

- **Mass structures**: Built from solid materials, these structures rely on their weight and bulk for support. Examples include stone monuments, dams and compact sculptures such as statues.
- **Frame structures**: Composed of interconnected elements forming a framework, these structures provide strength while using minimal material. Examples include bridges, scaffolding and the skeletons of buildings.
- **Shell structures**: Formed by thin, curved surfaces that enclose or protect spaces within. Examples include domes, car body, eggshells, and cereal and egg boxes.

MASS STRUCTURES

Mass structures rely on their own weight for strength and stability, using dense materials such as reinforced concrete, stone, brick or soil. These structures distribute their weight to resist external forces and remain durable over time (Figure 2).

Colosseum, Rome Large reservoir dam

∆ **Figure 2** Mass structures

DESIGN IN ACTION

Historical and modern examples of mass structures

Buildings like the Colosseum in Rome, Italy, were constructed using stone, where walls, **columns** and roofs depended on their sheer mass for support. This method ensured stability without the need for complex frameworks.

Dams are large-scale mass structures, built with soil, brick, stone or reinforced concrete to withstand immense water pressure. The weight and density of these materials prevent failure, ensuring the dam can effectively hold back vast amounts of water.

By utilising heavy, durable materials, mass structures remain stable, strong and resistant to external forces, making them essential for architecture and infrastructure.

FRAME STRUCTURES

Frame structures are built by connecting individual parts (called **structural members**) to form a rigid skeleton that supports loads (Figure 3). These structures are designed to withstand forces by distributing weight across their interconnected components.

Common examples include:

- Buildings: Skyscrapers and houses use steel frameworks for strength.
- Bridges: **Truss** bridges rely on frame structures to span large gaps.
- Cranes and pylons: Used in construction and power transmission.

Their key features include:

- Strength through connection: Each part alone is weak, but together they form a strong, stable structure.
- Cladding materials: Glass, metal or panels are attached to the frame for weather protection and aesthetics.
- Versatility: Frame structures can be built tall (skyscrapers) or span large distances (bridges).

△ **Figure 3** Frame structures form the basis of many modern buildings.

SKILLS ACTIVITY

Annotating frame structures

Find images of *two* bridges with different frame structures. Sketch each one and label key parts, explaining how they contribute to the bridge's strength and stability.

SHELL STRUCTURES

Shell structures are made from thin, curved materials like sheet steel, glass reinforced polymer (GRP) or concrete. Their shape provides strength while enclosing space to protect what is inside.

Examples of shell structures include:

- Natural: Eggshells, turtle shells
- Architectural: Domes, stadium roofs
- Transport: Car bodies, aircraft fuselages, ship hulls
- Everyday objects: Tents, cans, helmets

Shell structures are often strengthened by bending, folding or corrugating the material, increasing durability without adding extra weight (Figure 4).

Stadium roof

Aircraft fuselage

Domed tent

△ **Figure 4** Examples of shell structures

DESIGN IN ACTION

Frame and shell structures in bicycles

Bicycles combine frame structures for strength and shell structures for lightweight durability (Figure 5).

- *Frame structure:* The main frame is a rigid skeleton, built using **triangulation**, ensuring stability and load distribution.
- *Shell structure:* Some structures, such as carbon fibre wheels, saddles and cyclists' helmets, are designed as thin, curved shells to enhance aerodynamics and reduce weight.

△ **Figure 5** Bicycles combine frame and shell structures

- *Mechanical systems:* The cranks, chain, ring and chain function as a lever mechanism and a chain drive transferring power to the wheels.
- *Brakes and gears:* These are operated by lever systems, ensuring smooth control and speed adjustments.

NATURAL STRUCTURES

Nature is a blueprint for structural innovation in fields like construction, machinery and robotics. It provides valuable insights into strength, flexibility and stability. Through biomimicry – the study and imitation of natural forms and processes – engineers and architects develop efficient, durable and resilient designs. They apply principles observed in **natural structures** to create systems that are stronger, more adaptable, sustainable and efficient.

Nature-inspired architectural designs

Two world-famous examples of nature-inspired architectural designs (Figure 6) include:

- Beijing Olympic Stadium ('Bird's Nest'): Modelled after a woven bird's nest, this intricate framework enhances both lightness and structural integrity, ensuring even weight distribution.
- Taipei 101 Tower: Inspired by bamboo, which is naturally flexible yet strong, allowing the skyscraper to withstand strong winds and earthquakes.

△ **Figure 6** Examples of architectural structures inspired by nature: **a** Beijing Olympic Stadium **b** Taipei 101 Tower

Robotic design mimicking the human skeleton

The human skeleton is an excellent example of a natural structure engineered for strength and movement:

- Joints provide controlled movement, like the backbone enabling rotation and bending.
- Feet act as a foundation, supporting walking, running and standing.

Modern manufacturing robots use structural principles similar to the human body (Figure 7):

- Rigid frameworks ensure stability, much like bones support the body.
- Joints and pivots enable controlled movement, replicating human articulation for precision tasks such as welding car parts.

△ **Figure 7** A robotic arm, often used in factory work, mimics the functions of the human skeleton.

SKILLS ACTIVITY

Identifying natural structures

Choose an outdoor area you are familiar with. Identify *five* natural structures in that space. For each structure:

1. Describe its physical features – shape, material and how it was formed.
2. Explain its purpose – how it benefits the environment.
3. Discuss its interactions – how it connects with other natural or human-made structures.

TOP TIP

Take inspiration from nature when you design structures. When designing a system or product, studying natural structures can inspire strong, efficient and adaptable designs. See unit 1.2.3 for more context and ideas.

KNOWLEDGE CHECK

1. Identify **two** examples of each of the following: mass structures, frame structures, shell structures.
2. Identify the key characteristics that define a shell structure. How do these features contribute to its function?
3. Compare the difference between natural and manufactured structures. Give **one** example of each.
4. Explain an advantage of a frame in a frame structure. What are its advantages in construction and design?

KEY TERMS

Column: A vertical support that carries the weight of a structure

Frame structure: A structure made of connected parts, forming a strong framework (for example, bridges, towers)

Mass structure: A structure built by piling materials like stone or concrete, relying on its weight for strength (for example, dams, pyramids)

Natural structure: A structure formed in nature, created by animals, plants or geology (for example, nests, caves, coral reefs)

Shell structure: A thin, curved structure enclosing space while staying strong (for example, domes, car bodies, tents)

Structural member: A single component of a structure

Triangulation: Using triangular shapes to enhance structural stability

Truss: A triangulated framework that supports loads, commonly used in roofs and bridges

1·6·2 Forces and structures

LEARNING AIMS

By the end of this unit, you should:

✓ Show knowledge of static and dynamic loads

✓ Understand forces that act on structures:

- tension
- compression
- shear
- bending
- torsion

✓ Understand static loads and dynamic loads, and how they influence structures

✓ Explore different types of force and their effects on different materials

Structures must withstand a variety of forces to remain stable and functional. How do different loads and forces affect materials and construction? Engineers and designers carefully consider this.

FRAME STRUCTURES

A frame structure is a system of connected structural members designed to support loads and maintain stability. Each member has a specific role in spreading forces throughout the structure, helping it stay strong and resist bending or movement under pressure.

Load types in frame structures

Structures must withstand two main types of loads:

- **Static loads:** These are constant forces acting on the structure, such as its own weight.
- **Dynamic loads:** These are varying forces, such as vehicles moving across a bridge or wind forces acting on buildings.

Example: Road bridge

A road bridge is a classic example of a frame structure (Figure 1). It must:

- support vehicles that move across it
- stay strong and safe when the wind pushes against it
- stay stable even if the ground or foundation underneath shifts or moves
- be made of different parts (called members) that work together to carry the weight and keep the bridge steady.

△ **Figure 1** A bridge is a frame structure.

Frame structures are built using key members, each with a distinct function:

- **Beams**: Horizontal supports that carry loads.
- **Ties**: Members that resist tension forces.
- **Struts**: Members that resist compression forces.
- Columns: Vertical supports that transfer loads to the foundation.

FORCES IN STRUCTURES

All structures and structural components must withstand the forces acting on them to ensure stability and safety. For instance, a floor in a house should not bend excessively or collapse when walked upon.

Size of forces

Forces can vary widely in scale:

- Small forces, such as the grip used to hold a pencil.
- Large forces, such as the aerodynamic loads acting on an aircraft at high altitude.

Measurement units of force

The standard unit used to measure force is the **newton** (N). Larger units are often used for convenience:

- Kilonewton (kN) = 1000 N
- Meganewton (MN) = 1 000 000 N

Compression and tension

Forces can act in two primary ways (Figure 2):

- Tension (tensile force) pulls a material apart, stretching it.
- Compression (compressive force) pushes a material together, squeezing it.

Understanding stress and strain helps engineers predict whether a structural component will withstand these forces, ensuring its suitability for practical applications.

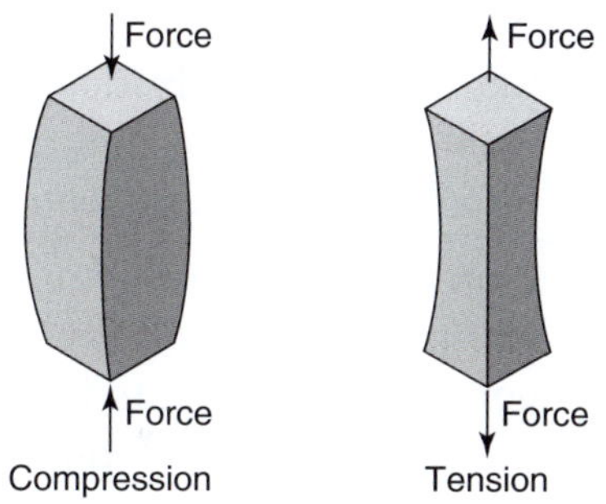

△ **Figure 2** Compressive and tensile forces

SHEAR, BENDING AND TORSION IN STRUCTURAL COMPONENTS

Structural and mechanical parts must be designed to withstand shear and torsion to ensure durability and performance. Torsion refers to the twisting effect on a component when **torque** is applied. Parts such as screwdriver blades, and bolts, need strong torsional properties to prevent failure during use.

When a part breaks due to torsion, the fracture typically occurs through shear failure, where the material twists and separates along a sliding plane. Shear strength determines how well a material can resist such forces. Unlike tensile failure, where the fracture surface is at right angles to the applied force, shear failure causes components to slide apart under stress.

Designers must carefully select materials based on their shear and torsional properties to prevent structural failure. Some materials, such as concrete, are weak in tension, highlighting the importance of material selection in engineering applications.

Structural elements must be designed to resist bending forces to maintain strength and reliability (Figure 3). Bending occurs when a load causes a material to curve around its neutral (resting) axis. Beams in bridges and cantilevered shelves need high **flexural strength** to prevent excessive deflection or breakage under load.

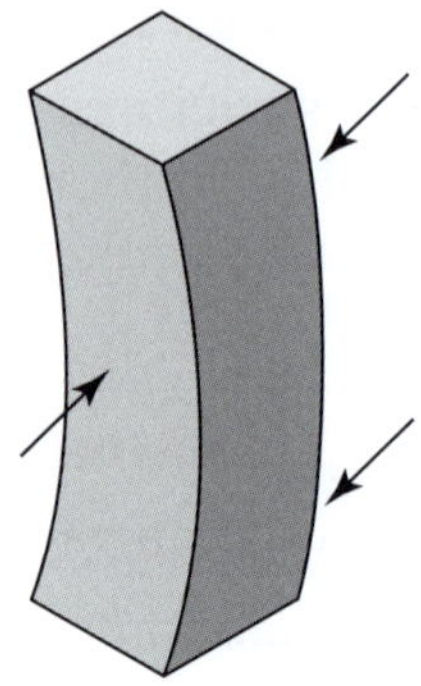

△ **Figure 3** Bending

SKILLS ACTIVITY

How do different forces affect structures?

In this skills activity, you will explore how different forces – **tension**, **compression**, **shear**, **bending** and **torsion** – affect structures. You will learn about the difference between static and dynamic loads through practical testing.

Design and build your own bridge to explore how structures respond to different forces:

1. Sketch a simple bridge design – consider how to make it strong and stable. Could you incorporate triangles or arches? Will your bridge be a beam, truss or arch type?
2. Construct the bridge using the materials provided. It should span a gap of at least 300 mm between two supports. To test for static load, gently place weights in the centre of the bridge and record how much weight it can hold before it begins to bend or break.
3. Test for dynamic load by dropping a small weight from a short height onto the bridge and observe how it reacts to the sudden force. As you test, observe and record where the bridge bends or fails. Identify which parts are under compression (being squeezed) and which are under tension (being stretched). Look for shear or torsion as well (Figure 4).
4. Finally, reflect on your design. What would you change to make it stronger? Consider how engineers use this kind of testing in real-world construction to ensure safety and performance.

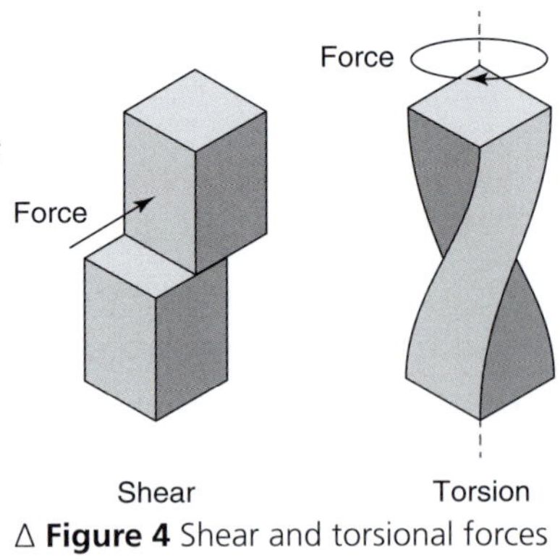

△ **Figure 4** Shear and torsional forces

STRESS–STRAIN GRAPH

A **stress-strain graph** shows how a material behaves when it is stretched (Figure 5). You can use it to understand how strong and durable a material is. The graph is made by pulling a sample until it breaks. At first, the material stretches and returns to its original shape when released – this is the *elastic region*. If it is pulled further, it starts to change shape permanently – this is the *plastic region*.

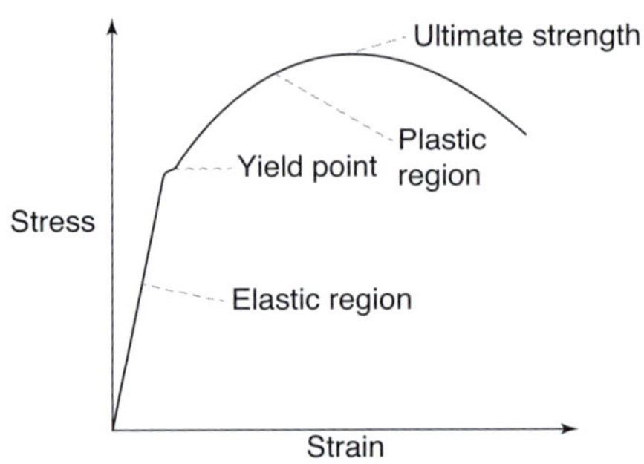

△ **Figure 5** A stress-strain graph

Two important points are the *yield point*, where permanent change begins, and the *ultimate strength*, where the material breaks. Engineers design bridge cables and turbine blades to stay below the yield point, so they stay safe and keep their shape.

TOP TIP

Understanding how forces act on structures is key to designing strong, stable and efficient systems:

- *Think about load paths*: Always consider how forces travel through a structure. A well-designed structure distributes loads efficiently, preventing weak points.
- *Balance opposing forces*: Structures must resist tension, compression, shear, bending and torsion. Identifying these forces helps you strengthen designs and avoid failures.
- *Observe real-world examples*: Look at bridges, buildings and natural structures, such as trees or bones, to see how forces are managed effectively.
- *Test and iterate*: Experiment with models or simulations to visualise force behaviour and refine structural stability.

REFLECTIVE LOG

Exploring framework structures

Identify framework structures in your local area. For each structure:

- List its name and location.
- Describe its purpose and how the framework supports it.
- Note the materials used in its construction.

For example:

- *Structure:* Suspension bridge
- *Purpose:* Supports traffic by distributing load through cables and towers
- *Materials:* Steel cables, concrete piers, reinforced beams

DESIGN IN ACTION

Designing a climbing frame for children

Before building structures such as bridges, designers use models and computer tools to test how the structure will handle different forces. For example, when engineers design a climbing frame, they need to make sure it is safe for children to use. Before building it, they create a computer model to test how the frame will react when children climb, hang or swing on it. These tests help them see if any part of the frame might bend or move too much.

The tests help engineers see how the structure might bend, twist or move under a force or load. By testing the design first, they can make changes – such as using stronger materials or adding extra supports – so the final structure is safe, stable and fun to use.

KNOWLEDGE CHECK

1. Describe the difference between static and dynamic loads.
2. Identify how tension force acts on a material and suggest **two** real-world examples where it plays a crucial role in structural stability.

KEY TERMS

Beam: A member which spans gaps and supports the loads acting on it

Bending: A force that causes an object to bend

Compression: A squashing force

Dynamic load: A changing force caused by movement, impact, or varying pressure over time

Flexural strength: A material's ability to resist bending before deforming or breaking under load

Newton: The unit of force (which has the symbol N)

Shear: A cutting or slicing force

Static equilibrium: An object is at rest, with no linear or rotational motion

Static load: A constant, unmoving force applied to a structure, like a resting weight which never increases or moves

Stress-strain graph: A graph showing how a material deforms under stress

Strut: A member designed to resist compressive forces

Tension: A pulling force that stretches a material, trying to make it longer or break it apart

Tie: A member designed to resist tension forces

Torque: A force that causes something to turn or rotate

Torsion: The result of a turning or twisting force

1·6·3 Reinforcing structures

LEARNING AIMS

By the end of this unit, you should:

✓ Understand reinforcement methods used in structures:
- triangulation
- corrugation

Strength comes from smart design. Triangulation and **corrugation** are used to reinforce structures in different ways.

TRIANGULATION IN STRUCTURAL REINFORCEMENT

Rectangular shapes can deform or collapse under applied forces due to their lack of stability. Triangulation strengthens frame structures by introducing diagonal members, which distribute forces more effectively and prevent distortion (Figure 1). By connecting a cross member between two corners of a frame, the structure gains rigidity, ensuring that loads are transferred efficiently. The members used for triangulation can experience either tensile or compressive forces, depending on how the structure is loaded. This principle is widely applied in bridges and scaffolding where stability is critical.

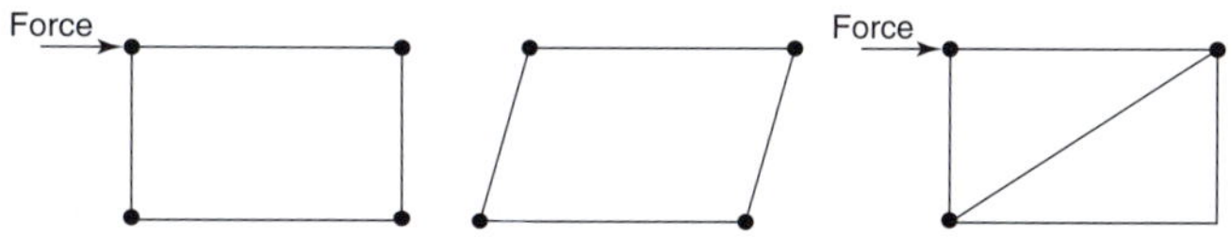

∆ **Figure 1** Triangulation in structural reinforcement

There are many well-known structures that use triangulation for strength and stability. For example:

- Eiffel Tower (Paris, France): Its iron lattice framework relies on triangulation to distribute loads efficiently and resist wind forces (Figure 2).
- Burj Khalifa (Dubai, UAE): The triangular core design enhances stability, reducing sway in high winds and earthquakes.
- Gherkin (London, UK): The diagonal bracing system forms triangular patterns, improving structural integrity and airflow.

∆ **Figure 2** The Eiffel Tower: An example of a frame structure

SKILLS ACTIVITY

Explore how reinforcement improves structural stability

Using drinking straws or similar, construct a basic rectangular frame to explore how reinforcement improves structural stability.

Triangulation in frames

1. Assemble a rectangular frame using straws.
2. Add one **cross-brace** diagonally between two corners and observe how it affects the structure when gently squeezed.

3. Introduce a second cross-brace, completing a triangular reinforcement. Test the frame again and note how stability improves.

Strengthening frame corners

1. Build a new rectangular frame using the same materials.
2. Strengthen the corners using **a** cross-bracing and **b gusset plates** made from cardboard.
3. Compare how each method affects the rigidity and load distribution when pressure is applied.

Observation and analysis

1. Describe the differences in stability before and after reinforcement.
2. Explain how triangulation and gusset plates help distribute forces.
3. Suggest how these methods apply to real-world structures such as bridges.

TRUSSES: STRUCTURAL FRAMEWORKS FOR LOAD SUPPORT

Trusses are strong frames made of connected parts. They are used in bridges, cranes and roofs to help spread weight and keep the structures stable. Roof trusses use beams, ties and struts to hold up the roof. Bridge trusses are more complex but work the same way. Each part either pulls (tie) or pushes (strut) to handle the load (Figure 3).

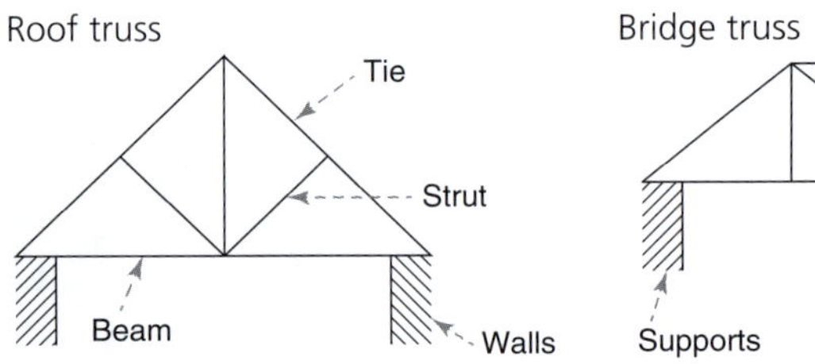

△ **Figure 3** Examples of trusses

Cross-bracing and gusset plates are common ways of strengthening the corners of the frames (Figure 4).

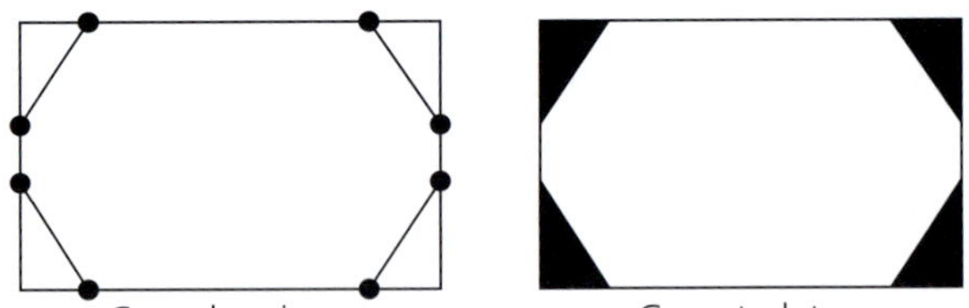

△ **Figure 4** Ways to strengthen the corners of frames

BEAMS

A beam is a structural element designed to resist bending, primarily caused by vertical forces (Figure 5). Beams are commonly used to span gaps, providing support in structures such as bridges, buildings and frames.

Common types of beam include:

- *Cantilever beam:* Fixed at one end only, extending freely at the other. Common in balconies and bridges.
- *Simply supported beam:* Supported at both ends, allowing for efficient load distribution. Often used in bridges and floor structures.

- *Overhanging beam:* A beam that sticks out past its support on one or both sides. You can see this in balconies or parts of a roof that overhangs.

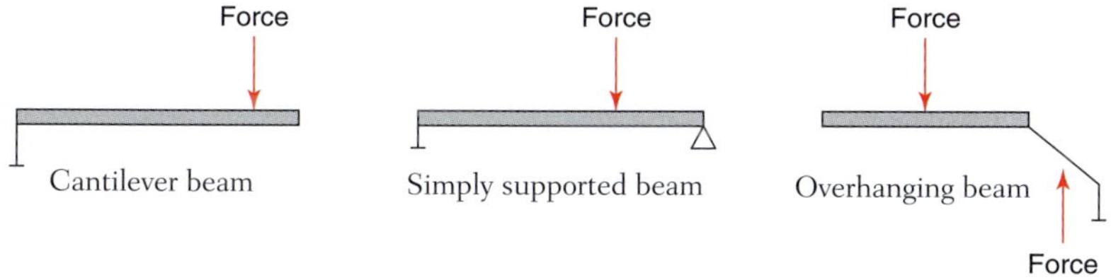

△ **Figure 5** Common types of beam

When a beam bends, its surfaces experience two opposing forces (Figure 6):

- The top surface is in compression, as it is being pushed together.
- The bottom surface is in tension, as it is being pulled apart.

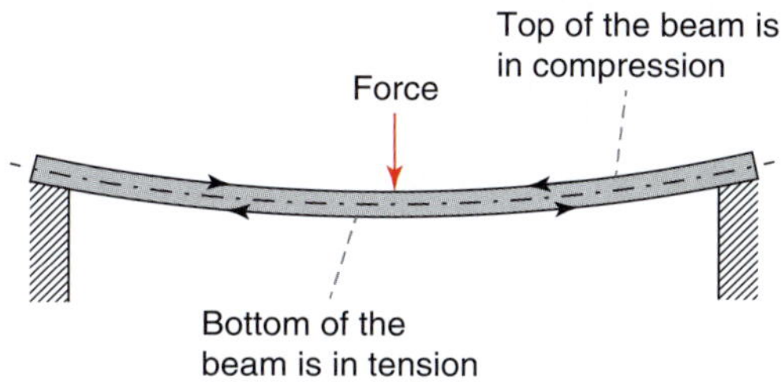

△ **Figure 6** A beam in tension and compression

Understanding these forces is essential for selecting suitable materials in beam design. Some materials – such as concrete and certain types of timber – are stronger in compression than tension, making them ideal for specific applications. Designers must consider these properties to ensure structural stability and optimise the beam's performance.

TIES

A tie is a structural member specifically designed to resist tension (tensile forces). It plays a crucial role in maintaining stability and preventing excessive deformation in various structures (Figure 7). Common examples of ties include:

- Rods and bars, which provide rigid tensile support.
- Guy ropes, used to stabilise towers and tents.
- Suspension bridge cables, which carry tensile loads over long spans.

While many ties are solid bars, they can also be made from cables, wires or ropes, which become stronger when stretched as they efficiently distribute tensile forces.

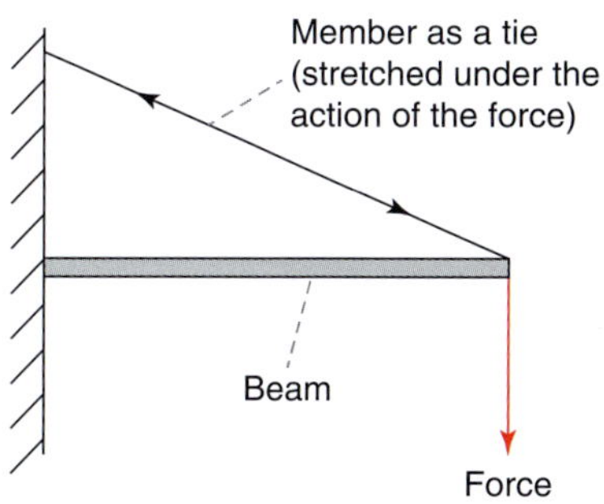

△ **Figure 7** A tie

STRUTS

Struts are structural components designed to resist compressive forces, helping to maintain the stability of a structure. These members are essential in load-bearing applications, preventing **buckling** or collapse under pressure (Figure 8). Struts:

- resist compression (squeezing forces)
- provide structural support in frameworks such as bridges, buildings and towers
- cannot be made from flexible materials (cables, wires or ropes), as they cannot support compression loads
- are commonly made from concrete and cast iron, which perform well under compression but may be weaker in tension.

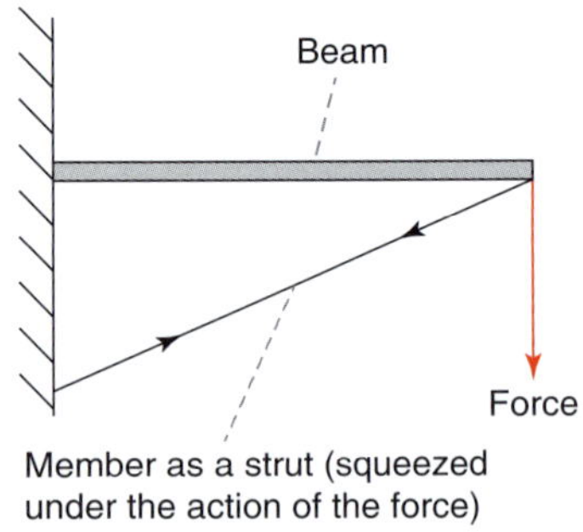

△ **Figure 8** A strut supporting a beam

SKILLS ACTIVITY

Analysing how members behave under applied forces

Use drinking straws or similar lightweight materials to build models of the frame structures shown in Figure 9. Connect the parts with glue, tape or other quick-assembly methods to keep them stable.

1. Build the frames based on the diagrams in Figure 9.

3. Place them on a flat surface (a table) for support.

3. Press at the marked loading points to see how they react.

4. Decide if each member is a tie (tension), strut (compression) or beam (load support).

Reflection and analysis

1. How do different members behave under applied forces?

2. Which parts of the structure experience tension and which experience compression?

3. How does altering the shape or connection points affect stability?

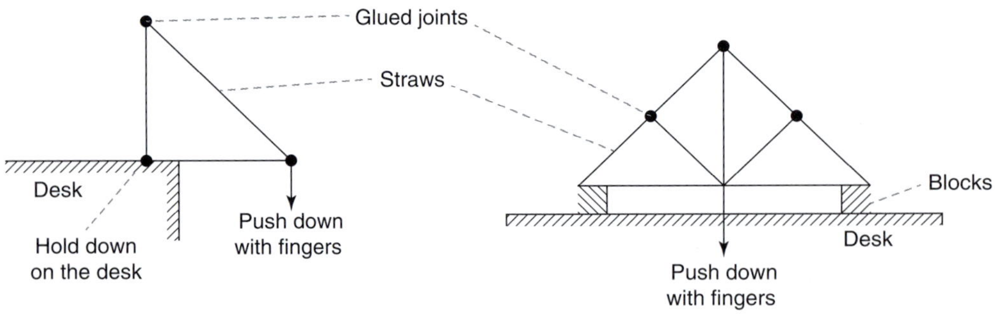

△ **Figure 9** Frame structures to build

COLUMNS

Columns are upright members designed to support beams and other loads. Their main function is to resist compressive forces from the weight pressing down on them. Columns:

- support vertical loads, helping to transfer weight to the foundation
- resist compression, preventing buckling or collapse

- may also need to withstand twisting and bending forces, such as wind acting on a lamp post.

CORRUGATION

Corrugation means a surface with ridges and grooves, like waves or folds. Corrugation makes materials stronger, as seen in the wavy layer of cardboard or metal roofing, because the alternating ridges and grooves act like tiny beams. These 'mini-beams' increase stiffness so the material resists bending and spreads loads evenly.

Everyday examples include:

- *Cardboard boxes:* The wavy layer between two flat sheets makes them strong and light.
- *Metal roofing:* Corrugated metal sheets are used on sheds and buildings to resist bending (Figure 10).
- *Plastic pipes:* Some drainage pipes have a corrugated surface to make them flexible and tough.
- *Packaging:* Boxes, trays or cup holder sleeves have a corrugated shape to protect the food inside, or help keep it hot or cold.

△ **Figure 10** A house roof using metal corrugation

TOP TIP

Strength comes from smart design. When reinforcing a structure, consider how forces act on different components and choose reinforcement methods that maximise stability. Triangulation prevents deformation; corrugation adds rigidity; cross-bracing strengthens weak points. Always think about material properties, ensuring the structure can withstand compression, tension and shear forces effectively. A well-reinforced design is not just stronger – it is more efficient and durable over time.

KNOWLEDGE CHECK

1. Identify **two** advantages of using triangulation in structural reinforcement commonly used in engineering.
2. Sketch a simple structure that uses triangulation for stability. State how the forces are distributed within the framework.
3. Analyse the difference between tensile and shear failure in reinforced structures. Suggest how corrugation or triangulation can help prevent collapse.

KEY TERMS

Buckling: Failure mode where a component bends out of shape due to excessive compressive force or heat

Corrugation: A surface that has ridges and grooves

Cross-brace: A diagonal support forming an 'X' shape to strengthen and stabilise a structure

Gusset plate: A flat metal plate at structural joints connecting beams, columns, and trusses for reinforcement

1·7 Mechanisms

1·7·1 Basic concepts of mechanisms

LEARNING AIMS

By the end of this unit, you should:

✓ Identify and sketch simple examples of first-, second- and third-class levers, and associated linkages

✓ Understand gears, pulleys and belts, sprockets and chain drives for practical applications

✓ Recognise the need to reduce friction between two surfaces by design, and describe the types of lubrication

Why use **mechanisms**? Mechanisms are essential for reducing **effort** and making tasks easier to perform. **Levers**, **pulleys** and **gears** serve as the building blocks for all mechanisms and machines.

WHAT ARE MECHANISMS?

Mechanisms consist of moving parts, such as gears, chain drives, and pulleys and belts (Figure 1), which work together to transfer and modify motion. Many mechanisms are designed to convert one type of motion into another, such as **rotary motion** into **linear motion**. In a bicycle, for example, the pedalling action generates rotary motion, which is then converted into linear motion as the bicycle moves forward (Figure 2).

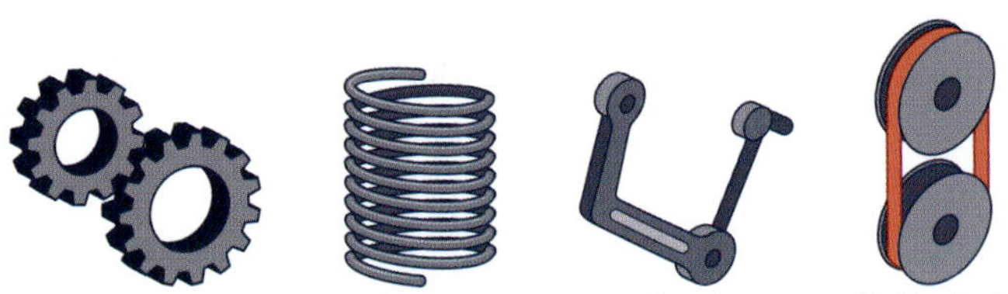

△ **Figure 1** Examples of mechanisms

△ **Figure 2** Bicycles turn rotary motion into linear motion.

FULCRUM, LOAD AND EFFORT IN LEVERS

Levers are fundamental components in many mechanisms, such as bicycle brake levers and scissors, allowing forces to be applied efficiently. They function by balancing three key elements:

- **Fulcrum**: the pivot point where the lever rotates
- **Load**: the force being moved or lifted
- **Effort**: the force applied to move the lever

The position of the fulcrum relative to the effort and load determines the lever class (Table 1).

Lever class	Relative positions	Examples
1	The fulcrum is positioned between the effort and load	Scissors, seesaw
2	The load is positioned between the effort and fulcrum	Wheelbarrow
3	The effort is positioned between the fulcrum and load	Spade, tweezers

∆ **Table 1** Classes of lever

The ability to lift a load using a lever is determined by its **mechanical advantage**. Class 3 levers do not provide a mechanical advantage, but they enhance precision and control in movement.

For Class 1 and Class 2 levers, the mechanical advantage depends on the relative distances between the effort, fulcrum and load (Figure 3). If the effort is applied farther away from the fulcrum than the load, the lever will have a higher mechanical advantage, making it easier to lift the load.

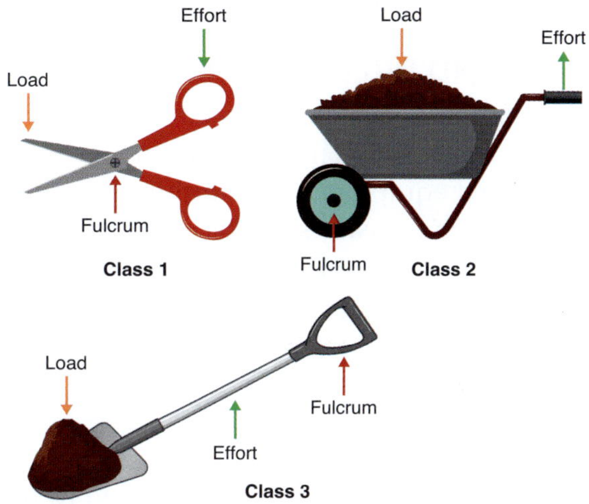

∆ **Figure 3** Examples of classes of levers

TOP TIP

Remember the rule: F-L-E (Fulcrum, Load, Effort) to classify levers:

- First-class → Fulcrum in the middle.
- Second-class → Load in the middle.
- Third-class → Effort in the middle.

LINKAGES IN MECHANICAL SYSTEMS

Linkages connect moving parts within a mechanism, enabling controlled motion and force transmission. Typically, they consist of rigid bars joined by pivoting joints, allowing movement while maintaining structural integrity (Figure 4). To enhance durability and **efficiency**, these joints often incorporate **bearings**, which minimise **friction** and reduce wear, ensuring smooth, quiet operation without unnecessary energy loss. Linkages are fundamental in machines, robotics and mechanical assemblies, for precise motion control.

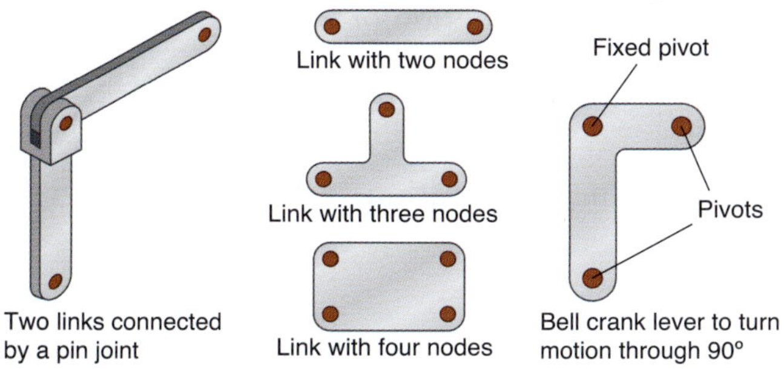

∆ **Figure 4** Examples of linkages

PULLEYS

A pulley is a simple machine that assists in lifting loads by changing the direction of force and reducing effort. There are different types:

- *Fixed pulley*: Changes the direction of the force but does not reduce the effort.
- *Movable pulley*: Reduces the effort by sharing the load.
- *Compound pulley*: A system combining multiple pulleys for greater mechanical advantage.

BELT AND PULLEY SYSTEMS

Belt and pulley systems transfer motion and power between rotating shafts efficiently. They are commonly found in machinery, vehicles and industrial equipment. The pulley – a grooved wheel – guides a flexible belt, which transmits rotational motion from one pulley to another. The belt can be made of rubber, fabric or metal, depending on its use.

There are different types of belt drive (Figure 5):

- *Open belt drive*: Both pulleys rotate in the same direction.
- *Cross belt drive*: The belt is twisted to reverse rotation between pulleys.
- *V-belt drive*: Uses a V-shaped belt for better grip and power transmission.
- *Timing belt drive*: A toothed belt that synchronises rotation precisely.

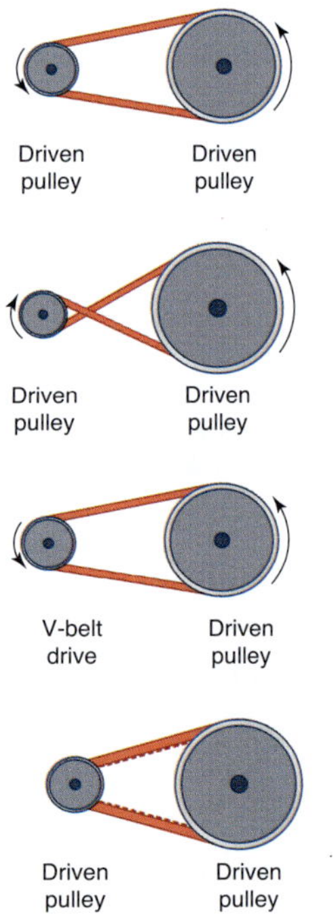

△ **Figure 5** Examples of belt and pulley systems

GEARS

Gears are mechanical components used to transmit motion and power between rotating shafts. They consist of toothed wheels that mesh together to change the direction, speed, or torque of rotation.

There are different types of gear:

- *Spur gear*: Has straight teeth and is used for parallel shafts.
- *Bevel gear*: Has angled teeth and is used to change the direction of rotation between intersecting shafts.
- *Worm gear*: Consists of a screw-like gear that meshes with a toothed wheel, used for large speed reductions.
- *Helical gear*: Has angled teeth for smoother and quieter operation.

GEARS AND CHAIN DRIVES

Gears and chain drives are used together to transfer motion and power over longer distances. A chain drive uses a metal chain to connect two or more gear wheels, ensuring synchronised rotation.

The toothed wheel in a chain drive is called a **sprocket**. Sprockets have specially shaped teeth designed to mesh precisely with the links of the chain. They are essential for a chain drive system to function effectively.

Chain drives are commonly found in bicycles, motorcycles, and industrial machinery.

There are different types of chain drive:

- *Roller chain drive:* Uses rollers to reduce friction and wear.
- *Silent chain drive:* Uses specially shaped links for quieter operation.
- *Leaf chain drive:* Used in lifting applications like forklifts.

SKILLS ACTIVITY

Exploring simple machines

Simple mechanisms can make tasks easier.

Experiment with the materials provided for different mechanisms – lifting weights with pulleys, moving objects using levers or connecting gears to see how they interact. Observe how changes in setup affect movement, effort and direction.

1. What changes when you add more pulleys?
2. How does the size of a gear affect how it turns?
3. What happens when you move the position of the lever's pivot point?
4. Can you find a way to make lifting or moving something feel easier?

EFFICIENCY

Efficiency is the ratio of useful output work produced by a machine compared to the input work supplied. A perfectly efficient machine would have 100 per cent efficiency, meaning no energy is lost, and output equals input. However, this is impossible in practice.

Friction, heat and sound generated by moving parts cause efficiency losses. Bearings help reduce friction at joints, while **lubrication** minimises wear and energy dissipation.

Bearings

△ **Figure 6** Bearings come in lots of different sizes

Bearings are machine components designed to reduce friction between a rotating shaft and its housing, allowing smooth, efficient motion (Figure 6). They are essential in machinery and equipment, enabling shafts to rotate freely while preventing excessive wear and heat buildup.

Common types of bearings include:

- *Plain bearings:* Operate with sliding contact instead of rolling elements.
- *Ball bearings:* Reduce friction in high-speed applications.
- *Roller bearings:* Support heavier loads with rolling cylinders.

Lubrication

Lubrication is essential for reducing friction and wear between two contacting surfaces. When surfaces rub together, they create friction, which can lead to heat buildup, increased resistance and gradual deterioration over time. Lubricants help prevent direct metal-to-metal contact by forming a thin protective layer that separates the surfaces, minimising wear and enhancing performance.

The two primary types of lubricants are oil and grease:

- Oil is fluid and can easily penetrate tight-fitting components like gear teeth, ensuring smooth movement while effectively dissipating heat generated by friction. However, oil must be changed regularly, as small metal particles from worn surfaces can contaminate it and cause further damage.
- Grease is a semi-solid lubricant that provides long-lasting protection, particularly for components exposed to heavy loads or slow-moving conditions, where continuous oil application may not be practical.

SKILLS ACTIVITY

Investigating appliances that rely on bearings

Identify household appliances that rely on bearings for smooth operation. Describe why bearings are necessary in each appliance – considering friction reduction, rotary motion and durability.

Copy Table 2 and record your observations.

Appliance	Where bearings are used	Purpose of bearings
Example: Washing machine	Drum and motor	Reduces friction, enables smooth rotation
1.		
2.		
3.		

△ **Table 2** Use of bearings in household appliances

Reflection questions

1. How do bearings improve the performance of household appliances?

2. What might happen if bearings fail or wear out in these appliances?

3. Can you think of any alternative solutions to reduce friction in machinery?

KNOWLEDGE CHECK

1. Sketch a simple example of a first-, second- and third-class lever, and identify the position of the fulcrum, load and effort in each case. How do the differences in lever design affect the force required to operate them?

2. Explain how gears, pulleys, belts and chain drives are used in practical applications. Give **one** example where each system is used to transfer motion or force efficiently.

3. Describe why reducing friction between two surfaces is important in mechanical systems.

KEY TERMS

Bearing: A mechanical device that reduces friction between moving parts, enhancing efficiency and longevity

Efficiency: The ratio of useful output work or power to the actual input work or power, expressed as a percentage

Effort: The force applied to the input side of a mechanism to produce movement or work

Friction: A force that resists movement between two surfaces touching each other, slowing things down

Fulcrum: The pivot point around which a lever rotates

Gear: A circular mechanical part with teeth that mesh with another gear to transmit motion or force

Lever: A rigid bar that rotates around a fulcrum, used to move loads with mechanical advantage

Linear motion: Motion that follows a straight line

Linkage: A system of rigid components connecting two or more parts of a mechanism, with each link having at least two attachment points

Load: The force that a mechanism supports or moves during operation

Lubrication: The application of oil, grease or other substances to minimise friction between moving components

Mechanical advantage: The ratio of output force to input force in a mechanism, indicating how much a tool or machine amplifies force

Mechanism: A system of moving parts designed to transform motion and force into a desired outcome

Pulley: A wheel with a groove that helps lift or move loads using a rope or belt

Rotary motion: Motion in a circular path

Sprocket: A toothed wheel designed to mesh with a chain; used to transmit rotary motion in a chain drive system

1·7·2 Conversion of motion

LEARNING AIMS

By the end of this unit, you should:

✓ Recognise, describe and give examples of the following types of motion:
- rotary
- linear
- reciprocating
- oscillating

✓ Explain and give examples of the conversion of motion

TYPES OF MOTION

There are four basic types of motion (Figure 1):

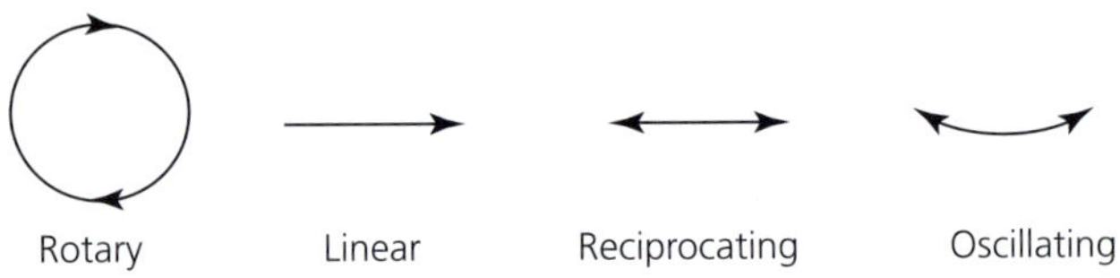

△ **Figure 1** The four types of motion

ROTARY MOTION

Rotary motion follows a circular path (Figure 2). It goes round in a circle like the hands of a clock, the blades of a fan or the wheels of a car.

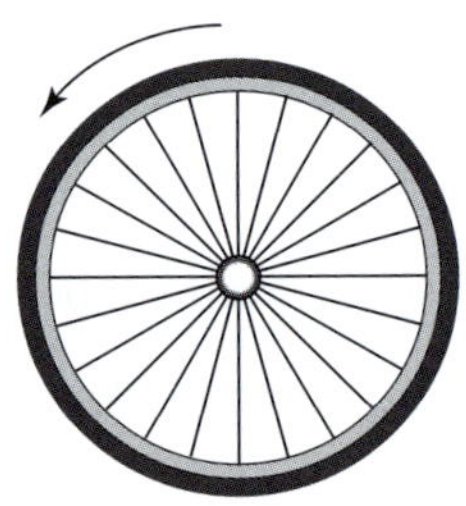

△ **Figure 2** Rotary motion

LINEAR MOTION

Linear motion is motion along a straight line (Figure 3). Examples of linear motion are a train travelling on a straight track, a free-falling object (for example, a stone dropped from a height or an apple falling from a tree) or a rocket launched into space.

△ **Figure 3** Linear motion

RECIPROCATING MOTION

Reciprocating motion is where a device moves back and forth or up and down in a straight line. Examples include the motion of a yo-yo, the piston in an engine or a needle on a sewing machine (Figure 4).

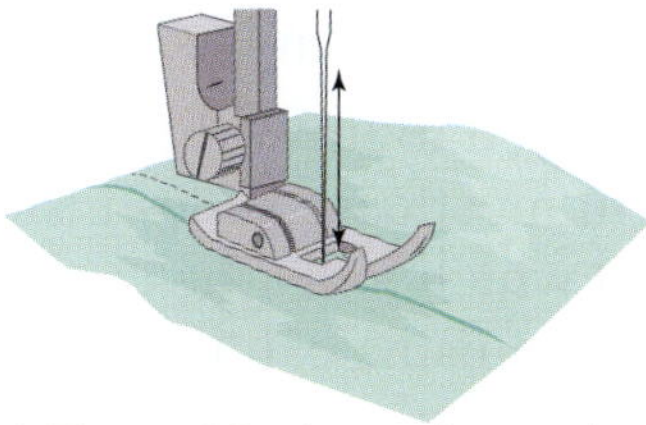

△ **Figure 4** Reciprocating motion

OSCILLATING MOTION

Oscillating motion is where a device swings back and forth, like the motion of a child on a swing (Figure 5) or the pendulum of a clock.

△ **Figure 5** Oscillating motion

CONVERTING ROTARY MOTION TO LINEAR MOTION

Conversion of motion is when one type of movement or motion changes into another. In a bicycle, for example, the pedalling motion (rotary motion) is converted into the movement of the bike (linear motion). In another example, wind (linear motion) can turn windmills or wind turbine blades (rotary motion), as shown in Figure 6.

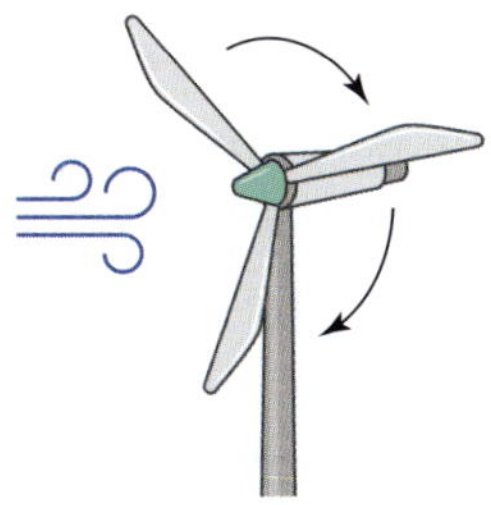

△ **Figure 6** An example of the conversion of motion

Converting one type of motion to another is a common feature of mechanisms. Converting rotary to linear motion and vice versa can be achieved using the following mechanisms:

- a **crank and slider** mechanism
- **cams**
- screw-thread mechanisms.

CRANK AND SLIDER MECHANISMS

Crank and slider mechanisms are frequently used to convert rotary to linear motion (Figure 7).

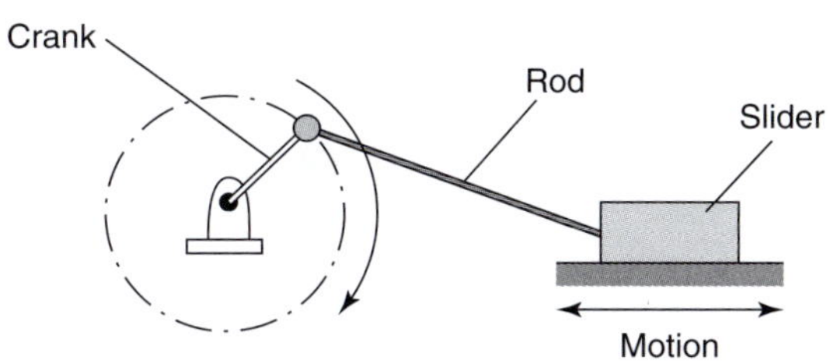

△ **Figure 7** A crank and slider motion

The crank and slider mechanism has three main parts:

- the crank which is used to drive the slider
- the slider (which in most case slides inside a guide)
- the connecting rod which joins the crank to the slider.

Crank and slider mechanisms can be used in one of two ways:

1. Where the crank rotates and drives the slider – for example, operating a sewing machine needle, producing the motion of a mechanical saw, and driving steam engine wheels.
2. Where power is applied to the slider which turns the crank via the connecting rod. This principle is used in internal combustion engines where pistons slide backwards and forwards to drive a crankshaft. This in turn can be used to drive the wheels of a vehicle.

TOP TIP

The frequency of the slider (the number of cycles it completes for one revolution or turn of the crank) depends on:

- the rotational speed of the crank (how fast it completes revolutions)
- the stroke length of the slider.

SKILLS ACTIVITY

Demonstrate a slider and crank mechanism

Using card, paper and split pins, design and make a card model of a slider and crank to demonstrate the mechanism.

Describe the motion of the slider when the crank is rotated through one revolution (360-degree turn).

ECCENTRICS

An **eccentric** is a circular disc or wheel attached to a rotating shaft, but with its centre positioned off-centre from the shaft's axis (Figure 8). This offset creates a displacement as the eccentric rotates, converting the circular motion of the shaft into linear motion. This mechanism is used in engines and pumps to drive valves or rams.

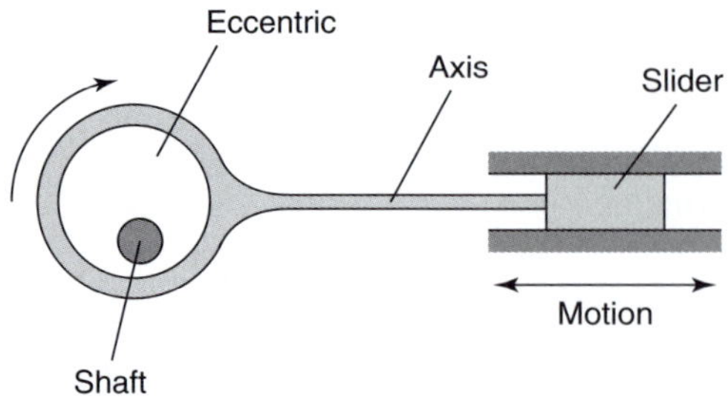

Δ **Figure 8** Eccentric motion

CAMS

A cam is another part of a mechanism designed to change rotary motion to linear motion. It is made up of three parts: the cam, the **slide and the follower** (Figure 9).

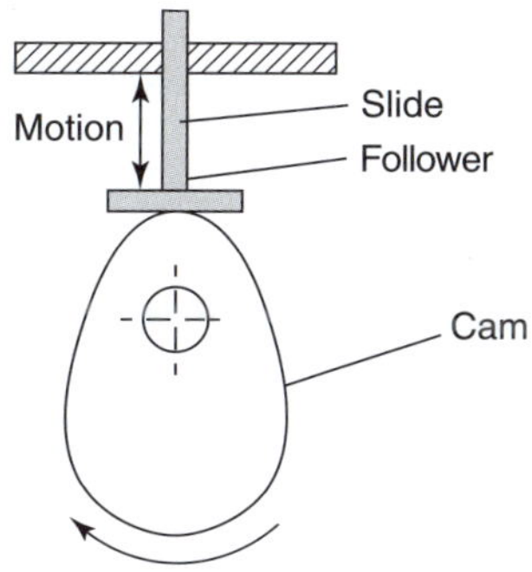

△ **Figure 9** A cam

The follower is a rod that rests on the cam. When the cam shaft rotates, the follower can either move up or down or dwell (stay still). Unlike the crank and slider mechanism, the output motion of a cam is different depending on the shape of the cam profile.

Cams are used in toys, household appliances, vehicles (cars, lorries, bicycles) and industrial equipment, such as packaging machines. They are useful in mechanisms because they have a small number of parts and can be designed to transmit different patterns of motion.

Cams tend to be reliable – they can work at high speeds and can operate relatively quietly.

There are several types of cams:

- Plate cams are common. They have a specific profile (edge) depending on the type of motion required. They are produced using materials such as sheet metal, polymers or timber. In many cases, it is necessary to machine the profile of the cam to a high precision so that it can operate effectively.
- Barrel cams have grooves machined into the cam to provide a track for the cam follower to follow.

The type of motion depends on the shape of the cam. The cam performs three basic actions (Figure 10):

- A rise, where the cam follower moves up.
- A fall, where the cam follower drops down.
- A dwell, where there is no rise or fall movement.

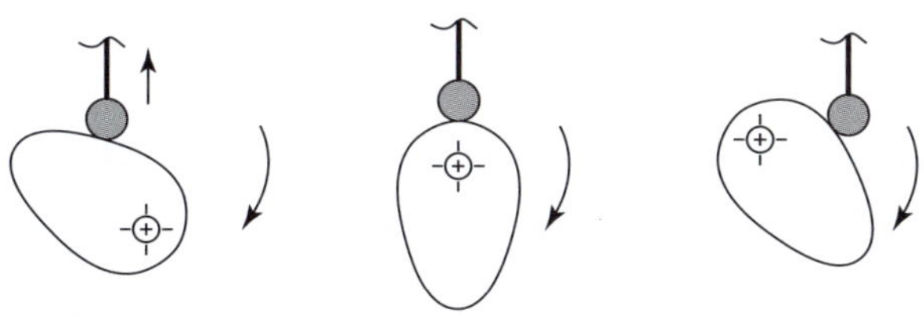

△ **Figure 10** Motions of different types of cam

The follower of a plate cam rests against the cam profile and moves according to its shape as the cam rotates. Followers come in various types, including flat, roller and knife-edge, or they may function as levers that amplify the movement generated by the cam.

The shape of the cam determines the type of motion produced. Cam profiles including pear-shaped, circular (eccentric), snail and multi-rise-and-fall cams (Figure 11). The snail cam can only operate in one direction. If it is turned the other way, it will lock against the follower. The snail cam produces a sudden drop when the follower reaches the vertical portion of the profile. If more than one movement is required for each revolution of the cam, a profile such as an ellipse, a square or a hexagon can be used to produce two, four or six lifts respectively.

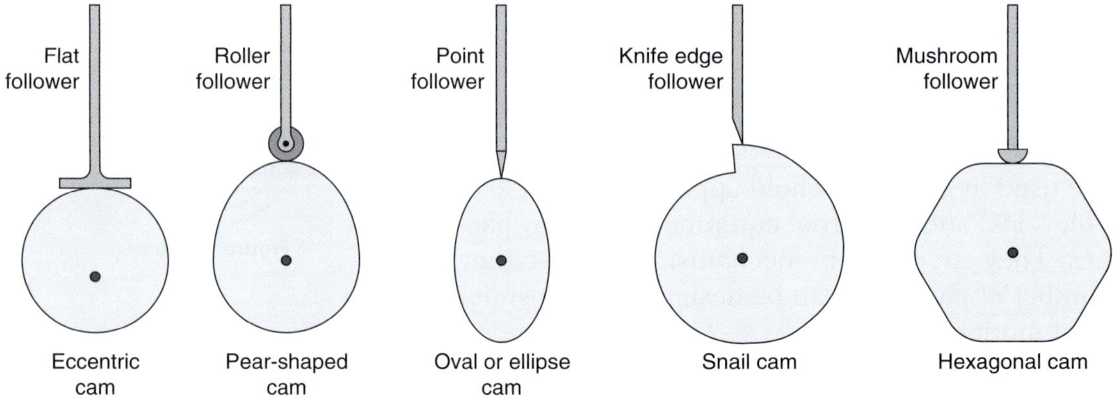

△ **Figure 11** Types of follower and cam profile

SCREW THREADS AND THE SCREW JACK

Screw threads are designed to convert rotary motion into linear motion. As the screw rotates, a collar (nut) moves along the thread's axis. The **pitch** – the distance between consecutive tops (or crests) of the thread – determines the mechanical advantage: a smaller pitch results in an increase in the effect of the force (a greater force multiplication).

Common applications of screw threads include **screw jacks**, turnbuckles and lead screws in machinery. A screw jack is a lifting device operated by turning a screw (Figure 12). It is often used to lift heavy objects, such as cars, machinery or even structural components in construction.

A screw jack works in the following way:

- The input force is applied using a handle, which functions as a lever.
- In the simplest form (using a single-start thread), one full turn of the handle moves the jack by a distance equal to the pitch of the screw thread.
- This mechanism allows large force multiplication, making it ideal for lifting heavy loads with minimal effort.

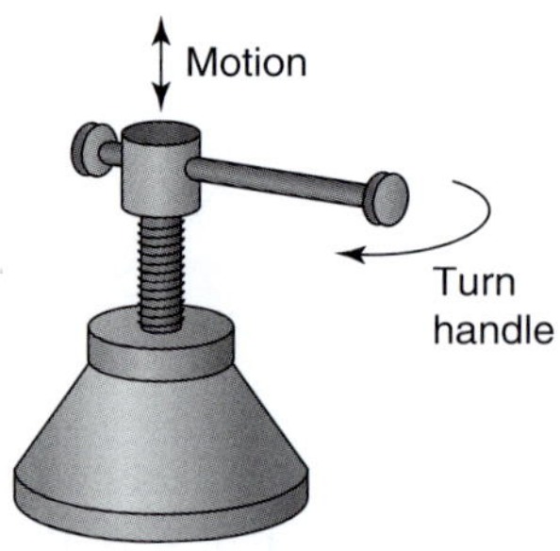

△ **Figure 12** A screw jack

WHEEL AND AXLE

Wheel and axle mechanisms are used in car steering wheels, wheel and axle parts of cars and locomotives, and other types of transport. Wheel and axle motion also describes the operation of screwdrivers and doorknobs.

To operate a wheel and axle, an effort is applied to a large diameter wheel which transmits a load to a smaller diameter wheel (Figure 13).

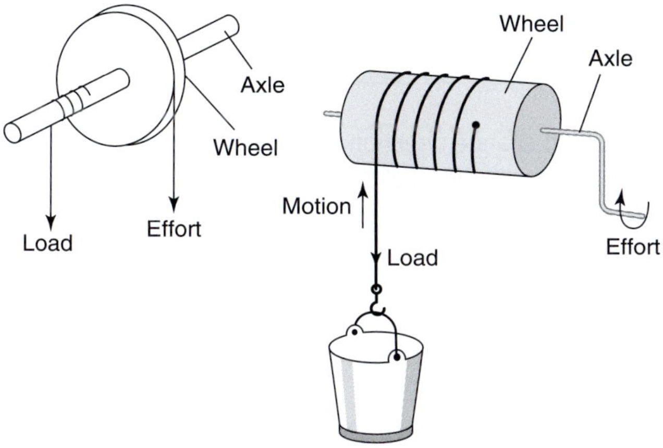

△ **Figure 13** Wheel and axle mechanism

KNOWLEDGE CHECK

1. Describe the following types of motion: rotary, linear, reciprocating and oscillating.
2. Give a real-world example of the following types of motion: rotary, linear, reciprocating and oscillating.
3. Sketch how rotary motion can be converted to linear motion.

KEY TERMS

Cam: A specially shaped part attached to a rotating shaft that imparts linear motion to a cam follower

Conversion of motion: When one type of movement or motion changes into another

Crank and slider: A mechanism used to change rotary motion to linear motion, or vice versa

Eccentric: A disc with the centre of rotation moved away from the centre of the circle

Oscillating motion: Repetitive movement that swings back and forth along a curved path

Pitch: The distance between consecutive tops (or crests) of a screw thread

Reciprocating motion: Repetitive straight-line movement back and forth along a linear path

Screw jack: A device designed to lift a load, operated by turning a leadscrew

Slide and the follower: A mechanism where one-part slides in a straight line while another part follows its motion, often used to convert rotary motion into linear motion

Wheel and axle : A simple machine part that consists of a wheel attached to an axle

1·7·3 Transmission of motion

LEARNING AIMS

By the end of this unit, you should:

✓ Understand how mechanisms can be used to change direction or force of motion
✓ Identify and describe the key components of mechanical, electronic and structural systems
✓ Compare the effectiveness of different system designs and suggest improvements

Motion can be transferred between rotating shafts and different parts of a machine in several ways. For example:

- Gears transfer rotary motion between shafts that are close together.
- Pulley systems and chains connect shafts that are farther apart, helping to transfer movement over longer distances.
- Rack and pinion systems change rotary motion into linear motion, or vice versa.
- These systems help machines work efficiently by controlling movement and direction.

GEARS AND GEAR SYSTEMS

Gears are essential components in many mechanical systems, such as in car engines, bicycles and industrial machinery. They are used to control speed, direction and power transmission:

- Gears can increase or decrease the rotational speed of shafts or change the direction of motion.
- In gearboxes, gears adjust power output for efficient performance, to do this they change the input speed to a faster or slower output speed (depending on the gears in the gearbox).

How gears work

Each gear has a specific number of teeth, which mesh with other gears to transfer motion. In a **gear system**:

- The gear that drives the gear train is called the **driver gear**. It is typically connected to a shaft powered by an electric motor, generator or engine.
- The gear that receives motion from the driver gear is called the **driven gear**.
- When two gears mesh, they rotate in opposite directions.
- An *idler gear* can be added between the driver and driven gear to ensure they rotate in the same direction (Figure 1).

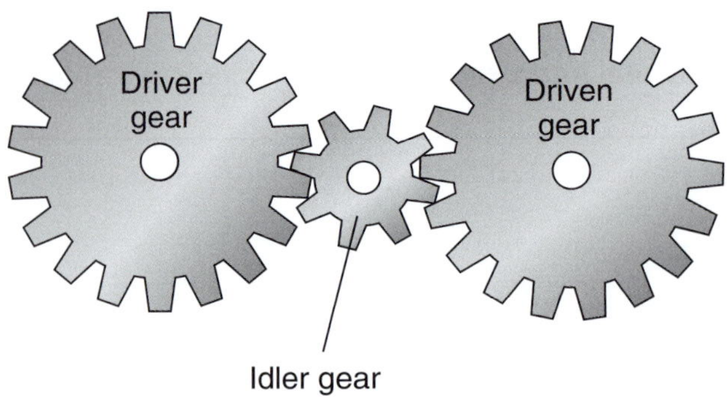

△ **Figure 1** An idler gear

There are two types of gear system (**gear train**):

- *Simple gear train:* Two meshed gears transferring motion between shafts (Figure 2).
- *Compound gear train:* Two or more gears fixed together on a single axle, allowing large speed reductions in a compact space (Figure 3).

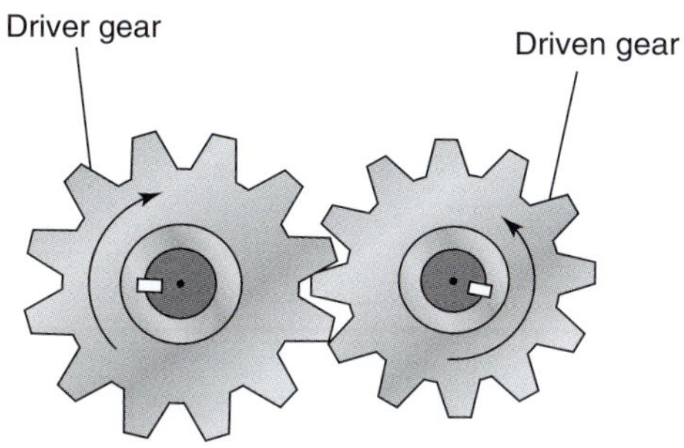

∆ **Figure 2** A simple gear train

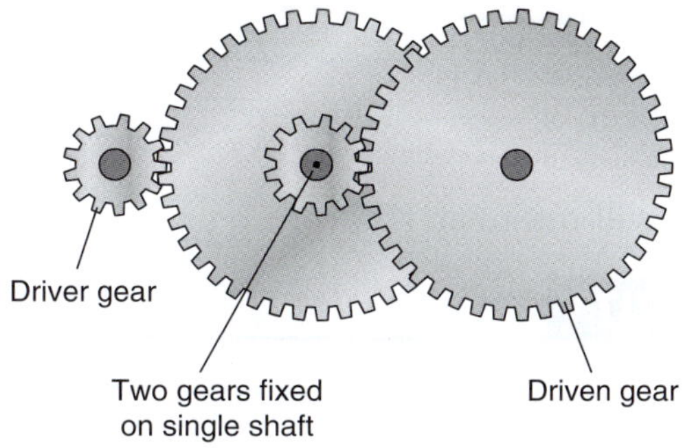

∆ **Figure 3** A compound gear train

By understanding gear interactions and **velocity ratio**, engineers can design efficient mechanisms tailored to different applications.

VELOCITY RATIO OF SIMPLE GEAR SYSTEMS

The velocity ratio, commonly known as **gear ratio**, determines the relative speeds of two gears. It is calculated using:

$$\text{Velocity ratio} = \frac{\text{Number of teeth on driven gear}}{\text{Number of teeth on driver gear}}$$

This ratio affects how speed and torque (turning force) are transferred in a system. Higher ratios result in greater torque but reduced speed, while lower ratios produce higher speed but lower torque.

Example 1: Calculating output speed

A simple gear train has a driver gear rotating at 200 rpm (revolutions per minute). The driver gear has 40 teeth, while the driven gear has 80 teeth. What is the output speed of the driven gear?

Step 1: Calculate the velocity ratio

Use the velocity ratio formula:

$$\text{Velocity ratio} = \frac{\text{Number of teeth on driven gear}}{\text{Number of teeth on driver gear}}$$

Substitute in the given values:

$$\text{Velocity ratio} = \frac{80}{40} = 2$$

Step 2: Calculate the output speed

Determine the driven gear's speed using:

$$\text{Output speed} = \frac{\text{Input speed}}{\text{Velocity ratio}}$$

Substitute in the values:

$$\text{Output speed} = \frac{200}{2} = 100 \text{ rpm}$$

The driven gear will rotate at 100 rpm.

SKILLS ACTIVITY

Calculate velocity ratios

Calculate the velocity ratios of the gear systems shown in Table 1.

Driver gear teeth	Driven gear teeth
50	100
30	90
20	80
60	30
40	80

△ **Table 1** Various gear systems

TYPES OF GEAR

There are different types of gear for different purposes (Table 2 and Figures 4–8).

Gear type	Purpose
Spur	Simple, straight-toothed gear used for basic power transmission
Helical	Angled teeth for smoother and quieter operation compared to spur gear
Bevel	Conical gear used to change the axis of rotation
Worm	A screw-like gear that provides high torque while reducing speed
Rack and pinion	Convert rotary motion into linear motion, commonly used in steering systems
Planetary	Compact gear system found in automatic transmissions for efficient torque distribution
Ratchet and pawl	Allow movement in only one direction while preventing backward motion, commonly used in winches and hand tools

△ **Table 2** Types of gear and their purposes

△ **Figure 4** Spur, helical and bevel gears

△ **Figure 5** Worm-wheel system

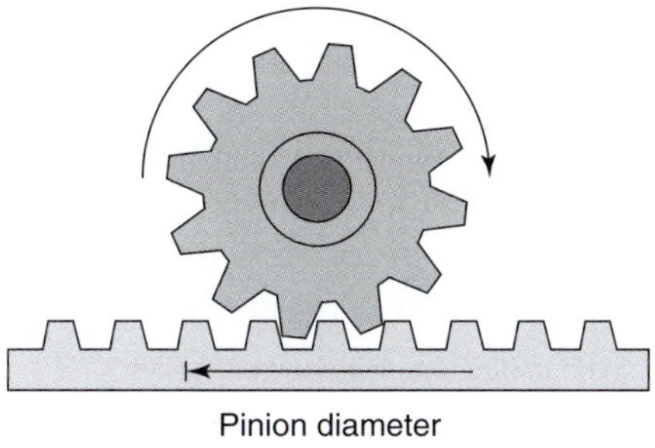

△ **Figure 6** Rack and pinion system

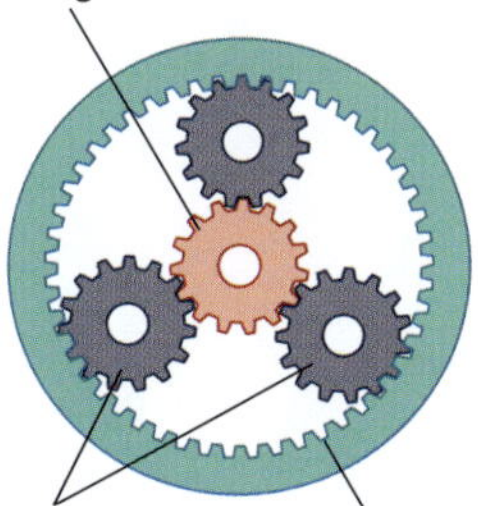

△ **Figure 7** Planetary gears

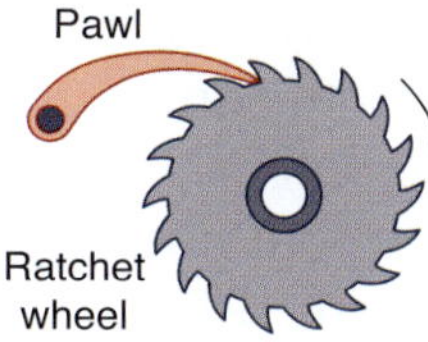

△ **Figure 8** Ratchet and pawl gear

BELT DRIVES

Belt drives are used to link two rotating shafts which are relatively far apart. In most cases, the shafts are parallel to each other. In a similar way to gear systems, belt drive pulleys are either driver or driven **pulleys**. The driver is generally attached to a motor or other power source. The driver then drives the driven pulley using a connecting belt.

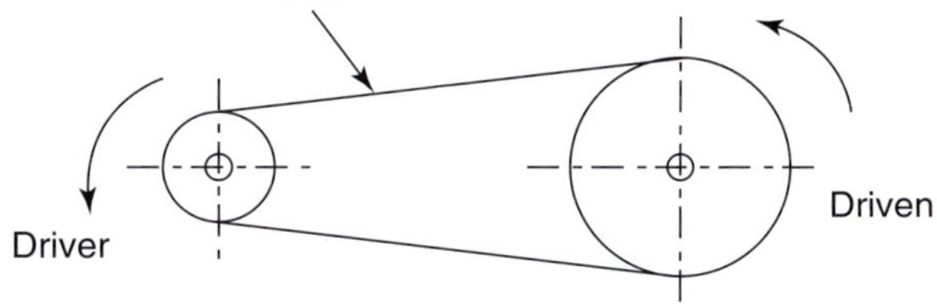

△ **Figure 9** A belt drive with pulleys rotating in the *same* direction

When a belt is used without crossing, the pulleys will rotate in the same direction (Figure 9). If the belt is crossed, then the pulleys will rotate in opposite directions (Figure 10). This is a way of changing the direction of rotating shafts.

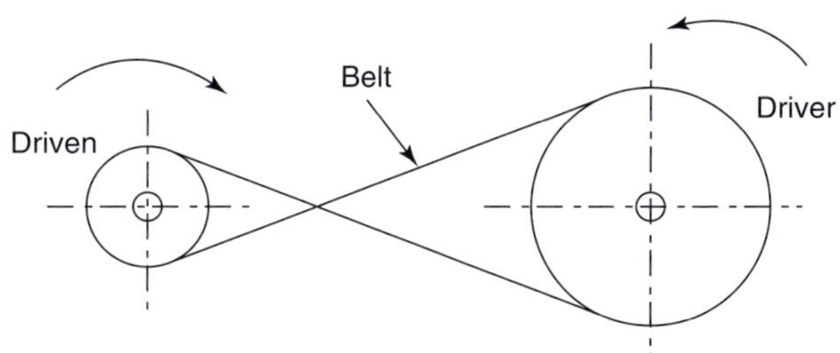

△ **Figure 10** A crossed belt drive with pulleys rotating in the *opposite* direction

Pulley systems tend to be cheaper than gear systems. However, the belts can slip and stretch over time. Therefore, most belt drive systems need a method of adjusting the belt tension.

TYPES OF BELT DRIVE

Belt drives are classified by the cross-sectional shape of the belt. They include:

- Flat belts
- Round belts
- Vee-belts
- Toothed belts

Flat belts

Flat belts are used to drive parts of textile machinery. They are found in household appliances (for example, vacuum cleaners) and are used in small electrical generators. This type of belt can 'climb' off the face of the pulley when used. To counter this, the pulley surface has a slight convex shape (Figure 11). This keeps the belt central when it is rotating.

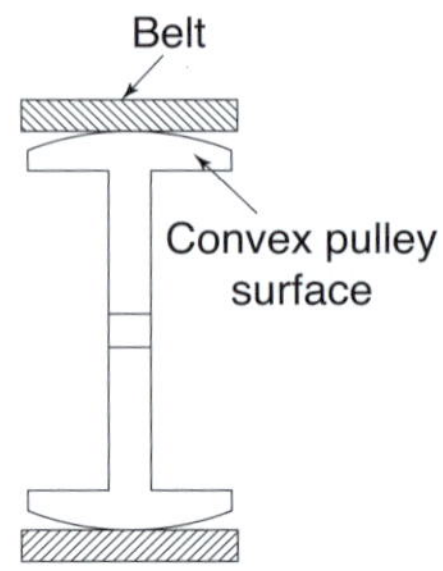

Δ **Figure 11** A flat belt

Round belts

Round belts are used for low power-transmission applications, such as driving the needle in sewing machines and also in small electrical fans. They have a circular cross-section and tend to run in pulleys with a vee-groove. When the belt is rotating, the sides of the belt 'squeeze' out and press against the sides of the vee (Figure 12).

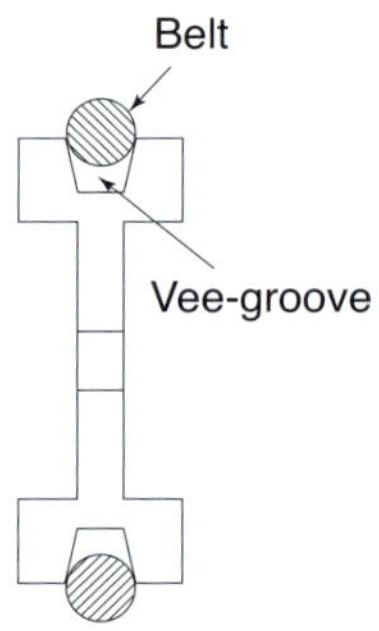

Δ **Figure 12** A round belt

Vee-belts

Vee-belts are used where high power-transmission forces are required – for example, in industry where high loads need to be driven at high speeds without the belt slipping. Typical uses are driving lathes, milling machines, industrial presses and industrial conveyors. The vee-shape of the belt fits into the vee-groove of the pulley (Figure 13).

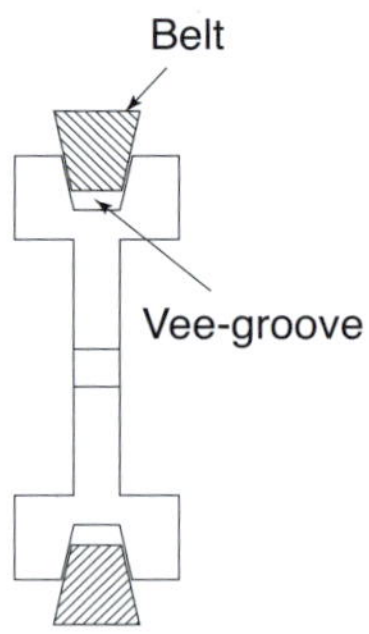

Δ **Figure 13** A vee-belt

Toothed belts

Toothed belts are often used for timing applications, such as in car engines and in computer printer equipment. They have teeth (Figure 14). These match up with the teeth in a toothed pulley. The teeth reduce belt slippage and keep two shafts of a mechanism running in time with each other.

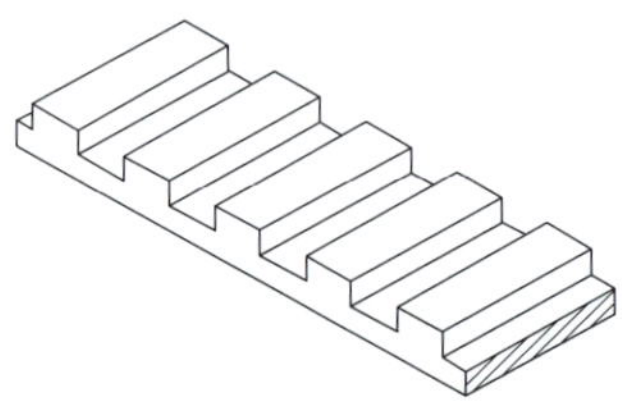

Δ **Figure 14** A toothed belt

SPROCKET AND CHAIN DRIVES

Sprockets and chains are used for driving the wheels of bicycles and motorbikes, and the timing belts for some motor car engines. The sprocket and chain allows power to be transmitted from one shaft to another without slippage. This means that relatively high power can be transmitted from one shaft to another. The sprocket is the toothed wheel in which the chain engages (Figure 15).

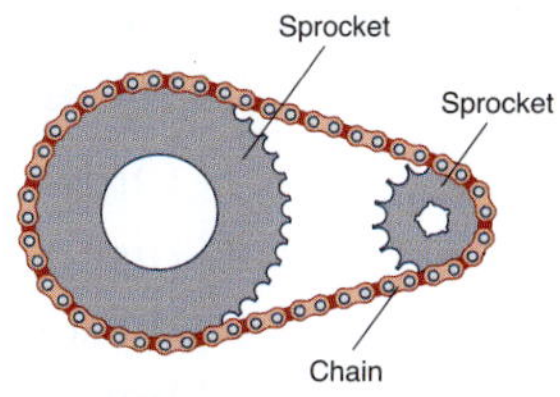

△ **Figure 15** A sprocket and chain drive

TOP TIP

Selecting mechanisms for design applications

When choosing parts for a mechanism, consider the following key factors:

1. *Type of movement:* Does it need linear, rotary or oscillating motion?
2. *Speed:* How fast should the parts move?
3. *Space:* Is there enough room for the mechanism?
4. *Load capacity:* What weight or force must it handle?
5. *Material:* Should you use a polymer, metal or another material?
6. *Environment:* Will it face heat, moisture or chemicals?
7. *Cost:* Is it affordable while still being effective?
8. *Maintenance:* Will it need regular servicing?
9. *Torque:* Does it require strong rotational force?
10. *Vibration:* Is stability important?

Thinking about these factors helps you choose the best parts for a strong and reliable mechanism.

SKILLS ACTIVITY

Comparing system designs

Compare the effectiveness of *two* different system designs. Discuss key factors such as cost, efficiency and reliability. Look at the example in Table 3 to guide you.

Factor	System 1 (gear train)	System 2 (pulley drive)	Comparison notes
Cost	Expensive; needs correct alignment and lubrication	Cheaper; requires lubrication	Which is more economical?
Efficiency	Can be highly efficient, depending on lubrication	The longer the belt, the lower the efficiency	Which delivers better performance?
Reliability	Can be very reliable, failure is often catastrophic if teeth shear off, as failure is instant and without warning	Belts wear over time, if one shaft becomes stuck (ceased) the belt will slip	Which system is more durable?

Factor	System 1 (gear train)	System 2 (pulley drive)	Comparison notes
Usage	Only useable over small distance, can convert direction of rotation between shafts	Can operate over large distances, belt requires tensioners in some cases, same input and output direction of rotation	How close are the two rotating shafts to each other?

△ **Table 3** An example comparing a belt drive and a chain drive

Copy and complete Table 4 to record your comparison.

Factor	System 1 (*name*)	System 2 (*name*)	Comparison notes
Cost			
Efficiency			
Reliability			
Best use case			
Improvement suggestion			

△ **Table 4** A comparison of two systems

KNOWLEDGE CHECK

1. State the purpose or function of an idler gear.
2. Give **one** advantage of using gears rather than belt drives.
3. Sketch the difference between a simple gear train and a compound gear train.
4. Explain how mechanisms can be used to change direction or force of motion.

KEY TERMS

Belt drive A system that transmits power using an endless belt wrapped over two pulleys

Driven gear: The gear that receives motion from the driver gear

Driver gear: Is the main gear in a system that makes other gears move; it turns first and transfers motion to the driven gear, controlling speed and direction

Gear system (gear train): A system of interlocking gears used to transmit motion and torque between rotating shafts

Sprocket and chain: A system that uses toothed wheels (sprockets) and a chain to transfer motion

Velocity ratio (gear ratio): The ratio of the distances moved by the effort and the load at the same time, influencing speed and force transmission

1·8 Electronics

1·8·1 Basic concepts of electronics

LEARNING AIMS

By the end of this unit, you should:

✓ Understand the terms and units for electrical current, voltage, resistance and power
✓ Understand how to use the relationships between current, voltage, resistance and power
✓ Understand the characteristics of direct and alternating current
✓ Recognise a range of circuit symbols
✓ Be able to interprete and draw simple direct current circuits
✓ Understand how to use meters to measure electrical current, voltage and resistance

Electronic circuits are widely used for operating and controlling products, systems and processes. There are many examples in the world around us, from mobile phones to more complex control systems, such as automated manufacturing processes and air-conditioned building systems.

These circuits, however complex, are made using components, conductors (for example, wires) and energy sources, such as batteries, which are the source of electricity. This unit covers the concepts electrical current, voltage / potential difference, resistance and power, including common component symbols, the basics of resistors and capacitors, and the use of multimeters.

CIRCUITS

Electronic circuits are the foundation of modern technology. From smartphones and computers to washing machines and traffic lights, circuits are everywhere. In this unit, you will explore basic electronic concepts. In order to understand these you need to know about component symbols (Figure 1) and circuit diagrams (Figures 2 and 3). An electronic circuit is a path through which electric current flows. It typically includes components such as resistors, capacitors, LEDs, switches, and transistors, all connected by conductive wires or tracks. Circuits can be as simple as turning on a light, or as complex as controlling a robot.

Electronic circuit diagrams can look complicated at first, but they make complex circuits easier to understand. A circuit diagram is a simplified drawing that shows how components are connected using standard symbols. These symbols represent parts like resistors, LEDs, switches, and batteries, and help engineers and designers communicate ideas clearly. For example, a resistor is shown as an elongated rectangle, while an LED is a triangle with a bar on the tip and arrows pointing outward (Figure 1). Learning to read and draw these diagrams is a key skill in electronics, and allows you to plan, build, and troubleshoot circuits without needing to physically assemble them first. Symbols are instantly recognisable, where different types of the same physical component can look quite different or the same as components with different functions. Once you understand the symbols, you can quickly interpret how a circuit works and even design your own.

Key concepts you will learn in this and the other electronics units:

- *Circuit types:* Series and parallel circuits, and how they affect current and voltage.
- *Components:* What each part does—resistors limit current, capacitors store energy, LEDs emit light, and switches control flow.
- *Symbols and diagrams:* How to read and draw circuit diagrams using standard symbols.
- *Input, process and output components:* Understanding how sensors (input), microcontrollers (process), and actuators (output) work.

Learning about electronic circuits helps you understand how everyday devices function and gives you the skills to design and build your own. Whether you're creating a simple alarm system or programming a microcontroller to control lights, circuit diagrams (sometime referred to as schematics) show how components are connected to create a functional electronic system.

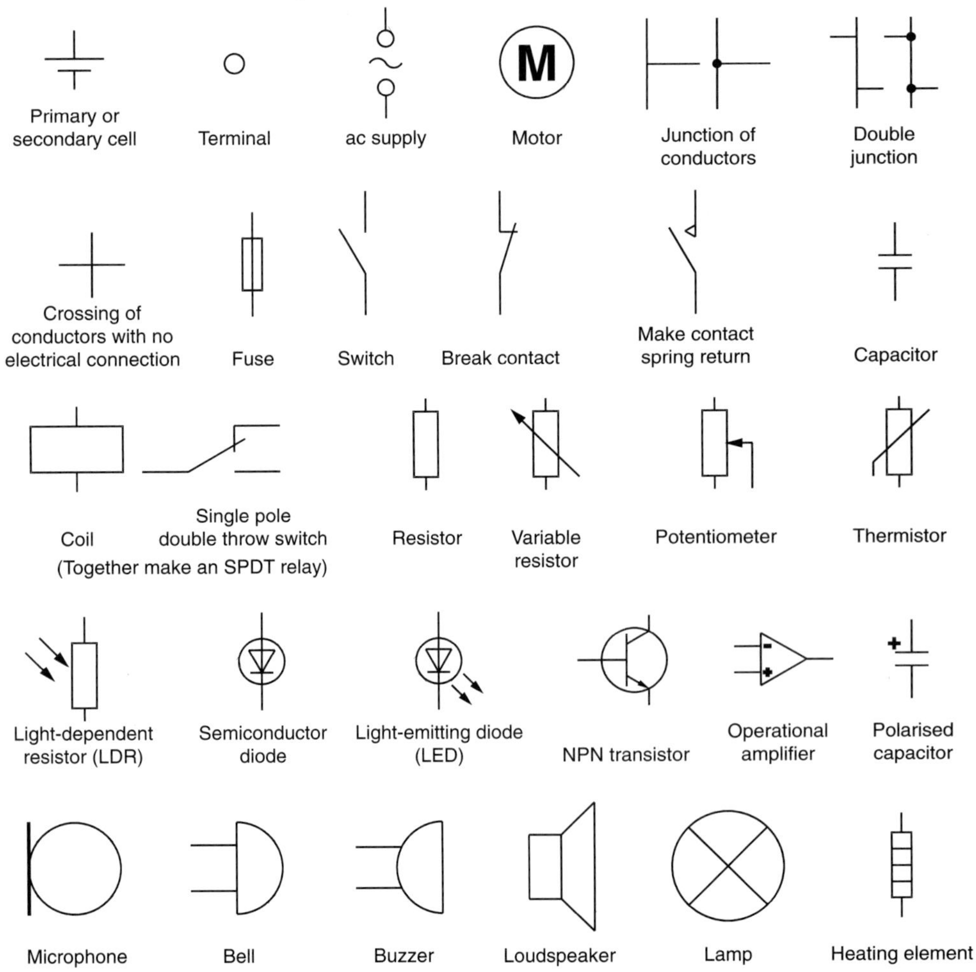

△ **Figure 1** Common electronic symbols

CURRENT

Electricity is the flow of negatively charged electrons in a circuit. A circuit is a combination of components connected in a specific pattern to perform a particular function.

There are two types of electrical flow (or **current**):

- **Direct current (DC)** is provided by power sources such as batteries, solar cells and direct current generators. In a DC circuit, electrical flow is in one direction only. DC tends to use lower voltages (typically 1.5–18 V) and is, therefore, safer than high voltage AC supplies. It is ideal for using with electronic devices in offices and the home (using AC to DC transformers), as well as portable appliances (using batteries).
- **Alternating current (AC)** is supplied through the mains supply in homes and schools. This comes from power plants (generated using renewable and non-renewable fuels). AC oscillates (moves back and forth) in both directions around the circuit. AC supplies tend to be high voltage (e.g. 240 V) and are more efficient to transmit over long distances. They also need to be transformed to lower voltage DC to be used locally with electronic devices.

Figure 2 shows a simple direct current circuit. The circuit includes a battery, a switch and a lamp (light bulb). Wires connect the components together.

The unit of measurement for current is the 'ampere' or amp (A). Most small circuits will have currents measured in milliamps (mA). When the switch is closed it is assumed that the current flows from the positive battery terminal to the negative terminal. This positive-to-negative direction is called *conventional current flow*. In doing so, it lights up the lamp.

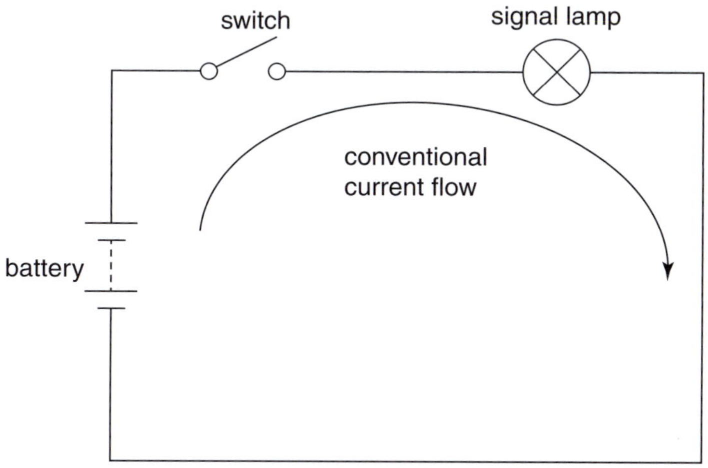

△ **Figure 2** A simple circuit diagram of a series circuit

Resistance is the 'force' that impedes (reduces) the flow of current through a conductor. Resistance is measured in 'ohms' (Ω or R).

ENERGY AND POTENTIAL DIFFERENCE

The energy from a power supply, such as batteries and generators, is what causes the current to flow in a circuit. This energy is measured in volts (V). The higher the **voltage**, the higher the potential energy supplied to a circuit.

Potential difference describes the voltage that is used by a component, or across a circuit, when a current flows through it. You can use a voltmeter connected in parallel (Figure 3) to measure the potential difference between two points in a circuit. The voltage at the 'negative' terminal of the power supply is said to be zero (0).

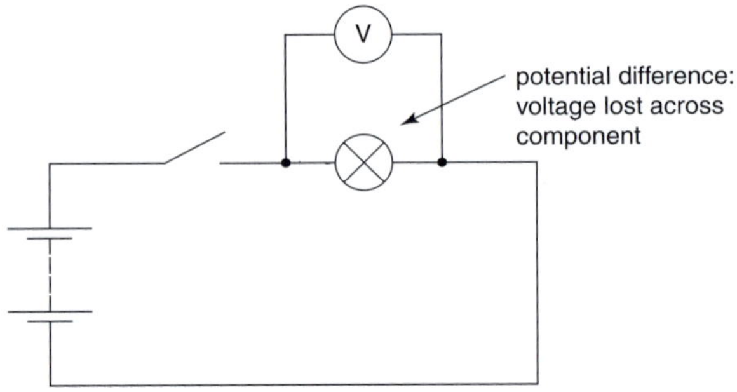

Δ **Figure 3** A parallel circuit diagram with a voltmeter

SERIES AND PARALLEL CIRCUITS

Understanding how components are connected in a circuit is essential for designing and troubleshooting electronic systems. The two most common types of connections are **series** and **parallel**.

Series circuits

In a **series circuit** (Figure 2), components are connected one after another in a single path. The current flows through each component in turn. Key characteristics include:

- *Current*: The same current flows through all components.
- *Voltage*: The total voltage is shared across the components. Each component gets a portion of the total voltage.
- If one component fails (like a bulb blowing), the whole circuit stops working.

If you connect two resistors in series to a 6 V battery, each resistor might get 3 V (depending on their resistance).

Parallel circuits

In a **parallel circuit** (Figure 3), components are connected across the same two points, creating multiple paths for current to flow.
Key characteristics include:

- *Current*: Splits between the paths depending on the resistance of each branch.
- *Voltage*: Each component receives the full voltage of the power supply.
- If one component fails, the others can still work.

If you connect two bulbs in parallel to a 6V battery, each bulb gets the full 6V and can operate independently.

Summary

Feature	Series circuit	Parallel circuit
Current	Same through all components	Splits across branches
Voltage	Shared between components	Same across all components
Reliability	One failure breaks the circuit	Other branches still work

WHAT ARE RESISTORS?

A **resistor** is an electronic component that limits the flow of electrical current in a circuit (Figure 4). It is used to protect components, divide voltages and control signal levels.

Resistors behave differently depending on whether they are connected in a series circuit (end-to-end) or a parallel circuit (side by side). Resistance can be calculated using the following formulae:

Resistors in series $R_{total} = R1 + R2 + R3\ldots$

Resistors in parallel $\frac{1}{R_{total}} = \frac{1}{R1} + \frac{1}{R2} + \frac{1}{R3}\ldots$

There are several types:

- **Fixed resistors** have a constant resistance value.
- **Variable resistors** (potentiometers) can be adjusted to change resistance.
- Special resistors include **thermistors** (temperature-sensitive) and **light-dependent resistors (LDRs)**.

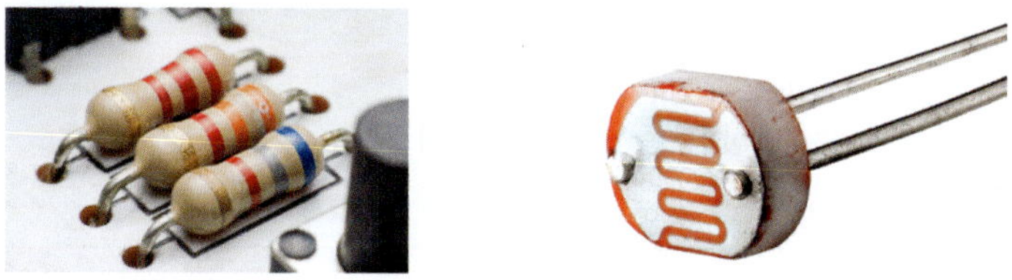

Δ **Figure 4** Resistors on a circuit board and an LDR

Reading resistor values

Resistors use colour bands to indicate their resistance value and tolerance. The *first two* bands represent digits, the *third* is a multiplier (number of zeros added), and the *fourth* is the tolerance (silver or gold) or percentage accuracy above or below the stated value.

In Figure 5, for example, the colour code for the resistor is: red, violet, orange, silver = 27 kΩ ±10%.

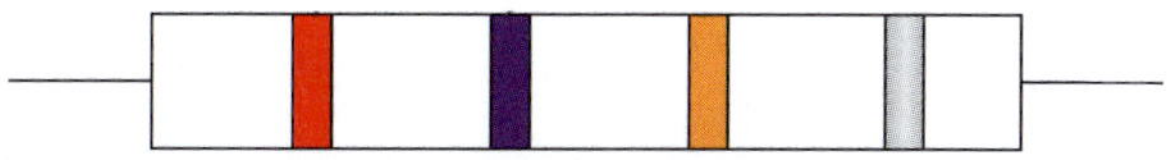

	1st digit	2nd digit	Multiplier	Tolerance
Black	0	0	×1	
Brown	1	1	×10	±1%
Red	2	2	$\times10^2$	±2%
Orange	3	3	$\times10^3$	±3%
Yellow	4	4	$\times10^4$	±4%
green	5	5	$\times10^5$	±0.5%
Blue	6	6	$\times10^6$	±0.25%
Violet	7	7	$\times10^7$	±0.1%
Grey	8	8	$\times10^8$	±0.05%
White	9	9	$\times10^9$	
Gold			$\times10^{-1}$	±5%
Silver			$\times10^{-2}$	±10%

Δ **Figure 5** Resistor colour codes

WHAT ARE CAPACITORS?

A **capacitor** is a component that stores electrical energy. It is used in timing circuits, filters and for smoothing voltage (reducing fluctuations).

Capacitors behave differently whether they are connected in *series* (end-to-end) or in *parallel* (side by side).

MEASURING VOLTAGE, CURRENT AND RESISTANCE WITH METERS

Meters are used to help check the current, voltage or resistance values of parts of circuits. They are also used to help find faults.

Ammeters measure the electrical current through components. To measure the current in a specific part of a circuit, the ammeter needs to be placed in series with the circuit. To do this, you break the circuit to add the ammeter.

Voltmeters measure the potential difference (voltage) between two points in a circuit. When measuring voltage, the meter is designed to be used in parallel with the component or device being measured.

Multimeters are more versatile because they can measure current, voltage and resistance in one instrument (Figure 6).

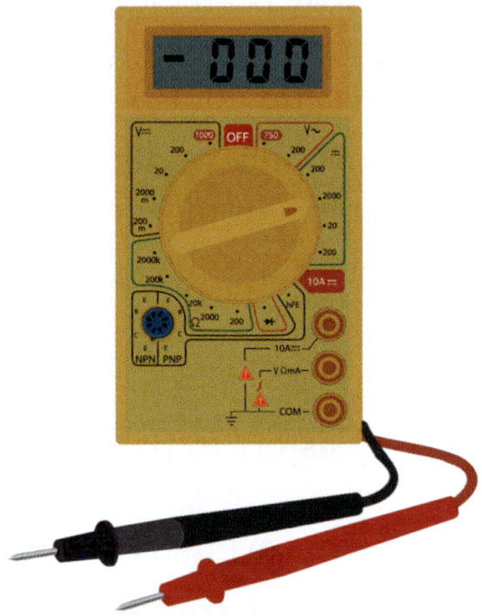

△ **Figure 6** Digital multimeter

KNOWLEDGE CHECK

1. State the units of potential difference, electrical current and resistance.
2. Define the term 'potential difference'.
3. How do you calculate total resistance in a series circuit?
4. A resistor has colour bands: brown, black, red, gold. Use Figure 5, p.133, to determine its resistance and tolerance.

KEY TERMS

Capacitor: A component that stores and releases electrical energy in an electric field

Current (electrical): The flow of electricity through a circuit or a measure of the rate of this flow – unit of measurement: amp (A)

Fixed resistor: A resistor with a constant resistance value

Light-dependent resistor (LDR): A resistor whose resistance changes with light intensity

Parallel circuit: A circuit in which components are connected along parallel paths

Potential difference: The difference in voltage between two points in a circuit – unit of measurement: volt (V)

Resistance: The extent to which a component or material reduces the flow of current through that part of a circuit – unit of measurement: ohm (Ω or R)

Resistor: A component that limits the flow of electrical current in a circuit

Series circuit: A circuit in which components are connected along the same path

Thermistor: A component whose resistance changes with temperature

Variable resistor: A resistor whose resistance can be adjusted; also known as a potentiometer

Voltage: A measure of electrical potential difference – unit of measurement: volt (V)

1·8·2 Output components

LEARNING AIMS

By the end of this unit, you should:

✓ Recognise a range of electronic output components

✓ Describe the use of output components to produce light, sound and motion

In the world of electronics, output components play a crucial role in transforming electrical signals into light, sound and motion, which our senses can detect. These components are the bridge between the hidden digital realm of electronic circuits and our everyday experiences, enabling us to see, hear and interact with electronic devices.

LIGHT

A signal lamp or light bulb is a basic output device used to show the presence or status of an electrical signal. It typically contains a fine metal filament inside a glass bulb and lights up when connected to a circuit. These bulbs are common in control panels, vehicles, appliances and industrial machines, serving as indicators for status, warnings or alerts. Types include traditional filament bulbs, incandescent bulbs, fluorescent bulbs and **light-emitting diodes (LEDs)** – each differing in brightness, efficiency and lifespan. LEDs are especially popular for their energy efficiency, long life and bright, colourful light.

Light-emitting diodes (LEDs)

An LED is a special kind of **diode** that gives out light when current passes through it. A diode only allows current to flow in one direction. The LED is made from a semi-conducting material, and it is possible to emit a range of colours including red (Figure 1), yellow and green light. LED arrays (arrangements) have effectively replaced light bulbs in a number of applications such as home and street lighting. Figure 2 shows the circuit symbol for an LED.

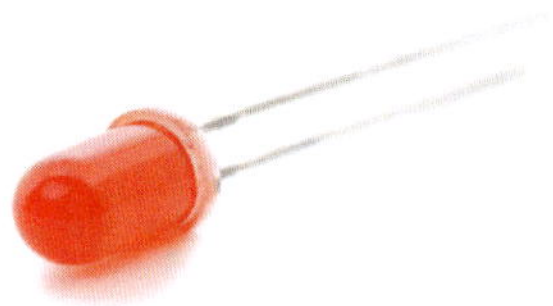

△ **Figure 1** A standard red LED

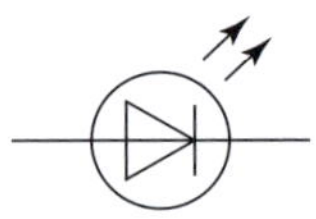

△ **Figure 2** Circuit symbol for an LED

Seven-segment displays

Seven-segment displays are a common form of display used for applications such as digital clocks, digital radios, car dashboard displays and other similar display features. A seven-segment display is made up of seven separate LEDs: one for each segment. In most cases, an eighth LED is used to show a decimal point. Figure 3 shows a typical example of a single digit display.

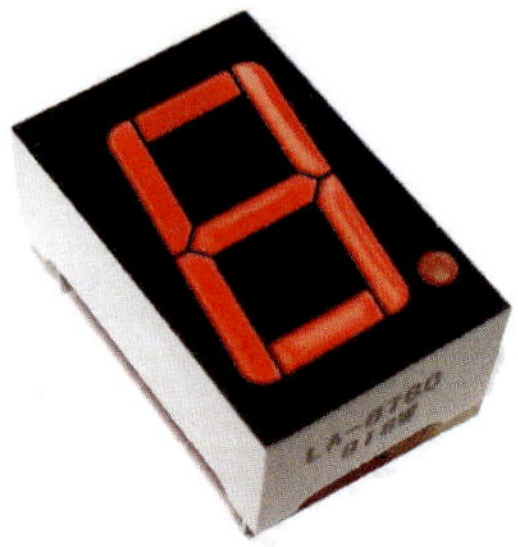

△ **Figure 3** Seven-segment display component

SKILLS ACTIVITY

Build a simple circuit

Build a simple circuit using a battery, switch, diode and bulb, and a prototype board or other component/wire connection method. Explore how current flows when the diode is connected in its **forward bias** mode, and how it prevents current flow when connected in its **reverse bias** mode. Record the outcomes of your findings.

SOUND

Sound output devices (or transducers) are essential components in electronic circuits, used to produce audible signals for various applications such as alarms, notifications and entertainment systems. Common sound output devices include piezo sounders, buzzers and speakers. Each of these devices has unique characteristics and applications.

Piezo sounders

Piezo sounders are compact and efficient devices that convert electrical signals into sound. They are often used in applications requiring high-pitched tones, such as alarms and timers. Piezo sounders consist of a piezoelectric material that vibrates when an electrical signal is applied, producing sound waves.

Buzzers

Buzzers are similar to piezo sounders, but are typically used for generating continuous or intermittent buzzing sounds. Buzzers often have a piezo sounder and a signal generating circuit housed in a casing to amplify the fixed tone. They are found in alarm systems, timers and notification devices.

Buzzers can be either active or passive:

- Active buzzers have a built-in oscillator and only require a DC voltage to operate.
- Passive buzzers need an external AC signal to produce sound.

Speakers

Speakers are used to produce a wide range of sounds, from simple tones to complex audio signals. They are used in multimedia devices, such as radios, televisions and computers. Speakers convert electrical signals into sound waves through the movement of a diaphragm.

TOP TIP

Follow these tips when using sound output devices.

- Piezo sounders: Mount securely to ensure optimal sound output (Figure 4).
- Buzzers: Choose the best type of buzzer based on the application requirements and ensure proper electrical contact methods.
- Speakers: Match the speaker's impedance with the circuit to ensure efficient sound output. Impedance is the effective resistance of a component and is measured in ohms (Ω or R). Design the speaker enclosure to prevent sound cancellation and enhance audio quality.

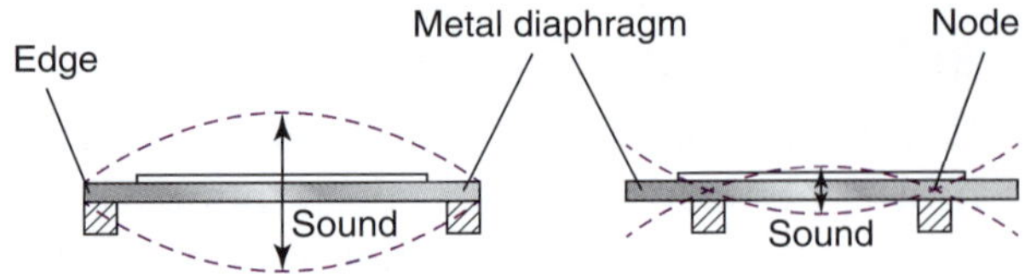

△ **Figure 4** Edge mounted and nodal mounted piezo devices

MOTION

Motion output devices are also crucial components in electronic circuits, used to convert electrical energy into mechanical energy (motion). These devices include motors, solenoids and **actuators** (Figure 5), each serving specific functions in various applications such as robotics, automation and control systems.

Stepper motor

Solenoid valve

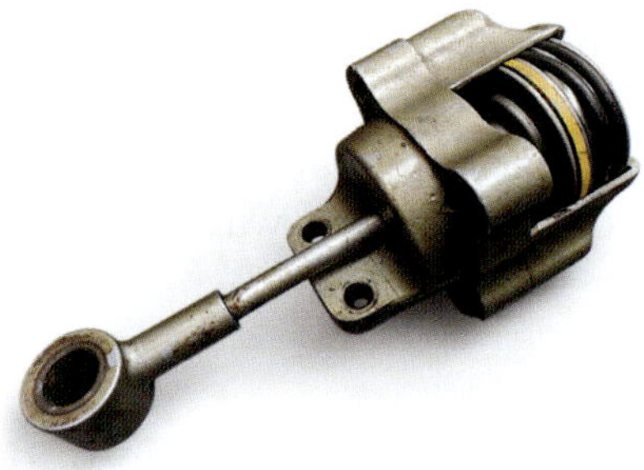
Turbo actuator

△ **Figure 5** Motors, solenoids and actuators

Motors

Motors convert electrical energy into rotary mechanical motion. They are widely used in applications requiring rotational movement, such as fans, pumps and robotic arms. There are several types of motors:

- DC motors operate by converting DC electrical energy into rotational motion. DC motors can also be connected to gearboxes to reduce the speed and increase the power, making them more useful in control systems.
- Stepper motors move in discrete steps, allowing precise control of angular position.
- Servo motors provide precise control of angular position, speed and acceleration.

Solenoids

Solenoids are electromagnetic devices that convert electrical energy into linear motion. They consist of a coil of wire wound around a movable core (plunger). When an electric current passes through the coil, it generates a magnetic field that moves the plunger. Solenoids are used in electronic door locks to control the locking mechanism. They are also used to control the flow of liquids or gases in valves.

Actuators

Actuators are devices that convert electrical energy into mechanical motion, similar to motors and solenoids. They can produce both linear and rotary motion. They are used in a wide range of applications, including robotics, industrial automation and aerospace.

Types of actuator:

- Linear actuators provide straight-line motion and are used in applications such as adjustable beds and conveyor belts.
- Rotary actuators provide rotary motion and are used in applications such as robotic arms and valve control.

TOP TIP

Follow these tips when using motion output devices.

- Motors:
  - Use variable resistors or pulse-width-modulated (PWM) signals to control the speed of DC motors.
  - Use H-bridge circuits to control the direction of rotation. An H-bridge is an array of four transistors, typically packaged in pairs in a dual in-line (DIL) integrated circuit (IC).
- Solenoids:
  - Ensure proper mounting and electrical connections to enhance the durability and performance of solenoids.
- Actuators:
  - Select actuators with the appropriate specifications for the required precision and load capacity.
  - Use feedback systems, such as encoders, to enhance the accuracy of actuator movements.

KNOWLEDGE CHECK

1. What is the function of an output component in an electronic circuit?
2. Describe how a light-emitting diode (LED) works and why a resistor is needed in series with it.
3. What is the difference between an active and a passive buzzer?
4. What is the purpose of a seven-segment display and how is it constructed?
5. How does a DC motor differ from a stepper motor in terms of movement and control?
6. What is the function of a solenoid in an electronic system? Give **one** example of its use.
7. Describe how a servo motor is controlled and what type of signal it uses.
8. What is the purpose of using a diode with output devices like motors or relays?

KEY TERMS

Actuator: A device that converts electrical energy into mechanical energy (motion)

Diode: An electronic component which allows current to flow predominantly in one direction only

Forward bias: The main direction of current flow through a diode

Light-emitting diode (LED): A type of diode which emits light when operating

Microcontroller: A compact integrated circuit designed to govern a specific operation in an embedded system

Relay: An electrically operated switch that uses an electromagnet to mechanically operate a switch

Reverse bias: The direction where there is no current flow until the diode breaks down

Transistor: A semiconductor device that can amplify or switch electronic signals and electrical power

1·8·3 Input components

LEARNING AIMS

By the end of this unit, you should:
✓ Identify and describe different types of switches and sensors
✓ Understand how input components are used in electronic circuits
✓ Explain the function of potential dividers in sensor circuits
✓ Apply knowledge of input components to design simple control systems

Input components are devices that detect changes in the environment and send signals to the rest of an electronic system. These signals can then be used to control outputs like lights, motors or alarms.

There are two main types of input component:

- **Switches** are manually or mechanically operated.
- **Sensors** produce electrical signals in response to a change in their surroundings such as light level, temperature or pressure.

SWITCHES

A switch is a device that opens or closes an electrical circuit. When closed, current flows; when open, it does not. Table 1 provides a list of common switches and their uses. Figure 1 illustrates the anatomy of switches.

Switch type	Description	Example use
Toggle switch	Flips between on and off positions	Light switches
Push switch	Push to make (PTM) or push to break (PTB) a connection	Doorbells
Microswitch	Activated by small movements or forces	Machine safety guards
Rotary switch	Selects between multiple circuits	Multimeter dials
Reed switch	Activated by a magnet	Bicycle speedometers
Relays	Electromagnetically activated switches (refer to unit 1.8.4 for more information)	High voltage outputs

Δ **Table 1** Types of switches

Switch states

A switch can be either open (not connected) or closed (connected) in its inactive state (normal):

- Normally open (NO): Current cannot pass until the switch is pressed.
- Normally closed (NC): Current is able to pass unless the switch is pressed.

Switch poles and throws

Switches can have multiple connections. The permanently connected terminal(s) is called the *pole* and the temporarily connected terminal(s) is called the *throw*:

- Single pole, single throw (SPST) switches are simple on/off switches.
- Single pole, double throw (SPDT) switches can have two outputs – NO or NC.
- Double pole, double throw (DPDT) switches have two parallel and unconnected poles between two separate outputs.

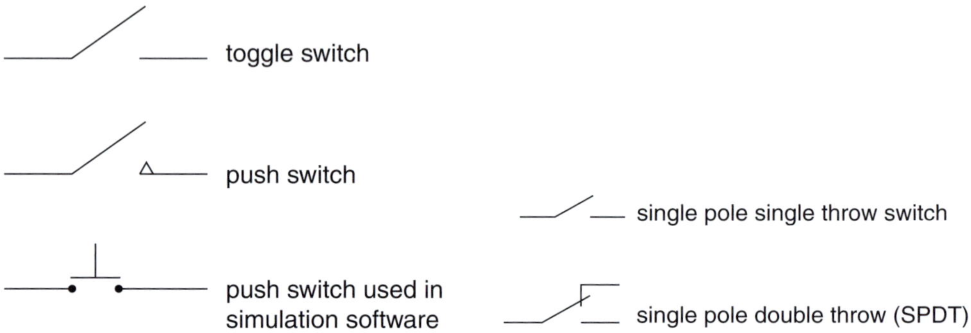

△ **Figure 1** Anatomies of switches

SENSORS

Sensors detect physical changes – such as temperature, light or movement – and convert them into electrical signals (Table 2).

Sensor	What it detects	Symbol
Light-dependent resistor (LDR)	Light levels	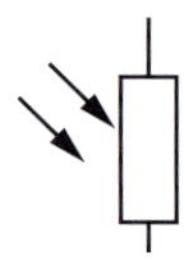
Thermistor	Temperature	

△ **Table 2** Types of sensor

WHAT IS A POTENTIAL DIVIDER?

A **potential divider** splits the voltage (the potential difference) from a power supply between two resistors (or electronic components/sensors) in series between positive and zero volts (Figure 2). The output voltage (taken from between the two resistors and ground, across R2) depends on the ratio of the resistors. The resistor with the higher value will have the high voltage drop across it. So, if the top resistor (R1) is twice the value of the bottom resistor (R2), the output voltage (V_{out}) will be one-third (1/3) of the supply voltage (V_{supply}), and vice versa.

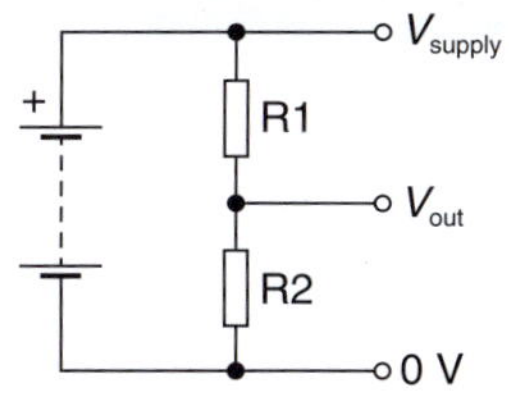

△ **Figure 2** Basic potential divider circuit

The formula to work out the output voltage from a potential divider array is:

$$V_{out} = \left(\frac{R2}{R1 + R2}\right) \times V_{supply}$$

Using switches and sensors in potential divider circuits

Switches and sensors are often used in potential divider circuits to produce a variable voltage depending on environmental conditions. In a dark detector, for example, an LDR and a fixed resistor form a potential divider. As it gets darker, the resistance of the LDR increases, raising the output voltage. This voltage can be used to turn on a transistor and light an LED.

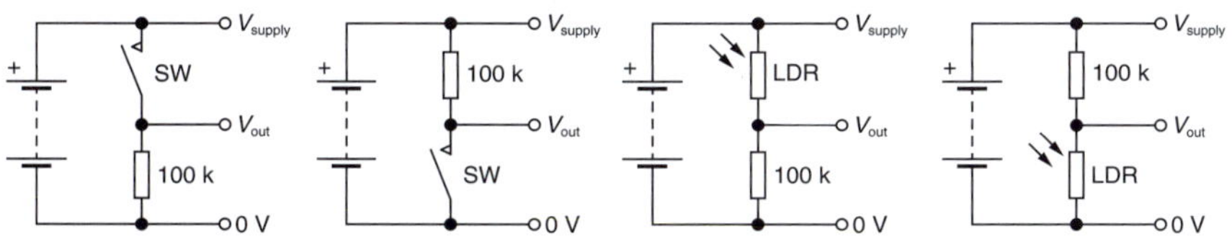

△ **Figure 3** Potential dividers with switches and sensors

Potential divider arrays are also used with switches as input devices. The input pin to the device it is triggering (for example, a transistor or microcontroller) is always either tied to +V or 0 V, depending on the function of the device and the desired trigger signal. Figure 3 illustrates the circuit diagrams for potential dividers for switches and sensors in both the top (R1) and bottom (R2) positions.

Potential divider circuits have many practical applications:

- LDRs in streetlights that turn on at night.
- Thermistors in thermostats to control heating.
- Microswitches in alarm systems to detect doors opening.
- Reed switches in security systems triggered by magnets.

SKILLS ACTIVITY

Designing and making a sensing application

Use the circuit diagrams in Figure 3 to design and make a light (or temperature) sensing application. Design a printed circuit board housed in a suitably designed package.

KNOWLEDGE CHECK

1. What is the difference between a PTM and a PTB switch?
2. How does an LDR behave in bright light?
3. Describe **one** use of a reed switch in a real-world application.

KEY TERMS

Potential divider: Two resistors in series splitting the voltage directly proportional to their resistance

Sensor: A device that detects physical changes and converts them into electrical signals

Switch: A device used to start or stop the flow of electricity in a circuit

1·8·4 Process components

LEARNING AIMS

By the end of this unit, you should:

✓ Identify and describe the function of transistors, relays and microcontrollers
✓ Understand how these components are used to process signals in electronic circuits
✓ Explain how transistors act as switches and amplifiers
✓ Understand the role of microcontrollers in modern electronic systems

Process components are the 'thinking' parts of an electronic system. They take signals from input components (such as switches or sensors), make decisions and send signals to output components (such as motors or lights). Process components add control to a system.

TRANSISTORS

A transistor is a small semiconductor component with three legs (Figure 1): the base (b), collector (c) and emitter (e). A small current applied to the base (**base current**) allows a larger current to flow between the collector and emitter. This makes them ideal for controlling outputs such as LEDs or buzzers using small input signals from sensors.

Transistors can act as:

- a switch, turning a circuit on or off
- an **amplifier**, increasing the strength of a signal.

The most common type used in schools is the **NPN transistor**, which is constructed using a sandwich of negative-positive-negative (NPN) semiconductor substrates (Figure 1).

△ **Figure 1** An NPN transistor

MICROCONTROLLERS

A microcontroller is a small computer-like device on a chip (integrated circuit or IC). It can be **programmed** to perform a wide range of tasks (Table 1). A microcontroller takes inputs from sensors or switches, processes the information using a program (coding) and controls outputs such as LEDs, motors or displays. Think of it as a tiny computer that can be programmed to perform tasks automatically – that is, you can design the function of the microcontroller to meet the requirements of your design solutions.

Application	Description
Washing machines	Controls water level, temperature and spin cycles
Microwave ovens	Manages cooking time, power level and safety locks
Remote controls	Sends coded signals to TVs or other devices
Alarm systems	Monitors sensors and triggers alarms
Traffic lights	Controls timing and sequencing of lights
Robotics	Processes sensor data and controls movement

Δ **Table 1** Applications of microcontrollers in everyday life

Programmable interface controllers (PIC) are commonly used by engineers for prototyping and in school projects. They are programmable microcontrollers with 8 to 40 pins for inputs and outputs (I/O), can store thousands of lines of code and are very accurate for timing and control tasks.

Microcontrollers are programmed using software on a computer. The program is then uploaded to the chip.

Microcontroller code can be written in several ways. For example:

- Visual blocks: For example, flowcharts, ladder diagrams, Scratch blocks: Flowcharts are used in educational tools like Flowol or PICAXE.
- Text-based code (computer language): For example, C/C++, Python or BASIC. Figure 2 shows an example of coding (in pseudocode).

```
If temperature > 30°C
  Turn on fan
Else
  Turn off fan
```

Δ **Figure 2** An example of pseudocode (computer language)

There are many different types of microcontroller (platforms), including PICAXE, Crumble, Arduino, BBC Micro:bit and Raspberry Pi Pico (Figure 3).

Arduino Raspberry Pi Pico

Δ **Figure 3** Popular microcontrollers

There are many advantages of using microcontrollers in Design and Technology:

- You require fewer components.
- It is relatively easy to update or change the program.
- They can handle complex tasks like counting, timing and decision-making using the same device (rather than using traditional discrete components).

Table 2 summarise the advantages and limitations of microcontrollers, and their key features.

Advantages	Limitations
• Reduces component count – one chip can replace many logic gates and timers • Versatile – can handle multiple inputs and outputs • Flexible – easily reprogrammed for different tasks • Accurate – excellent for timing and counting • Compact and efficient – save space (all essential components are built into one chip) and run on low power	• Requires programming knowledge • May need additional components (for example, sensors, drivers) • Can be overkill for very simple tasks

△ **Table 2** Advantages and limitations of microcontrollers

SKILLS ACTIVITY

Programming a microcontroller

Program a microcontroller to control various output devices in response to input signals.

KNOWLEDGE CHECK

1. Explain how a transistor can be used as a switch.
2. Give an example of a real-world application of a microcontroller.
3. Explain the role of the base current in the operation of an NPN transistor.
4. What are the advantages of using microcontrollers in electronic systems?
5. How can a microcontroller be programmed to perform specific tasks?

KEY TERMS

Amplifier: An electronic device that increases the power of a signal

Base current: The current that flows into the base terminal of a transistor to activate it

NPN transistor: A component used for switching or amplifying electronic signals; constructed from negative-positive-negative layers of semiconductive materials

Program/Programming: The process of designing and building an executable computer program to accomplish a specific task

1·8·5 Systems

LEARNING AIMS

By the end of this unit, you should:

✓ Identify and show knowledge of open and closed loop systems

✓ Describe the characteristics and main features of input, process, output and feedback

WHAT IS A SYSTEM?

A **system** is a set of interconnected parts that work together to achieve an output. For example, mechanisms are systems which typically consist of motors, gears, levers, cams, and belts and pulleys found in various products such as washing machines, cars, bicycles, sewing machines, lifts and automatic doors. Structures like buildings, cranes and bridges are systems designed to support an object, load or set of forces.

Many systems are control systems, which use equipment to manage and regulate system functions. For instance, a thermostat controls the temperature within an air conditioning system. Most modern control systems are electronic and regulate a wide range of machines, devices and processes.

This section focuses on three main systems areas:

- structures
- mechanisms
- electronics.

These systems often integrate into complex designs rather than functioning independently. For example, a modern car integrates multiple systems:

- *Electronic system:* The onboard computer manages satellite navigation and fuel consumption calculations, enhancing efficiency and user experience.
- *Mechanical system:* The transmission and braking systems work together to control speed and safely stop the vehicle.
- *Shell structure:* The car body provides a protective space for passengers while ensuring safety in case of impact.

These systems work together to create a functional, efficient and safe vehicle.

System diagrams

System diagrams (or **block diagrams**) visually represent systems by dividing them into individual blocks. Each block has an input, performs an operation and generates an output. The *block diagram approach* simplifies system analysis by focusing only on inputs and outputs, without requiring an in-depth understanding of each internal function. These details can be refined later in the design process.

When a system has more than one stage, it is known as a 'multi-stage system'. Each stage processes its input, generates an output and passes it as input to the next stage. This concept is common in both mechanical and electronic systems, such as washing machines, air conditioning systems and microwave ovens, where different components work sequentially to achieve the intended outcome.

Example 1: Multi-stage system in a washing machine

Input:

- The user selects the wash settings, including temperature, spin speed and cycle type.
- Water is supplied based on the selected program.

Process:

- The drum rotates, mixing detergent and water to clean clothes.
- Dirty water is drained, and freshwater refills for rinsing.
- The drum spins at high speed to remove excess water.

Output:

- Clothes are cleaned and excess water removed, ready for drying.

Feedback:

- Sensors monitor water level, temperature and spin speed, adjusting settings as needed.
- The system ensures the correct wash cycle completes based on user input and detected conditions.

Each stage's *output* becomes the *input* for the next stage, ensuring a structured process (Figure 1).

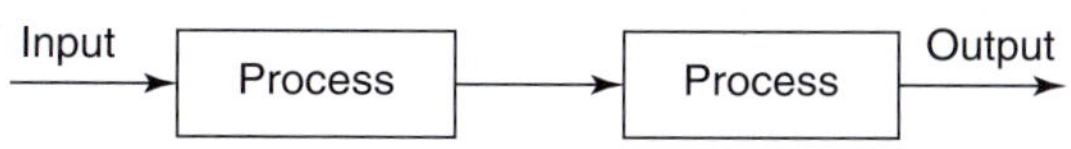

Δ **Figure 1** A system diagram

SKILLS ACTIVITY

Analysing how a system functions

Identify a product or appliance. Analyse how it could be broken down into a system, considering the input, process, output and feedback.

Sketch a systems (block) diagram for your chosen product or appliance, that represents the functional stages, breaking it down into input, process, output and feedback.

For example, if you choose a microwave oven, the block diagram might include:

- Input: User selects cooking time and power level.
- Process: Microwave generator activates, heating food.
- Output: Heated food is ready.
- Feedback: Temperature sensor ensures even heating and auto-adjusts power.

Each stage helps explain how the system functions in a logical sequence. When analysing and designing systems, it is common to consider the *outputs* (the actions produced by the system) first, then the *inputs* (the interactions with the system) second, followed by the process(es) (the connection between the inputs and the outputs that controls the systems function) third; rather than in a linear order (i.e. input-process-output).

OPEN AND CLOSED LOOP SYSTEMS

Open loop systems operate without feedback (Figure 2), meaning their accuracy depends solely on how well they are set up before operation.

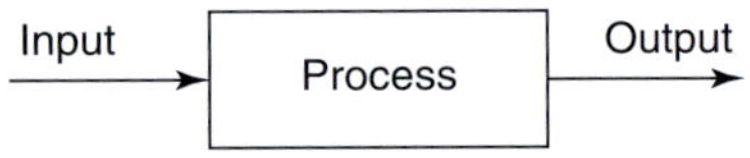

Δ **Figure 2** An open loop system

Closed loop systems use sensors to monitor output values and provide feedback (Figure 3), allowing the systems to adjust inputs as needed for greater accuracy and control (Figure 4).

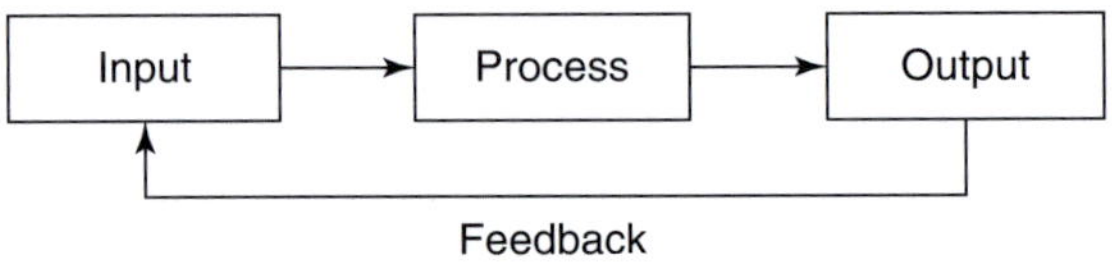

Δ **Figure 3** A closed loop system

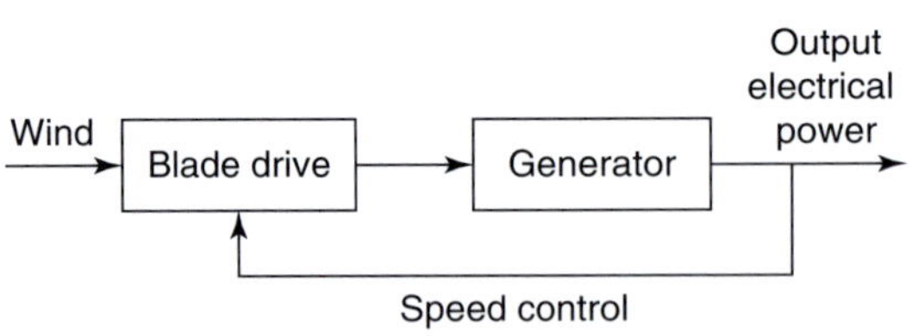

Δ **Figure 4** A system (block) diagram for a wind turbine

TOP TIP

When sketching a systems (block) diagram, consider how the whole system can be broken down into smaller parts or stages. Remember that each system block will have an input, process and output, and that these relate to what each part of the system is trying to achieve. Also remember that closed loop systems use *feedback* to control the system.

KNOWLEDGE CHECK

1. Describe the difference between an open loop and a closed loop system.
2. How does feedback influence the operation of a closed loop system?
3. Describe the roles of input, process, output and feedback in a system, and how they interact.

KEY TERMS

Closed loop system: A system that incorporates feedback to continuously regulate and adjust its operation, ensuring the desired output is achieved

Feedback: A key feature of a closed loop system that monitors the output and sends a signal back to the input, enabling adjustments to maintain the desired performance

Open loop system: A system that operates without feedback, meaning its output does not affect its input during operation

System: A collection of interconnected components or processes that interact to perform a specific function or achieve a desired outcome

System or block diagram: A visual representation that outlines the main components, processes or functions of a system, typically using blocks and arrows to show inputs, operations and outputs

1·8·6 Circuit modelling

LEARNING AIMS

By the end of this unit, you should:

✓ Show knowledge of building and testing of simple circuits through physical and/or virtual modelling

✓ Identify good and safe practice when soldering

✓ Explain why prototype boards are used for building and testing circuits

CIRCUIT BOARD MODELLING

Have you heard the terms 'breadboard' and 'ironing out'? Before manufacturing a circuit, **prototype boards** ('breadboards') may be used to experiment with different circuits during the early stages of design. Faults can be 'ironed out' and different circuit configurations can be tested.

Components, wires and integrated circuit components are pushed into holes on the top of the board (Figure 1). They are held in place by solderless clips. This allows the components to be easily removed so that circuits can be changed quickly.

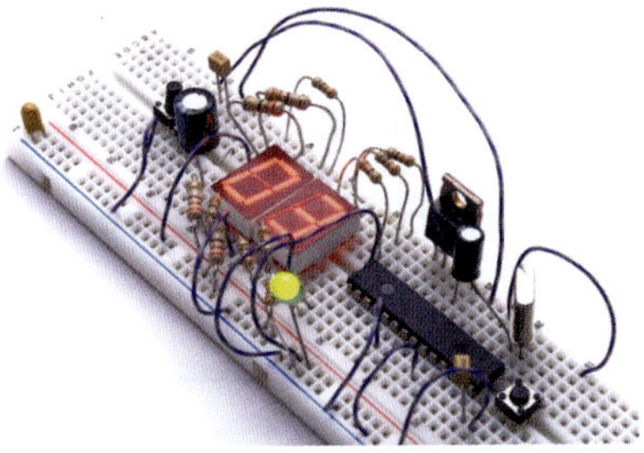

△ **Figure 1** A prototype board

PROCEDURE FOR DESIGNING A PRINTED CIRCUIT BOARD (PCB)

Best practices for PCB design

When designing a **printed circuit board (PCB)**, it is good practice to begin by creating a circuit diagram (schematic) that outlines how components are connected. This diagram ensures that all electrical connections are correctly planned before proceeding to the physical layout.

A systems diagram approach using blocks can be helpful in the early design stages (refer to unit 1.8.5). This method ensures that different circuit sections are properly integrated before moving to the board layout phase.

Methods for PCB design

- *Hand-drawn PCB layouts:* Use an etch resist pen to sketch circuit traces directly onto the board.
- *Transfer sheets:* Pre-made pads, tracks and circuit features can be applied to the board surface to create an accurate layout.
- *PCB design software:* A range of computer-based tools allow for digital circuit design, helping to refine layouts before production.

Prototype testing

Before manufacturing the PCB, it is good practice to test the circuit using a prototype board. This allows adjustments to be made before committing to a final design. If you are using PCB design software, many programs offer simulation features that allow circuits to be tested virtually, reducing the risk of errors in the physical build (Figure 2).

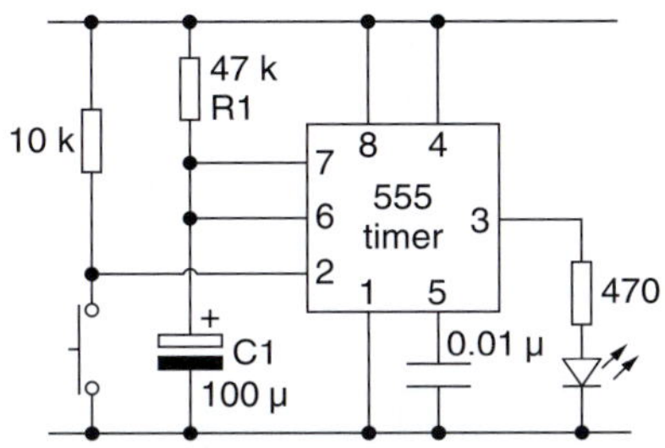

△ **Figure 2** Example of a circuit diagram

Using simulation software has several advantages compared with making PCBs by hand:

- It can save time. Changes can be made quickly, and there is no need to start the process again if you make a mistake. It is easy to make mistakes when designing boards by hand.
- It allows designs to be changed quickly and can help reduce material waste.

At the end of the process, the design should be checked to make sure it follows the schematic circuit precisely.

Component sizes are important and can vary depending on the type, manufacturer and application. Standard resistor sizes, for example, often follow industry norms, such as 0.4 inches for through-hole resistors, but surface-mount resistors are much smaller. Similarly, diodes and terminals come in different package sizes.

For the most up-to-date and precise dimensions, it is best to refer to manufacturer datasheets or industry standards. If you are working on a PCB design, checking the exact specifications of the components you are using is essential. Table 1 shows some typical dimensions (note that 0·1 inch is approximately 2·5 mm).

Component	Dimensions (imperial)	Dimensions (metric)
Resistor	0·4 inch	10.16 mm
Diode	0·3 inch	7.62 mm
Preset	0·4 inch × 0·2 inch	10.16 mm × 5.08 mm
Terminal	0·2 inch	5.08 mm

△ **Table 1** Typical dimensions for circuit components

Integrated circuits (ICs) have pin connections with specific pin distances (spacings) between them:

- Most dual in-line package (DIP) ICs have a 0.1inch (2.54 mm) spacing between adjacent pins in a row.

- The distance between the two parallel rows of pins is typically 0.3 inches (7.62 mm), although wider packages (such as 0.6 inches) exist.

For example, the 555 timer has eight pins, arranged in two columns with four pins per column. The columns are 0.3 inches apart, forming an 8-pin dual in-line (DIL) layout.

Pad spacing is important for several reasons:

- Checking component dimensions accurately is essential to ensure correct pad placement on a PCB.
- Referring to datasheets helps confirm the exact specifications for different IC packages.

TOP TIP

Digital callipers are an excellent tool for measuring pin spacing on electronic components or circuit boards (Figure 3). They provide precise measurements down to fractions of a millimetre, making them ideal for ensuring accurate spacing in PCB designs or component placement.

When using digital callipers to measure pin spacing:

- Ensure the callipers are properly zeroed before measurement.
- Measure from centre to centre of adjacent pins for consistency.
- Be gentle to avoid damaging delicate components.

△ **Figure 3** Measuring using digital callipers

Testing the prototype board

Once the board has been made, it should be tested to make sure it has been manufactured correctly. It is also a good idea to add test points so that each stage of the circuit can be individually tested.

These test points can be simple connection points for a multimeter probe, or indicator LEDs that light up if the circuit is working. You should think about track widths and pad sizes during the PCB design stage in order to make sure they can carry the current which will flow through them when used. A wider track or larger pad will be able to carry a larger current safely than a thinner track or smaller pad. Also, larger track and pad sizes give you larger surface areas for **soldering** the component.

To help identify parts of a circuit, it is useful to include some written information on the board. This may be your initials, the name of the circuit or letters indicating where components will go. This lettering is printed onto clear film or tracing paper. Remember that the writing on the film or tracing paper will need to be reversed (mirror writing). If the print is held against the back of the circuit board, the writing will appear on the track side the right way round. Mirror writing ensures correct orientation when the text is applied to the PCB. However, modern PCB design software automatically handles this, so manual reversal is rarely needed.

Tracks should run horizontally or vertically as far as possible for efficient routing. Rounded corners may help protect components and wires when the circuit is assembled. Finally, check the finished design against the schematic circuit.

SOLDERING

There are two types of **solder**: soft solder and hard solder.

In electronic work, you should use soft solder and flux. Within electronics, many solder wires have flux embedded within their core. Flux in soldering is necessary to help clean metal surfaces by removing oxides (preventing re-oxidation) and improving solder flow, ensuring a strong and reliable joint.

The soldering iron is used to heat the parts that are to be joined (Figure 4). When the soldering iron tip is hot enough to melt the solder, the solder is introduced to the soldering iron and joint from the opposite side of the soldering iron tip (Figure 5). Unwanted solder can be removed using a desoldering tool sometimes known as a 'solder sucker'. This uses a vacuum to suck up the unwanted molten solder. Braided copper wire can also be used to draw the unwanted solder away.

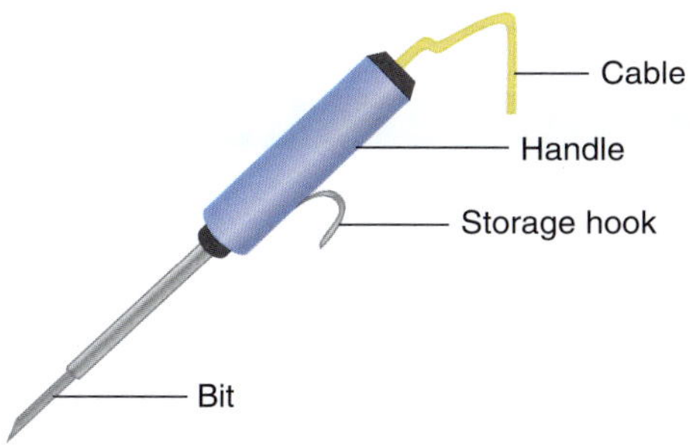

△ **Figure 4** Parts of a soldering iron

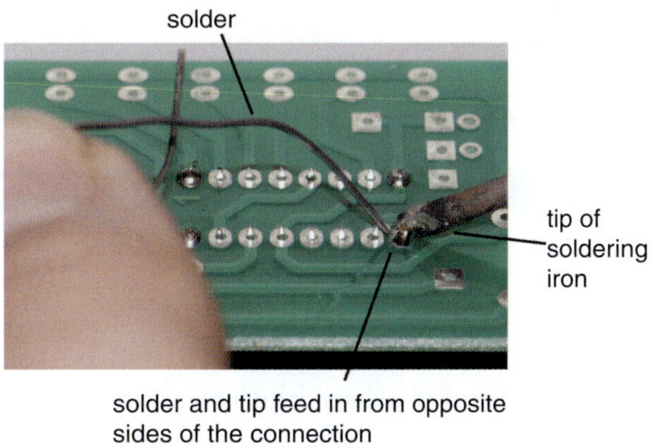

△ **Figure 5** Soldering an IC

SKILLS ACTIVITY

HEALTH AND SAFETY

In this skills activity, you are going to practise soldering.

You need to be very careful when soldering, as it can be dangerous. Make sure you follow these health and safety guidelines before you begin, during the soldering process and after you have finished.

Before you begin:

- Check the soldering iron, including the cable and plug for damage.
- Use an extractor fan to take away any fumes.

During the process:

- Keep your hands away from the hot parts of the soldering iron. The tip temperature is approximately 200 °C, which is twice as hot as boiling water. So, take care.
- Do not breathe in fumes. Place the soldering iron in the stand when it is not in use. Take care that the hot tip does not rest against the soldering iron cable by mistake.

After finishing:

- Switch the iron off, and make sure that it is placed in the stand. Remember that it will remain hot for some time.
- Components that you have been soldering will also stay hot for some time. The larger the soldered joint, the longer it will remain hot.
- Wash your hand thoroughly after soldering.

If you do burn yourself, wash the burn under cold water immediately, keeping it under the cold water for a few minutes, and inform your teacher.

Now, follow the guide on how to solder (Figure 6).

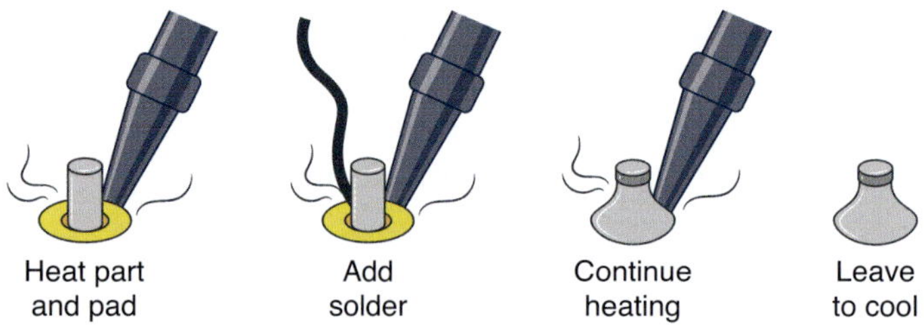

△ **Figure 6** How to solder

TOP TIP

Soldering technique: How to make better solder joints

1. **Keep the tip clean and tinned**
   A clean soldering iron tip transfers heat better. Wipe it on a damp sponge or brass wool to remove burned stuff (oxidation), then melt a little solder on it. This 'tinning' helps solder flow more easily when you work.

2. **Heat the joint properly**
   Touch the tip to both the metal pad and the component lead at the same time. Wait a second or two until they're hot enough, then add solder. The solder should flow smoothly onto the joint. Do not overheat – it can damage parts.

3. **Use the right amount of solder**
   You want just enough solder to cover the joint and make a small, shiny cone shape. Too much solder can cause blobs or short circuits, leading to weak connections; too little might not hold the connection well.

KNOWLEDGE CHECK

1. Explain the key difference between building and testing circuits using physical versus virtual modelling. How does each method impact the design process? What are their advantages and limitations?
2. State **three** important things you must consider before, during and after soldering.

KEY TERMS

Printed circuit board (PCB): A thin, insulated board with copper tracks etched onto its surface, used to mount and connect electronic components, forming a functional electrical or electronic circuit

Prototype board: Also known as a breadboard or stripboard; it is a thin, insulated board with a grid of electrically connected holes for prototyping circuits without soldering; used for temporary circuit development

Solder (electrical): An alloy, typically made of tin and lead (or lead-free alternatives), with a low melting point used to create secure electrical connections

Soldering: Bonding components or wires by melting and solidifying, ensuring conductivity and mechanical strength in circuits

Practice questions

Question 1

Figure 1.1 shows a design for a new portable water filter bottle.

△ **Figure 1.1**

COMMENTS

1) a) The command word Explain means you need to include reasoning or evidence in your answer. For each question part, the sample answer identifies a relevant consideration for the designer, then explains how it influences the design of the water filter bottle.

a) Explain **one** way each of the following would have influenced the design of the portable water filter bottle:

i) user needs

The designer would consider the age and abilities ✓ (1) of the primary user, such as ensuring the bottle is easy to open and hold ✓ (1) for all ages, or if it needs specific features for adventurers requiring quick access.

(2)

ii) where the product will be used

If used outdoors, the bottle must be durable and resistant to impacts ✓ (1) so it can withstand drops or rough handling ✓ (1) during activities such as hiking.

(2)

iii) sustainability.

The designer would consider using recyclable or biodegradable materials ✓ (1) to minimise environmental impact at the end of the product's life ✓ (1)

(2)

b) Use sketches and notes to show how the design for the water filter bottle could be developed to make it more suitable for users with limited hand strength.

Your idea will be assessed on the communication and suitability of the idea. (6)

c) Use sketches and notes to show how a loop handle or attachment point could be integrated into the water filter bottle to make it easier to carry or clip onto a bag.

Your idea will be assessed on the communication and suitability of the idea. (6)

d) State **two** reasons why a prototype model would be made of the water filter bottle before it is manufactured in quantity. (2)

e) Explain **one** reason why it is crucial for a designer to consider 'iterative design' when developing a new product. (2)

Question 2

Figure 2.1 shows a child's wooden toy. The pull-along toy is made from three different materials.

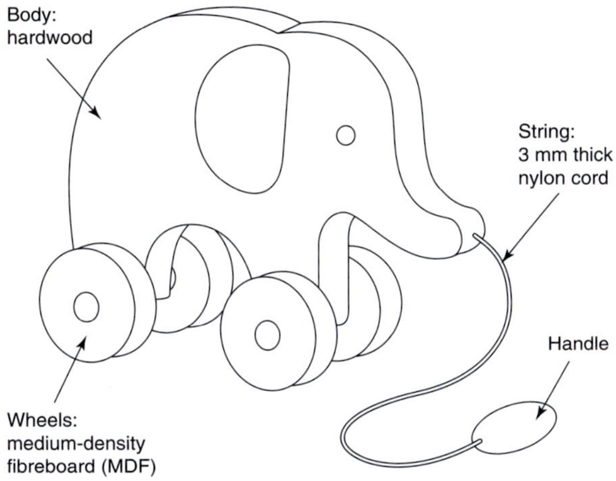

△ **Figure 2.1**

a) Complete Table 2.1 to show details of the materials used to make the parts of the toy.

Part	Classification	Material	Two suitable reasons of using the material
Body	Timber	Hardwood	1. High hardness 2. ....
String	Polymers	Nylon cord	1. Strong 2. ....
Wheels	Timber	....	1. Come in sheet stock forms 2. ....

△ **Table 2.1** (4)

b) Name **two** digital tools that can be used to mark out the body of the toy using computer aided-design CAD) software. (2)

c) Name **one** appropriate hand tool and **one** computer aided manufacturing CAM) machine that could be used to accurately cut out the wheels. (2)

d) Explain why the choice of finish is important for the child's toy. (2)

e) Describe why tolerances are important when joining the different parts of the child's toy. (2)

f) Complete Table 2.2 to show two drawing techniques for the toy and their uses.

Table 2.2

Drawing technique	Use
....	To show three different views and exact dimensions of the toy for manufacturing
Exploded drawing	....

∆ **Table 2.2** (2)

Question 3

Figure 3.1 shows a child's bicycle. The bicycle converts rotary motion into electrical energy using a dynamo to power a light on the bicycle.

Figure 3.2 shows the circuit diagram of the dynamo-powered light.

∆ **Figure 3.1**

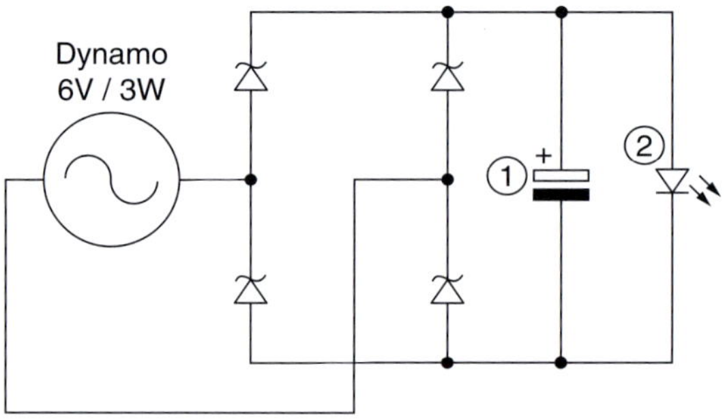

∆ **Figure 3.2**

a) Identify the following components in the diagram in Figure 3.2 **and** state their purpose:

i) component 1. (2)

ii) component 2. (2)

Figure 3.3 shows an outline of a child's bicycle.

Δ **Figure 3.3**

b) i) Use sketches and notes to show one example of a compressive force in the child's bicycle in Figure 3.3. (2)

ii) The child's bicycle uses a chain drive mechanism to drive the wheels. Add labels and arrows to Figure 3.3 to show the conversion of rotary into linear motion in the child's bicycle. (2)

c) The bicycle is an example of a frame structure. Use sketches and notes to show a design of a product that uses a shell structure to help carry or store items while riding the bike.

Include:

- a suitable material for the shell structure
- a suitable method of manufacture
- a modification for joining the shell structure to the child's bicycle frame. (6)

INTRODUCTION

Get hands on with materials!

In this section, you will look more closely into the world of making – learning how to choose the right materials, use the right tools and apply the right techniques to bring your design ideas to life.

You will explore how different polymers, metals, timbers and boards behave, and discover how to shape, join and finish them using both traditional methods and commercial manufacturing methods. You will also get to grips with smart and modern materials, exploring their role in today's design world – from biodegradable plastics to shape-memory alloys – and how materials are keeping up to date with technological changes.

By linking practical knowledge with real-world impact, this section encourages you to become, not just a skilled maker, but a thoughtful, responsible designer who understands the wider role of designing and making for the user, society, sustainability and the market.

STARTING POINTS

- How can you tell which material is best for a specific product or function?
- What are the differences between physical and working properties of polymers, metals, timber and boards?
- How do you safely and correctly use different tools and equipment when working with materials?
- How can your material and process choices affect the environment and sustainability of your product?
- What are some common problems that can happen during making, and how can you avoid them?
- Why is it important to consider the final appearance and quality of your product?

SECTION CONTENTS

2 Materials

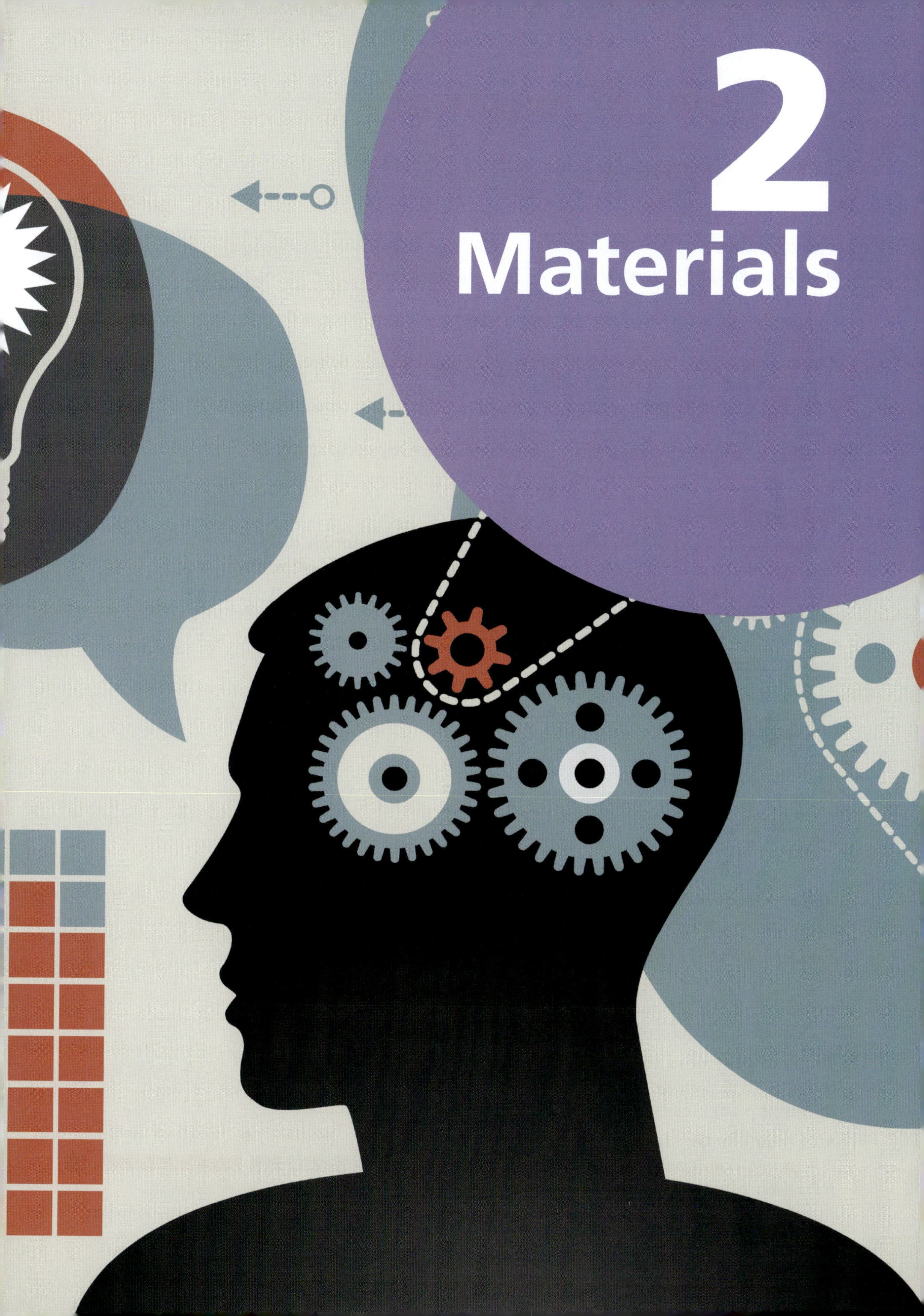

2·1 Types of material

2·1·1 Polymers

LEARNING AIMS

By the end of this unit, you should:

✓ Understand the different types of polymer
✓ Understand the properties of thermo polymers, thermosetting polymers and biopolymers
✓ Identify the working properties, stock forms and application of the different types of polymer and their environmental impact
✓ Discuss the environmental considerations associated with polymer production, usage and disposal
✓ Apply your understanding of polymer properties to choose appropriate materials

TYPES OF POLYMER

You will have heard of the term 'plastic' – it refers to materials made from polymers. Polymers are formed of molecules bonded together in long chains (Figure 1). Most polymers are synthetic, derived from petroleum oil, such as nylon, although there are some found naturally, such as silk. There are two types of synthetic polymer: thermo polymers and thermosetting polymers.

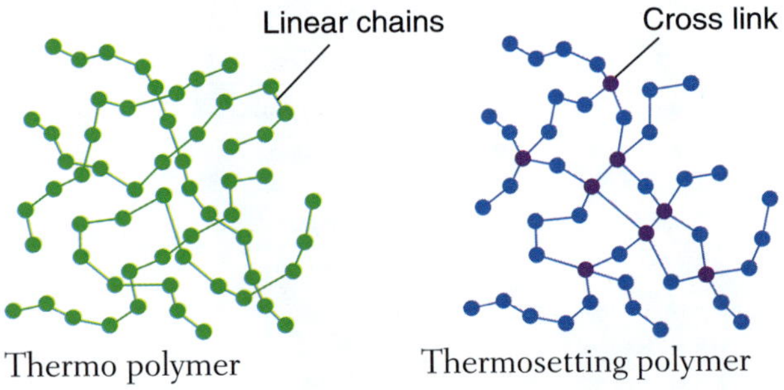

Δ **Figure 1** The molecular structure of thermo polymers and thermosetting polymers

THERMO POLYMERS

Thermo polymers are formed when heated, as they soften and become malleable. Each polymer has a particular temperature range where the material can be deformed and moulded (Figure 2).

Thermo polymers can be reheated and reformed, but repeating this too often will damage their structure. They can be shaped using different processes:

- In their **elastic state** by line bending, vacuum forming, dome blowing or blow moulding.
- In their **plastic state** by rotational moulding and injection moulding.

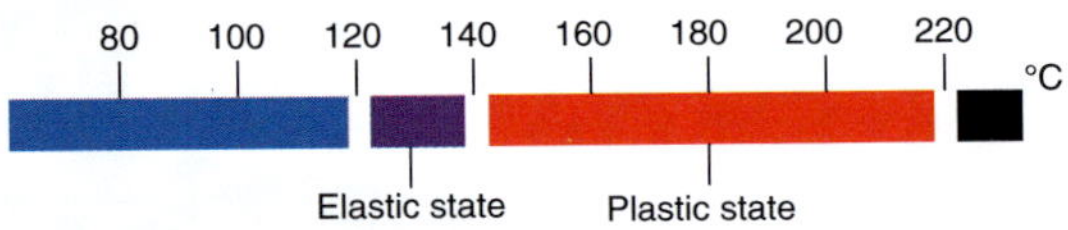

Δ **Figure 2** Heating characteristics for extruded acrylic (PMMA)

Properties, stock forms, environmental impact and uses of thermo polymers

Table 1 shows details of different thermo polymers.

Thermo polymers	Properties and some uses	Stock forms	Environmental impact
Nylon (polyamide)	Used for electric toothbrushes, etc. Strong and tough	Rods Fibres Sheets Granules	Not biodegradable; limited recyclability; microplastic shedding (textiles)
Low-density polyethylene (LDPE)	Used for food storage bags, etc. Lightweight and flexible	Film rolls Sheets Bottles Tubing Granules	Not biodegradable; recyclable but not widely accepted in facilities
High-density polyethylene (HDPE)	Durable; used for containers Stiff and strong	Bottles Sheets Pipes Containers Granules	More widely recycled than LDPE
Polyethylene terephthalate (PET)	Used for water bottles, etc. Strong and lightweight Transparent	Sheets Bottles Films Fibres	Widely recyclable; microplastic risk when used in textiles
Polyvinyl chloride (PVC)	Durable; used for window frames, etc. Durable and rigid (or flexible with additives) Weather and chemical resistant	Pipes Sheets Films Granules	Chlorine-based so produces toxic by-products during production and disposal; harder to recycle than other thermo polymers
Acrylic/Perspex (PMMA)	Used for cotton bud containers, etc. Rigid Good weather resistance Lightweight	Rods, sheets, tubes	Less harmful than PVC; not biodegradable; can be recycled mechanically or chemically
Polystyrene (PS)	Lightweight; used for food trays, etc. Brittle	Sheets (for thermoforming) Foam blocks/ sheets Granules/pellets	Non-biodegradable; difficult to recycle; often ends up as litter/ marine pollution
Polypropylene (PP)	Durable; used for hangers, etc. Tough resistant Chemical and heat resistant	Granules	Recyclable
Acrylonitrile-butadiene-styrene (ABS)	Used for 3D printing filaments Tough Good surface finish	Granules	Emits **volatile organic compounds (VOCs)** when heated (e.g., during 3D printing); limited recycling
Polylactic acid (PLA)	Used for compostable food containers Biopolymer made from renewable resources stiff brittle	Film, filament	Made from renewable resources (corn, sugarcane); industrial composting only; not biodegradable in landfills

△ **Table 1** Properties, uses, stock forms and environmental impact of thermo polymers

THERMOSETTING POLYMERS

Thermosetting polymers set as a result of a chemical reaction between a resin and a hardener. Unlike thermo polymers, which can be melted and reshaped multiple times, thermosetting polymers undergo a chemical change that creates a cross-linked structure (refer to Figure 1). Once set, they cannot be reheated or reformed.

Properties, stock forms, environmental impact and uses of thermosetting polymers

Table 2 shows details of different thermosetting polymers.

Thermosetting polymer	Properties	Stock forms	Environmental impact	Example of use
Epoxy resin	Strong and durable Chemical and heat resistant	Liquid resin and hardener (two parts), adhesive films, powder coatings	Releases VOCs during use; long-lasting but not biodegradable	
Melamine formaldehyde (MF)	Durable and heat-resistant	Powder and granules (for moulding), laminated sheets (e.g., countertops), coatings	Contains formaldehyde (toxic); non-recyclable; safer once cured	
Urea formaldehyde (UF)	Hard and brittle Good electrical insulation	Powder, adhesives (especially in plywood and MDF), electrical casings	High formaldehyde emissions, especially during manufacture; not biodegradable	
Phenol formaldehyde (PF)	Excellent durability reduces need for replacement	Powder, laminates (e.g., Bakelite), moulding compounds, electrical insulators	Formaldehyde-based – emits toxic fumes when burned; not recyclable	
Polyester resin	Stable; low cost and easy to use; good mechanical and chemical resistance; good electrical properties	Glass reinforced for boat hulls, car body panels, adhesives, coatings, printed circuits boards	Not biodegradable, can release styrene vapours - gases from the chemical used to make the polymer (toxic) and is difficult to recycle (composites)	

Δ **Table 2** Properties, stock forms, environmental impact and uses of thermosetting polymers

TOP TIP

When working with thermosetting polymers, think through your manufacturing plan carefully, as there is no going back!

BIOPOLYMERS

Biopolymers are made from renewable resources such as plants, animals and microorganisms. They are an important part of the effort to create more sustainable materials in place of traditional, petroleum-based plastics. They can be biodegradable or non-biodegradable. However, production costs are higher, performance in some cases is lower, and recycling difficulties remain. They are used in packaging, medicines, biomedical devices and agriculture.

Table 3 shows details of different biopolymers.

Biopolymer	Properties	Uses	Environmental impact	Example of use
Polylactic acid (PLA) Source: corn starch, sugarcane	Transparent, tough, rigid, thermo polymer	Packaging (films, bottles), 3D printing filament, medical devices (stitches, implants), food packaging	Renewable but non-biodegradable in landfills without optimal conditions; lower carbon footprint compared to other polymers PP,PVC,PE,PS	
Polyhydroxy-alkano-ates (PHA) Source: microbial fermentation of sugars or lipids	Flexible, high production cost	Biodegradable packaging, agricultural films, biomedical devices, water filtration	Biodegradable in soil and marine environments	
Starch-based polymers Source: corn, potatoes, wheat	Water-soluble (and so limited water resistance for some uses), low-cost, flexible	Packaging materi-als (foam, trays), loose-fill packag-ing, food packaging	Biodegradable	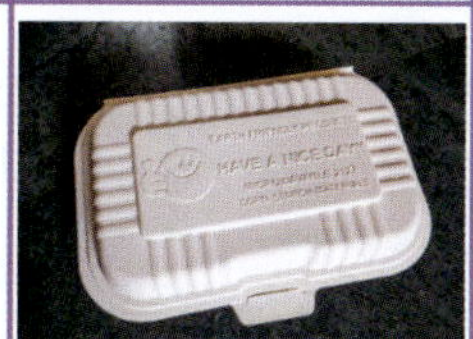
Cellulose-based plastics Source: wood pulp or cotton fibres	Strong, flexible, transparent, but limited by water resistance and cost	Cellophane (packaging), film coatings, medical devices	Biodegradable	
Bio-based polyeth-ylene (Bio-PE) Source: sugarcane or other plant-based sugars	Durable, flexible, water-resistant, non-toxic	Packaging (bottles, bags, films), containers, toys, agricultural films	Non-biodegradable; lower carbon footprint; recyclable like traditional PET	
Bio-based PET (polyethylene terephthalate) Source: sugarcane, corn	Strong, lightweight, impact-resistant	Bottles, clothing fibres (recycled PET), food packaging	Not biodegradable; recyclable like traditional PET; lower carbon footprint than fossil-fuel PET	

Δ **Table 3** Properties, stock forms, environmental impact and uses of biopolymers

DESIGN IN ACTION

Recycling materials

One concern about the use of synthetic polymers is that most are not biodegradable – they do not break down or decompose over time.

Sustainable use of materials tries to reduce, reuse or recycle materials. To help with this, there are international symbols to show if the plastic is recyclable. The 'triangle loop' symbol (Figure 3) indicates whether a material is recyclable. For plastic objects or containers, each element should be marked with a number (resin indication code) indicating the material used. For example, 1 is PET, 2 is HDPE.

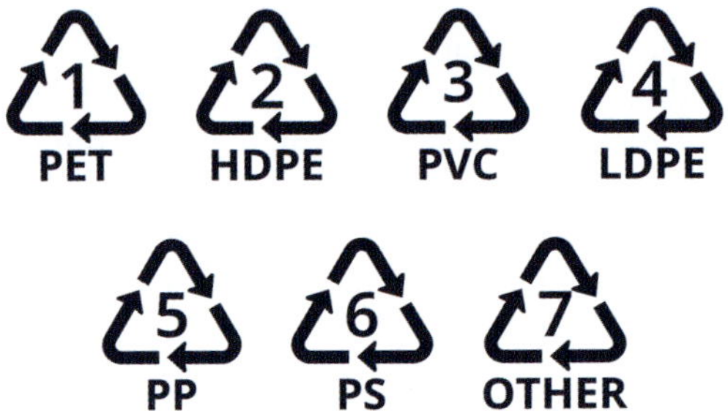

△ **Figure 3** International recycling symbols

SKILLS ACTIVITY

Analysing a household product

Pick a range of polymer household products.

1. Name the polymer materials you can identify using the recycling symbols.

2. Evaluate the recyclability of the product, including how easily it is for polymer components to be disassembled and recycled.

KNOWLEDGE CHECK

Giving examples of products manufactured from polymers:

1. Explain the advantages of polymers when designing and making everyday products.

2. Explain the disadvantages of polymers when designing and making everyday products.

3. Explain why polymers are commonly used in everyday products.

KEY TERMS

Elastic state: The condition of a thermo polymer when heated; it can be shaped, but will return to its original form

Plastic state: The condition of a thermo polymer when heated to a higher temperature than its elastic state; it will not return to its original form

Thermo polymers: A polymer that softens when heated and can be repeatedly reshaped upon cooling

Volatile organic compound (VOC): An organic chemical that, at room temperature, releases fumes into the air. Many synthetic resins, including polyester resin and epoxy resin, release VOCs during curing or processing

2·1·2 Timbers and boards

LEARNING AIMS

By the end of this unit, you should:

✓ Understand the classification, stock forms, properties, environmental impact and uses of natural timbers
✓ Demonstrate knowledge of softwood and hardwood timbers
✓ Demonstrate knowledge of manufactured boards
✓ Understand the advantages and disadvantages of working with manufactured boards

Timber is the term used for trees that are grown to then be harvested for their wood. The wood is manufactured for different products, such as furniture, houses or boats.

Natural timbers are categorised into two groups: **hardwoods** and **softwoods**.

Did you know that these classifications have nothing to do with how hard the wood is? These classifications are used to group timbers that come from similar types of trees:

- Softwood comes from trees that are coniferous – evergreen trees that bear cones and have needles (Figure 1).
- Hardwoods come from deciduous trees – trees that shed leaves (Figure 2).

△ **Figure 1** Softwood trees, such as pine

△ **Figure 2** Hardwood trees, such as oak

Before timber can be used, trees must be cut and then processed. Trees tend to grow at different rates and speeds, depending on the species. Generally, hardwoods grow much more slowly than softwoods.

Depending upon how you cut planks from the tree, you can change the properties of the planks. This is because planks produced from different parts will have a different **grain** structure (Figure 3). Planks that have a wood grain that is closer together are stronger and denser (heavier) than those with a wider-spaced wood grain running through it.

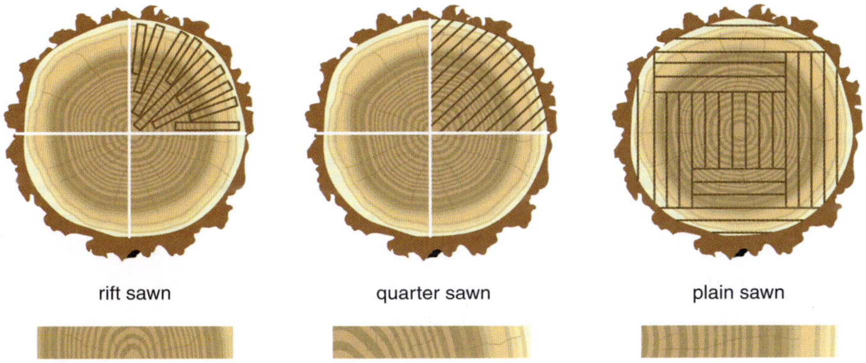

Δ **Figure 3** How planking trees can affect grain structures in finished lengths of timber

SEASONING TIMBER

Once a tree has been felled, it is then cut into planks. Timber needs to be seasoned to allow it to fully dry out. **Seasoning** is traditionally undertaken by stacking planks of wood and allowing air to circulate between the planks in order to dry them out. This process happens by using a kiln (Figure 4).

A kiln is used for seasoning timber by allowing air to be warmed and circulated by fans to speed up the seasoning process. As the warm air circulates around the inside of the kiln, it dries the timber placed inside it. Timber seasoned in this way is referred to as 'kiln dried'.

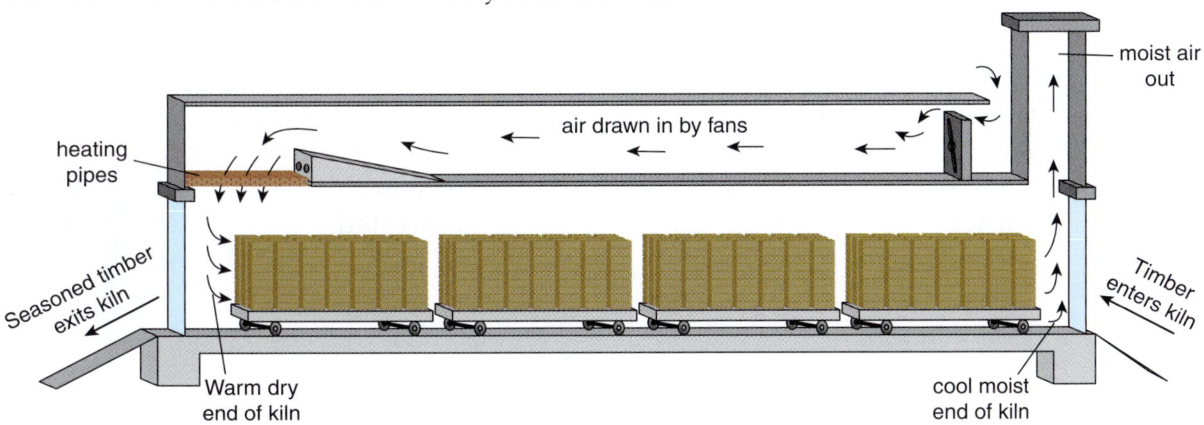

Δ **Figure 4** An automated kiln used for seasoning timber

VENEERS

Veneers are thin slices of wood, usually less than 3 mm thick, that are glued onto core panels (such as plywood, particleboard or MDF) to provide the appearance of solid wood at a lower cost and with greater stability.

SOFTWOOD EXAMPLES

Table 1 shows details of different types of softwood.

Type of softwood	Properties	Uses	Stock forms	Environmental impact	Example of use
Pine	Pale in colour, strong yet easy to work with, cheap and readily available	Low-cost furniture, construct-ion work	Planks, boards, beams, mouldings, veneer, plywood	Fast-growing; sustainably farmed in many regions; widely available	
Spruce	Creamy-white, not very hardwearing	Indoor furniture, including bedrooms and kitchens	Dimensional lumber, plywood, panels	Common in sustainable forestry; renewable; susceptible to pests; may require chemical preservatives	
Cedar	Very pale in colour, light in weight yet rigid	Furniture, boat building and veneers	Boards, planks	Naturally rot-resistant, so no need for chemical treatment; renewable	
Redwood	Relatively strong, durable when treated with a suitable coating or treatment, low cost	General woodwork, cupboards, shelves, roofs	Decking boards, beams	Naturally decay-resistant; often responsibly harvested	
Local equivalents (e.g., Douglas fir, larch, hemlock, native pine)	Varies by species; generally lightweight, strong, and workable; some species are naturally durable	Construction, joinery, interior and exterior applications	Similar stock forms depending on species; often available as rough-sawn or planed timber	Lower transportation footprint; environmental impact varies by species and forestry practices	

△ **Table 1** Properties, stock forms, environmental impact and uses of softwoods

HARDWOOD EXAMPLES

Table 2 shows details of different types of hardwood.

Type of hardwood	Properties	Uses	Stock forms	Environmental impact	Example of use
Oak	Light brown colour, strong and tough, open-grained, corrodes steel screws and fittings, reacts with certain adhesives	High-quality furniture, interior woodwork	Boards, beams, veneer, flooring, furniture compon-ents	Sustainable in Europe/USA (FSC-certified); slow-growing; can contribute to deforestation	
Mahogany	Rich reddish-brown colour, strong and durable, interlocking grain	Good-quality furniture	Planks, veneer, furniture panels	High risk of illegal logging; often linked to tropical deforestation	
Meranti	Durable, strong, reddish-brown colour	Interior and exterior use	Plywood, boards, veneer, doors and panelling	Widely used in Southeast Asia; deforestation risk in some regions; FSC-certified	
Jelutong	Stable, workable, soft, lightweight	Interior use, popular for model-making and pattern-making	Carving blocks, model-making wood, veneer-	Soft and overharvested in some areas; risk of habitat loss (especially in rainforests)	
Local equiva-lents (e.g., teak, sal, beech, rubber-wood, mango wood)	Varies by species; often durable, easy to work, and visually appealing	Similar uses to imported hard-woods—furniture, joinery, and interior fittings	Similar stock forms: boards, planks, veneers, dowels, turning blanks	Using locally available species lowers transport emissions; impact depends on forestry practices and species' growth rate	

△ **Table 2** Properties, stock forms, environmental impact and uses of hardwoods

MANUFACTURED BOARDS

There are some disadvantages to working with natural timber. One is the widths it is available in – the limiting factor is the thickness of the tree trunk it is cut from. Most softwoods come from fast-growing trees with a small diameter trunk (refer to Figure 1).

What happens if something larger is required, but the cost of using an expensive hardwood is not an option?

You could join a few pieces of timber together yourself, or you could buy something that has already undergone this process commercially.

There are a number of different types of **manufactured board** available, each with different properties. The most common manufactured boards are shown in Table 3.

Type of board	What it looks like	Properties
Chipboard		Chipboard is made up of small chips of wood bonded together with resin and compressed to form sheets. Chipboard is often used for indoor furniture, and it is covered in a plastic coating or veneer for a more aesthetically appealing timber.
Medium density fibreboard (MDF)		MDF is made up from very fine wood dust and resin pressed into a board. This material can be worked, shaped and machined easily and has considerably more strength than hardboard due to the use of a resin as a bonding agent. It is used in many applications, indoors, and it can be easily finished with veneers or paint.
Plywood		Plywood is made from veneers of timber with the grain of each layer being at right angles to the layers either side of it. The layers are bonded together by resin and pressure. A number of different types of plywood are available, and these are often referred to as grades. They are manufactured differently and designed for different purposes, including: • boil resistant plywood • flexible (flexi) plywood (typically three layers thick with a very thin middle layer) • interior plywood • laser plywood (non-toxic adhesive for use with laser cutters) • marine plywood, which is moisture-resistant • weather and boil-proof plywood.

Δ **Table 3** Common manufactured boards

Advantages of manufactured boards

There are many advantages to working with manufactured boards as opposed to natural timber:

- Availability of different sizes and thicknesses
- Cost effective
- Versatile – boards are designed for specific purposes, so have specific properties (for example, marine plywood is glued together using waterproof adhesive)
- Aesthetics – smooth surfaces, manufactured boards are uniform with few imperfections
- Unlike natural timbers, they do not split
- Available in ready finished formats (with veneers or self-finish).

Disadvantages of manufactured boards

There are also some disadvantages of working with manufactured boards such as:

- They can blunt tools quickly
- Produce harmful dust
- Weak edges – prone to chipping or crumbling when cut or screwed
- Poor screw/nail holding strength, especially near edges
- Highly moisture-sensitive – can swell, warp
- Lack natural wood grain – usually needs veneer or paint for appearance
- Lower structural strength than solid timber – not suitable for heavy-load applications
- Difficult to recycle due to adhesives being used in the board being manufactured.

SHAPING AND JOINING TIMBER

Timber can be joined in different ways (see unit 2.2.3). However, many methods involve a wasting process, such as cutting or machining, or a mechanical fastening, such as a screw or a nail.

What happens if a curved piece of timber is required?

There are two common methods of forming such shapes: steam bending and laminating.

Steam bending

Thin layers of timber (veneers) are placed into a steam chamber. Steam is introduced at one end and travels through the chamber, heating the veneer and absorbing into the timber as it does so. As the steam cools, and condenses, it turns back into water and it simply drains away.

△ **Figure 5** A chair produced using steam bending

After a period of time immersed in the steam, the veneers are removed and are malleable and flexible. This change in their properties makes it possible to bend them to a different shape. They are positioned around a former and clamped, or held, into place and left to cool. Upon being unclamped and cooled, they will retain this new shape (Figure 5).

Laminating

This is a process that involves no heat. It involves using a number of thin laminates of timber and bonding them to each other over a former. Unlike steam bending, there is no need to try to get the sections into a steam chamber, and they retain their shape by being bonded to other layers of laminates. While the adhesives used in this process cure and set, the layers of laminates need to be held in place (Figure 6).

△ **Figure 6** A product that has been laminated

Adhesive curing times and strengths vary from product to product. PVA (polyvinyl acetate) adhesive is commonly used to bond timber in the school workshop as it is relatively cheap, non-toxic and easy to work with. Typically, PVA is left to set for a period of 24 hours before removing the clamps, to ensure that it is fully set.

TOP TIP

If you are trying to bend and form shapes in timber, consider using either a ratchet clamp or the opposing half of the former tool. This holds the parts in place while they set or cool during curing, if you are steam bending (Figure 7).

△ **Figure 7** Ratchet clamp holding timber

DESIGN IN ACTION

Environmental considerations

Trees are a natural resource. They remove harmful gases such as carbon dioxide from the atmosphere, replacing it with oxygen. It is essential that we replant them so that the ecological impact is minimised and the cycle can continue for years to come.

◁ **Figure 8** Timber from an accredited FSC supplier displays the FSC logo. Look out for it when you are buying timber.

Some tropical hardwoods, such as teak and mahogany, take hundreds of years to grow. It is therefore essential that we continue to plant new trees to take their place. The **Forest Stewardship Council (FSC)** is a global organisation set up to ensure this happens (Figure 8).

TOP TIP

Consider what you are going to use the timber for (for example, a chair or a table). Look for a timber or manufactured board that matches your product needs (properties). This will give you a range of materials to work with. You can then make your final decision based on either cost or availability.

SKILLS ACTIVITY

Flat-packed furniture

A flat pack is a product (usually furniture) that is sold unassembled in a flat box, with all the parts and instructions included for the customer to put it together at home.

Think of a piece of flat-packed furniture. Sketch the item. Identify where you could use hardwood, softwood and manufactured boards in its construction. Suggest two different types of timber or manufactured board for each of the components you have identified.

REFLECTIVE LOG

Identify and justify the types of timber and manufactured boards you have used in your own work. Suggest different timbers and manufactured boards that could be substituted for the ones you used.

Comment on the relative costs that these changes would bring about. Would it make the product cheaper or more expensive?

KNOWLEDGE CHECK

1. Explain when wood is referred to as 'timber'.
2. Give **three** examples of softwood trees. Suggest a use for each one.
3. Give **three** examples of hardwood trees. Suggest a use for each one.
4. Explain **one** use for manufactured boards.
5. Explain how you would know if timbers have come from a sustainable forest.

KEY TERMS

Forest Stewardship Council (FSC): A logo showing the paper comes from well-managed forests

Grain: The pattern you see in wood created by how the tree grew. The grain can be straight, wavy, spiral, or irregular

Hardwood: Wood that comes from broad-leaved trees, such as oak, beech and ash

Manufactured board: Sheet material made from wood particles, fibres, or veneers bonded with adhesive

Seasoning: The process of drying out timber so that it becomes strong and stable to use

Softwood: Wood from coniferous trees (trees with needles and cones), like pine, spruce, or fir

Timber: Wood that has been processed and turned into a form that can be easily used, often planks

Veneer: A thin layer of wood that is glued on top of another material (like plywood or MDF) to make it look like solid wood

2·1·3 Metals

LEARNING AIMS

By the end of this unit, you should:

✓ Understand the different metals and their classification, stock forms, properties, environmental impact and uses

✓ Understand where metals come from

✓ Understand the molecular structure of a metal

Metal is found throughout the world. It is mined from the rock that makes up the surface of our planet and comes from the earth in raw form called 'ore'.

Metal is extracted and processed from ore. The ore is crushed and then heat and chemicals are used to further refine it (Figure 1).

△ **Figure 1** Iron ore extraction

Sometimes the ore from which a metal is extracted is evident, other times it is not. Iron comes from iron ore, while aluminium comes from bauxite. Pure metals fall into one of two main categories:

- **ferrous** (those containing iron)
- **non-ferrous** (those that do not contain iron).

Pure metals do not often have the exact properties that are required for the specific functions needed in products. Therefore, it is necessary to combine a number of metals to give the desired properties. This is done in a process called 'alloying'. An **alloy** is a mixture of two or more pure metals.

PROPERTIES OF METALS

Metals have many different characteristics. These are described by the various properties they possess (Table 1).

Some examples of alloys and their uses are shown in Table 2 (ferrous) and Table 3 (non-ferrous) metals.

Property	Description	Example
Brittleness	Something that has no flexibility: when it breaks, it shatters into multiple pieces	
Ductility	The ability to be stretched, bent, deformed and shaped without breaking	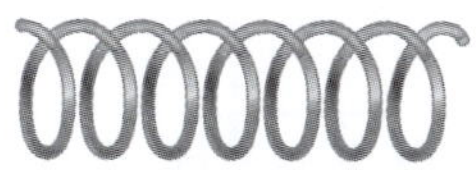
Hardness	Resistance to scratching, cutting and wear	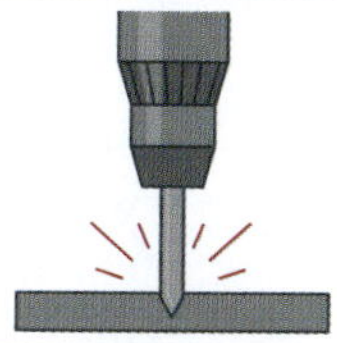
Elasticity	The ability to return to its original shape after it has been deformed	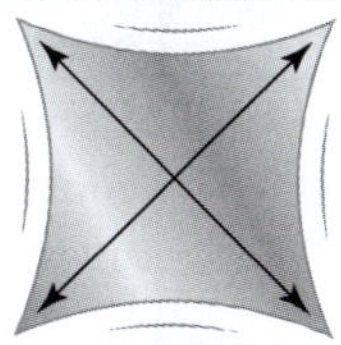
Malleability	Something that can be easily shaped, spread, flattened, hammered and deformed	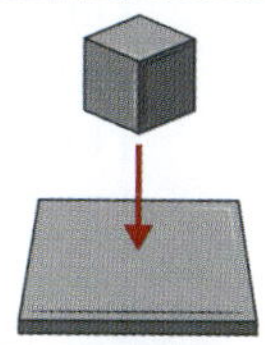
Toughness	Resistance to impact without breaking; opposite of brittleness	

△ **Table 1** Properties of metals

FERROUS METALS

Any alloy that contains iron is a ferrous metal (see Table 2).

All ferrous metals have some common properties which relate to iron: they conduct heat and electricity, and they react with oxygen and corrode (rust) unless they are treated to prevent this. Due to the iron content, ferrous metals also have high melting points (1200 °C and greater).

Name and melting point (°C)	Properties	Uses	Stock forms	Environmental impact	What it looks like
Cast iron (1200)	Brittle, corrodes by rusting	Casting and base metal for all steel alloys, manhole covers, car brake discs	Castings (engine blocks, cookware, machine parts), bars (limited use)	High carbon content, high CO_2 emissions during production; recyclable; heavy; less efficient in transport	
Stainless steel (1400)	Hard, corrosion and wear – resistant to a large extent; typically, an alloy of iron with 18% chromium, 8% magnesium and 8% nickel added	Cutlery, kitchen equipment, sanitary equipment, surgical equipment	Sheets and plates, rods and bars, tubes and pipes, wire, foil	High **embodied energy** due to alloying elements; recyclable; long-lasting	
High-speed steel (HSS) (1400)	Contains a high content of tungsten, vanadium and chromium alloyed with iron; very brittle and very resistant to wear	Drill bits, lathe tools, milling cutters	Round bars, flat bars, tool blanks, preformed cutting tools (drills, taps, end mills)	Contains rare alloying metals; harder to recycle; long tool life offsets some impact	
Mild steel (1600)	Tough, ductile, malleable, good tensile strength, poor resistance to corrosion; an alloy of iron combined with 0.15–0.30% carbon	General purpose engineering and construction material, nuts, bolts, car body panels	Sheets and plates, bars (round, flat, square), tubes, structural sections (I-beams, angles)	Energy-intensive production; moderate CO_2 emissions; highly recyclable (most used metal globally)	
High carbon steel (1800)	Hard and tough, but the increase in carbon makes it more brittle; can be heat-treated to further enhance its properties	Cutting tools, ball bearings, hand tools; screwdrivers, hammers, chisels and saws	Sheets and plates, bars (round, square, flat), structural sections, wire	Moderate CO_2 emissions; recyclable (varies with carbon content); harder steels require more energy to process	

Δ **Table 2** Properties of ferrous metals – these are all alloys

NON-FERROUS METALS

These are metals and metal alloys that do not contain iron (see Table 3).

Name and melting point (°C)	Properties	Uses	Stock forms	Environmental impact	What it looks like
Lead (160)	Very soft and very malleable; has one of the lowest melting points of a metal that is solid at room temperature	Roofing, construction, casting, lead acid batteries (at one time, used in paints and water pipes, but it is toxic and no longer used for these)	Sheets (roofing, shielding), ingots, wire, pipe, bars	Highly toxic to humans and wildlife; recyclable but strict controls needed	
Tin (230)	Very ductile and very malleable; is resistant to corrosion from moisture; bright silver in appear-ance, often used as a coating on a base metal	Used as a coating on food cans, drinks cans, and tin foil for use in the kitchen	Ingots, foil, coating (e.g., tinplate), powder (for solder or alloys)	Low toxicity, but mining can cause soil and water quality to decrease; recyclable	
Zinc (420)	By itself, very weak; however, highly corrosion-resistant	Used as a coating on screws, nails, nuts and bolts; also used to weatherproof steel in the process 'galvanising'	Ingots, sheets and plates, rods, powder (galvanising, batteries)	Moderate impact from mining – air pollution; recyclable; can leach into water if not managed	
Duralumin* (630)	Very strong, hard, lightweight alloy of aluminium, copper (3%), manganese (1%) and magnesium (1.5%); soft and workable in normal state	Widely used in aircraft construction, boat building and car manufacture	Sheets and plates, rods and bars, tubes, extrusions	Similar to aluminium; recyclable; strong and light; improves energy efficiency in transport	
Aluminium (660)	Light in colour although it can be polished to a mirror-like appearance; it is very light in weight and the most abundant metal in Earth's surface	Saucepans, cooking foil, takeaway containers, window frames, ladders, bicycles	Sheets and plates, foil, rods and bars, tubes, extrusions, wire	High energy to extract; highly recyclable; low weight; energy savings in use	

Name and melting point (°C)	Properties	Uses	Stock forms	Environmental impact	What it looks like
Brass* (925)	An alloy often machined from cast ingots and billets of raw material; golden yellow in colour: typically a mixture of copper (65%) and zinc (35%)	Decorative metal work such as handles, candlesticks, ornaments, pins on electrical plugs, and musical instruments	Rods and bars, tubes, sheets and plates, wires, castings	Impact depends on copper/zinc sources; recyclable; less toxic than base metals	
Pewter** (tin + copper/ antimony/ bismuth) (230)	A tin-based metal alloy, typically consisting of 85–99% tin, with additional metals such as copper, antimony, bismuth (and, in the past, lead); modern pewter is lead-free for safety and often used in schools as it is more stable, readily available, comparatively cheaper and more predictable in use	Known for its low melting point, ease of casting, and use in non-structural applications such as tableware, decorative items, and medals	Bars, ingots, cast items (figurines, jewellery, tableware)	Low toxicity (modern, lead-free versions); some environmental impact from tin and alloying metals; recyclable	
Copper (1080)	Very ductile and malleable metal; often red/brown in colour and goes green when it corrodes, forming a substance 'verdigris'; an excellent conductor of heat and electricity	Used for plumbing, cookware, electrical fittings and roof coverings	Rods and bars, sheets and plates, pipes and tubes, wire, strip	Mining is destructive to the environment; recyclable	

△ **Table 3** Properties of non-ferrous metals (* indicates that these are alloys.)

CHANGING THE STRUCTURE AND PROPERTIES OF A METAL

Work hardening

Work hardening happens when a non-ferrous metal is continually deformed through processes like bending, hammering, rolling or drawing – without heating the metal over a period of time. This is often referred to as 'working the metal'. Work hardening can be both desirable and undesirable.

Annealing

Annealing is a process that is often undertaken after a piece of material is work hardened, and it is in a state where it can no longer be worked as required (Figure 2). When a metal is annealed, it is heated to a specific temperature and then cooled – it does not involve working with the material in a hot state. Heating and cooling changes the molecular structure of the material, and these changes result in the metal being softened. This means that a metal that has been annealed can be cut and shaped more easily than if it had not been.

∆ **Figure 2** Annealing

Molecular structure

Metals are made of atoms arranged in a repeating pattern called a crystal lattice, held together by freely moving electrons called metallic bonds (Figure 3). Metals do not form molecules.

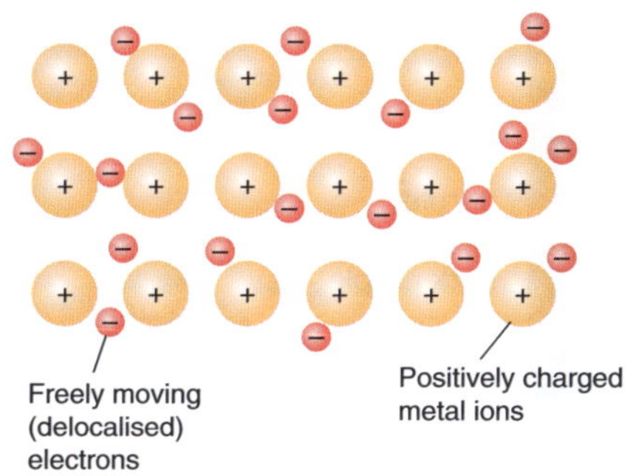

∆ **Figure 3** A metal's molecular structure

During the annealing process, the metal needs to be heated to a specific temperature. As you heat a piece of metal, it changes colour. These changes in colour occur at specific temperatures. It is often easier to look at the colour of a piece of heated metal and use this to know the temperature rather than try to measure it with a thermometer. For example, the alloy *mild steel* needs to be heated to a red colour and allowed to cool in order to anneal it.

However, metals with lower melting points, such as aluminium, will melt if heated for too long. Aluminium can be annealed but care must be taken while heating.

Hardening and tempering of tool steel

Tool steel is a type of high-quality steel used for making tools due to its strength, hardness and resistance to wear. To achieve these properties, it goes through two key heat treatment processes because hardening alone makes the steel brittle to be of any use. So, it has to go through:

- Hardening
- Tempering

An example of a product that goes through this process is a screwdriver. It needs to be strong and hard, yet not brittle or it will not be able to withstand the turning force (torque) generated in turning a screw. To harden the screwdriver blade, the tool steel is formed into the desired shape and then it is heated until it is at a temperature of around 900 °C. This can be easily seen as the metal will turn red with the heat. Once it reaches this temperature it is plunged into clean, cold water.

To remove the brittleness but retain the strength, the tool steel must now be tempered. In order to do this, the metal must first be thoroughly cleaned, then gradually reheated. As it is heated, it changes colour and heating continues until a blue coloured line is seen on the screwdriver blade, which signifies that the metal is now at the correct temperature. It then needs to be cooled, either by putting it in cold water again or in oil.

△ **Figure 4** As steel is heated, it changes colour.

Table 4 shows the temperature and colour for tempering tool steel.

colour	temperature (°C)	example
pale yellow	230	scriber
dark yellow	250	twist drill bit
brown	260	plane blades
purple	270	knives
dark purple	280	saws
blue	300	screwdrivers

△ **Table 4** Temperature and colour chart for tempering tool steel

Case hardening of mild steel

Case hardening is a heat treatment process used to harden the outer surface (case) of the mild steel, while keeping the core soft and tough. This makes the steel wear-resistant on the outside and shock-absorbent inside.

Case hardening is quicker and less complicated, but less precise, than the hardening and tempering process used on tool steel. This process hardens the surface of the metal only, unlike hardening and tempering, which hardens the material throughout. This process only hardens the outer 0·05 mm.

Case hardening also has the advantage of leaving the core unhardened, so it retains greater malleability and flexibility, allowing the material to still be easily worked.

The mild steel is heated to a red colour. Following this, it is removed from the heat and plunged into a case hardening compound that is high in carbon, as this element hardens the steel. Once the metal has been put in the hardening compound, it is returned to the heat and again its temperature raised until it glows red. At this stage, it is removed from the heat and plunged into clean, cold water to complete the process. (See Figure 5)

△ **Figure 5** Case hardening of a mild steel product

TOP TIP

Always know your metal type before cutting, welding or heat treating – different metals behave very differently!

SKILLS ACTIVITY

Identifying metals

Identify *four* uses of metal in tools that you know and have used. Determine a suitable metal for each tool. Work out if they are likely to be ferrous or non-ferrous – could they be alloys?

Looking at the tools again:

1. Work out if they need to be hardened. If so, which processes would be suitable.
2. Note any specific metal features, such as a saw blade. List the properties that the metals must have in order to fulfil their function.

DESIGN IN ACTION

Planishing sheet metal for everyday products

Various metals are used in everyday objects. Products such as cars or aeroplanes are brilliant examples of the process of hardening and how it helps increase the performance of real-world products.

Another example is your everyday cooking-ware pot and pans. These also go through the process of hardening. Manufacturing a product with copper is a quicker process as it becomes really malleable and easy to shape. Once it is in the desired shape, it will need to be hardened to retain this shape. A process called 'planishing' is often used to do this.

Planishing is a metalworking technique used to smooth and refine the surface of sheet metal by lightly hammering it with a planishing hammer or mallet over a hard surface like an anvil. Planishing involves intentionally hardening the metal.

REFLECTIVE LOG

Explain why you think it is necessary to recycle metals, thinking specifically about alloys. Why are these harder to recycle than metals in their pure form?

KNOWLEDGE CHECK

1. Explain how to determine if a metal is ferrous or non-ferrous.
2. Describe in simple terms what an alloy is.
3. Put these metals in order according to their melting points: aluminium, pewter, cast iron, copper, duralumin, lead, mild steel, stainless steel, tin, zinc.
4. What is the purpose of annealing metals?
5. When and why would a metal be tempered?
6. Typically, how thick is the hardened layer on mild steel that has been case hardened?
7. Identify **four** steps in the process of case hardening, in sequence. Draw a picture of each step, labelling the parts in each drawing.
8. Justify which metals are more environmentally friendly.

KEY TERMS

Alloy: A mixture of two or more metals

Embodied energy: The total energy required to extract, process, manufacture, transport, and install a material or product — from raw resource to final use

Ferrous metal: A metal that contains iron

Non-ferrous metal: A metal that does not contain iron

2·1·4 Composites

LEARNING AIMS

By the end of this unit, you should:

✓ Understand the term 'composite'

✓ Demonstrate knowledge of composite materials and understand their classification, properties, environmental impact and uses

What is a composite? A composite is a material made from two or more different substances that, when combined, create a material with better overall properties than the individual components.

A composite material is made by combining a **matrix** (binder) with a **reinforcement** (strengthener) to create a strong, durable and lightweight product.

WHY ARE COMPOSITES USED?

Composites are used because they can be engineered to meet the exact requirements of a specific application. By combining individual materials, each becomes enhanced and, typically, the advantages of the new material mean it is more efficient, stronger and lighter.

EARLY COMPOSITES

Composites are not new! One of the earliest known examples is combining mud (wet soil or clay) with plant material, such as straw, to make bricks for building walls and houses. In this example:

- the mud is the matrix
- the straw acts as the reinforcement.

Concrete, which comprises small stones and gravel with cement and sand, is another early example of a composite material. In many buildings today, concrete is further reinforced by embedding metal wires or rods into the concrete during construction (Figure 1).

△ **Figure 1** Steel-reinforced concrete

MODERN COMPOSITES

Continuous research is helping to ensure that new innovative composite materials are developed. Within resistant materials there are three main composite groups:

- Glass reinforced polymers (GRP or GFRP)
- Carbon-fibre reinforced polymers (CFRP)
- Aramid-reinforced polymers (Kevlar®)

Glass reinforced polymers (GRP)

GRP is a strong, lightweight material made by mixing glass fibres (fibreglass) with plastic (polymer resin such as polyester or epoxy), which forms the matrix. The glass fibres give strength and stiffness, while the plastic (resin) holds the fibres together and provides shape by using a mould.

△ **Figure 2** GRP components being manufactured

During the manufacturing stage, different weights and strengths of GRP are produced by creating layers of glass fibres of different thicknesses. This is achieved by placing the GRP material into a mould: placing the fibreglass strands and adding polyester resin. Once the resin has **cured**, the process is repeated. This creates layers of GRP which are lightweight and very strong (Figure 2).

The process can be repeated to create the set design of a product. Then, the GRP can be smoothed via sanding and a finish applied.

△ **Figure 3** GRP is widely used to make boat hulls.

GRP is a popular composite which is widely used to make car bodies, water tanks, swimming pool slides, canoes and boat hulls (Figure 3).

Carbon-fibre reinforced polymers (CFRP)

CFRP is a strong, lightweight composite material made by embedding carbon fibres in a polymer resin matrix (such as epoxy). It combines high strength, stiffness and low density, making it ideal for high-performance applications.

CFRP is one of the most expensive composite materi-als, but has the best strength-to-weight ratio of any construction material. Carbon fibres are resistant to stretching and the result is a rigid material, light in weight yet very strong.

△ **Figure 4** CFRP is used in the manufacture of Formula 1 car bodies.

CFRP is used extensively within the aerospace industry, as it has a high tolerance to heat, and is used to replace traditional, heavier metal-based materials. Other examples include marine, automotive, defence, and sports and leisure industries (Figure 4).

Kevlar®

Kevlar® is another high-strength fibre. It is known for its exceptional strength, lightweight properties, and resistance to heat, impact and wear. See unit 2.1.5 for more information about how Kevlar® is made and what it is used for.

PROPERTIES, USES, AND ENVIRONMENTAL IMPACT OF COMPOSITES

Table 1 shows the environmental impact of some composites.

Material	Properties	Uses	Environmental impact	Product
CFRP	Extremely strong, lightweight, high stiffness, corrosion-resistant	Aerospace, automotive, sports equipment, marine	High production energy; difficult to recycle; research into sustainable production methods	
GRP	Strong, flexible, weather-resistant, good insulation	Marine, construction, automotive, electrical	Moderate energy use; difficult to recycle; research into greener resins and reuse	
Melamine formaldehyde (MF)	Hard, scratch-resistant, heat-resistant, durable	Furniture, kitchenware, electrical components	Uses formaldehyde (toxic); non-recyclable; potential for eco-friendly alternatives	

△ **Table 1** The environmental impact of composites

TOP TIP

Remember that composites combine the best properties of two materials – one gives strength (reinforcement), the other gives shape and support (matrix).

Think of it like this: *'One holds it together, the other makes it strong.'*

A good example would be reinforced concrete, where the metal rods are inserted to increase strength, retain their shape and size, and are clearly visible within the concrete.

SKILLS ACTIVITY

Investigating composites

Choose *one* example of a composite material and complete the following:

1. Name each individual material utilised in its construction.
2. Describe how the composite is formed, and explain the purpose of each individual material. Which is the matrix and which is the reinforcement?
3. Explain the advantages of using this composite over traditional materials, and give examples of its application.

REFLECTIVE LOG

Consider the materials you have used in your own work. Have you used, or could you consider using, a composite? Explain the advantages a composite material choice would have over other more traditional materials.

DESIGN IN ACTION

Carbon-fibre prosthetic limbs

Van Phillips is an American inventor and amputee who revolutionised prosthetic limbs by creating the flexible carbon-fibre prosthetic foot – most famously, the 'Flex-Foot®', used by Paralympic athletes worldwide (Figure 5).

They can be made specifically to meet the requirements of the individual athlete, taking into account their weight, height and leg length in order to maximise their performance on the track.

Δ **Figure 5** CFRP is used to make sporting prosthetic limbs.

KNOWLEDGE CHECK

1. Give an example of an early composite and name the individual materials used.
2. Give **three** benefits of using composite materials.
3. What material was Van Phillips famous for using?
4. Name a disadvantage of an environmental impact of GRP.

KEY TERMS

Cure: The chemical process of allowing a substance, such as a polymer resin used within a composite, to harden and set

Matrix: The material in a composite that performs the binding function

Reinforcement: The material in a composite that adds tensile strength and toughness

2·1·5 Smart, modern and alternative materials

LEARNING AIMS

By the end of this unit, you should:

✓ Develop an awareness and understanding of 'smart', modern and alternative materials

✓ Understand the key properties of common 'smart', modern and alternative materials

What are smart and modern materials? These are materials whose properties change depending on the external (environmental) conditions in which they are placed.

Smart materials change their properties in response to heat, light, pressure or electricity – and then return to normal when the condition is removed. Some smart materials appear to have a '**memory**': for example, deforming and returning to their original shape/structure under certain conditions, such as heat from an electrical current (shape memory alloys and the effect of heat on **shape memory polymers**).

Modern materials are newly developed or improved materials designed to meet specific performance needs, often used in advanced engineering, medical or technology products. These include materials manufactured by making changes to the structure at molecular level or using **nanoparticles**, such as graphene or hydrophobic surfaces that repel water.

Some smart and modern materials are inspired by nature; this is called biomimicry (Figure 1). Alternative sustainable materials include biopolymers and bamboo.

Δ **Figure 1** Smart or modern materials change their properties in response to external conditions, just like some animals.

EXAMPLES OF SMART AND MODERN MATERIALS

There are many different materials that can be classed as being either smart or modern. Some common examples are shown in Table 1.

Name	Properties	Uses
Shape memory alloy (SMA) or nitinol	An alloy composed of nickel and titanium, which will when deformed (bent), **(a)** return to its original shape when heated beyond 90 °C, and **(b)** contract when an electric current is passed through it	Used in stents, which are tubes inserted into damaged blood vessels: inserted cold and expand to the correct size in response to the patient's body temperature, strengthening the blood vessel; also used in some spectacle frames and dentures
Shape memory polymer (SMP)	A variety of polymer (plastics), which deform in response to an external stimulus, such as when an electric voltage is applied or there is a change in temperature	Potential uses: valves or pumps for liquids where mechanical components are not desirable
Thermochromic inks	Materials with these properties change colour in response to changes in temperature	Commonly used in forehead thermometer strips and in the food industry to indicate the temperature of a packaged food product
Photochromic inks	Materials with these properties change colour in response to changes in light level, including ultraviolet (UV) or infrared (IR)	Light-reacting sunglasses or spectacles, which darken in response to UV light
Polymorph	Available in small pellets which fuse when heated to 62 °C and can be moulded, resulting in a tough polymer	Can be used by designers and engineers to prototype difficult shapes, such as components, joints and handles
Bamboo	A natural composite material with self-healing capability (limited): can recover from minor deformations due to its high elasticity; its natural hygroscopic behaviour (absorbs moisture) allows it to expand or contract slightly, making it responsive to humidity; its fast growth rate and carbon sequestration make bamboo a sustainable and *smart ecological choice*	Can be used in construction (scaffolding, flooring), textiles, toothbrush handles and biodegradable packaging

Name	Properties	Uses
Metal foam	A cellular solid (metal with gas-filled pores); provides excellent shock absorption and is lightweight and strong; offers good thermal management for dissipating heat effectively and acoustic damping	Can be used for aerospace and automotive components, and is excellent for crash protection, as well as blast protection and military armour; often used for prosthetics and biomedical implants, as well as for soundproofing buildings
Graphene	An allotrope of carbon (single-atom-thick 2D material), stronger than steel with extreme electrical and thermal conductivity; is flexible and transparent, with sensing capabilities that can detect single molecules or small pressure changes	Often used for flexible electronics and sensors, energy storage (supercapacitors, batteries), water filtration and desalination, and for biomedical devices
Kevlar®	A high-strength synthetic fibre made from aromatic polyamide (aramid), Kevlar® is resistant to impact, heat and wear; its smart textiles include self-healing fabrics, energy-harvesting garments and wearable technology for health monitoring	Can be used for ropes and cables, body armour and personal protective equipment (**PPE**) such as fireproof gear; is often used in the aerospace and automative industries
Hydrochromic materials	Can create hidden images or patterns that become visible when wet and disappear when dry; the colour change is reversible: the material returns to its original state as it dries	Often used for automotive applications, such as car trims that change colour in the rain to increase visibility, or for moisture indicators for agriculture or construction; can be used for promotional materials, interactive art or clothing that change colour or reveals hidden designs when exposed to water or sweat
Biopolymers	Natural or synthetic polymers derived from living organisms: biopolymers are biodegradable, and decompose naturally, reducing environmental impact; some biopolymers can change shape or behaviour in response to pH, temperature or light (for example, hydrogels); they are biocompatible, and suitable for medical applications	Often used for medical implants and drug delivery systems; can be used for food packaging and agricultural films, and for tissue engineering scaffolds

△ **Table 1** Common examples of smart or modern materials

Kevlar®

Stronger than steel, Kevlar® is a high-strength synthetic fibre made from aromatic polyamide (aramid). It is known for its exceptional strength, lightweight properties, and resistance to impact, heat and wear. It is commonly used in bulletproof vests, helmets and composites.

Kevlar® is one of a group of materials developed from a synthetic fibre created by chemist Stephanie Kwolek in 1965. It is manufactured by combining paraphenylenediamine (PPD) and terephthaloyl chloride (TC), the result is a super stiff, heat-resistant polymer, nine times stronger than nylon.

This material has 20 times the strength of steel. A common use for this synthetically engineered material is personal protective equipment (PPE), to protect people working in hazardous jobs (Figure 2).

△ **Figure 2** Kevlar® is heat resistant and used in PPE garments.

TOP TIP

Always consider the environment and the intended use of materials. Choose materials that perform well and last a long time in the specific conditions your product will face.

SKILLS ACTIVITY

Investigating smart and modern materials

Explore different smart materials used in commercial products, analyse their properties, applications, and environmental impacts, and present your findings using a mind map. What is your favourite smart and modern material?

DESIGN IN ACTION

Smart and modern materials in health and medicine

Smart and modern materials have numerous applications in health and medicine. A 'stent' is a small mesh tube, made from a shape memory alloy, which is inserted into damaged blood vessels to strengthen or keep them from collapsing (Figure 3).

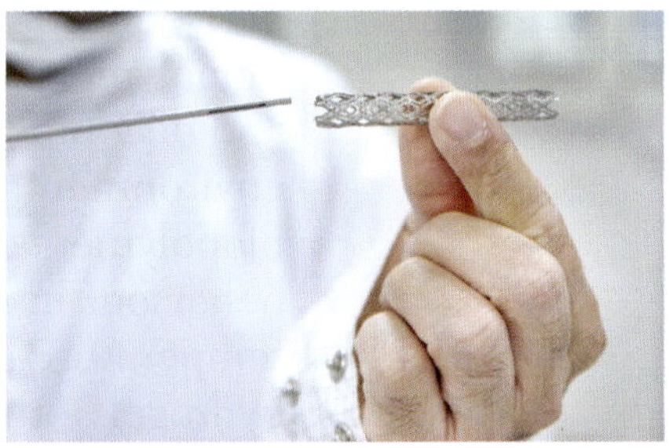

△ **Figure 3** The stent is inserted cold and expands into the desired size with the patient's body heat.

KNOWLEDGE CHECK

1. Explain how a smart and modern material differs from a natural material.
2. Describe the properties of a smart and modern material, and give examples of how these could be used to add functionality to a product.

KEY TERMS

Memory: The property by which a material returns to its original shape under environmental conditions such as heat

Nanoparticles: Very tiny particles. Materials made with nanoparticles have special properties

PPE: Personal protective equipment (PPE) such as eye protection, gloves and face masks*

Photochromic: Changes colour with light

Shape memory polymer: A polymer that returns to its original shape when heated

Thermochromic: Changes colour with temperature

2·2 Making processes

2·2·1 Measuring and marking out

LEARNING AIMS

By the end of this unit, you should:

✓ Understand the importance of consistent and accurate measuring and marking out, using appropriate hand tools and equipment, and/or CAD tools

✓ Be aware of the correct measuring and drawing tools

What is setting and marking out? This is the process of measuring, drawing and marking lines, shapes or points onto a material (such as wood, metal or plastic) before it is cut, shaped or assembled.

It is the first and most important step in making a product accurately.

WHY IS ACCURACY IN MEASUREMENT IMPORTANT?

Inaccurate measuring could mean that pieces do not fit together! This can reduce both the function and the aesthetic appeal of your product.

Accurate measuring means taking correct and precise measurements so that parts, or materials, are made to the exact size and shape needed for the task.

MEASURING AND MARKING OUT

Measuring and marking out is the process of accurately measuring material and marking lines, points or shapes onto it before cutting, shaping or assembling.

To help ensure accuracy, setting, measuring and marking out should always be done in a clean and well-lit area. The tools and equipment needed to ensure precision will differ depending upon the material and intended processes of manufacture. Before beginning, all tools and equipment should be checked to ensure they are in good working order.

Figure 1 shows an example of marking out for making a phone stand.

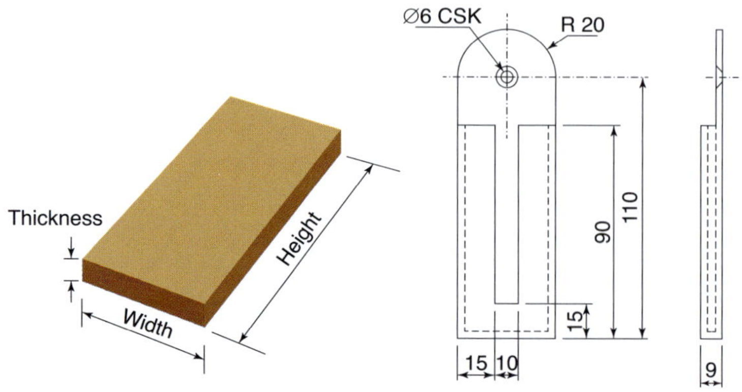

△ **Figure 1** How you could mark out for making a phone stand

SELECTING THE CORRECT TOOLS AND EQUIPMENT

Table 1 shows the correct methods, tools and techniques to use to ensure accuracy when you set, mark out and measure different materials.

Type of mark	Correct tool/equipment			What it looks like
	Timber	**Plastic**	**Metal**	
A sharp, straight line (any angle)	Sharp pencil, marking knife or sliding bevel	Permanent marker pen	Straight steel edge and scriber	
A parallel line	Marking gauge	Odd-leg callipers	Odd-leg callipers	
A perpendicular/ 90° angle	Try square	Try square	Engineer's square	
A 45° angle	Mitre square/ combination square	Mitre square/ combination square	Mitre square/ combination square	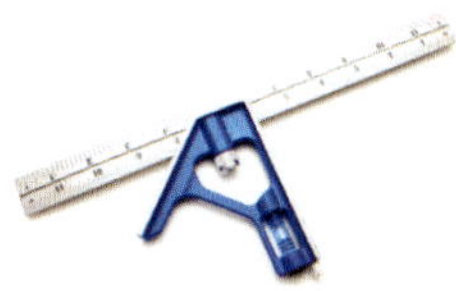
The centre of a hole	Sharp pencil and a centre punch	Permanent marker pen	Dot/centre punch	
Arches, curves and circles	A pair of compasses	Dividers	Dividers	
An irregular shape	Template	Template	Template	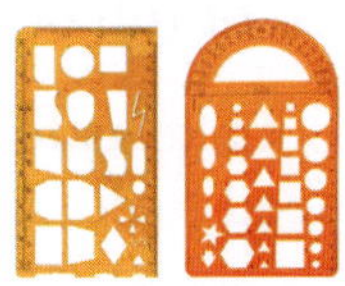
A mortise and tenon joint	A mortise gauge for both mortise and tenon	—	—	

Δ **Table 1** Tools for measuring and marking out

Precise instruments for measurements

Where measurements of fractions of a millimetre are required, it is necessary to use a micrometre or callipers. These are explained in Table 2.

Precise instrument	Uses	What it looks like
Inside and outside callipers	Used to measure the inside or outside of material	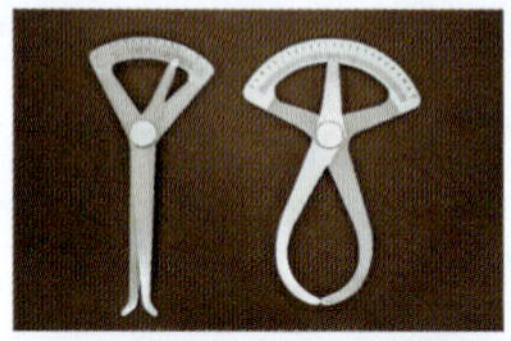
Micrometer	Sometimes known as a micrometer screw gauge, this is a precision device used to measure depth, length or thickness to a high degree of accuracy	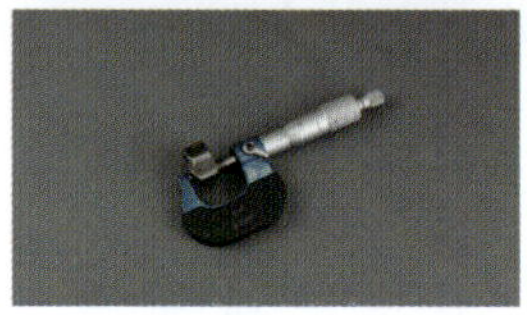
Vernier gauge	A manual calliper used to measure internal and external distances with precision and accuracy; it is less easy to read than the digital calliper but does not require any power source	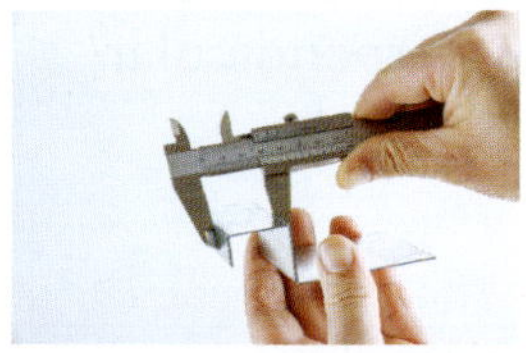
Digital vernier calliper	A precision instrument used to accurately and easily measure internal and external distances; the LCD display can be set to measure either imperial or metric units	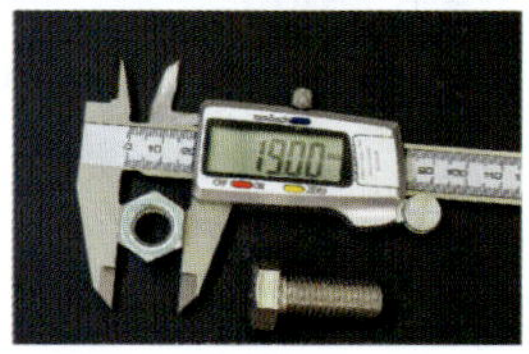

∆ **Table 2** Precise instruments for measurements

TOP TIP

Always measure twice and mark once. This helps avoid mistakes!

Incorrect equipment, such as using a pencil or pen to mark out instead of a scriber or marking knife, can vary the thickness of the line, and may lead to making the wrong cut.

Do not use non-permanent marker pen on plastic, as it will result in marks that become blurred or rub off.

Try to make as few marks as possible. Numerous marks may make it unclear which line you need to cut along.

SKILLS ACTIVITY

Marking out a piece of mild steel

In preparation for cutting, you are going to mark out a piece of mild steel. List the tools and equipment you would use. Explain your choices. Name each stage of the process you would follow.

REFLECTIVE LOG

Using an example from your own work, write about one occasion when you measured and marked out material.

- What preparation did you do?
- Name the tools and equipment you used.
- If you were marking out a different material, would you have used the same tools and equipment?

DESIGN IN ACTION

Mars Climate Orbiter

Everyone makes mistakes! There have been lots of mathematical errors that have led to catastrophe over the years, but probably one of the most memorable measurement mishaps occurred in 1999, and resulted in NASA losing its $125 million Mars probe.

The Climate Orbiter was designed to relay environmental data about Mars back to Earth (Figure 2), but engineers failed to convert British imperial measurements into metric units. Two hundred and eight-six days into its mission, the simple error was discovered when the probe fired its engines to push itself into orbit. The mistake caused the satellite to veer 60 km off course, pushing it beyond Mars and out into space.

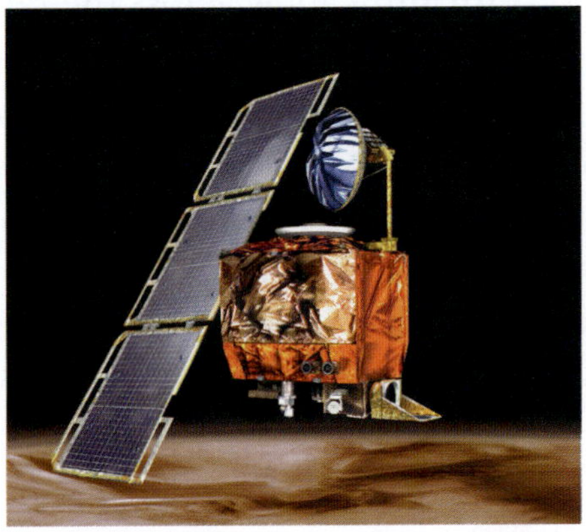

△ **Figure 2** The Climate Orbiter

KNOWLEDGE CHECK

1. Explain why accurate measurement is important.
2. Give **two** methods of setting and marking out wood, and list the tools required.
3. Give **two** methods of setting and marking out metal, and list the tools required.
4. Suggest **two** potential consequences of inaccurate measurement.

2·2·2 Cutting, shaping and forming

LEARNING AIMS

By the end of this unit, you should:

✓ Understand the different ways of cutting and removal of materials, using appropriate hand tools, power tools and machinery

✓ Understand how computer-aided design (CAD) / computer-aided manufacture (CAM) can be used for shaping and cutting

Different tools and equipment are used to shape different types of material. However, the principles of **wastage**, **addition**, **deforming** and **reforming** apply across the range of resistant materials (Figure 1).

In school workshops, the most common tools used to shape materials by wastage are saws, files and other abrasives (for example, glass paper).

Deforming processes, such as laminating woods or vacuum forming, are used to create shapes while retaining (or enhancing) structural integrity.

Reforming processes, such as casting metals or injection moulding plastics, are used to form complex shapes without the need to employ wastage techniques.

a b c

△ **Figure 1** Shaping materials: **a** laminated wood is often used for furniture; **b** vacuum formed plastic is often used for packaging; **c** injection moulded plastic is often used in machinery components.

SHAPING BY WASTAGE AND ADDITION

This process shapes a material by removing material (waste) from a larger piece to form the required shape.

Designers, technologists and engineers need to be aware of a range of tools and methods for cutting and removing material, as well as methods for joining materials to produce desired shapes, forms or contours. This knowledge provides a wider understanding when designing and making high-quality products and prototypes. The tools for shaping woods, metals and plastics (for example, hand, portable, power, machine or CAD) are used differently, due to the properties of materials (See Tables 1 and 2).

Hand tools

Process	Woods	Metals	Plastics	What it looks like
Cutting straight lines	Tenon saw (shown on right)	Hacksaw or junior hacksaw	Scoring tool or hacksaw	
Cutting curved lines	Coping saw (shown on right)	Piercing saw	Abrafile or piercing saw	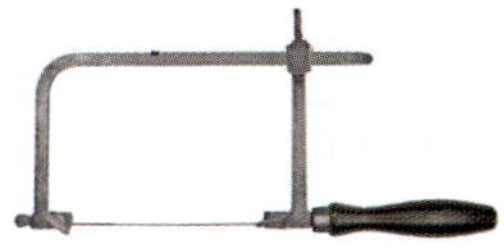
Shaping edges	Planes (shown on right), spokeshaves, rasps	Files	Files	
Smoothing surfaces	Abrasive papers	Abrasive papers and cloths, polish	Abrasive papers and cloths, polish	
Hollowing	Chisels (shown on right), gouges	Bossing mallet	N/A	
Drilling holes	Wheel brace and bit	Hand drill and twist bit (shown on right)	Hand drill and twist bit	

△ **Table 1** Hand tools

Machine tools

Computer-Aided Manufacture (CAM) uses computer-controlled machines to shape, cut, or build materials.

Most CAM processes are wastage (subtractive), but some use addition (additive). CAM allows for accurate, repeatable production. Commonly used for prototypes, custom parts, and precision manufacturing.

These machines remove material to create the required shape.

Laser Cutter – Uses a focused laser beam to cut or engrave materials such as wood, acrylic, and metal.

Plasma Cutter – Uses a jet of hot plasma to cut through conductive metals like steel and aluminium.

3- and 4-Axis Milling Machines – Use rotating cutters to remove material from solid blocks, producing complex 3D shapes.

3- and 4-Axis Routers – Similar to milling machines but mainly used for cutting wood, plastic, and foam.

CNC Lathes – Spin the workpiece while cutting tools shape it, ideal for making round or cylindrical parts.

This process builds up material layer by layer to make the shape.

3D Printing (Fused Deposition Modelling – FDM) – Melts and deposits plastic filament (such as PLA or ABS) to build models or prototypes.

Process	Woods	Metals	Plastics	What it looks like
Cutting straight lines	Circular saw (shown on right)	Guillotine, metal cutting bandsaw	Circular saw, bandsaw	
Cutting curved lines	Bandsaw	Bandsaw	Bandsaw	
Shaping edges	Router, disk/ belt sander, lathe	Off-hand grinder, centre lathe (shown on right)	Disk/belt sander	
Smoothing surfaces	Planer, thicknesser, belt sander	Polishing machines, belt sander	Polishing machines	
Hollowing	Router	Milling machining	Milling machining, router	
Drilling holes	Pillar/bench drill	Pillar/bench drill	Pillar/bench drill	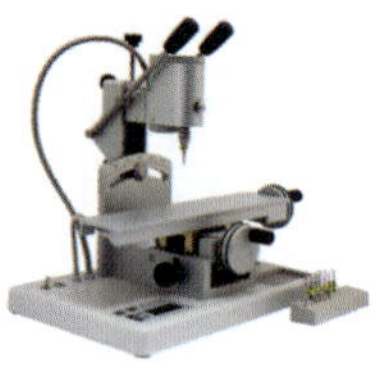

Δ **Table 2** Machine tools

Drilling

Drilling is useful for making a hole all the way (through hole) or part way (blind hole) through a material (such as wood) (Figure 2). Table 3 shows the different elements of a hole used for joining two materials.

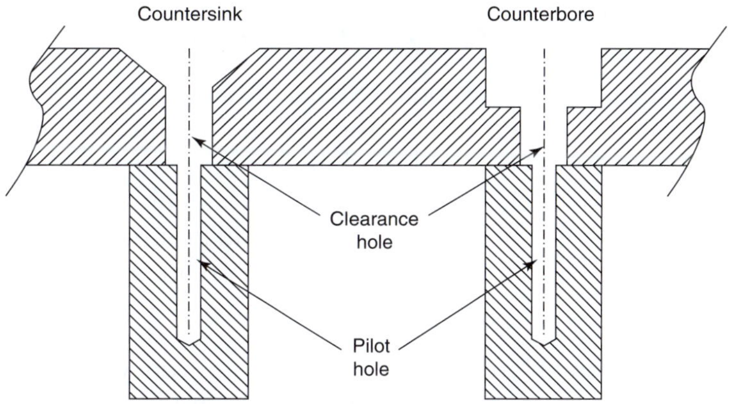

Δ **Figure 2** Drilling holes in cross section

Process	What it does
Pilot hole	Smaller than the screw being used, so that the thread cuts in and holds (usually in the bottom piece so that it is pulled against the top piece)
Clearance hole	Larger than the thread and shank of a screw (usually in the top piece), so that the screw does not grip or 'bite' into the sides, allowing the two pieces to pull together
Tapping	Usually used with metals, this is where a screw-thread is added to the inside of a pilot hole, using a tool called a 'tap', so that it accepts a machine screw; a thread can be added to the outside of a rod using a tool called a 'die'
Countersunk hole	A conical shaped indentation at the top of a hole to accept a countersink headed screw, with the screw head being 'flush' (level) with the surface, usually with a 90-degree inclusive angle
Counterbored hole	A larger diameter recess at the top of a hole to accept a cheese or fillister headed screw, with the screw head being recessed below the surface

Δ **Table 3** Drilling holes

SHAPING BY DEFORMING AND REFORMING

The material is bent, stretched, compressed or reshaped into the required form – often while it is hot or under pressure. This involves changing the shape of a material without removing material (as in cutting).

Deforming (Table 4) and reforming (Table 5) are used in industry to form complex shapes and gain strength from an object being formed as a single piece.

Deforming processes

Process	Materials	Description	Applications	What it looks like
Steam bending	Hardwoods, such as beech and oak	Strips of hardwood are heated in a steam chamber until the wood is pliable enough to easily bend around a former to create a specific shape	Wooden furniture	
Lamination	Hardwoods, such as birch and ash	Thin sheets (veneers) of hardwoods are layered with strong adhesive and pressed in a former until the adhesive cures	Wooden furniture, decorative roof beams	
Press forming	Sheet materials (woods, metals and plastics)	Sheet materials are pressed between a male and female (or saddle and yolk) former, until they cool, to take on a new shape; some materials need to be heated to become 'plastic' (malleable) prior to forming, or in the case of metals they can be annealed	Metal vehicle panels	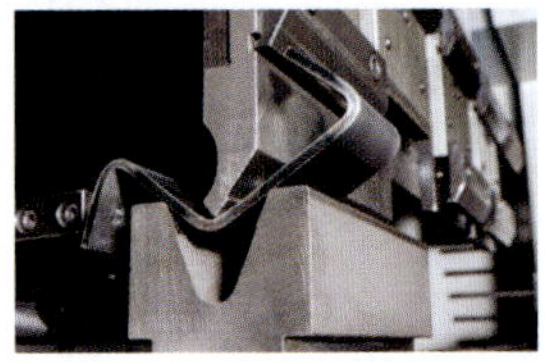
Vacuum forming	Thermo polymers	Plastic sheets are heated to their elastic state, then a former is pressed into the sheet and the air below is evacuated; the external pressure presses the plastic onto the former	Food packaging/ trays	
Blow moulding	Thermo polymers	Tubes of plastic are heated and fed through a mould; the air is blown into the tube, forcing it to expand out and form against the mould	Plastic milk bottles	

△ **Table 4** Deforming processes

Reforming processes

Process	Materials	Description	Applications	What it looks like
Injection moulding	Thermo polymers	Plastic beads are heated to their plastic state and injected into a mould to form complex shapes	Toys, consumer goods, such as mobile phone cases	
Extrusion	Thermo polymers	The material is heated to its plastic state and pushed through a 'die' to create components or parts with a fixed cross-sectional profile	Pipes, tubes, beams and rods	
Sand casting	Metals	Non-ferrous metal (for example brass, aluminium) is melted and poured into a mould made of a special sand	Engine blocks, gas and water valves	
Die casting	Non-ferrous metals	The metal is melted and forced into a hardened tool steel mould (or die)	Toys, brackets, engine parts	

△ **Table 5** Reforming processes

TOP TIP

Choose the shaping method that best suits the material type and product design – for example, do not try to bend brittle materials like cast iron!

SKILLS ACTIVITY

Identifying cutting, shaping and forming

Think about the most recent design-and-make assignment you have completed. What tools and equipment did you use? Sketch your product and label or annotate where wastage, addition, deforming and/or reforming were used.

REFLECTIVE LOG

Look at Tables 1–5 in this unit, make a note of the tools and equipment that you have used. Identify them in a Design and Technology workshop and locate tools and equipment that you have not used. Investigate, and ask your teacher (a) how they are used, (b) what they do and (c) what materials they are used with.

DESIGN IN ACTION

Nike shoes

Nike use shaping materials combining traditional moulding with cutting-edge technologies such as 3D printing and textile engineering. This creates a product that is high performance and that strives to be sustainable by being made using a proportion of recycled materials (Figure 3).

△ **Figure 3** Nike's Air VaporMax shoe

This product is a perfect example of how shaping materials – from moulded foams to knitted textiles – can create innovative, high-performance footwear.

KNOWLEDGE CHECK

1. Explain the differences between wastage, addition, deforming and reforming.

2. Which of these is an example of a wastage method used in manufacturing?

A) Vacuum forming a plastic tray
B) Turning a metal rod on a lathe to make a bolt
C) Spot welding a car body panel
D) Folding a sheet of aluminum to make a box

KEY TERMS

Addition: When material is added to build or make a product

Deforming: When a material is shaped without adding or removing material

Reforming: When a shaped material is shaped again without adding or removing material

Wastage: The process of cutting away material to leave the shape you want

2·2·3 Joining

LEARNING AIMS

By the end of this unit, you should:

✓ Understand both permanent and temporary methods of joining different materials

✓ Be able to select and justify the use of appropriate methods of permanently or temporarily joining different materials together for a product

Joining and assembly are used to connect two or more parts, or materials, together to make a complete product or structure. These processes can be *temporary* (can be taken apart) or *permanent* (cannot easily be separated without damage).

TEMPORARY JOINING

Temporary joining of materials can be achieved using components that have a screw thread. Examples include screws, nuts and bolts, set screws (Figure 1) and knock-down (KD) fittings (commonly found in flat-packed furniture).

Δ **Figure 1** There are lots of different types of nuts, bolts and set screws

PERMANENT JOINING

Permanent joining of materials can be achieved using a process that is not easily reversed. Processes such as welding (Figure 2), brazing and soldering involve using heat to create a bond between metals. All forms of riveting are also considered to be permanent joining processes. Nailing pieces of timber together is a method of permanent joining, along with any type of adhesive added between parts of material.

Δ **Figure 2** Welding steel

HOLDING DEVICES: JIGS

A **jig** is a custom-made fixture or device that guides the position and movement of a tool (such as a drill or saw) during a manufacturing or woodworking process (Figure 3). It ensures accuracy, repeatability and speed when making multiple identical parts.

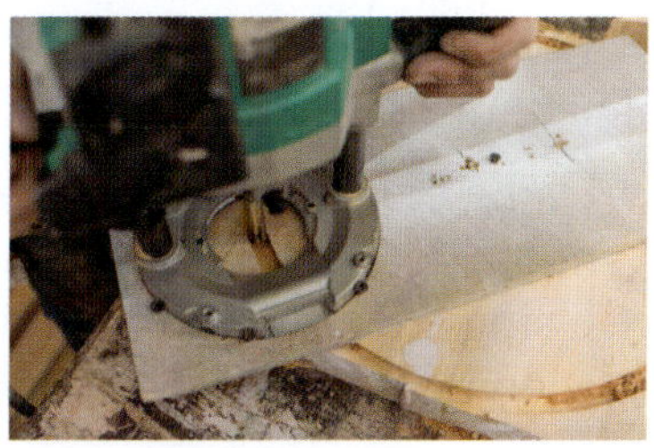

Δ **Figure 3** A jig being used to create a new product

JOINING METAL

Brazing

Brazing is a process of joining two or more pieces of metal by melting and flowing a filler metal into the joint (Figure 4). The process involves melting a third metal (often brass) over, and into, the two pieces to be joined. This only works if the two pieces to be joined together have a higher melting point than the brass being used to join them.

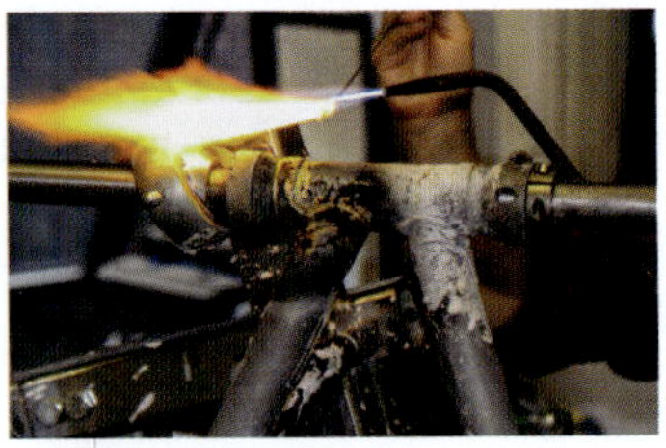

△ **Figure 4** Brazing is used to create bike frames.

The pieces are heated together using a brazing torch, the brass is introduced into the joint, and the heat source remains in place until the brass melts. Once the brass is molten (melted), the heat is removed and the brass cools and solidifies, bonding the two pieces being together.

Soldering

Soldering is a type of brazing which uses a lower-melting-point alloy as its filler material. Soldering is often weaker than brazing, so it needs to be selected with this in mind.

Soft soldering is used to join copper, brass or tinplate. It is also the way electronic components are joined (Figure 5). Soft solder typically melts at around 200 °C. Once heated, solder will 'flow' along the cleaned components, bonding them together once it solidifies.

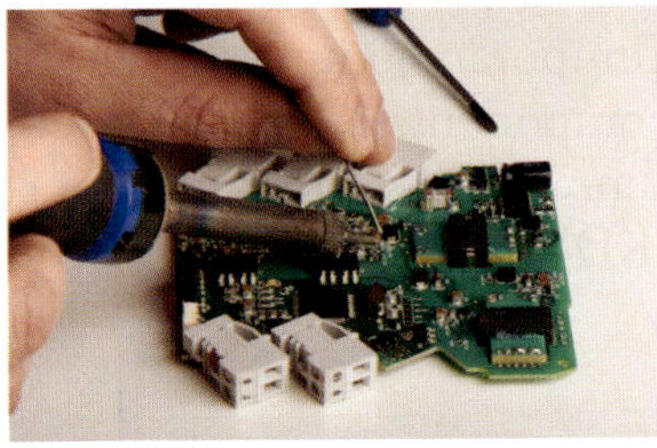

△ **Figure 5** Soldering is used in making circuits for electrical products.

Welding

Welding differs from soldering as the metals to be joined are heated to extreme temperatures, causing the edges of the components to melt. A filler material is used in the process to fill any gaps between the edges of the parts being joined. Inert gas is often blown over the weld as it forms to keep the molten material clean and free from oxidation during cooling. Oxidation is the name given to the process whereby oxygen interacts with the surface of a metal, and it causes that metal to corrode.

There are different types of welding process:

- Using electricity (electric-arc) to generate a spark to melt the metals to be joined.
- Using a flammable gas mixed with oxygen (oxy-acetylene) to achieve the same outcome.

Different methods are more suited to different types of metal due to the differences in melting points of metals (Figure 6). As the temperatures generated in welding are very high, it is very important that people joining materials by welding wear appropriate eye protection.

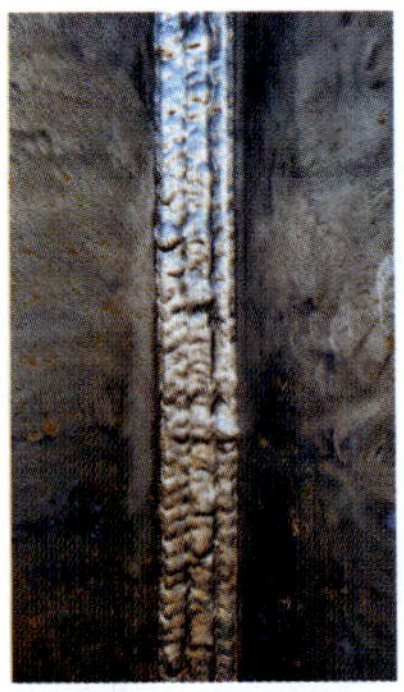

a

b

△ **Figure 6 a** Weld filler and **b** electric-arc weldin

Riveting

Riveting is a method of permanently joining two or more pieces of material (usually metal or leather) by inserting a metal pin (called a rivet) through holes and deforming the end to hold the parts together (Figure 7).

△ **Figure 7** Riveted structural steel

Once set, a rivet forms a strong, durable joint that resists loosening under vibration. (See Figures 8–11.)

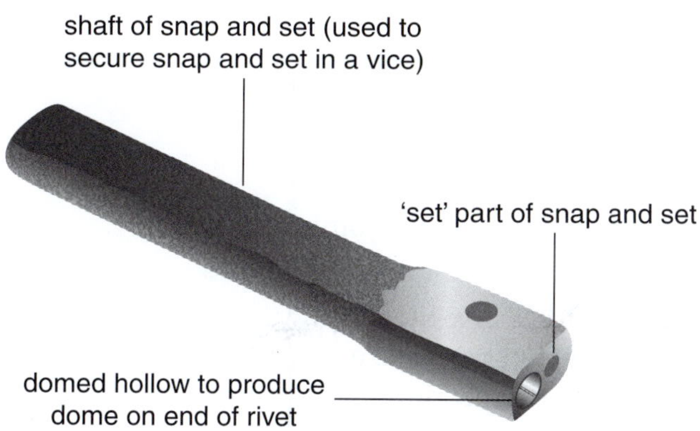

△ **Figure 8** A rivet snap and set

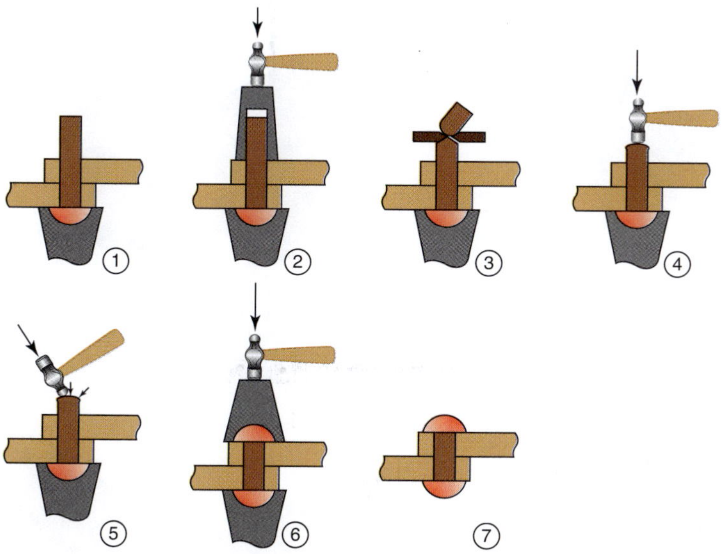

△ **Figure 9** Seven key stages for creating a riveted joint using a ball pein hammer and a snap and set.

△ **Figure 10** A rivet gun

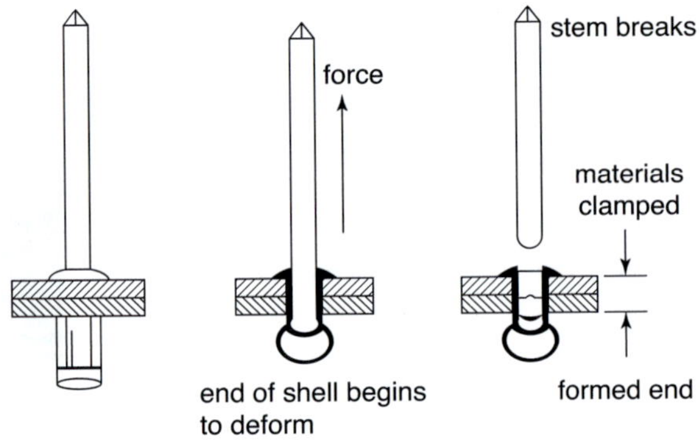

△ **Figure 11** How a pop rivet works

JOINING TIMBER

Wood joints

There are many different types of wood joint. Some require little or no adhesive to hold them together (for example, dovetail joints). Other joints with a bigger surface area will need more adhesive to be used to help with strength (for example, comb/finger joint).

There are also joining mechanisms designed to be used in manufactured boards. These provide a positive mechanical lock joining the two pieces together (for example, a cam lock).

Consider a piece of carcase furniture (furniture with a box-like construction, such as chest of drawers or bookcases). There are a number of broad types of joints that can be seen in the product: corner joints and joints where pieces of timber join each other (Figures 12 and 13).

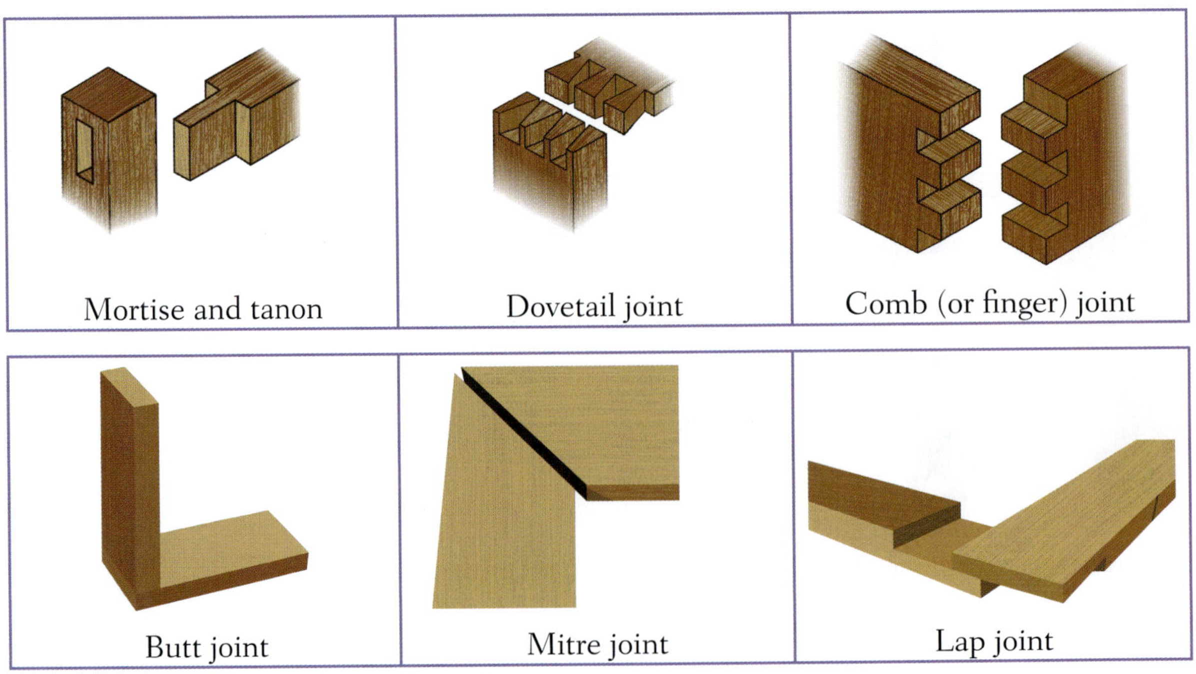

△ **Figure 12** Common corner joints used in wood

Δ **Figure 13** Mortise and tenon joints are often used for chair corners.

Knock-down (KD) fittings

Wood joints have been around for thousands of years! However, as technology has advanced, so have the methods available for joining wood. The rise in the popularity of flat-packed furniture has led to a need for different methods of joining components that can be easily carried out in the home with the minimum amount of equipment.

When products are shipped with knock-down (KD) fittings, it is beneficial to try to minimise the number of different fittings used. This is cheaper for the manufacturer as they do not have to carry large stocks of different components, or use a lot of different machinery in order to machine out the holes and slots into which the fittings locate. Also, from an end-user perspective, there is less chance of using the wrong fitting if a lower number of fitting types are used.

The simplest form of KD fitting is a corner block (Figure 14). These are usually manufactured in plastic. However, a square section piece of timber can be used if it is drilled in the appropriate places. Both are applied in the same way (Figure 15).

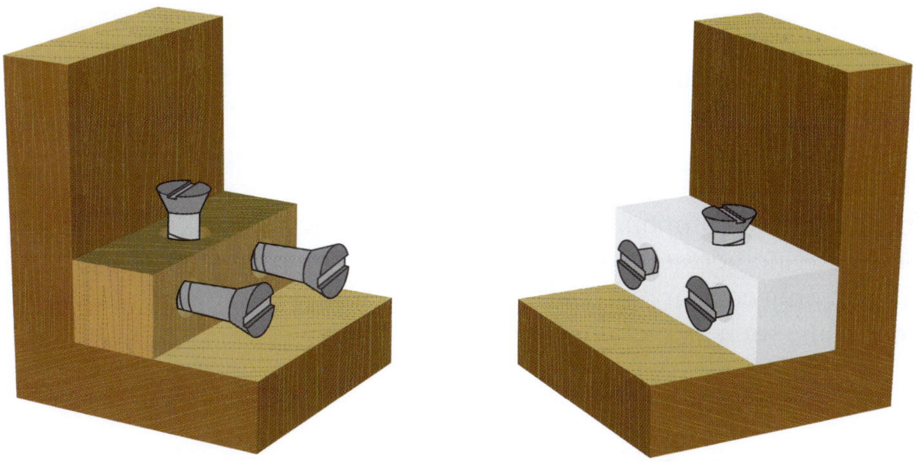

Δ **Figure 14** A wooden corner block (left); a plastic corner block (right)

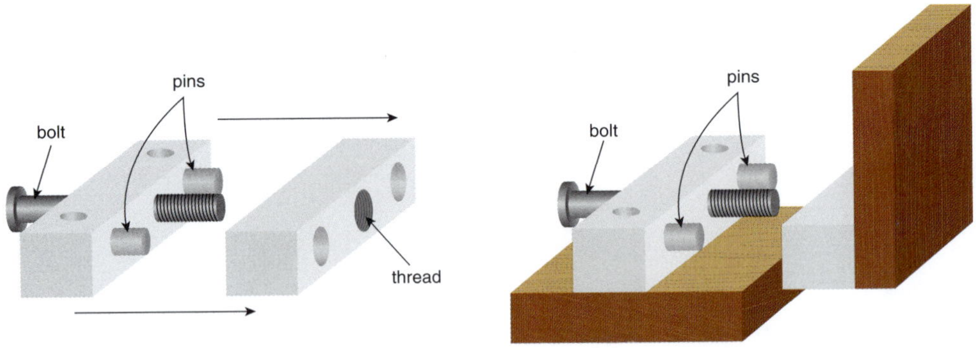

△ **Figure 15** A two-piece corner block technique

Scan fittings are used to pull together pieces securely (Figure 16). They are so effective that the join they create can be considered permanent in some cases. A steel barrel fitting is inserted into one piece of the work. In the middle of it is a threaded hole into which a screw is inserted through the second piece of work and tightened.

One of the more favoured types of KD fitting, in manufactured boards and sheet material, is a cam lock (Figure 17). This requires drilling a shallow hole, into which the cam is located, and another hole in the adjoining piece, into which a specially manufactured bolt type piece is located. These two pieces of the fitting are brought together and then the cam is turned, locking the pieces in position.

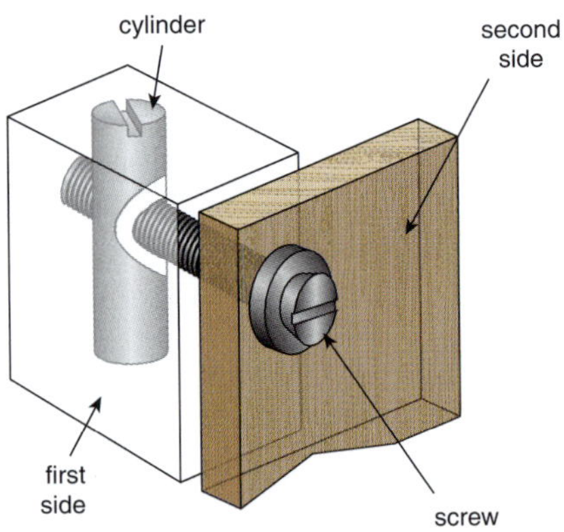

△ **Figure 16** A scan fitting

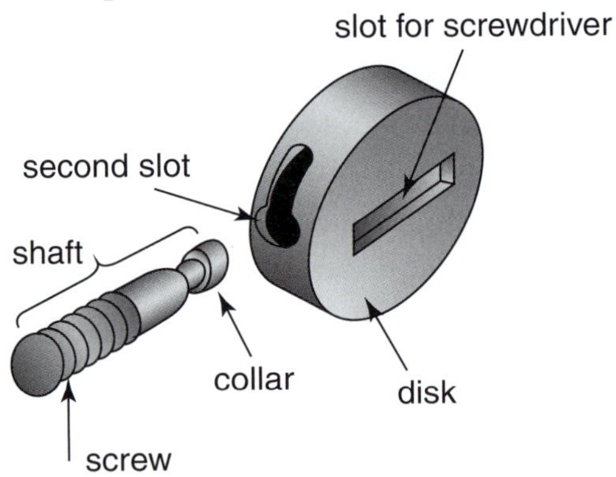

△ **Figure 17** A cam lock in an open position

PRE-MANUFACTURED COMPONENTS

There are a few pre-manufactured components that can also be used to join materials together. These include screws, nails, nuts, bolts, hinges and catches. Some will join only certain materials, and others will join a range of dissimilar materials, such as metal to wood, for example.

Threaded fasteners

There are a large range of screws and bolts with different profile head shapes (Table 1). Some of these are designed to lie flush (there is no part sticking out or sunk in). Screws have a pointed tip and are designed to locate and drive into a surface, so they are not suitable for use on metal.

Often it is necessary to drill a pilot hole into the material before driving in the screw. This makes it locate in the right place and avoids splitting the material. Bolts have a flat profile at the end opposing the head. The thread is uniform all the way down the bolt, as it is designed for the nut to be attached.

Type of threaded fastener	How it works	What it looks like
Wood screw	Screws with a smooth shank below the head, they have a tapered point and are used in wood	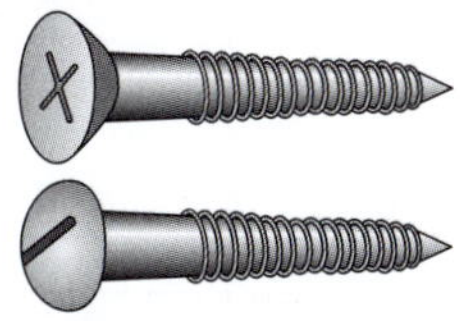
Machine screw	Screws with threads up to the head; they do not taper and are designed to be used with nuts or threaded holes	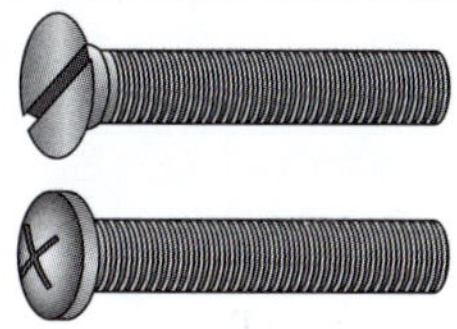

△ **Table 1** Threaded fasteners

As well as a range of threaded fasteners, there is a range of different types of screwdriver (Figure 18). These vary by having different shaped end profiles to meet different shaped holes and slots in the head of the screw. In addition to slotted screwdrivers, there are Pozidriv and Phillips screwdrivers, both of which are cross-headed screwdrivers. There are spanners and sockets for use with bolts. There are unusual and unique head shapes and fittings to prevent casual users without specialist tools from removing them. These are mostly used for security and safety.

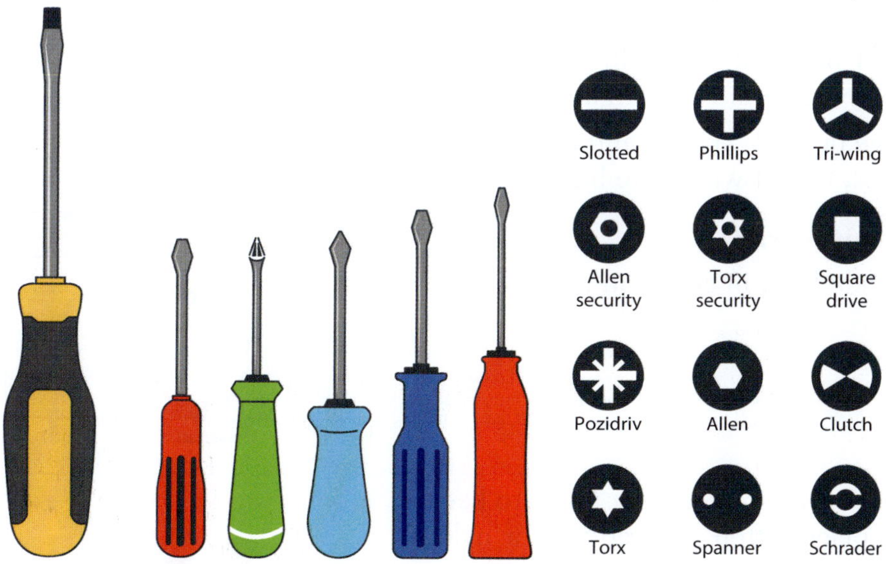

△ **Figure 18** Types of screwdriver and head

Woodscrews come in sizes called 'gauges'. This is a measurement of the diameter of the metal from which the screw is manufactured (Table 2). In addition to this measurement they also come in a range of set lengths, usually specified in millimetres (Table 3).

Diameter	
Gauge	**Metric (mm)**
2	2·0
3	2·5
4	3·0
6	3·5
8	4·0
10	5·0
12	5·5
14	6·5

△ **Table 2** Woodscrew diameters

Common lengths	
Imperial (inches)	**Metric (mm)**
$\frac{1}{4}-\frac{1}{2}$	6·5–13
$\frac{3}{8}-1$	10–25
$\frac{1}{4}-\frac{11}{2}$	6·5–38
$\frac{3}{8}-\frac{21}{2}$	10–65
$\frac{3}{8}-\frac{31}{2}$	10–90
$\frac{1}{2}-4$	13–100
$\frac{3}{4}-4$	19–125
$\frac{11}{4}-6$	32–150

Table 3 Woodscrew lengths

Nuts and bolts are much simpler. They are described by their length and their diameter. If they are metric (in millimetres), then the diameter has the letter 'M' before it. For example, a bolt that is M5 × 45 mm has a thread diameter of 5 mm and a length of 45 mm.

Nuts also come in a range of sizes, shapes and profiles, each being designed for different jobs, two of which are highlighted in Table 4.

Type of nut	How it works	What it looks like
Hex	Six-sided nut in common usage	
Nylon insert lock	A nut with a nylon inner piece to keep it in place (often referred to as a 'nyloc nut')	

△ **Table 4** Types of nut

Nails

Nails are used in timber, or to fix things to timber (Table 5). They tend to be used more in softwood than hardwood, as they can bend and distort in hardwoods due to the dense nature of hardwoods. Nails come in sizes specified by their length in millimetres.

Type of nail	How it works	What it looks like
Oval wire nail	A long nail used to make timber products. Its oval shape means it does not tend to split the timber when hammered in. The longer it is, the harder it becomes to drive deeper into timber. The head lies flush with the surface of the wood into which it is being hammered.	
Panel pin	By far the most common method of joining timber with nails in schools, these are small and light and often used in conjunction with an adhesive. They are designed to lie flush with the surface of the material into which they are being secured.	

Δ **Table 5** Types of nail

Hinges

Hinges also come in a variety of different shapes, materials and sizes (Figures 19 and 20). They are used to connect two pieces of material that need to move. Hinges can be mounted onto wood and screwed into place or mounted onto metal and secured with nuts and bolts.

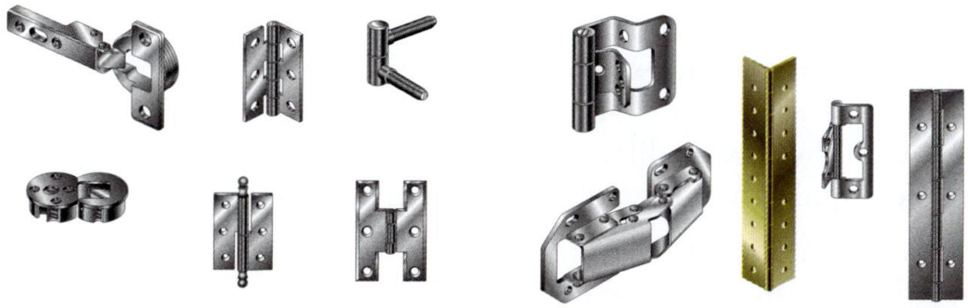

Δ **Figure 19** Types of hinge

a **b**

Δ **Figure 20** Hinges: **a** mounted in a rebated slot, so it is virtually hidden; **b** surface mounted and decorative

Catches, locks and latches

These are used to secure lids to boxes and close doors on cabinets. They come in different shapes, sizes and materials (Table 6).

It is important to know what the exact function of the catch is to ensure the correct one is selected:

- Is it to hold something in place, open or closed?
- Or is it to secure something needing a key?

It is also important to consider the thickness of the material being joined by the catch. Can the catch be placed into the material, or must it be placed inside, or outside?

Type of lock or latch	How it is used	What it looks like
Decorative swing latch	These can be very simple and plain, or decorative and ornate. They are quick to fix and easy to open and sit outside of the product.	
Mortise chest lock	These provide a secure locking mechanism between two pieces of material, and they require a key to operate them.	

△ **Table 6** Types of lock and latch

ADHESIVES

Adhesives are used to join materials by gluing them together. There are many different types of adhesives. Some set by exposure to the air (they dry out), some have a spirit-based element that evaporates allowing the adhesive to harden, and others work by mixing different chemicals and forcing a chemical reaction to occur, allowing the adhesive to set.

As a result of this, some adhesives take longer to set than others. It is also important to consider health and safety here. As spirit-based adhesives dry, the fumes produced during the drying process will often be flammable and not good to human health if inhaled. This is one of the reasons it is very important to use adhesives in a well-ventilated room. (See Table 7.)

TOP TIP

Always choose a joining method suitable for the material, strength required, and whether the joint needs to be permanent or temporary.

Always consider the wood's grain direction and allow for expansion and contraction to prevent cracking or weakening the joint.

Adhesive	Used for
Acrylic cement	Joining of acrylic and some other types of plastic; the adhesive dissolves the surface of the plastic parts being joined and it fuses
Contact adhesive	Joining Polystyrene and fabrics; it can also be used for fixing layers, or coatings, of plastic to a wooden base
Epoxy resin	Joining metals and plastics; it is waterproof and comes in different parts that need to be mixed by the end user
PVA (polyvinyl acetate)	Construction and assembly of timber products; some PVA adhesives are water-resistant
Synthetic resin	Joining timber where PVA is not suitable; it is water-resistant and it needs to be mixed prior to application

△ **Table 7** Types of adhesive

SKILLS ACTIVITY

Fixtures and fittings for flat-packed furniture

Design a piece of flat-packed furniture with a hinged section (a door or a lid). Justify which fixings you would use to assemble the piece you have designed. Then, using the internet, work out the total cost of the fixtures and fittings you need.

KNOWLEDGE CHECK

1. Compare the differences between permanent and temporary fastenings.
2. Describe **one** difference between welding and brazing.
3. Name **three** different types of corner joints that can be made from wood. Suggest **two** alternative KD fittings that could be used in their place.
4. Explain what the gauge of a screw represents.

KEY TERMS

Jig: Holds something in place for the same task to be performed repeatedly or more accurately – for example, drilling a hole

2·2·4 Finishing

LEARNING AIMS

By the end of this unit, you should:

✓ Be able to select and use appropriate decorative and protective finishes
✓ Understand the use of self-finishing materials

Finishing is the final process carried out on a product's surface to improve its appearance, protect it or prepare it for use.

It is the last step that enhances function, durability and aesthetics, to:

- protect the material (from moisture, rust, UV, wear)
- improve appearance (shine, colour, smoothness)
- make cleaning easier
- add special properties (for example, anti-slip, waterproofing).

TYPES OF FINISH

There are many different types of finish that can be applied to a product or material. The finish used depends on what it is designed to achieve – for example, improve how it looks or strengthen the surface.

Tables 1–3 are grouped by material: timber, metal and polymer. They show a range of suitable finishes for each material, giving examples and a brief description of the application process needed.

Timber

Finish	Material	How it is applied	Why it is applied	Examples in action	What it looks like
Wax polish	Any wood	Buffing or by hand with a cloth	Aesthetic appeal; wax adds a dull sheen to bring out the grain of the timber	Interior doors, furniture	
French polish	Usually, hardwoods like mahogany	Several very thin layers are applied, usually by hand with a cloth	Gives a high-gloss finish	Expensive furniture	
Varnish	All wood	Spray, brush or roller in thin coats	Weather protection	Boat decking	

Finish	Material	How it is applied	Why it is applied	Examples in action	What it looks like
Wood stain	All wood	Spray or brush	To apply colour or to bring out the wood grain	Indoor and outdoor furniture	
Exterior wood stain	Used on both hardwood and softwood	Applied with a brush or spray	Used as a preservative to protect the wood	Garden furniture, fencing panels	
Oil (teak, Danish, vegetable or linseed)	Any wood	Often applied with a cloth, although it can be sprayed onto larger surfaces for an even coat	Longer lasting than surface finishes; enhances the aesthetic appeal of a material	Tradition-ally lin-seed oil is used on cricket bats; vegetable oil can be used on cooking utensils	
Paint (oil- or water-based)	Any wood	Brush or spray	To add a protective coating that improves visual appeal	Internal doors and frames	
Cellulose sealant	Any wood; particularly good for porous surfaces such as MDF	Brush or spray	To seal the surface, usually prior to a further finish being applied	Furniture	

Δ **Table 1** Finishes for woods

Metal

Finish	Material	How it is applied	Why it is applied	Examples in action	What it looks like
Galvanis-ing	Iron, steel	Via a chemical process which coats the base material with zinc	Provides a good rust and corrosion-resistant finish	Hinges and locks, nails, nuts and screws, car bodies	
Anodising	Typically aluminium	Via electrolysis, using acid and electrical current to build protective layers onto the base material	To increase resistance to corrosion; also an opportunity to add colour	Torches, smartphones, cookware and jewellery	
Electro-plating	Typically iron and steel	Chemically, using electricity, to add layers of other metal (typically nickel or chromium) over the top of the base layer	The additional layer helps to prevent rust and corrosion, and the finish can be highly polished	Chrome plating of motorbike wheels or engine parts	
Paint	Any metal	Spray or brush	Prevent corrosion or enhance the appearance	Metal gates	
Oil/grease	Any metal	Sprayed, rubbed or smeared onto exposed surface areas	Applied as a protective layer to prevent corrosion	Moving engine parts	
Polish	Any metal	Machine buffing or by hand using a cloth	To add shine to the material	Copper, bronze or brass ornaments, jewellery	
Plastic dip coating	Any metal	Usually the metallic object is dipped into a tank of thermo polymer coating, removed, and left to cool	To enhance ergonomic features (make things easier or safer to hold), or make weather-resistant	Plastic-coated handles	
Powder coating	Any metal	Powder is applied via an electrostatic spray gun; the product is then heated, and the powder melts	To add a hard, protective coating	Washing machines and fridge freezers	

△ **Table 2** Finishes for metals

Polymer

Finish	Material	How it is applied	Why it is applied	Example in action
Buffing compound/ polish	Injection moulded and shaped plastics	Buffing wheel or hand-polished with a soft cloth	To remove any rough or sharp edges, remove static dust, to add extra shine for visual appeal	

Δ **Table 3** Finishes for plastics

CHOOSING AN APPROPRIATE FINISH

Choosing the most suitable finish is very important. To decide, there are two key considerations:

- *The material*: Before you can select an appropriate finish, you need to know which type of material it will be applied to. Use Tables 1–3 to support your choice, as well as reading the manufacturer's instructions to ensure an appropriate finish is selected. Selecting an incompatible finish may damage the material or make it ineffective.
- *Function*: In selecting a finish, you must understand why you are applying it. Is the finish required for aesthetics or visual appeal? Is it for indoor or outdoor use? You need to know how the product will be used and select a finish that will enhance its function.

SELF-FINISHING MATERIALS

New specialist materials are being developed constantly. These plastic-based materials have been engineered specifically to have a 'self-finish'. For example, rather than spraying it with a finish after manufacture in order to make it waterproof, Gortex® is a **self-finished** fabric that has been engineered to be water-resistant.

A common use for these new synthetic materials is personal protective equipment (PPE), to protect people working in hazardous and dangerous jobs. Another example of a self-finished material is Nomex®, which has been engineered to be resistant to heat (Figure 1).

Δ **Figure 1** A firefighter's PPE clothing is made from Nomex®.

HEALTH AND SAFETY

Before using any finish, it is very important to read the manufacturer's instructions carefully. **Preparation** is not just about the material, it also means thinking about yourself and the environment you are working in.

Some finishes may be solvent-based and may be flammable, hazardous or toxic. You must follow the manufacturer's recommendations and take precautions to protect yourself (Figure 2). You may need to:

Δ **Figure 2** Always read the health and safety instructions on products you use.

- wear gloves, a face mask or overalls
- consider the environment you are working in: Is it well ventilated? Do you need to protect the work surface?

Refer to unit 2.2.5 for more on health and safety.

TOP TIP

A common mistake made in the application of a finish is the lack of thorough preparation.

A really high-quality outcome takes time. If applying multiple coats of a paint, varnish or stain, apply a series of thin, even coats. Allow each coat to fully dry before applying the next.

Always prepare the surface properly (for example, clean, sand, degrease) before applying any finish – good preparation gives the best result.

SKILLS ACTIVITY

Identifying finishes and their functions

Choose an industrially manufactured product that is in the room where you are working. List all the materials used in its construction. For each material, list the type of finish used and explain its function. Why has it been applied? Describe the process for each finish you have listed.

REFLECTIVE LOG

Write about a finish that you have used in your own work.

- How did you decide which finish to apply? What preparation did you undertake? How was the finished applied?
- If your product were manufactured on a larger scale through commercial production, would the same finish be appropriate? Would the finish be applied in the same way?

KNOWLEDGE CHECK

1. Give **four** reasons why a finish is applied.
2. Name a finish that can be applied to timber, and state how and why it is applied.
3. Explain a commercial method of finishing metal. Name the type of metal and a reason why the finish is applied.
4. Name **one** example of a self-finishing material and explain **one** advantage.

KEY TERMS

Preparation: The process of making the surface of the material ready before applying a finish

Self-finishing materials: Materials that have their desired finish built in during manufacture and do not need additional finishing processes

2·2·5 Safe working practices

LEARNING AIMS

By the end of this unit, you should:

✓ Show safe use of hand tools, power tools, machinery and computer-aided manufacture (CAM) equipment

✓ Select and use appropriate PPE when working practically

Why is health and safety important? Health and safety ensures that everyone can work safely without unnecessary risks to their wellbeing. It protects people from harm at work, in workshops, factories and other environments. Owners and managers have a responsibility to ensure that people working in these environments are safe.

In most countries, there are important health and safety laws, legislation and guidelines to protect employers and employees (workers) in the workplace. Health and safety organisations are responsible for the encouragement, regulation and enforcement of workplace health, safety and welfare.

Most schools will have a set of health and safety workshop rules and regulations. These are put in place to make the school workshop a safe place to work, be creative and make products.

RISK ASSESSMENT

A **risk assessment** involves evaluating potential hazards and implementing necessary safety measures (Figure 1). It helps keep people safe by thinking ahead about what could go wrong and how to prevent harm.

△ **Figure 1** Example of a risk assessment

SKILLS ACTIVITY

Safety check hunt

Complete a 'Safety check hunt'. Identify a safety hazard in a design and technology space and record the safety steps that should be put in place to keep people safe. How many different types of safety controls can you record around your school or classroom? Here are some examples to get you thinking:

- Where is the storage area for chemicals (Figure 2)?
- Where is your storage area for tools, equipment and materials?
- Where are the emergency stop buttons to cut the power to machines (Figure 3)?
- Can you locate how many fire extinguishers there are?
- What do the safety signs inform you of?
- What personal protective equipment (PPE) is located in your design and technology space?

△ **Figure 2** A chemical cupboard

△ **Figure 3** Know where the emergency stop button is

PERSONAL PROTECTIVE EQUIPMENT (PPE)

PPE is the clothing or gear worn to protect you from hazards when working (Table 1). It helps prevent injury or harm when working with tools, machinery, chemicals or in hazardous environments.

Goggles, aprons/overalls, dust masks, visors, sensible footwear and ear defenders are all useful pieces of equipment depending on the activity taking place. Table 1 summarises the symbols you will need to know.

Workshop operation	Hazard/Risk	Suitable PPE	Sign/Symbol
General practical activity in the Design and Technology environment	Sharp tools or edges of materials causing cuts; protection of clothing from dust, paint, chemicals	Apron or overall	
Drilling, wasting, sanding, polishing	Dust, sparks, particles in your eyes	Goggles/visor	
Handling hot or sharp materials, using adhesives	Potential to burn fingers, cutting hands when handling materials, solvents on skin	Leather gloves / disposable gloves	
Drilling, wasting, sanding, polishing	Breathing in dust, sparks, particles	Dust mask	
General workshop noise, specific noisy task (grinding)	Ear damage from prolonged exposure to noise	Ear defenders	

△ **Table 1** Suitable PPE for particular workshop operations

WORKSHOP SAFETY AND SIGNAGE

As well as the symbols for PPE, there are many other safety symbols that you may see in a workshop environment (Figure 4).

a

b

△ **Figure 4** Safety symbols you might see in a workshop: **a** fire extinguisher symbol; **b** First Aid symbol

COSHH symbols and signage

In the workshop, you will see symbols relating to **control of substances hazardous to health (COSHH)** (Figure 5).

COSHH is a UK regulation that requires employers and workers to control exposure to substances that could harm health. It helps protect people from hazardous substances at work, such as chemicals, dusts, fumes and biological agents.

a **b** **c**

∆ **Figure 5** COSHH symbols warn of hazardous substances: **a** corrosive; **b** flammable; **c** toxic

DEMONSTRATING SAFE USE OF HAND TOOLS

It is important when using saws (Figure 6), chisels, files, screwdrivers and hammers, etc., to:

- Inspect tools for damage (cracks, loose handles, worn edges).
- Use the correct tool for the task.
- Cut, strike or push *away* from your body.
- Keep tools sharp and clean.
- Secure the workpiece using a vice or clamp.
- Wear safety goggles to protect your eyes.
- Return tools to storage after use.

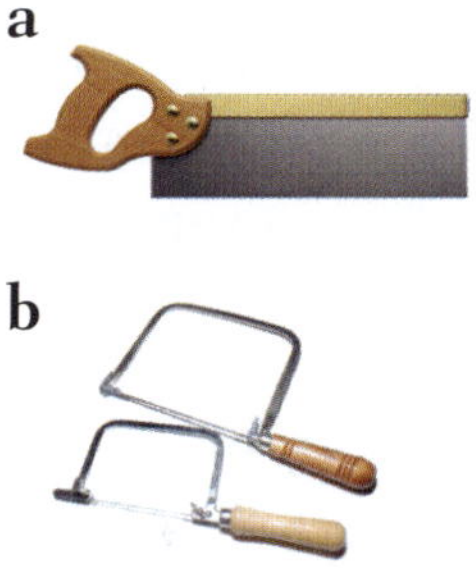

∆ **Figure 6** Examples of saws you might use
a tenon saw
b coping saw

DEMONSTRATING SAFE USE OF POWER TOOLS

It is important when using a hand drill (Figure 7a), jigsaw (Figure 7b), sander and cordless screwdriver, etc., to:

- Check cables, plugs and battery packs for damage.
- Make sure guards and safety features are in place.
- Use both hands to hold and control the tool.
- Let the tool reach full speed before starting to cut or drill.
- Disconnect power before changing bits or blades.
- Wear PPE – goggles, ear defenders and dust mask, if needed.
- Keep workspaces free of clutter.

∆ **Figure 7** Examples of tools you might use
a hand drill
b jigsaw

DEMONSTRATING SAFE USE OF MACHINERY

It is important when using a pillar drill (Figure 8), bandsaw, disc sander and lathe to:

- Only use machinery if you are trained and authorised.

- Check that guards are fitted and working.
- Set up and secure material properly (clamps, jigs).
- Adjust machine settings before switching on.
- Keep hands clear of moving parts (use push sticks if needed).
- Tie back long hair, remove jewellery, no loose clothing.
- Wear PPE – goggles, ear defenders.
- Stand in a safe position (not directly in line with cutting blades).
- Use emergency stop button if needed.
- Never leave machine running unattended.

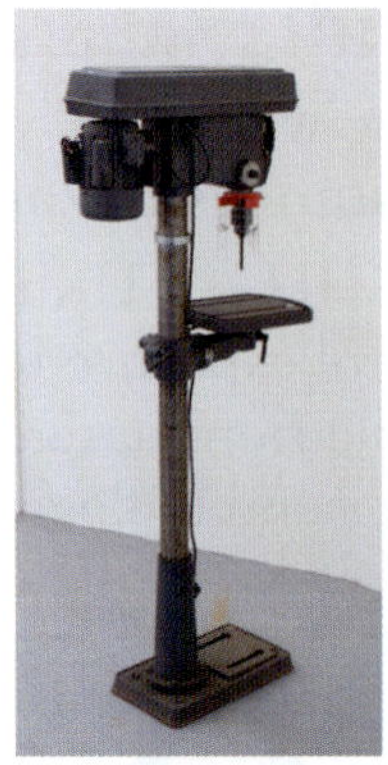

△ **Figure 8** A pillar drill

DEMONSTRATING SAFE USE OF COMPUTER-AIDED MANUFACTURE (CAM)

CAM equipment includes laser cutters, CNC routers, CNC lathes and 3D printers (Figure 9). These machines are computer-controlled, but they still need careful setup and safe operation.

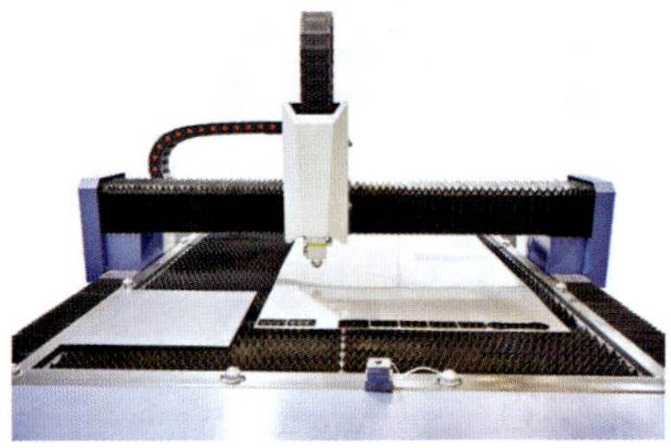

△ **Figure 9** A laser cutter

Demonstrating the safe use of CAM software focuses less on physical safety. It focuses more on ergonomic practices, data security and operating the software correctly:

- Only use CAM equipment after training and permission from a supervisor or teacher.
- Double-check the design file – make sure dimensions, toolpaths and settings are correct before starting.
- Place and secure material accurately on the machine bed (for example, with clamps or magnets if required).
- Ensure machine covers, shields and guards are closed and in position before starting the job.
- Stand clear while the machine is running – do *not* open its doors or reach inside during operation.
- Keep the area around the machine clean and free from obstacles.
- Watch for warning signs – if the machine makes unusual noises or something seems wrong, *pause or stop immediately* and get help.
- Wear appropriate PPE:
  - o Laser cutter: goggles (if required by the machine type), no loose clothing, good ventilation.
  - o CNC router/lathe: goggles, ear defenders, tie back hair, no jewellery.
- Do not leave CAM equipment running unattended unless permitted and safe to do so.

TOP TIP

1. Always wear PPE as required (for example, goggles, gloves, ear defenders).
2. Keep your workspace clean and tidy.
3. Report any faults or damage immediately.
4. Follow instructions and risk assessments for each tool or machine.
5. PPE must fit properly and be used correctly – damaged or worn-out PPE will not provide proper protection.

SKILLS ACTIVITY

Assessing health and safety

Health and safety is a serious issue for businesses and industry. Consider what impact sustaining injuries have on employers and employees.

1. Think of a range of specific tasks you may undertake in your Design and Technology classroom, and list the appropriate risk assessments and actions that you may consider.
2. Health and safety signs are usually placed in workshops. Can you find any in your workspace? Identify the safety signs and explain what they mean.
3. Look around your Design and Technology classroom at school. Make a list of at least 10 potential health and safety hazards, and the risk assessments you would put in place to avoid any accidents.

DESIGN IN ACTION

The seatbelt

Volvo, the car manufacturer, has always been innovative when it comes to safety. They introduced the seatbelt in 1959 (Figure 10).

Δ **Figure 10** Volvo introduced the seatbelt in 1959.

KNOWLEDGE CHECK

1. Name **two** safety factors that need to be considered when using adhesives to join two pieces of acrylic together.
2. Name **five** items of PPE.
3. Explain what PPE and safety precautions you should consider when soldering an electronic circuit.
4. In school, why are health and safety rules put in place?

KEY TERMS

Control of substances hazardous to health (COSHH): A set of regulations designed to ensure the safe use of hazardous substances

Risk assessment: Process of identifying hazards and evaluating risks to ensure safe working practices

2·3 Commercial manufacturing processes

2·3·1 Commercial manufacturing methods

LEARNING AIMS

By the end of this unit, you should:

- ✓ Demonstrate knowledge of how products can be commercially manufactured from timbers, polymers, metals and smart materials
- ✓ Demonstrate knowledge of forming processes, including injection moulding, steam bending and press forming
- ✓ Demonstrate knowledge of casting processes, including resin, sand and die casting
- ✓ Understand how commercial manufacturing includes assembly aids, automation and heat treatments

What is **commercial manufacturing**? This entails making products in large quantities that are then sold in shops for use in everyday life. This process involves turning materials such as metals, timber and polymers, or components, into finished products, using labour, machinery and tools. Examples of commercial manufacturers include Johnson and Johnson, IKEA, Jaguar and Land Rover.

Producing goods in large quantities helps meet global user demand, but this process also has a significant impact on the environment. The use of assembly lines in factories allows for fast and efficient production, but it often involves high levels of energy consumption, resource use and waste.

Industries, such as pharmaceuticals, automotive, electronics, food and consumer goods, manufacture items including clothing, furniture, packaged foods, mobile phones, cars and medicine. These products are essential to modern life. However, their **mass production** contributes to air and water pollution, greenhouse gas emissions and excessive use of natural resources. Sustainable practices and cleaner technologies are increasingly important to reduce the environmental footprint of manufacturing.

(Refer to unit 2.4.1 for information on different scales of manufacturing production.)

FORMING PROCESSES

Forming processes are important in commercial manufacturing because they allow the transformation of materials (such as metals, plastics, ceramics or composites) into useful products or components.

The goal of forming is often to produce parts that meet specific design needs and material quality for products such as construction (Figure 1).

Injection moulding bottle caps | Compression moulding machine | Blow moulding plastic bottles

△ **Figure 1** Examples of forming processes on plastics

Injection moulding

Injection moulding is a method where molten plastic is injected into a mould to create complex shapes. This process is fast. It can produce complex shapes precisely – creating various products such as phone cases, bottle caps and plastic toys.

Compression moulding

Heated plastic is placed in a mould, then compressed into shape with pressure and heat. The process produces strong products/parts and low waste. This type of moulding can be in seen in electrical parts, car bumpers and panels, and rubber mats.

Blow moulding

Blow moulding creates hollow plastic objects by blowing air into a heated plastic tube inside a mould. The process allows for high output of a specific product to be manufactured and is ideal for hollow-shaped products such as water bottles, containers and fuel tanks.

Steam bending

Steam bending is a woodworking technique where wood is softened with steam, making it flexible enough to bend into curved shapes without breaking (Figure 2). This process is mainly used for bending wood (although it can be used for some plastics) by applying steam to make the material more flexible.

△ **Figure 2** Wood steamed and bent over a form

Press forming

Press forming is a manufacturing process where sheet metal is shaped by being pressed between two dies using high pressure. It uses a mechanical or hydraulic press to shape it into a specific form (Figure 3).

Press forming is also known as 'pressing'.

△ **Figure 3** Press forming a metal sheet

Rolling forming

Metal is gradually shaped by passing it through a series of rollers (Figure 4). Rolling is a metalworking process. Metal is passed through one or more pairs of rolls to reduce the thickness and shape it into a flat sheet or other forms.

△ **Figure 4** Rolling forming a metal sheet

CASTING PROCESSES

Casting is the process of pouring a liquid material (often metal or plastic) into a mould to create a desired shape (Figure 5). It solidifies into the design of the product, or parts of it. This process can create a wide variety of products, ranging from simple to complex shapes.

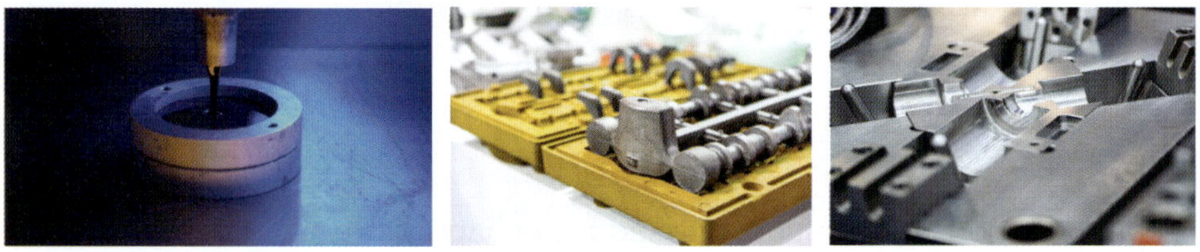

Casting resin into a mould | Sand-casted cam shaft | Die mould for casting automotive parts

△ **Figure 5** Examples of casting processes

Resin casting

Resin casting is a process where liquid plastic (resin) is poured into a mould, allowed to harden (cure), and then removed to create a solid shape. It is useful for making detailed, small-scale items.

Sand casting

Sand casting is a metal casting process where molten metal is poured into a mould made of compacted sand. This shapes the metal as it cools and solidifies. This process is ideal for making large or simple metal parts and is cost-effective.

Die casting

In die casting, molten metal is forced under high pressure into a reusable steel mould (die). It creates precise, smooth and detailed metal parts. This process is best used for high-volume production of precise, durable parts.

HEAT TREATMENTS

Heat treatment is a controlled process used in manufacturing to change the shape of materials, such as metals (Figure 6). This is done by heating and cooling the material. Heating the metal can improve the material's properties, such as strength, hardness, toughness and ductility, making it suitable for products. In commercial manufacturing, heat treatment is used in aerospace, construction, electronics, and other industries.

Heat treatment helps products by:

- improving the materials' properties of hardness, strength, toughness and wear resistance
- extending the lifespan of products due to their improved resistance to wear, fatigue and corrosion – thus, making them more durable
- reducing costs associated with wear, failures and replacements.

Some common heat treatments used in commercial manufacturing include annealing, quenching and tempering.

△ **Figure 6** Heat processes are used to commercially manufacture products, from cutlery to energy supply pipelines.

Annealing

Annealing is a heat treatment process used to soften metals, making them easier to work with. It involves heating the metal to a specific temperature and then cooling it slowly, usually inside the furnace.

Quenching

In quenching, metal is heated to a high temperature and then rapidly cooled by putting it in a cooling medium like water, oil or air. This sudden cooling changes the metal's internal structure, increasing its hardness.

Tempering

Tempering is performed after quenching to reduce brittleness and improve the toughness of a hardened metal. It involves reheating the quenched metal to a lower temperature and then cooling it slowly.

ASSEMBLY AIDS IN COMMERCIAL MANUFACTURING

Fixtures

A fixture is a custom-made tool used to securely hold a workpiece in place during the manufacturing or assembly process (Figure 7). For example, in the automotive industry, a fixture might hold the frame of a vehicle in place during the welding process, ensuring precise welds in a consistent pattern across all vehicle frames.

△ **Figure 7** A welding platen table with fixtures

Jigs

A jig in a school workshop is a custom-made, device used to help perform an operation on a workpiece safely, accurately and repeatedly.

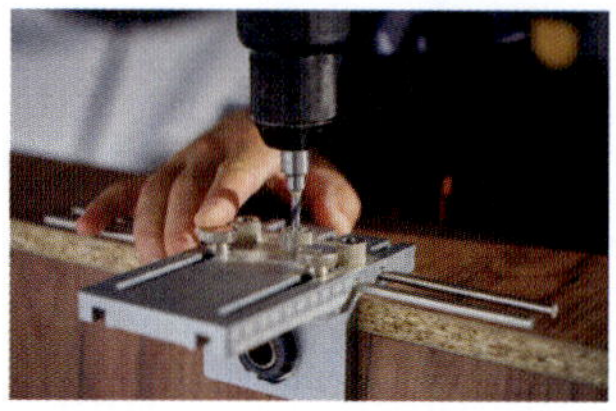

◁ **Figure 8** A jig can be used to ensure accurate and repeatable cutting and drilling

ROBOTICS IN COMMERCIAL MANUFACTURING ASSEMBLY

Commercial manufacturing uses many different systems and computers to help make products. Robotic systems perform tasks in the manufacturing process. These tasks range from simple repetitive actions to complex, high-precision operations. The use of robotics in commercially made products helps improve efficiency, safety and quality.

Robotics are used by many companies, including Apple, Samsung, Ford and BMW. Examples of high-street products made by robotics include mobile phones, cars and food (Figure 9).

△ **Figure 9** Robotics can be used to help make mobile phones

TOP TIP

You will need to carry out good quality control checks for designing and making products.

No customer wants poorly made products! Making and selling these will only lead to customer dissatisfaction, and customers will not buy more products in the future.

SKILLS ACTIVITY

Deconstructing commercial manufacturing

Select an existing product that could be commercially manufactured. Consider its aesthetics, function, materials and how it has been manufactured. Deconstruct the processes that the product has gone through, creating a list as you go.

REFLECTIVE LOG

Justify what you think is the most important commercially manufactured product that is manufactured.

DESIGN IN ACTION

Use of robotics in BMW

BMW operates smart factories globally, including in Germany, USA, China and South Africa. These factories use advanced robotics systems to:

- assemble cars
- paint vehicle bodies
- install electric powertrains
- conduct real-time quality control.

△ **Figure 10** BMW use robotics in manufacturing.

Welding robots

- Assemble car bodies by welding panels with extreme precision (Figures 10 and 11a).
- Improve strength and safety.

Painting robots

- Apply consistent, flawless coats of paint (Figure 11b).
- Reduce material waste and environmental impact.

Assembly line automation

- Robots assist with engine installation, seat mounting and dashboard placement

Collaborative robots (cobots)

- Work side by side with human technicians (Figure 11c).
- Help with tasks such as screwing, gluing and light-fitting.

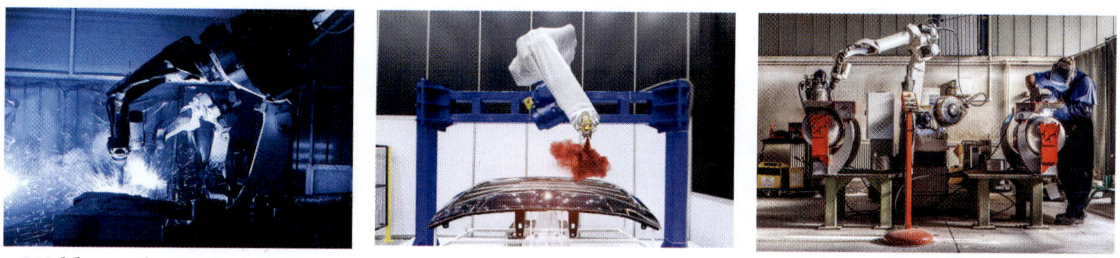

a Welding robot **b** Painting robot **c** Collaborative robot

△ **Figure 11** Use of robotics in commercial manufacturing

KNOWLEDGE CHECK

1. Explain what 'commercial manufacturing' means.
2. Explain what would happen if commercial production did not have robotics available in assembly lines. What would be the impact on production of products on different industries – for example, on the car industry – and the wider impact on society?

KEY TERMS

Commercial manufacturing: Manufacturing method used to produce products in quantity*

Mass production: Manufacturing large quantities of identical products using mechanised processes efficiently

2·4 Product analysis

2·4·1 Understanding product analysis

LEARNING AIMS

By the end of this unit, you should:

✓ Demonstrate an understanding of how to analyse real-world products, the different scales of production and the importance of quality control in a product's life

✓ Demonstrate an understanding of planned and unplanned obsolescence

Real-world products are made from lots of different materials and are a part of everyday life. They range from shoes, bags and clothes to smartphones, cars, Dyson vacuums and everything else we interact with.

Product analysis is the process of looking at a real-world product and analysing it. This requires understanding all the product parts and thinking about the product more deeply than what it is manufactured from. Things you will need to consider are:

- how it works
- who it is for
- how it is made
- how it looks
- how well it does its job.

MAIN SCALES OF PRODUCTION

Scales of production refers to how many products are made and the methods used to make them – from a single handmade item to millions produced by machines.

Different scales of production are chosen depending on:

- the number of products needed
- the complexity of the item
- available tools and labour
- cost-effectiveness
- time.

One-off production or prototype model

One-offs are products that are designed and made for a specific use or situation that will only happen once. Most one-offs are generally handmade, using a wide range of techniques and equipment. Examples include a custom-made bicycle for a particular competition, or an exclusive piece of jewellery (Figure 1).

A prototype is similar to a one-off. A prototype is an early model or sample version of a product that is created to test and evaluate an idea before full production.

△ **Figure 1** One-off production – a precious jewellery Faberge egg.

Batch production

Batch production is when a product is manufactured in a batch of a specific quantity. A batch can range from a few items to many thousands. Batch production usually takes place over a series of workstations. A slight change can be made at one workstation to create a slightly different batch. For example, a baker making 100 loaves of bread might make a batch of 50 wholemeal loaves and 50 ciabattas for sale in a shop (Figure 2).

△ **Figure 2** Batch production of bread

The use of jigs, moulds and templates speed up the process of making batches.

Mass production

Mass production is when identical products are made in large quantities. This could be from a thousand up to millions, depending on the product. For example, nuts and bolts would be made in large amounts for sale (Figure 3). Specialist machines and assembly lines are used for mass production. Assembly line machines are usually expensive to set up. However, the ability to quickly manufacture thousands of copies increases the ability to get the product into shops to sell. This, of course increases sales turnover and profit.

△ **Figure 3** Mass production of hex nuts

Continuous production

Continuous production is when products are made for weeks and even months on end, 24 hours a day, seven days a week. This type of production is heavily automated. The product range is typically small and specialised. An example of continuous manufacturing is the production of fuels, oils, plastics and lubricants from crude oil, such as petrol/gasoline (Figure 4).

△ **Figure 4** Oil refinery plant producing petroleum products 24/7

When designing, it is important to consider the commercial processing that will take place, as this will influence the materials you use and the form and overall aesthetic of a product.

Table 1 illustrates the increasing or decreasing effect that various production methods have on certain aspects of manufacturing products, such as cost and efficiency.

Level of production	Efficiency of process	Labour costs	Workers' skills	Equipment, machines and tooling costs	Product costs
One-off	↓	↑	↑	↓	↑
Batch					
Mass					
Continual					

△ **Table 1** Level of production and costs in relation to scale of production

QUALITY CONTROL AND QUALITY ASSURANCE MEASURES

When manufacturing products, quality control (QC) and **quality assurance** (QA) checks are carried out. This is a process whereby products that have been manufactured are checked to ensure they are of good quality and they meet the required standards to be considered fit for purpose. There are key differences between these checks:

- *Quality control (QC):* Checking products during manufacture to find any faults.
- *Quality assurance (QA):* The system to prevent mistakes and ensure the whole process meets quality standards.

These checks are used to find and fix problems. They are important to protect user safety (Figure 5), as well as maintaining the designer/manufacturer's reputation, reducing waste and saving costs by highlighting mistakes in designs to ensure customer satisfaction.

QA is focused on preventing problems by making sure that the processes used to make products are correct, controlled and consistent. Ensuring everything is going to plan throughout the manufacturing process, by using plans, manufacturing specifications and testing throughout the process.

QC focuses on checking the final product (and sometimes parts during production) to make sure it meets quality standards and is free from errors. This can be achieved throughout the manufacturing process by visually inspecting the parts of the product, ensuring the correct measurements materials, tools, processes and appropriate testing is carried out throughout the manufacturing process. So, once the product is completed, it should meet the requirements of the design brief and manufacturing specification, leading to successfully passing final checks.

◁ **Figure 5** Design meets standards: the child's wooden high chair has been examined to ensure it is safe, reliable, and high quality

PRODUCT LIFE STORY

Think about your phone, your trainers or even a simple pen. Every product has a life story (Figure 6). Knowing these stages helps designers think about how to be kinder to the environment.

The main stages are:

- *Design:* This is where the idea comes from. Designers figure out what the product will do, what it looks like, and what it is made of.
- *Manufacture:* Time to make it! This involves getting the raw materials and turning them into the finished product in a factory.
- *Use and maintenance:* This is when you own and use the product. It includes looking after it and fixing it if it breaks.
- *End-of-life:* What happens when you are done with it? Does it get disassembled? Will it be reused? Will it be recycled into something new? Or will it just end up in landfill?

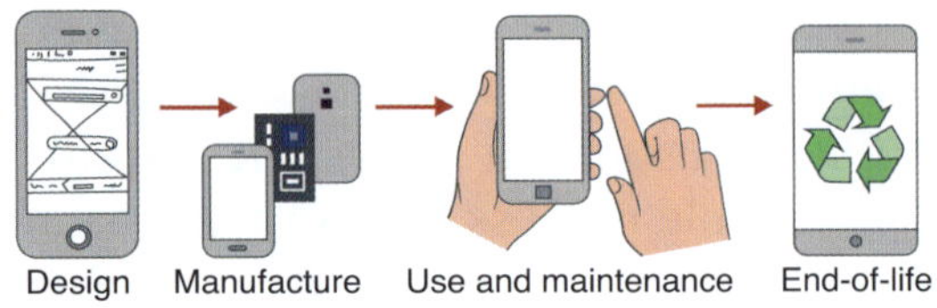

Δ **Figure 6** Product life story of a mobile phone

WHY DON'T THINGS LAST FOREVER? OBSOLESCENCE EXPLAINED

It can be frustrating when products break or get old too quickly. Sometimes this happens by accident, but sometimes it is planned. This is called 'obsolescence'.

Planned obsolescence

Have you ever felt like companies *want* you to buy the newest gadget? Often, they do! This is when products are deliberately designed to stop working well or go out of fashion after a while. Planned obsolescence involves:

- using materials that break easily
- making things hard or impossible to repair (such as gluing parts together or hiding fasteners)
- releasing firmware updates that slow down older models
- bringing out slightly different new versions so your old one feels outdated.

Unplanned obsolescence

Unplanned obsolescence is when a product breaks down unexpectedly. It was not planned, but happens because of:

- mistakes in the design
- a vital component failing sooner than expected
- accidental damage (such as dropping your phone!).

Both types of obsolescence mean more stuff gets thrown away, which uses up resources and creates more waste (Figure 7).

Δ **Figure 7** Much of the waste that ends up being thrown away is difficult to recycle.

Damian's story: Designing for disassembly

Damian, an international school student, conducted product analysis by taking apart a games controller (Figure 8). He found:

- hidden fasteners and glued parts made it difficult to repair
- mixed materials could not be recycled effectively
- non-durable materials.

Δ **Figure 8** Product analysis: Taking apart a games controller

Using design for disassembly principles, Damian designed a modular games controller with the following features:

- *Replaceable parts:* Buttons and joysticks can be swapped out when damaged.
- *Temporary joining methods:* Enables easy disassembly, replacement and repair.
- *Durable materials:* Long-lasting materials increase the lifetime of the controller.
- *Customisation:* Parts can be replaced with new colours or designs.

To communicate his ideas, Damian used exploded drawings to show how the parts fit together (Figures 9 and 10). This made his design easy to understand.

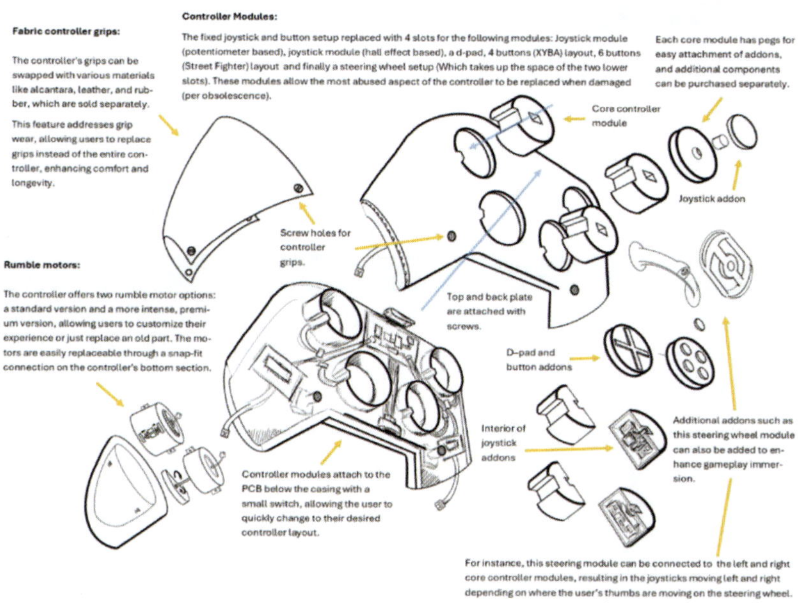

Δ **Figure 9** Damian used exploded drawings to communicate his ideas.

△ **Figure 10** CAD can also be used to create exploded drawings.

Damian used 3D printing to test his models with users and develop his idea further (Figure 11).

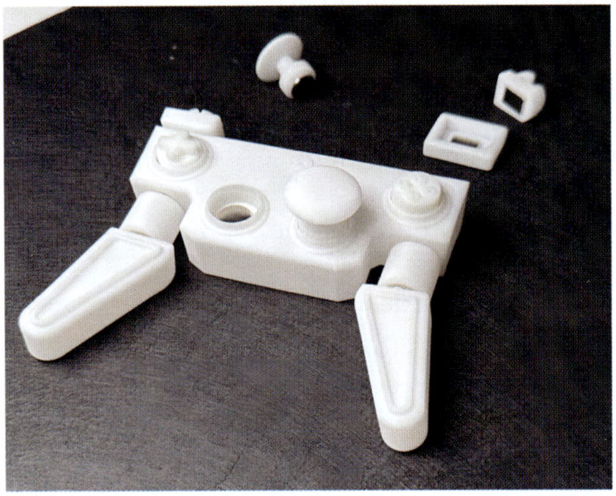

△ **Figure 11** Damian used his CAD files to 3D print his prototypes to test with users.

Damian's work demonstrates how design for disassembly can reduce waste and combat planned obsolescence while inspiring creative, sustainable solutions.

TOP TIP

When analysing a product, think of the person/user it is intended for. What problem does it solve? There are also quick frameworks to help with this process such as: ACCESSFM (refer to unit 1.2.2).

DESIGN IN ACTION

Cool idea: Repair cafes!

Instead of just throwing broken things away, what if you could fix them? That is the idea behind 'Repair Cafes'. These are free meet-ups where volunteers help people fix their broken stuff – for free! – anything from toasters to clothes to bikes. Repair Cafes fight against planned obsolescence by:

- making repair normal – showing that fixing things is possible and worthwhile
- cutting down waste – less stuff ends up in landfills
- sharing skills – people learn how to fix things themselves
- bringing people together – they are friendly places that build community.

Repair Cafes are a great way to make products last longer, saving resources and helping the environment. They challenge the idea that we always need something new.

Students can make a difference too! Marc, a design student, started a Repair Cafe in his international school (Figure 12). Marc and his team of repairers fix broken items for teachers and students. Could you start something similar in your school? It is a great way to think about planned obsolescence, practise design and technology skills, and help your school community.

△ **Figure 12** Marc's Repair Cafe

SKILLS ACTIVITY

Product manufacture

Look at the products in Figures 13 and 14. Discuss with a partner how you think each is manufactured.

△ **Figure 13** A set of disposable biro pens

△ **Figure 14** A stack of magazines

KNOWLEDGE CHECK

1. Identify the four stages of a product's life.
2. Explain how planned obsolescence impacts the environment.
3. Justify which method of production is best for manufacturing an aluminium drinks can.
4. Identify **three** advantages of mass production.
5. Explain a disadvantage of a one-off product.
6. Suggest **two** ways Damian's design follows design for disassembly principles.

KEY TERMS

Quality assurance: Checks that are done during a manufacturing process to ensure the product meets the customers' expectations*

Scale of production: The number of identical products made - one-off/prototype, batch, mass, continuous

Unplanned obsolescence: A product breaks down unexpectedly

2·5 Use of technology

2·5·1 Understanding the use of technology

LEARNING AIMS

By the end of this unit, you should:

- ✓ Understand the advantages and disadvantages of using technology and digital tools to communicate and share design work on media platforms: text, emails and social media
- ✓ Demonstrate knowledge of remote working software and digital tools for communicating design proposals
- ✓ Understand the advantages and disadvantages of computer-aided design (CAD) and computer-aided manufacture (CAM) to design and make products
- ✓ Understand the benefits and risks of using artificial intelligence

Using technology has transformed how we communicate at work! There are lots of ways designers work with clients, both collaboratively and remotely (working together or alone). Technology has made the way we connect both personally and professionally speedier and more accessible than traditional communication methods, such as writing letters and face-to-face meetings. Designers can now share **design proposals** in a variety of ways.

WHAT IS A DESIGN PROPOSAL?

A design proposal is a formal document (a plan) or presentation/pitch that explains what you aim to create, how you plan to do it, what it will cost and why it is needed. Designers communicate this to the client in a variety of ways:

- *Communication platforms:* Instant messaging apps allow people to connect in real time globally via text, voice and video.
- *Email:* Formal communication for business, schools and workplaces.
- *Social media:* Platforms enable networking and sharing news, updates and professional networking.
- *Video conferences:* Platforms allow for the user to meet remotely by video, instead of traditional phone lines, for webinars and meetings.
- *Digital whiteboards:* For mind-mapping ideas.
- *File sharing/cloud collaboration:* Allows multiple users to share documents and work on them in real time securely online.
- *Document collaboration:* Allows multiple users to edit documents and spreadsheets at the same time.
- *Project management tools:* For setting deadlines, tracking progress and organising tasks.

Using different forms of technology to communicate (for example, design proposals), has some advantages and disadvantages (Table 1 and Figure 1).

Form of communication	Advantages	Disadvantages
Text messages 	• Speed • High interaction rate of client • Convenient • Instant feedback • Easy to follow up • Good for short design proposals	• Lack of professionalism • Limited space to share detailed designs • Can be easily overlooked • Not a formal written record • Formatting issues of text or images • A text message can be misinterpreted
Email  	• Professional • Written record • Can attach files easily • Cost effective	• Can be overlooked • Limited engagement • Delayed response • Barrier with building relationships with clients – too formal
Social media 	• Some platforms can make your work look more creative • More relatable to your audience • Wider reach • Instant feedback • Free marketing • Allows for networking opportunities • Allows for engagement through content shared	• Lack of professionalism • Limited depth in showing short posts making it hard to explain complex proposals • Allows for negative feedback, which can damage reputations
Video conferencing 	• Face-to-face interaction • Real-time discussion • Visual presentation tools – for example, sharing screen • Saves time and costs • Recordable sessions • Engagement – facial/body reactions within the meeting • Collaborative features – chat box to ask questions during the discussion	• Technical issues, perhaps a poor connection • Less natural interaction, which can feel awkward • Distractions for team members or clients in the video call from their surroundings • Privacy risks • Time zone scheduling difficulties • Dependent on technology – relying on good hardware (camera, microphone) for the users

Form of communication	Advantages	Disadvantages
Document collaboration	• Real-time collaboration makes teamwork faster • Version control can track changes • Allows for faster feedback to users and can track changes • Secure sharing options can control who views documents • Allows for better organisation – collected in place and can remain neat	• Internet dependency – needing a stable internet connection • Security risks – can be shared with the wrong person • Confusion if too many edits • Distracting if too many real-time comments pop-up
Remote working software	• Instant communication • Real-time collaboration • One place to store work • Flexibility • Better and easy to organise • Cost-effective • Increased productivity	• Technical issues • Security risks • Reduced personal connection face-to face meetings, communication gaps, misunderstandings • Software fatigue – switching between too many tools • Time zone differences when collaborating with other people in different locations

△ **Table 1** Advantages and disadvantages of the use of technology in communication

△ **Figure 1** Collaborative communication

TECHNOLOGY FOR DESIGNING AND MAKING

Computer-aided design (CAD) and computer-aided manufacturing (CAM)

Computer-Aided Design (CAD) is software used by designers and engineers to create products on a computer instead of drawing them by hand.

CAD simplifies the design process by letting you:

- Draw and Build: Create detailed, accurate 2D drawings and complex, virtual 3D models of parts and products.
- Test Virtually: Generate realistic images of the finished product and test its performance (like how much stress it can handle) before building a physical sample.

Computer-aided manufacturing (CAM) is the use of computers and machines to make products automatically from **digital designs** created on computer aided-design software programmes.

Computer-aided manufacturing (CAM) is used to manufacture and produce graphic products like packaging, signage, and promotional materials.

There are advantages and disadvantages of using CAD and CAM during product design (Table 2).

Advantages	Disadvantages
CAD • The ability to draw in 2D and 3D and then change a design quickly without redrawing from the beginning • Allowing the designer to see a drawing from different angles by rotating and zooming • Being able to render a drawing to make it look photo-realistic and in 3D • The ability to send a design to a machine to make individual parts using CAM • The ability to test a design, such as stress and strain, through testing software before manufacture, saving money on expensive models • Managing production schedules through CAD to control workflow through a factory carrying out QC, so that goods are produced to the right standards	**CAD** • *Cost:* Professional CAD software requires powerful computers and licences to use the software which are costly to set up • *Training is required:* Designers need training on CAD programmes, which takes time • *Challenging software:* Some CAD software is very complex and can be overwhelming for beginners to learn • *Limited creativity:* The tools within the programme may limit freehand and traditional creative approaches to designing products • *Software errors:* Crash or glitch causing design work to be lost or damaged • *Maintenance costs:* CAD systems need regular updates and upgrades which can add to long term costs

Advantages	Disadvantages
CAM	**CAM**
• *Accuracy:* CAM systems ensure high accuracy and repeatability, which is crucial for detailed graphic products (e.g. die-cut packaging, intricate prints) • *Speed:* Machines like CNC cutters, laser cutters, and digital printers work faster than manual methods, speeding up production • *Complex designs:* CAM allows the creation of intricate, complex designs that would be difficult or impossible to do by hand • *Reduced human error:* Automated systems reduce mistakes that occur in manual production • *Scalability:* Once a design is programmed, CAM can produce large quantities consistently, making it ideal for mass production	• *High set-up costs:* Buying and setting up CAM equipment can be expensive, especially for small businesses • *Training required:* Operators need technical skills to use CAM systems, which may require time and investment in training • *Maintenance:* CAM machines require regular maintenance, and any breakdowns can delay production • *Software issues/updates:* Compatibility or software glitches can affect production if the CAM software isn't updated or well-integrated

△ **Table 2** Advantages and disadvantages of using CAD and CAM in product design

In terms of product development, CAD can be two-dimensional (2D) or three-dimensional (3D). Two-dimensional CAD packages allow the user to produce accurately scaled, dimensioned technical drawings that can, if required, include text, photographs, bitmap images and vector graphics (Figure 2). This is very useful for producing designs such as logos, point of sale displays, packaging nets, menus and PCB circuit layouts. Two-dimensional CAD drawings can also be output to a variety of CAM devices.

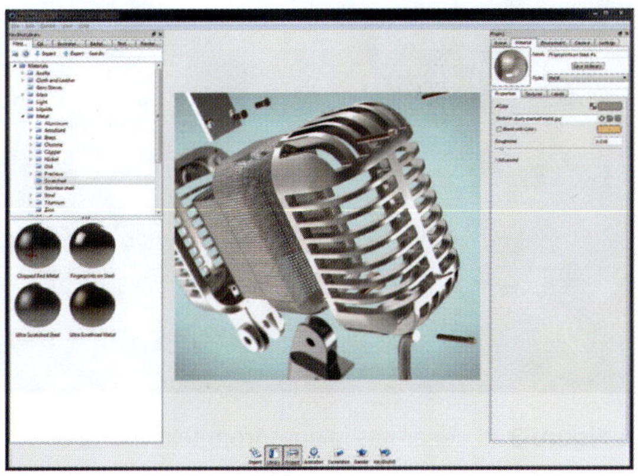

△ **Figure 2** A professional rendering using CAD

DESIGNING PRODUCTS USING ARTIFICIAL INTELLIGENCE (AI)

Artificial intelligence (AI) is a type of computer technology concerned with making machines work in an intelligent way; similar to the way that the human mind works. It uses computers or systems to assist humans complete certain tasks. Using AI technology in designing is becoming a rapidly evolving field. AI tools can analyse data from a range of sources and predict the user's preferences (who you are designing for).

Understanding the preferences and behaviour of the user is crucial for **user experience (UX)** and **user interface (UI)** design. Designers can use data from AI tools to design products that meet user needs and increase sales. There are advantages and disadvantages of using AI in designing (Table 3).

Advantages	Disadvantages
• *Efficiency:* Design tasks can be completed with speed • *Data informed decisions:* Leading to more success in the product's outcome	• Loss of human interaction when designing and making products • Heavy reliance on data to inform decisions and generate ideas • *Ethical challenges:* Certain data used by AI tools may not have been agreed to be shared by people

Δ **Table 3** Advantages and disadvantages of using AI in product design

AI has been used successfully in the real world for creating designs or design ideas. By using the user's input prompts, AI can generate complex images (Figure 3).

Δ **Figure 3** AI generates images from text prompts

TOP TIP

Keep your communication clear, simple and organised – and always check that it has been shared correctly.

Good communication equals fewer mistakes and helps with smoother teamwork.

SKILLS ACTIVITY

Reviewing the use of CAD

Pick an object in the room you are working in. Where could CAD have been used for in the manufacturing of this product?

REFLECTIVE LOG

Make a list of the technology you have used for communicating, designing and making in your own work. Are there other types of technology that you would like to try?

DESIGN IN ACTION

An example of remote design and manufacture

The book you are reading is an example of remote design and manufacturing. The book was written in the UK, Brunei and Hong Kong. The editing was completed in the UK, typesetting in India and the manufacturing in China. All correspondence was completed by email, video conferencing, document collaboration and remote working software. Distribution is worldwide.

DESIGN IN ACTION

Dyson

James Dyson is a British designer, engineer and inventor. He founded Dyson Ltd, a company famous for using technology and engineering to solve everyday problems. Dyson invests heavily in developing smart, self-directed products such as robotic vacuum cleaners (Figure 4).

△ **Figure 4** A robotic vacuum cleaner

KNOWLEDGE CHECK

1. Identify the advantages of CAD designing over traditional drawing techniques.
2. Explain how artificial intelligence assists designers.
3. Identify **two** advantages of technology used with design communication.

KEY TERMS

Design proposal: Suggestion(s) for a design of a product that is developed using the criteria and needs given*

Digital design: Digital design uses computers, graphics tablets, and various electronic devices to design and create products in a digital format*

User experience (UX): Designing products that provide meaningful and relevant experiences to users

User interface (UI): Visual and interactive elements of the product, such as colour, typography and layout

Practice questions

Question 1

Figure 1.1 shows a disposable plastic water bottle, which is often thrown away after one use.

△ **Figure 1.1**

a) State why throwing away plastic water bottles is harmful to the environment.

They can pollute oceans and harm marine life. ✓ ① (1)

b) Give **one** way a manufacturer can reduce the environmental impact of disposable water bottles.

Making materials easier to separate. ✓ ① (1)

COMMENTS

1) a) The sample answer directly identifies a key environmental harm caused by disposable plastic bottles – pollution of oceans and harm to marine life. It is clear, focused, and concise, which is exactly what is needed for the command word State.

b) The question asks for exactly one way in which a manufacturer can reduce environmental impact. The sample answer gives exactly one specific and accurate method.

Question 2

△ **Figure 2.1**

Figure 2.1 shows a stock form of wood.

a) Name the stock form of wood shown in Figure 2.1. (1)

b) Give **two** design uses for the material shown in Figure 2.1. (2)

Question 3

Explain what is meant by the term *PPE*. (2)

Question 4

Figure 4.1 shows a drawing of a bottle holder. The bottle holder will be made from a manufactured board.

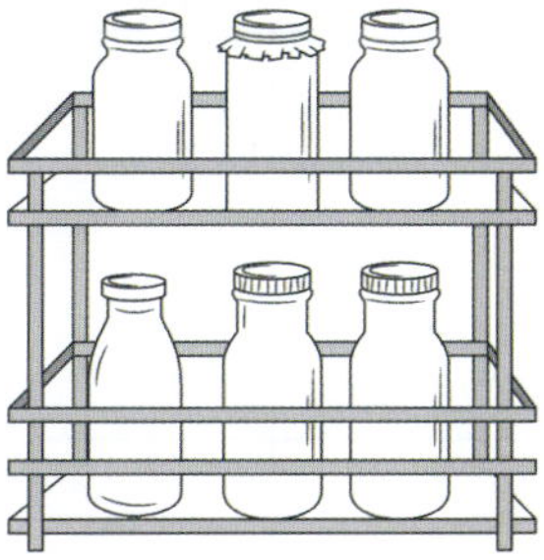

△ **Figure 4.1**

a) Name a suitable computer-aided-manufacturing (CAM) method that could be used to cut the holder shown in Figure 4.1. (1)

b) Use sketches and notes to show how to apply a suitable finish to the bottle holder, made from a manufactured board. (4)

Question 5

Designers often use email to share design proposal with other designers and clients.

Give **one** advantage and **one** disadvantage of this form of communication. (2)

Question 6

a) Explain what is meant by the term *planned obsolescence*. (1)

b) Circle the deforming process from the list. (1)

die casting   **sand casting**   **press forming**   **injection moulding**

Question 7

Give **one** example of a permanent joining method for metal and explain why it is used. (2)

Question 8

Explain what is meant by 'end of life' in a product's life cycle. (2)

Question 9

Complete Table 9.1 by naming a suitable material for each product. (3)

Product	Suitable material

∆ **Table 9.1**

Question 10

Add the correct property from the list to complete the following sentence.

hardness **toughness** **softness** **brittleness**

Quenching ferrous alloys, such as steel or cast iron, increases the .... of the metal. (1)

Question 11

Figure 11.1 shows details of a child's balance bike. The bike is manufactured from timbers and boards.

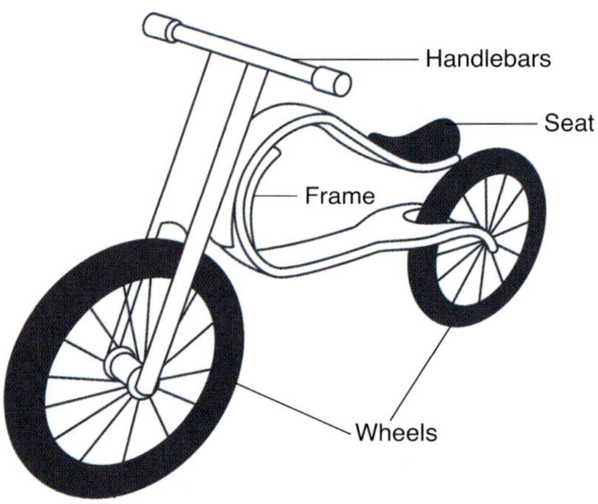

∆ **Figure 11.1**

a) i) Give **two** reasons why a manufacturer might choose timbers and boards for making a child's balance bike. (2)

ii) Explain **two** advantages of using robotics in manufacturing a child's balance bike. (4)

b) i) The balance bike is designed for disassembly. Name a suitable joining method that can be used to join the parts in Figure 11.1 (1)

ii) Explain the process of creating the 'frame', labelled in Figure 11.1. (2)

c) Use sketches and notes to show how a prototype of the 'frame' could be produced from the material stated in **11(b)(i)**, using workshop tools and equipment.

Include the following details:

- measuring and marking out
- cutting and finishing
- forming or joining
- health and safety considerations. (8)

d) The child's balance bike is to be commercially produced from a composite material.

Use sketches and notes to show and describe the process that could be used to commercially produce the balance bike.

Include the following details:

- Consideration of the manufacture of multiple copies.
- What tools and processes could be used.
- What materials could be used.
- Reduction of waste. (6)

e) Give **three** health and safety precautions you should take when using workshop tools to produce a prototype of the wooden frame for the child's balance bike. (3)

Graphic products are everywhere, silently communicating, telling stories and guiding you through modern life. From a cereal box to an app icon, these meticulously designed solutions address real-world challenges, meet user needs and evoke emotions. They are crucial for branding, packaging, information and user experience, directly influencing how you interact with products, services and the world.

The design landscape is evolving fast. We have moved beyond traditional materials into an era of smart materials, sustainable alternatives like biopolymers, and automated manufacturing.

Artificial intelligence (AI) is reshaping the design process, offering incredible opportunities for innovation. However, this rapid advancement also brings uncertainty for future design careers. As AI automates various tasks in the design process, the roles of designers will undoubtedly shift, demanding new skills and a deeper focus on uniquely human contributions. While AI can process vast amounts of data and generate numerous options, it is the human designer who truly understands the emotions, cultural contexts and unspoken needs of users. A designer's ability to connect with users empathetically, observe their behaviours and interpret their feedback ensures that designs remain focused on solving real human problems with genuine care.

Designers today face the exciting challenge of creating visually compelling and highly functional solutions, while addressing critical issues such as environmental impact, material life cycles and ensuring accessibility for all. This section provides the knowledge and skills to navigate this dynamic field – empowering you to design for a more sustainable, user-centric and impactful future.

STARTING POINTS

- How can graphic product designers balance aesthetic appeal with the urgent need for environmental sustainability in packaging and promotional materials?
- In what ways might AI enhance or fundamentally change the role of human creativity in graphic design?
- Beyond traditional paper, what emerging materials or technologies will have the greatest impact on the future of graphic products?

SECTION CONTENTS

3 Graphic Products

3·1 Types of material

3·1·1 Paper and card

LEARNING AIMS

By the end of this unit, you should:

- ✓ Understand the properties of paper and card
- ✓ Understand stock forms in which paper and card are available
- ✓ Discuss the environmental considerations associated with paper and card
- ✓ Apply your understanding of paper and card properties to choose appropriate materials
- ✓ Identify a range of paper and card types and describe their typical uses in graphic products

Paper and card are not just flat and boring. They are useful materials for graphic designers (Figure 1). Think about the packaging for your phone, the cover of your favourite comic or the birthday card you received. Each of these used paper or card.

Paper and card mostly come from wood pulp (tiny fibres from trees) or from recycled paper. Knowing about different types of paper and card helps you choose the perfect one to make your design ideas real.

△ **Figure 1** Paper and card are used everywhere in graphic design.

PROPERTIES

Weight and thickness

Is the paper/card light like a feather or thick like a board?

Paper weight is measured in **gsm (grams per square metre)**. A higher GSM means heavier and, usually thicker, paper (Figure 2). Everyday printer paper is light (about 80 gsm). The card for a sturdy birthday card is much heavier (160 gsm or more).

Thickness can also be measured in **microns**. Really thick boards are measured this way. Thicker materials are stronger and don't bend easily. They are great for boxes or book covers.

△ **Figure 2** A measurement in gsm tells you how heavy and thick paper or card is.

TOP TIP

Master the fold! Paper and card have a **grain direction**. This is the direction in which most fibres lie. Try folding a piece of paper gently both ways. It will fold much more easily and neatly *along* the grain. Knowing this makes your models and cards look more professional.

Finish

How does the paper/card look and feel (Figure 3)? Smooth? Shiny? Bumpy?

- Matt paper is smooth but not shiny (glossy). It is easier to read text on matt paper than on glossy paper.
- Glossy paper makes colours pop and look vibrant.
- Textured paper and card have an interesting feel, sometimes like fabric or with tiny lines.

△ **Figure 3** Different finishes give paper and card unique looks and textures.

Opacity

If a piece of paper has high **opacity**, then you cannot see through it. Opacity refers to how well a material prevents light from travelling through it.

Strength and durability

How tough is the paper or card? Can it survive being handled a lot? Card and board are tougher than paper.

Absorbency

Does the paper soak up ink like a sponge, or does the ink sit nicely on top? Glossy paper absorbs less ink, making prints look sharp. Newsprint soaks up ink quickly.

STOCK FORMS

Table 1 shows the standard ways paper and card are sold.

Stock form	Description
Sheets	Flat pieces in sizes you probably know, such as A4 (your normal printer paper size), A3 (double A4), A2, A1. Using standard sizes saves time and waste.
Rolls	Imagine giant toilet rolls of paper! Newspapers and wrapping paper often come like this.
Boards	Thick, strong card is sold in large flat sheets, which are perfect for big models or mounting your artwork.

△ **Table 1** The stock forms in which paper and card are available

ENVIRONMENTAL IMPACT

Making paper can affect our planet.

△ **Figure 4** Look for the FSC logo or choose recycled paper and card to protect the planet.

- *Source*: Where does it start? It mostly comes from trees. Cutting down too many trees without planting new ones (deforestation) is bad for the environment, wildlife and the climate. Look for the **Forest Stewardship Council (FSC)** logo when you are sourcing paper and card (Figure 4). It means the paper or card comes from forests that are responsibly managed.
- *Recycling*: Using old paper to make new paper saves trees and energy, and stops waste going to landfill.
- *Bleaching*: Making paper white often uses chemicals. These need to be handled carefully to protect rivers and lakes.
- *Biodegradability*: Most paper and card break down naturally over time. This means they do not stay around forever like some plastic does.

SKILLS ACTIVITY

Material detective

Become a material detective! Collect some samples of different paper and card – for example, copier paper, card, corrugated card, a cereal box, or anything else you can find made of paper or card. Complete the following investigations:

1. **The tear test**: Carefully tear each sample – first down, then across. Which way is easier? That's the grain direction.
2. **The fold test**: Fold each sample along the grain, then against it. Look closely at the fold line. Is it sharp or a bit messy/cracked?
3. **The strength test**: Gently push a pencil point into each sample. Which ones resist the most?
4. **The absorbency test**: Place one drop of water on each sample. Does it vanish instantly or sit there?

TYPES AND USES

There are many different types of paper and card, each with unique properties that make them suitable for specific purposes. Here are some common examples – as you read through each one, think like a designer to match the right material to the job.

Types of paper

Table 2 lists some types of paper and their uses.

Paper type	Description	Questions to consider	Uses
Tissue paper (10–35 gsm)	This is very thin and delicate	Why would a designer choose such a fragile material? What are its limitations?	Wrapping delicate gifts, colourful crafts
Newsprint (45–55 gsm)	A cheaper, less refined paper	Think about a newspaper. Does the paper quality matter? Why or why not?	Newspapers
Copier paper (80 gsm)	This is the paper you probably use every day in your printer	Why is it so common? What jobs is it good at, and not so good at?	Printing notes, quick drawings
Cartridge paper (100–150 gsm)	A bit thicker than copier paper, with a slightly textured surface	How does this paper feel different from copier paper? What kind of drawings or artwork might suit this better?	Sketching, art projects, nicer printouts
Glossy paper (150–300 gsm)	This is smooth and shiny	What happens to colours and images printed on this type of paper? Where have you seen it used?	Printing photos, brochures, magazine covers

Δ **Table 2** Different types of paper and their uses in graphic products

Types of card and board

Table 3 lists some types of card and board and their uses.

Card/board type	Description	Questions to consider	Uses
General card (160–400 gsm)	Noticeably thicker and stiffer than paper; available in a huge range of colours and finishes	What kind of graphic products need to be sturdy? How does the wide range of colours and finishes expand design possibilities?	Birthday cards, invitations, model making, covers for booklets
Corrugated card/ board	A 'wavy' layer (**fluting**) is sandwiched between flat sheets	How does the fluting affect the strength of this material? Why is this so useful for packaging?	Delivery boxes, packaging for TVs or computers, pizza boxes (keeps it warm)
Solid white board	High-quality and bright white	What does the use of 'solid white' suggest about the desired look and feel of a product?	Fancy packaging (e.g. perfume boxes), quality book covers
Duplex board	Made of two layers stuck together, often with a white top and a grey underside	Why combine two layers? What does the grey underside tell you about this material?	Cereal boxes, shoe boxes
Mount board (500–2500 microns)	Very thick and rigid	Where have you seen this used? What does it add to the presentation of artwork?	Picture mounts, sturdy models
Foamboard	A lightweight 'sandwich' of foam between two card sheets; it is light but strong	Have you seen this used for a display or model? Why is the lightweight property important?	Making models, displays

△ **Table 3** Different types of card and board and their uses in graphic products

SKILLS ACTIVITY

Material match-up challenge

Imagine you have been asked to design each of the following products:

- A lightweight but sturdy display stand for a school project
- Packaging for a delicate glass ornament
- A set of colourful party invitations
- A magazine cover

Complete the following tasks:

1. Think about which paper and card types would be most suitable for each of the products.
2. Collect samples of as many different paper and card types as you can (at least five). Try to find examples from Tables 2 and 3.
3. For each product, decide which paper or card sample from your collection would be the *most* suitable.
4. Write a short explanation for each match, considering:
    - Properties (weight, thickness, finish, strength and durability)
    - Appearance
    - Cost (think about this even if you don't know the exact price).
5. Compare your choices and justifications with a classmate. Are there different 'right' answers?

KNOWLEDGE CHECK

1. State what 'gsm' means when describing paper.
2. Identify **one** property of glossy paper.
3. Explain why corrugated cardboard is suitable for packaging fragile items.
4. Describe what is meant by 'stock form' and give **one** example for paper or card.
5. Explain **one** benefit of recycling paper for the environment.

KEY TERMS

Fluting: The zigzag wavy layer in corrugated card

Forest Stewardship Council (FSC): A logo showing the paper comes from well-managed forests

Grain direction: The way the fibres line up in paper

gsm (grams per square metre): A measure for the weight of paper; the higher the gsm, the heavier or thicker the paper

Micron: Tiny unit to measure thickness (often for boards)

Opacity: How much you can (or cannot) see through paper

3·1·2 Polymers

LEARNING AIMS

By the end of this unit, you should:

✓ Identify a range of polymers and describe their typical uses in graphic products
✓ Understand the properties of polymers, including thermo polymers, thermosetting polymers and biopolymers
✓ Understand standard stock forms in which polymers are available
✓ Discuss the environmental considerations associated with polymer production, usage and disposal
✓ Apply your understanding of polymer properties to choose appropriate materials

What do your phone case, a colourful sign and a squeezy bottle have in common? The answer is polymers – those incredibly versatile materials we more often call plastics. Polymers allow designers to make everything from super-tough packaging that protects your products to vibrant displays that grab your attention (Figure 1).

△ **Figure 1** Polymers are widely used in graphic design.

Choosing the right polymer for a product is not just a detail – it's *key*. Designers must weigh up each polymer's unique properties *and* its impact on the planet when designing a product. Before you learn more about polymers and their use in graphic design, read through unit 2.1.1 on polymers. This provides an essential guide to the wide range of different polymers you will come across.

Polymers are great, but they create some big environmental challenges. Most polymers come from fossil fuels, and they can hang around in the environment for a very long time. That is why biopolymers are so exciting, as they point the way to a greener future!

PROPERTIES

Each polymer has defining properties: thermo polymers can be melted and remoulded, thermosetting polymers stay strong (Figure 2), and biopolymers are sustainable.

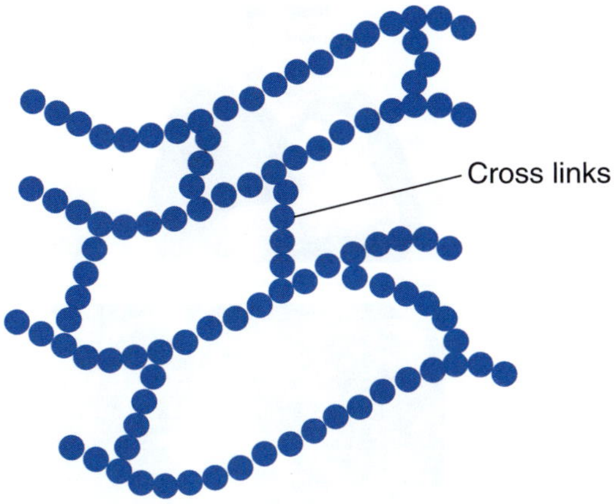

Δ **Figure 2** Cross links in thermosetting polymers, hold it in shape and make it strong.

Thermo polymers

Thermo polymers can be melted and remoulded repeatedly. They are versatile – using heat, they can be shaped into many things. PET and PVC are just two examples of thermo polymers; there are many more.

Thermosetting polymers

These plastics are all about strength and stability. Once they are set, they cannot be remoulded. Epoxy resins are a good example of thermosetting polymers, and are often used when you need a solid material.

Biopolymers

Biopolymers are derived from renewable resources, such as corn starch or sugarcane. PLA is a common biopolymer, offering a more sustainable alternative to traditional plastics.

There is much more to polymers than just how they react to heat. They have other properties, including those listed in Table 1.

Additional properties	Description	Example
Strength and flexibility	Some polymers are the bodybuilders of the material world – strong and rigid; others are the acrobats, flexible and bendy	
Transparency	Do you want to see right through it, or have a solid, opaque look? Polymers can do both	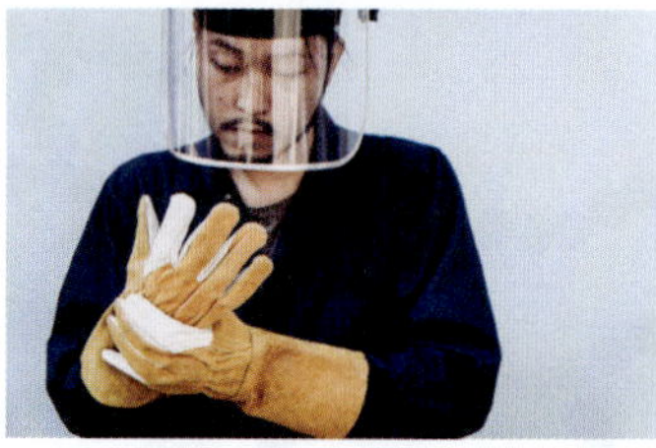
Resistance	Polymers can be designed to resist all sorts of things: weather, harsh chemicals, bumps and scrapes	
Printability	Can you get a crisp, vibrant print on it? This is critical for some graphic products	
Density	Polymers vary in density from low-density foams to high density stock forms	

△ **Table 1** Additional properties of polymers

SKILLS ACTIVITY

Plastic packaging sort

Find out more about plastic packaging by completing these tasks:

1. Collect a variety of used plastic packaging items from your home or a school recycling bin (for example, drinks bottles, food containers, packaging film). Make sure they are clean.
2. Look for the **recycling codes** on each item (refer to unit 1.1.3).
3. Sort the packaging items into groups based on their recycling codes.

4. For each group, try to identify the type of polymer (for example, PET, PP) using the recycling code and any other clues (such as flexibility or rigidity and other properties).
5. Finally, discuss:
   - Which polymers are most common in your collection?
   - Are there any items without recycling codes? What does this tell you?
   - Research the recyclability of each polymer type in your local area (Figure 3).

△ **Figure 3** Different types of plastic need to be separated for recycling.

TOP TIP

Did you know that different polymers have different sounds? Try squishing, bending and tapping a range of plastics, then check the recycling code on the bottom.

STOCK FORMS

Polymers are supplied in standard or stock forms, ready to be transformed by designers and manufacturers (Table 2).

Stock form	Description	Example
Sheets	Flat, even pieces; sheets of acrylic are cut for many uses, including making signs	
Films	Thin and flexible layers; PVC film is used for wrapping food or creating adhesive decals	
Rolls	Self-adhesive vinyl comes in rolls, ready to stick	
Filament	The raw material for 3D printing; a fine thread of polymer that can be built up layer by layer to create complex shapes	

△ **Table 2** The stock forms in which polymers are available

ENVIRONMENTAL IMPACT

Polymers have a complicated relationship with the environment. We cannot ignore the challenges.

- *Source*: The majority of traditional polymers are made from fossil fuels such as oil and gas. Those are non-renewable resources, meaning they will eventually run out.
- *Recycling*: Recycling polymers varies. Some, like PET, are relatively easy to recycle. Others are not so. Also even the ones we *can* recycle don't always get recycled.
- *Biodegradability*: Most polymers do not break down naturally. They can remain in the environment for hundreds of years, causing major problems. Biopolymers, such as PLA, are designed to be biodegradable, but they usually need very specific conditions (such as industrial composting) to break down.
- *Waste*: Plastic pollution is a global crisis. From overflowing landfills to plastic choking our oceans (Figure 4), it is a serious issue we need to tackle.

△ **Figure 4** We have to be responsible about how we use and dispose of polymers, but some responsibility also lies with the manufacturer.

SKILLS ACTIVITY

Polymer design challenge

Choose **one** of the following design challenges.

Option 1: Sustainable food packaging

Your mission is to design packaging for a new line of organic food.

Research:

Become an expert on PET, PP and PLA, with a focus on their environmental credentials. Don't forget to revisit unit 2.1.1 to understand how their properties align with sustainability.

Consider:

- What does food packaging *have* to do? (Keeping food fresh, being tough enough to survive transport, and maybe even letting you see the goodies inside.)
- Which polymer(s) would work for different packaging parts (container, lid, label)? Can they be separated for disposal?
- What happens to your packaging after you are finished with it? (Recycling? Composting?) How do end-of-life options drive your material decisions?

Design:

Sketch your packaging. Label all the materials and use annotations to justify your decisions.

Option 2: Custom phone case

You are designing a phone case that is protective, but also a style statement.

Research:

Get to know ABS, PP and PS inside and out. How do they stack up for phone case duty? How do their properties from unit 2.1.1 influence their strengths and weaknesses?

Consider:

- What does a phone case need to do? (Protect the phone from drops and scratches, feel good in your hand, look awesome.)
- Which polymer would work for the main body of the case?
- Could you mix it up with a different polymer for design details or inserts? (Remember that PS comes in different forms.)

Design:

Sketch a phone case that is both stylish and functional. Annotate all the materials you would use and sell your design choices with compelling arguments from your research.

KNOWLEDGE CHECK

1. Identify **three** common polymers that graphic designers use to make their creations come to life.
2. Explain the difference between a thermo polymer and a thermosetting polymer.
3. Identify **one** advantage and **one** disadvantage of using polymers in graphic design.
4. Describe **two** different stock forms in which polymers are typically supplied to manufacturers.
5. Explain why recycling is an important strategy for managing polymer waste and reducing its environmental impact.

KEY TERMS

Recycling code: A numerical symbol used to identify the type of polymer for recycling classification

3·1·3 Foam materials

LEARNING AIMS

By the end of this unit, you should:
✓ Identify a range of foam materials
✓ Understand the properties of foam materials
✓ Understand standard stock forms of foam materials
✓ Discuss the environmental considerations associated with foam materials
✓ Demonstrate knowledge of shaping and joining foam materials

Foam materials are light and easy to shape. This means they are very useful for displays and quick prototypes. This section explores foamboard and **Styrofoam**, two important materials of the graphic design and model-making world.

WHAT ARE FOAM MATERIALS?

Foam is a solid material with lots of tiny air pockets. This structure gives it some advantages in graphic products:

- It is low density and rigid, making it ideal for large, portable displays and structural models.
- It is easily shaped and can be cut or sanded into complex forms and intricate details.
- It is **impact resistant** and so provides excellent cushioning and protection for delicate items.

FOAMBOARD AND STYROFOAM

Foamboard and Styrofoam are the two most common foam materials in graphic products.

Foamboard

Foamboard is a low density foam core (often polystyrene) sandwiched between card or paper sheets. Its stock form is sheets. Foamboard is ideal for:

- mounting posters and prints
- exhibition displays
- detailed architectural models (Figure 1)
- 3D lettering and signage.

△ **Figure 1** Foamboard is a versatile material, allowing graphic designers to be creative in 3D form.

Styrofoam

Styrofoam is extruded polystyrene foam.
Its stock form is in blocks, which can be used to create:

- 3D models and prototypes (Figure 2)
- large-scale lettering.

◁ **Figure 2** Styrofoam is a quick and easy way to develop prototypes.

Cutting and joining foam materials

Use a **hot wire cutter** to slice through Styrofoam blocks effortlessly, and then file and sand the foam to shape. Ensure you wear a mask to avoid breathing in plastic fumes. Alternatively, use a craft knife – always use a cutting mat and keep your fingers away from the blade (Figure 3).

△ **Figure 3** Foam is easily cut and shaped.

You can join foam materials together using:

- adhesives – but make sure you choose the right glue for foam
- tape, which is useful for quick exploratory modelling
- fasteners, which are useful for temporary assembly.

ENVIRONMENTAL IMPACT

Foam materials present some significant environmental challenges:

- Shaping foam creates waste.
- Foam materials have a low recycling rate.
- Sanding and cutting foam can release **microplastics**.

Designers have a responsibility to address these issues. When you plan any projects using foam materials, plan them carefully to cut down on waste. Look into sustainable foam options or biodegradable materials.

TOP TIP

Safety first! Use a mask when sanding or using power tools on Styrofoam to avoid inhaling microplastic particles.

DESIGN IN ACTION

An alternative to Styrofoam

A major environmental concern is that most Styrofoam waste is not recycled and ends up in landfills. To address this, 'Refoam' offers a sustainable alternative to current Styrofoam processing. Refoam softens waste locally and uses the recycled material to create textured furniture.

SKILLS ACTIVITY

Foamboard challenge: Shape exploration

Using foamboard and a craft knife, make the following shapes (Figure 4). Try making them *without* using tape or glue. Instead, rely on making clever cuts.

- *Cube (four walls)*: Can you make it sturdy, with clean corners?
- *Hinge*: Create a working hinge.
- *Prism*: Use as many sides as you want.

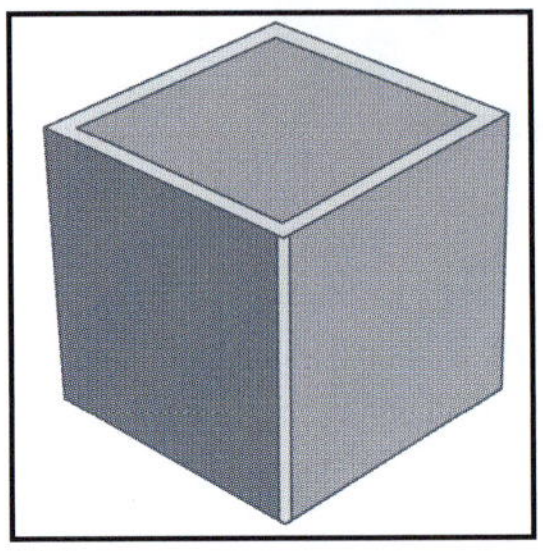

Cube

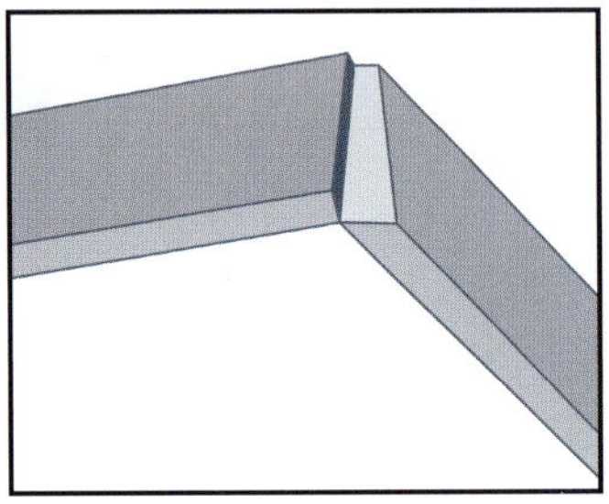

Hinge

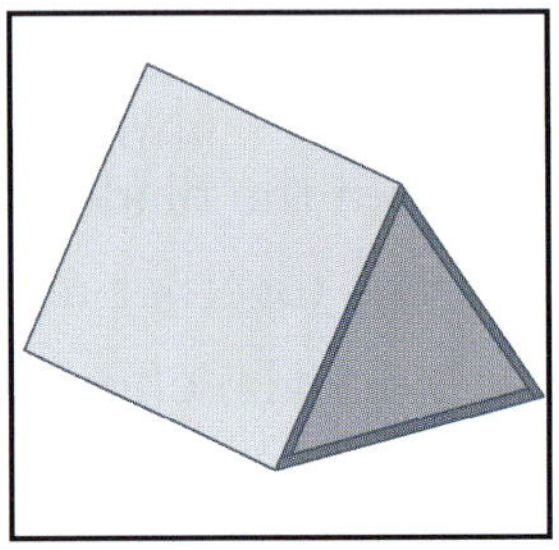

Prism

△ **Figure 4** Creating shapes using foamboard

KNOWLEDGE CHECK

1. Describe **three** advantages of using foam materials in graphic products.
2. Describe **three** typical uses of foamboard in graphic applications.
3. State **two** techniques for shaping Styrofoam.
4. Explain the environmental concerns around foam materials and how designers can tackle them.

KEY TERMS

Hot wire cutter: Tool with a heated wire for smooth cuts to a foam material

Impact resistance: Material's ability to withstand shock without damage

Microplastics: Tiny plastic particles that pollute the environment

Styrofoam: Extruded polystyrene foam available in blocks

3·1·4 Composites

LEARNING AIMS

By the end of this unit, you should:

✓ Understand what a composite material is
✓ Explain how composite properties make them suitable for specific uses
✓ Identify different types of composite materials in graphic products
✓ Describe foil-based and particle-based composites
✓ Discuss the environmental impact of composite materials

Combining materials can improve them. Composites are made from two or more different materials with very different properties. They often create a new material with improved properties.

Think about the properties required by a juice box (such as a **Tetra Pak®**). It needs to be strong, lightweight and waterproof. It also needs to keep the juice fresh and have a surface on which to print designs. No single material has all of these properties. Instead, the designers of juice cartons use a composite material, combining layers of paper, plastic and aluminium foil (Figure 1). Composites are all around us in graphic products, especially in packaging.

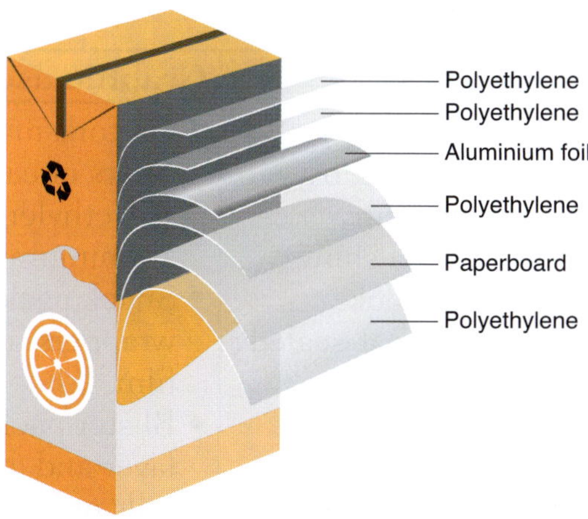

Δ **Figure 1** Composites like this juice carton combine materials to get the best properties.

WHAT MAKES A COMPOSITE?

Composites usually have two main parts:

- **Matrix**: the main material that holds everything together (for example, glue or plastic)
- **Reinforcement**: the fibres, particles or layers added to the matrix to make it stronger, lighter or give it special properties (such as foil or paper layers).

By carefully choosing the matrix and reinforcement, designers can create materials perfect for a specific job.

PROPERTIES

Why use composites in graphic products? Composites offer a mix of benefits, including those listed in Table 1.

Properties	Description
Barrier properties	Many composites, especially those with foil or plastic layers, successfully block out light, air and moisture. This keeps food and drinks fresh for longer.
Strength and rigidity	Combining materials can make packaging strong but still lightweight. Paperboard gives structure, while plastic layers add toughness or a liquid barrier.
Printability	The outer layer of a composite is often chosen in order to print high-quality graphics and information on it. The paper or plastic outer layer on juice boxes is perfect for colourful designs.
Flexibility	Some composites can be flexible for pouches or wrappers, while others are rigid for boxes.
Special finishes	Composites allow for shiny metallic finishes or specific textures.

△ **Table 1** Properties of composites

DIFFERENT TYPES OF COMPOSITES

You need to know about two types of composites: **foil-based composites** and **particle-based composites** (Table 2).

Composite	Description	Properties	Graphic uses
Foil-based	Includes a thin layer of metal foil, usually aluminium	• Excellent barrier against light, oxygen and moisture • Provides a shiny, metallic look • Can be heat-sealed	• Cartons made up of layers of card, polyethylene and aluminium foil • Snack packets and wrappers use metallised film • Blister packs have a foil layer and are used for pills or small items
Particle-based	Has small particles (e.g. wood dust or mineral powders) mixed into the matrix; they are less common than foil composites in graphic products	Properties depend on the particles and matrix used. They can: • increase strength or rigidity • change texture • add visual effects	• MDF display boards: MDF is made from wood particles mixed with resin (matrix) and pressed into sheets (Figure 2) • Textured papers/cards: Some specialist papers or cards include particles to give them a unique texture or visual effect

△ **Table 2** Different types of composites, their properties and uses in graphic products

∆ **Figure 2** Raw MDF boards showing the wood particles bonded together with resin

SKILLS ACTIVITY

Snack packets and blister packs

Cartons have layers of:

- paper for strength and a good print surface
- polyethylene for waterproofing and to help stick the layers together
- aluminium foil, which provides a light and oxygen barrier to keep drinks fresh.

Consider snack packets and blister packs (Figure 3). Research what properties the individual materials have and what benefit they bring to the packaging.

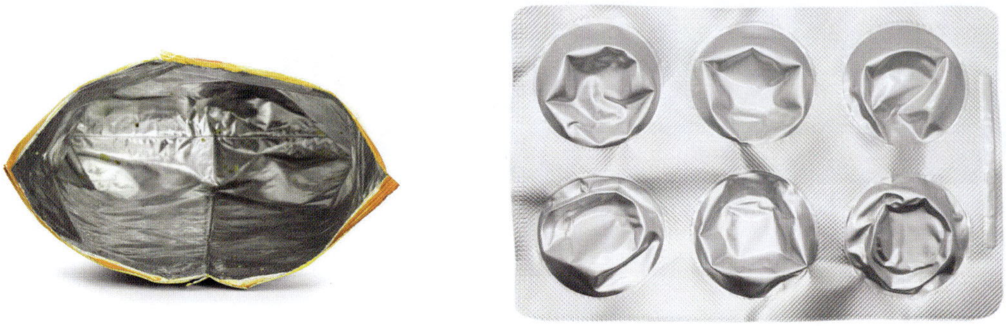

∆ **Figure 3** Foil layers give composites barrier properties and a shiny look.

TOP TIP

Look around! Next time you are shopping, look closely at packaging. Can you spot composites? Try to guess what materials might be combined and why. Is it shiny? Does it feel like paper and plastic? Is it keeping something fresh?

ENVIRONMENTAL IMPACT

Composites have great properties, but they can be bad for the environment. Why do you think this is?

Some companies are working hard to:

- use more recycled materials in composites
- develop composites that are easier to recycle or made from renewable resources (like biopolymers)
- design packaging that uses fewer layers or only one type of material.

DESIGN IN ACTION

The Tetra Pak® recycling puzzle

Recycling Tetra Pak® is difficult because the bonded paper, plastic and foil layers need special separation factories. When cartons *do* get recycled, the paper fibres are 'downcycled' into paper towels or cardboard rather than new cartons. The leftover mix of aluminium and plastic is made into 'PolyAl' pellets (Figure 4).

Designers are giving waste a new life. Designer Ed Chew created a TetraBox lamp crafted from discarded drink cartons, saving them from landfills. How can you creatively reuse your old cartons?

△ **Figure 4** Tetra Paks® can be recycled into fibres and PolyAl pellets, but it is a difficult process.

SKILLS ACTIVITY

Composite disassembly challenge

Carefully take apart a composite to see how it is made.

1. Find an example of layered composite packaging, such as a clean juice carton.
2. First, examine the outside and inside of the carton. What materials can you already identify? What job is the packaging doing?
3. Carefully disassemble the carton – try to peel apart the layers at an edge or corner. You might need to soak a piece of it in water for a while to help separate the paper layer.
4. Try to separate the different materials (paper/card, plastic films, foil layer). Be patient – layers can be thin and well stuck together.
5. Lay out the pieces you manage to separate and analyse the layers:
   - Can you identify paper/cardboard?
   - Can you find a thin, shiny foil layer?
   - Can you see clear or coloured plastic film layers?

KNOWLEDGE CHECK

1. Sketch a diagram illustrating the layered structure of a typical composite material used in packaging.
2. Give **two** reasons why composite materials are frequently chosen over single-material alternatives in graphic product packaging.
3. Identify the **three** main materials typically found in a Tetra Pak® carton.
4. Compare the disposal of composite materials to the disposal of single-material packaging.

KEY TERMS

Barrier properties: The ability of a material to block things like light, oxygen, or moisture

Foil-based composite: A composite containing a thin layer of metal foil, usually aluminium

Matrix: The material in a composite that performs the binding function

Particle-based composite: A composite where small particles of one material are mixed into a matrix material

Reinforcement: The material in a composite that adds tensile strength and toughness

Tetra Pak®: Brand name that refers to both a multinational food packaging and processing company and the multi-layered carton containers it produces for liquid food products

3·1·5 Smart, modern and alternative materials

LEARNING AIMS

By the end of this unit, you should:
✓ Develop an understanding of 'smart', modern and alternative materials
✓ Identify examples of smart materials
✓ Identify examples of modern and alternative materials
✓ Describe the properties and uses of smart materials and inks in graphic products

Graphic design is constantly evolving. To create more exciting and effective products, designers continuously explore new materials. This drive for innovation has led to the development of smart, modern and alternative materials which are opening up a world of new possibilities.

WHAT ARE SMART MATERIALS?

Smart materials respond to changes in environmental conditions, such as changes in temperature or light. They respond by changing their properties. Smart inks are 'smart' materials. As well as responding to environmental changes, they possess other unique properties. Smart materials and inks offer exciting possibilities for graphic design.

Thermochromic materials

Thermochromic materials and inks change colour with temperature. For example, you may have seen designs on mugs, clothing or packaging change colour with increases in temperature (Figure 1).

How could thermochromic materials and inks be used in packaging or printing to make products more useful or fun, or to add security or safety features?

Δ **Figure 1** Thermochromic materials change colour with temperature.

Photochromic materials

Photochromic materials change colour with ultraviolet (UV) light. For example, photochromic materials are used in cosmetics, children's toys and lenses in sunglasses (Figure 2).

Imagine a poster or label that changes colour in sunlight to reveal a hidden message or design. What possibilities does this open up?

△ **Figure 2** Photochromic materials change colour with light.

Shape memory polymer

Shape memory polymers (SMPs) can be shaped and deformed, but they return to their original shape when heated. SMP is useful in packaging to protect fragile products during shipping. They are also used in medicine and dentistry (Figure 3).

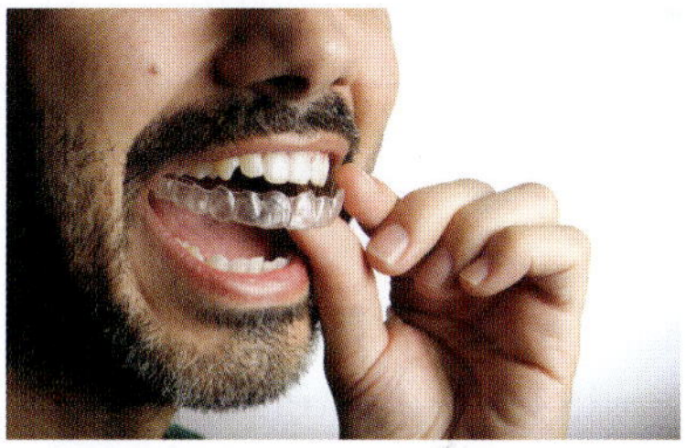

△ **Figure 3** Shape memory polymers are an innovative aligner material.

MODERN AND ALTERNATIVE MATERIALS

Modern materials are recently developed substances engineered to have special properties and improved performance over traditional materials.

Alternative materials are used as substitutes for common materials, often chosen for benefits like sustainability, cost, or performance.

Polymorph

Polymorph is a special polymer that becomes mouldable when heated in hot water (Figure 4). You can shape it with your hands! Polymorph allows for exploratory modelling of 3D forms, enabling designers to test the feel and shape of a product (such as a handle or tool grip) before committing to more expensive manufacturing methods.

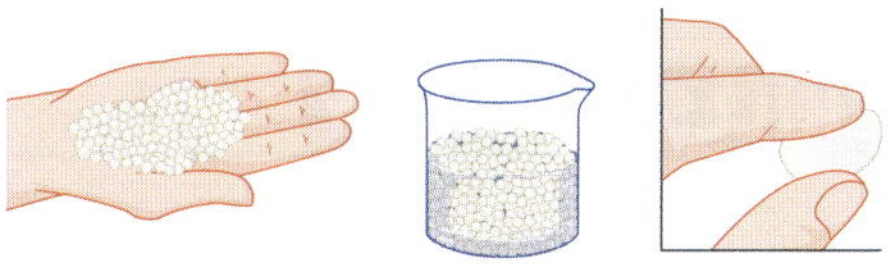

△ **Figure 4** Polymorph can be easily shaped when heated.

This is particularly useful for ergonomics, where designers can quickly create and modify models to assess how comfortably a product fits the hand or body.

Biopolymers

As you learned in unit 3.1.2, biopolymers are made from renewable resources, such as corn starch. They are a more environmentally friendly alternative to traditional plastics (Figure 5). Remember that, as a designer, it is important to consider the environmental impact of your material choices.

△ **Figure 5** Disposable cutlery and cup made from biopolymers.

TOP TIP

Word breakdown

Sometimes, breaking down the words of materials can help you recognise their properties:

- Thermo*chromic*: 'Thermo' relates to heat and 'chromic' to colour. So, thermochromic materials change *colour* with heat.
- Photo*chromic*: 'Photo' relates to light. So, photochromic materials change *colour* with light.
- Bio*polymer*: 'Bio' means it comes from living things. A polymer is a plastic. So, a biopolymer is a *plastic* from a natural source that was alive once.
- Shape memory *polymer* means a *plastic* that remembers its original shape.

SMART USES IN GRAPHIC PRODUCTS

Smart, modern and alternative materials can be used to make graphic products more interactive, functional and sustainable.

- *Interactive*: How could packaging use smart materials and inks to communicate information to users (for example, freshness, temperature, authenticity)? How could smart materials be used to create fun interactive elements?
- *Functional*: Can you think of ways smart materials can be used to make packaging easier to use or more protective?
- *Sustainable*: How do biopolymers help to make graphic products more sustainable?

Find out more about smart, modern and alternative materials in unit 2.1.5.

SKILLS ACTIVITY

Design a smart packaging concept

Choose a product and think about how smart or modern materials could be used to revolutionise its packaging.

1. Carry out research to answer the following questions:
   - What are the current challenges with packaging your chosen product?
   - Which smart or modern material has the potential to address these challenges? Why?
   - Research existing examples of smart packaging (if any). What can you learn from them?

2. Sketch your innovative packaging design. Clearly label the smart or modern material(s) you have incorporated.

3. Write a detailed paragraph justifying your design choices. Focus on how the smart or modern material(s) enhances functionality, user experience and/or sustainability.

KNOWLEDGE CHECK

1. Describe the key characteristic that defines a 'smart' material.
2. Explain how thermochromic materials and inks can be used in packaging or printing.
3. Describe how photochromic materials and inks could be used to enhance the functionality or user experience of a graphic product.
4. Discuss the environmental advantages of using biopolymers in graphic product design.

KEY TERMS

Alternative materials: Used as substitutes for common materials, often chosen for benefits like sustainability, cost, or performance

Modern materials: Recently developed substances engineered to have special properties and improved performance over traditional materials

Photochromic: Changes colour with light

Shape memory polymer: A polymer that returns to its original shape when heated

Thermochromic: Changes colour with temperature

3·2 Drawing techniques

3·2·1 Technical drawing methods

LEARNING AIMS

By the end of this unit, you should:

✓ Demonstrate a working knowledge of dimensioning and drawing to recommended scales and standards

✓ Understand and apply the following drawing techniques in designing and making:
- geometrical constructions
- orthographic projection
- three-dimensional drawing
- assembly drawings
- developments (nets)

Designers and engineers use computers to create amazing things. But, before the software, there is usually a drawing. Technical drawing teaches you the essential skills of visualising and representing objects. It helps you understand how things are built, not just how they look.

In this unit, you will explore dimensioning, scaling and important drawing techniques. You will learn to draw precise shapes, create 3D views and design packaging. You will discover that drawing by hand forms the foundation of design. Remember – practise makes perfect!

DIMENSIONING AND SCALE

Dimensioning is about adding *exact* measurements to your drawings. Dimensions are instructions for manufacturers, ensuring every part fits perfectly. Dimensions are usually in millimetres (mm).

How do you draw a building on paper, or a tiny circuit in detail? Scale is the ratio between your drawing's size and the object's actual size. For example, 1:2 means the drawing is half the size of the object; 2:1 means it is double the size.

Dimensioning standards

Since many products are made in different parts of the world, it is important that a common form of drawing and adding dimensions is used so that the drawings can be understood by designers and manufacturers worldwide. In your drawings, it will be expected that you use **British Standards**, as shown in Figure 1.

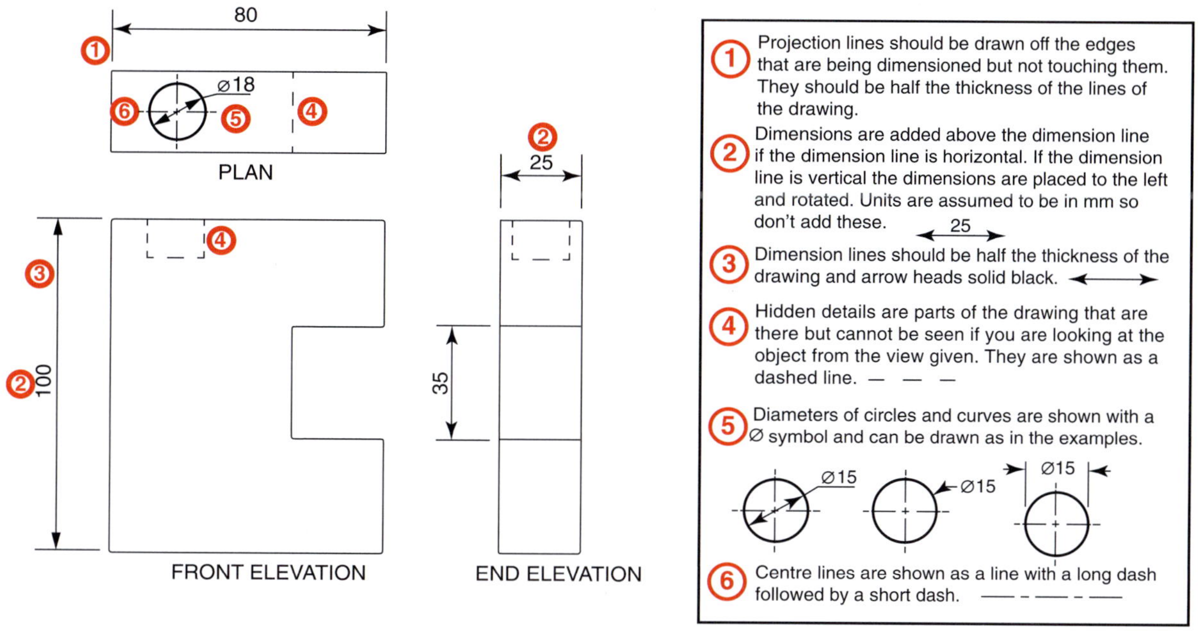

△ **Figure 1** British Standards are one of the conventions used for working drawings.

TOP TIP

CAD takes the complexity out of dimensioning and scaling by automating calculations and ensuring that design changes are reflected accurately throughout the drawing. Some CAD software even uses AI to allow you to automate the layout of the dimensions on the drawing!

GEOMETRICAL CONSTRUCTIONS

In geometrical constructions, you use only a compass, protractor and ruler to create precise shapes, lines and angles. It is a fundamental skill for developing accuracy in your drawing. Here, you will learn about dividing lines and angles, and constructing **regular plane linear shapes** (triangles, quadrilaterals, pentagons, hexagons, octagons), as well as circles, **tangents**, **tangential arcs** and **ellipses**.

Lines and angles

Dividing a line (line **bisection**) means splitting a line segment into two equal parts (Figure 2). Follow these steps to divide a line:

1. Open the compass to more than half the line's length.
2. Draw arcs above and below the line from one endpoint.
3. Repeat from the other endpoint, so the arcs intersect.
4. Connect the intersections with a straight line.

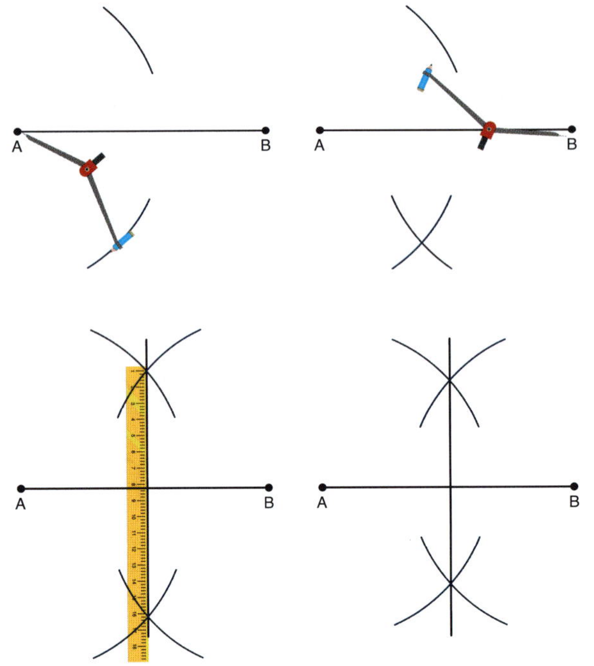

△ **Figure 2** Line bisection steps

Dividing an angle (angle bisection) means splitting an angle into two equal angles (Figure 3). Follow these steps to divide an angle:

1. Draw an arc across both angle sides from the vertex (where the lines meet).
2. Draw intersecting arcs from those intersections within the angle.
3. Draw a line from the vertex to the intersection of the arcs.

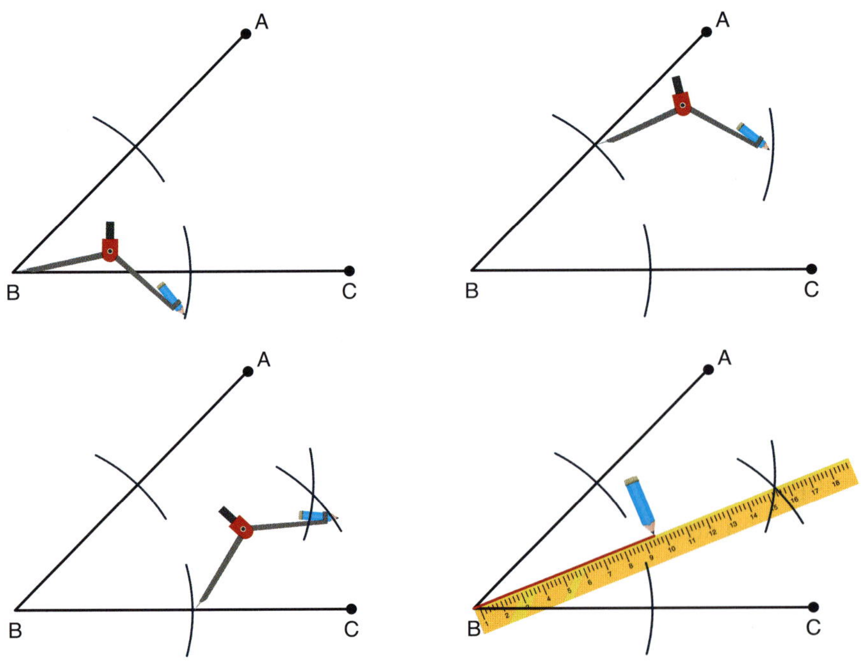

△ **Figure 3** Angle bisection steps

SKILLS ACTIVITY 1

Bisecting lines and angles

Practise bisecting lines and angles.

To create accurate design drawings, you must be able to construct basic shapes such as circles, ellipses and regular plane linear shapes. Even though CAD can produce these shapes with high precision, mastering the basics by hand is essential.

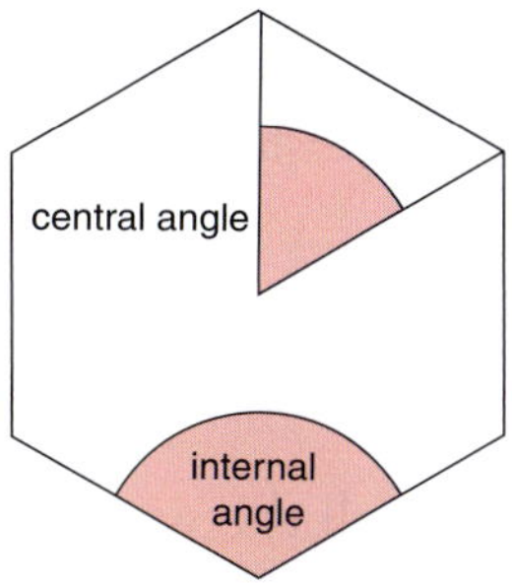

Δ **Figure 4** A hexagon showing the internal and central angles

Regular plane linear shapes

A regular plane linear shape has sides of equal length and internal angles of equal size (Figure 4). To find the central angle, you can divide 360° by the number of sides.

SKILLS ACTIVITY 2

Identifying regular plane linear shapes and their features

Copy and complete Table 1, showing some regular plane linear shapes and their central angles.

Number of sides	Name	Central angle (°)
3	Triangle	120
4	Quadrilateral (square)	90
5	Pentagon	?
6	?	60
7	Heptagon	?
?	?	45
9	?	?

Δ **Table 1** Regular plane linear shapes and their central angles

Drawing a hexagon using a compass and a protractor

1. Draw a circle with the same radius as your intended hexagon.

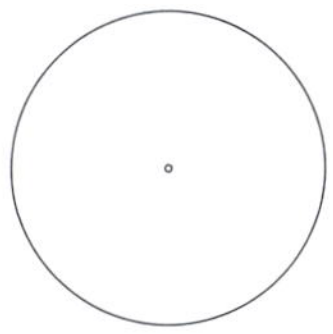

2. Place the protractor on the circle lining up the centre. Mark out 60° on the circle and draw a line from the centre.

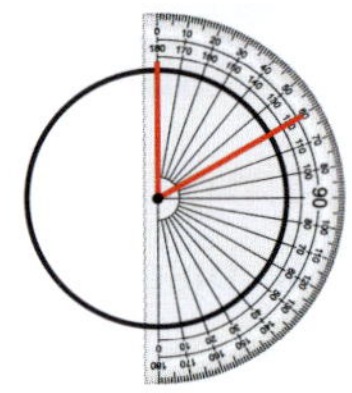

3. Rotate the protractor so it is lined up with the line you have drawn. Repeat the previous step.

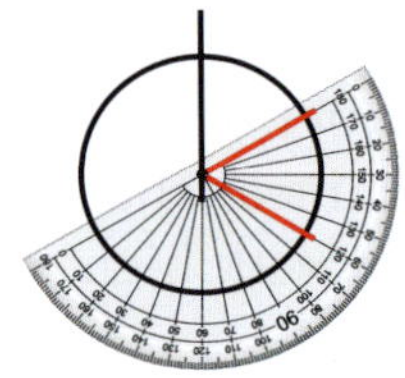

4. Repeat all the way round the circle.

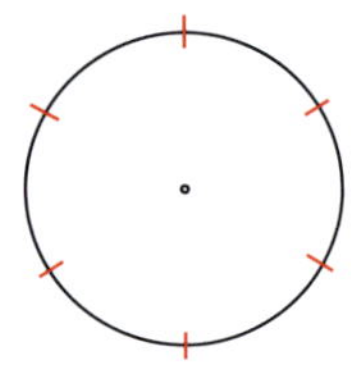

5. Join up the areas where the lines intersect the circle.

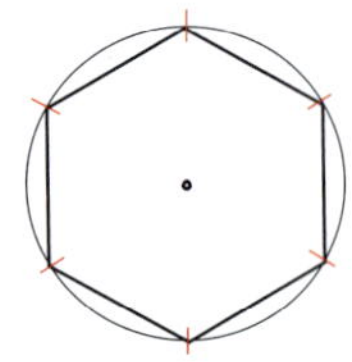

TOP TIP

Another way of drawing a regular plane linear shape is to use a compass to measure the distance between the first two lines. Then mark out the remainder of the points of the regular plane linear shape on the circle, before joining them up (Figure 5).

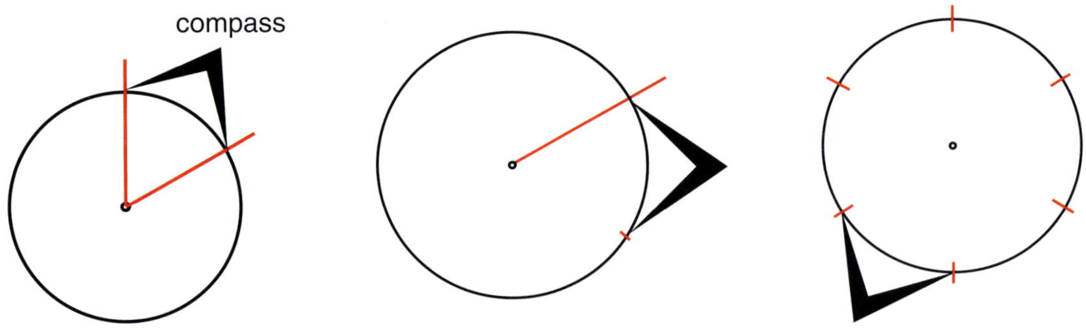

Δ **Figure 5** You can use a compass instead of a protractor to mark out the points after the first two lines have been drawn.

Drawing circles and ellipses

You can draw a circle by drawing lines of equal distances and angles and connecting the end points (Figure 6). Draw six lines as a minimum, and increase the number of lines for greater accuracy.

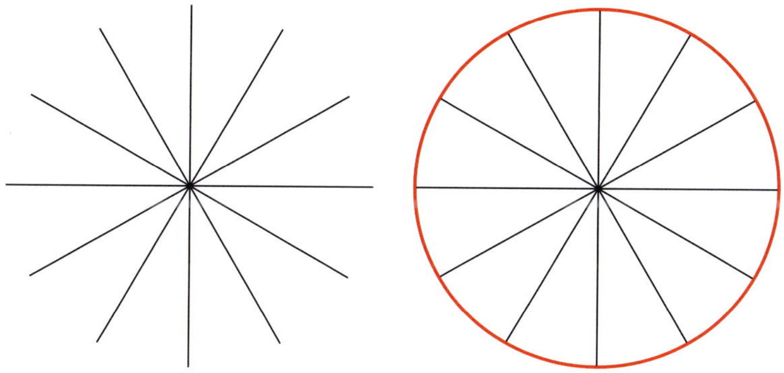

△ **Figure 6** Drawing a circle by drawing lines

To draw an ellipse, start with the same angled lines as you would for a circle and draw two circles with the diameters of the intended minor and major axis of the ellipse. Where the angled lines intersect the smaller circle, draw horizontal lines. Draw vertical lines where they intersect the larger circle. Make a point where these two lines intersect, then join up all of the points (Figure 7).

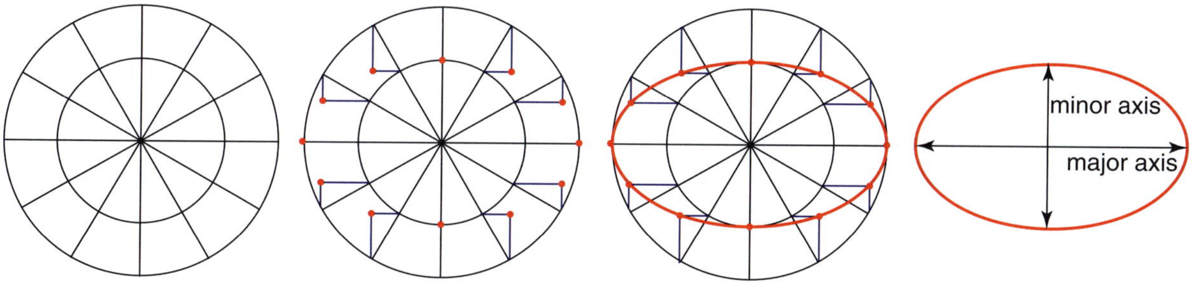

△ **Figure 7** Drawing an ellipse

Another way you can draw circles and ellipses is to use a template or stencil. However, these limit the sizes you are able to draw.

Drawing an ellipse using a trammel

A third way of drawing an ellipse is by using a trammel. A trammel can be made from a folded piece of paper or strip of card. This is an easy and accurate method of drawing an ellipse (Figure 8).

1. Draw two intersecting lines the lengths of the intended diameter of your minor and major axes.
2. Lay a folded piece of paper or strip of card (your trammel) against the minor axis with the corner of the card touching the top of the minor axis.
3. Mark (a) on the card where the axes intersect.
4. Rotate the card and mark (b) where the axes intersect.
5. Keeping (a) somewhere on the major axes and (b) on the minor axes, make a mark at the top corner of the card.
6. Repeat this several times around the axes.
7. Join up the marks for an ellipse.

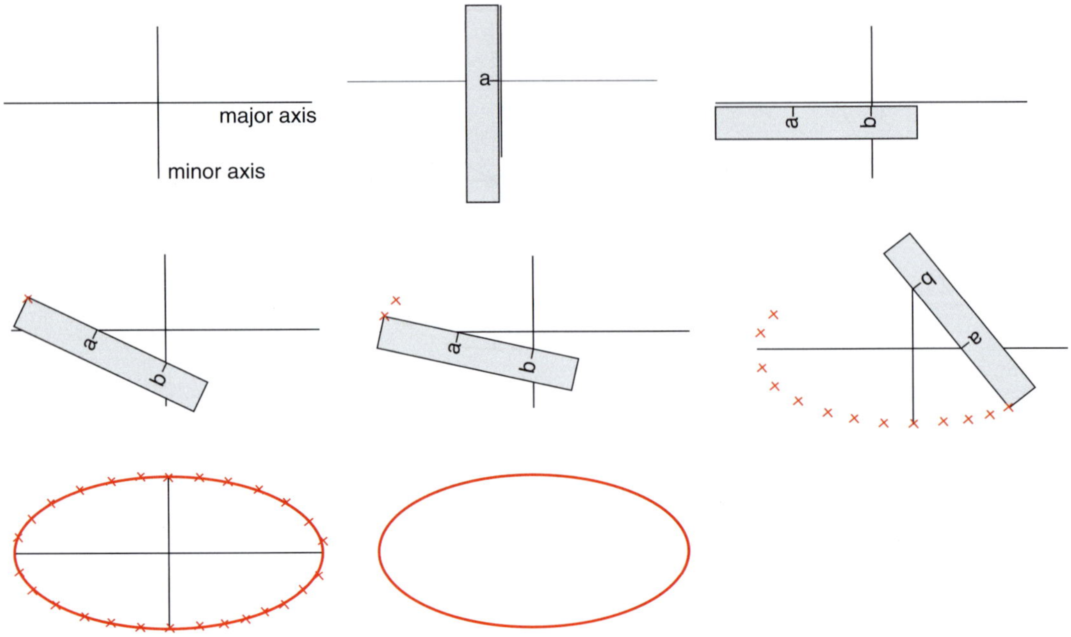

△ **Figure 8** Ellipses can also be drawn using the trammel method.

SKILLS ACTIVITY 3

Drawing circles and ellipses

Now it's your turn. Practise drawing circles and ellipses using one of the methods described.

Drawing tangents and tangential arcs

A tangent is a line that touches a circle or curve at a certain point (Figure 9). To draw a tangent:

1. Draw a circle with a point where you want the tangent.
2. Draw a line from the centre through the point.
3. Place the centre line of your protractor on this line and the bottom of the protractor just touching the circle.
4. Draw the tangent.
5. You can also use these lines to draw a tangential arc. Draw a perpendicular line from the centre of the circle through the part of the circle you want your tangential arc to be. Set your compass to the correct radius and draw the tangential arc, making sure the point of your compass is on the perpendicular line you have drawn.

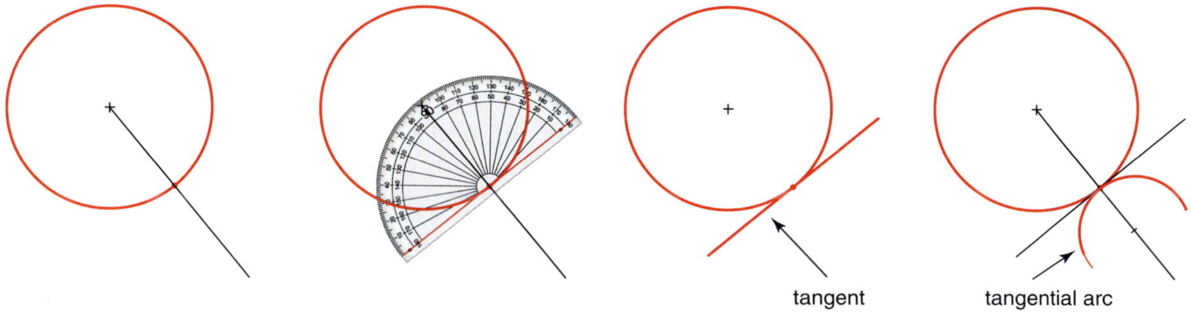

Δ **Figure 9** Drawing tangents and tangential arcs

SKILLS ACTIVITY 4

Skills practice

Practise drawing tangents and tangential arcs using the steps described.

ORTHOGRAPHIC DRAWING

To communicate designs effectively, designers use formal drawing techniques. Orthographic drawing is a formal drawing technique that shows three sides of a product at a specific scale. Orthographic drawings help other people make or manufacture our designs.

First and third angle projections

There are two main types of orthographic projection: **third angle projection** and **first angle projection**. There are different projection symbols for each (Figure 10). See Figure 11 for a pictorial view.

In a third angle projection, the top view is top left, above the front view (Figure 12).

In a first angle projection, the top view is bottom right, below the front view (Figure 13).

Dashed lines in the drawings indicate **hidden details**. These are parts you would not normally see, but they need to be shown on the drawing (Figures 12 and 13).

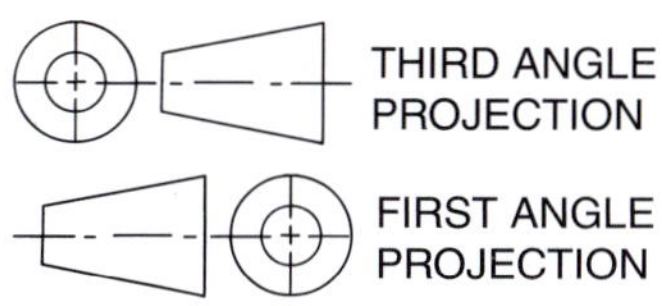

Δ **Figure 10** Projection symbols

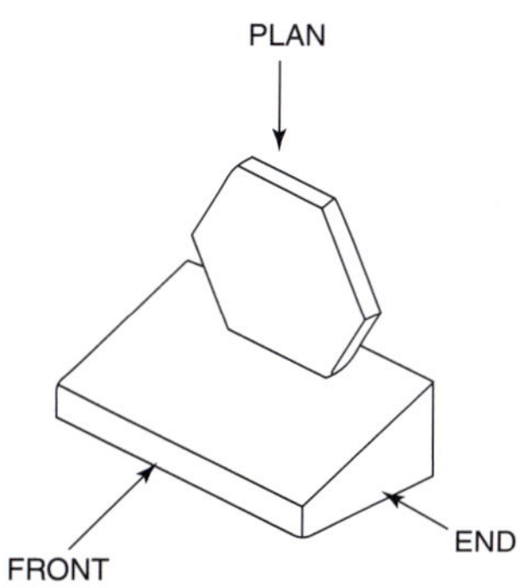

Δ **Figure 11** A pictorial view of a product

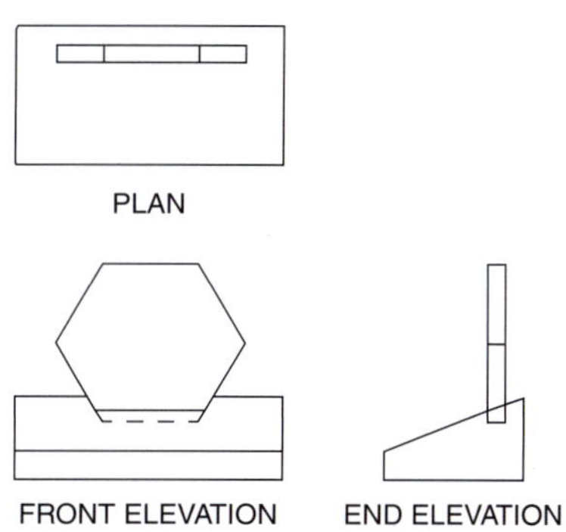

Δ **Figure 12** Third angle projection

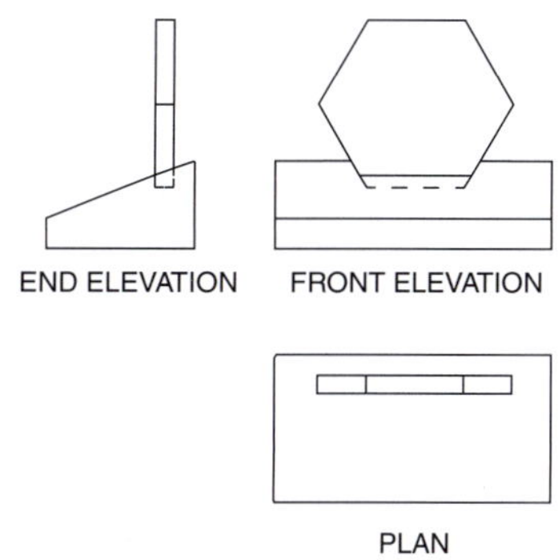

Δ **Figure 13** First angle projection

SKILLS ACTIVITY 5

Making an orthographic drawing

Find an object in your bag or pencil case, such as a pencil sharpener. Keeping one eye closed, look at it from the top and sketch what you see. Now turn it to the front and sketch what you see. Do the same from the side. Make sure you only draw the one side you are looking at. These three views would form the plan, front elevation and end elevation of an orthographic drawing.

REFLECTIVE LOG

Scale and standard conventions

Do you remember how to add scale and dimensions to your drawings? What is the standard that you will use?

SKILLS ACTIVITY 6

Drawing a third angle projection

It is now time to apply dimensions to our drawings. Try the following skills activity to get practising.

Figure 14 shows a trophy. The trophy consists of two parts: a circular base and a shape which slots into the base. The assembled trophy is shown on the left of Figure 14. Draw the assembled trophy in third-angle projection at a scale of 1:2. Remember to add dimensions.

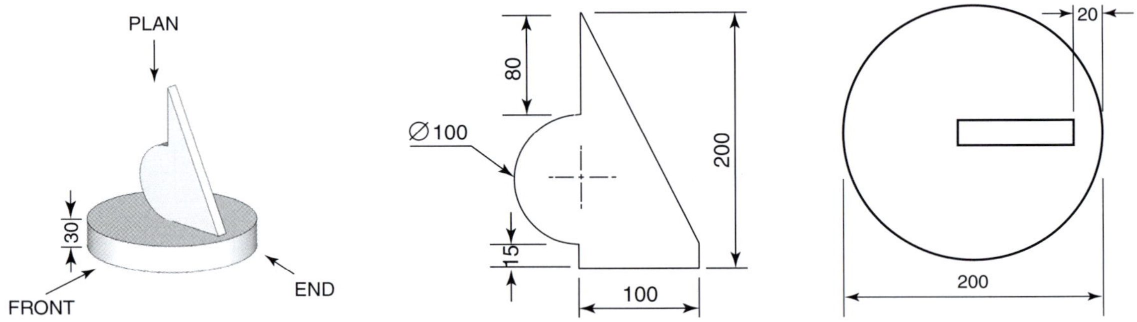

∆ **Figure 14** Views of a trophy

Sectional views

Sometimes, you need to see what's going on *inside* an object. For this, you need sectional views. This is like using a saw to slice through the object so you can see its internal details. The 'slice' is called the **cutting plane**.

Imagine an object with a hidden hole and a peg inside (Figure 15). A sectional view lets you clearly show how the peg fits into the hole, which you cannot see from a regular view.

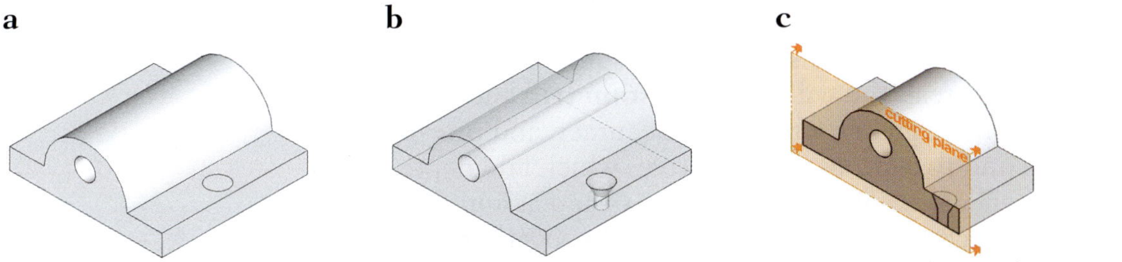

△ **Figure 15** The object: **a** with a hole through the middle; **b** shown as a see-through view; **c** showing the cut view

Figure 16 shows the plan of the object with a line through the middle (A–A) indicating where the cutting plane is. Figure 17 is a sectional view. In a sectional view, the part of the object that has been cut is cross-hatched at 45°. There is no hatching where the hole is, as it is empty space. Notice the hatching on the peg – it is in the opposite direction since it is a separate, solid object.

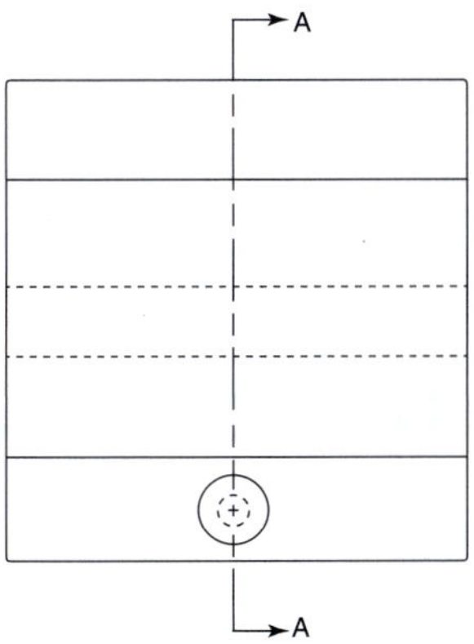

△ **Figure 16** A plan of the object and cutting plane A–A

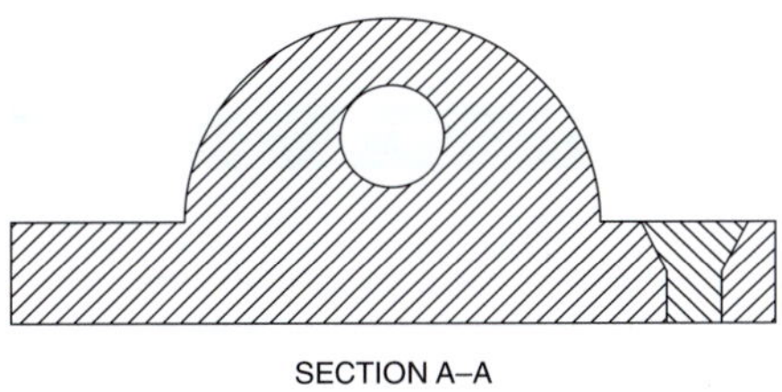

△ **Figure 17** A sectional view

SKILLS ACTIVITY 7

Drawing a sectional view

Figure 18 shows a pictorial drawing of an object. Draw the object as a sectional view along A–A, using the scale 1:1.

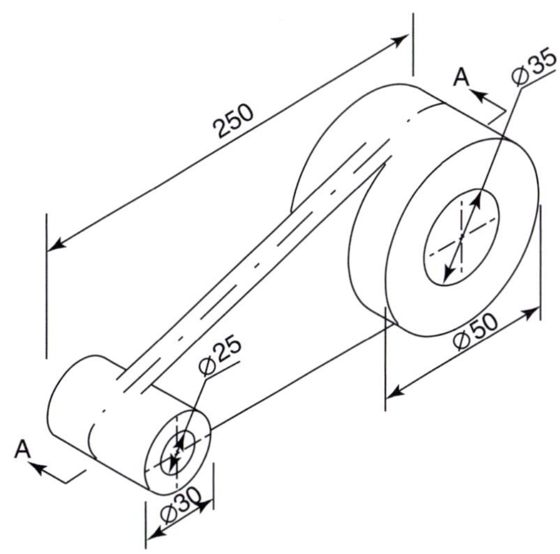

△ **Figure 18** A drawing of an object

THREE-DIMENSIONAL DRAWING

Ready to draw in three dimensions? Learn some techniques to make your designs look real. You will discover **isometric** and **planometric** drawings, which are great for technical accuracy, and **one-point perspective** and **two-point perspective**, which add depth and realism. You will also explore exploded views and assembly drawings – both are great ways to show how a product fits together.

Isometric and planometric

Isometric drawings are three-dimensional drawings at 60° and 30°. Isometric drawings are usually used to visualise products in three dimensions.

Planometric drawings are commonly used for interior rooms of buildings, as they can be drawn from the plan view of a room. Planometric drawings are drawn at 45° (Figure 19). You can use isometric paper underlay or a set square to help you draw in either isometric or planometric.

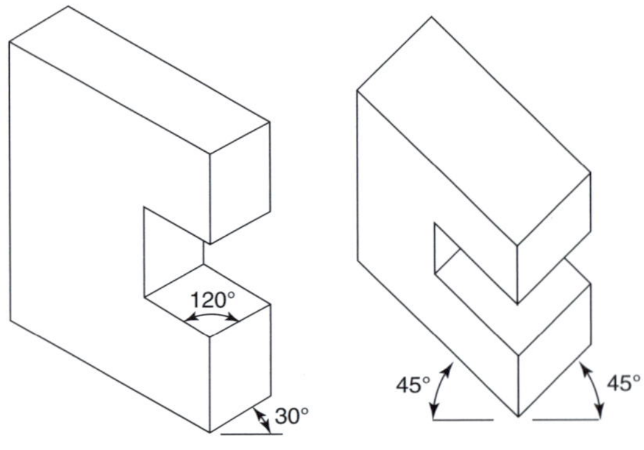

Δ **Figure 19** Isometric and planometric drawings

TOP TIP

Crating

Whatever the object you are drawing in isometric, it is important that you draw a constructional cube or cuboid first, which is the total length, width and height of the object you are drawing. You can then draw the object inside this cuboid. This is called **crating** (Figure 20). This will help you get the sizes and proportions right when you draw the object.

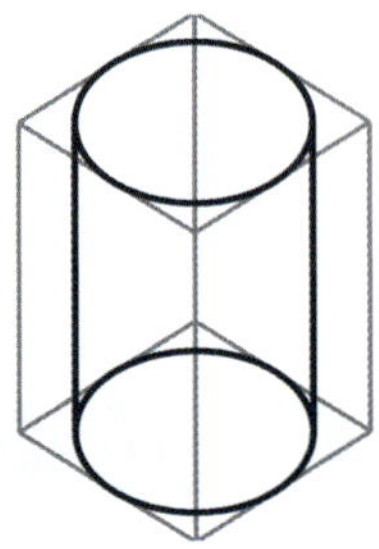

Δ **Figure 20** An example of crating

Perspective drawing

Perspective is a great way to create realism (Figure 21). It creates a convincing three-dimensional effect with a horizon line and vanishing points. In one-point perspective, depth lines converge on one vanishing point. Two-point perspective uses two vanishing points to represent both depth and width, resulting in a more realistic image.

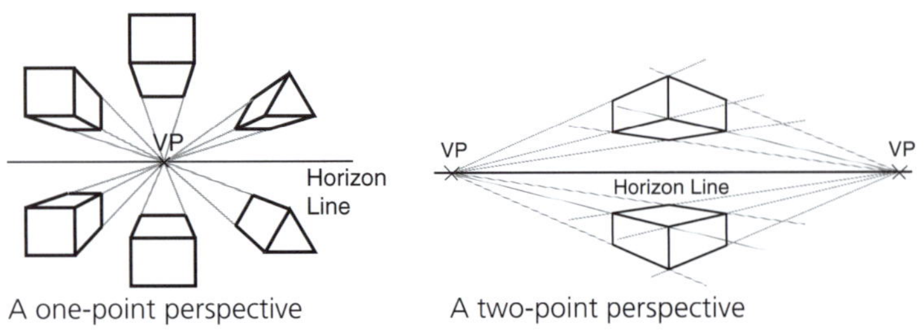

Δ **Figure 21** Perspective drawings

Notice that by drawing the object above or below the horizon line, it makes it look like you are looking at the object from above or below.

EXPLODED VIEWS AND ASSEMBLY DRAWINGS

An exploded view shows different components separated from each other by a certain distance. The parts appear to be floating in space. An assembly drawing is the opposite, and shows all the parts assembled. Exploded views are useful for showing how pieces fit together and in which order. They can often be found as instructions for assembling flat-packed furniture.

Exploded views should be drawn as line drawings in isometric. The components should line up with each other correctly, so you need to draw construction lines before completing an exploded view.

The object in Figure 22 has three pegs and an additional plug for the hole. The first image is the object with all the parts assembled. The second image shows all the parts separated.

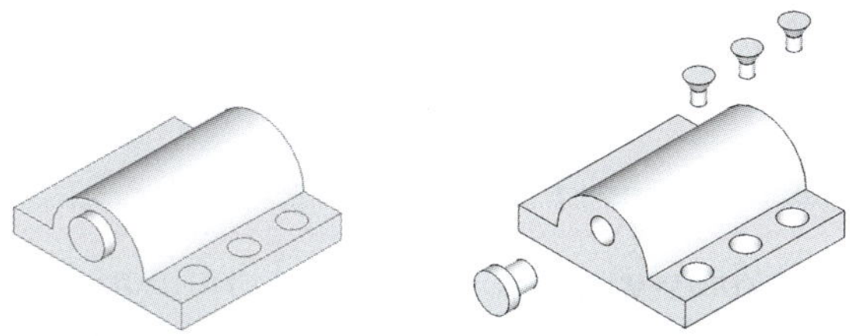

A pictorial view of an assembled product

An exploded drawing showing the separate parts

△ **Figure 22** An exploded view

TOP TIP

To construct an accurate exploded view, you need to use crating as constructional lines in the first image. Make sure these are at the correct angles and in line with the holes or slots on the drawing. In Figure 23, image **a** shows the object drawn using crating, while image **b** shows the completed exploded view.

a **b**

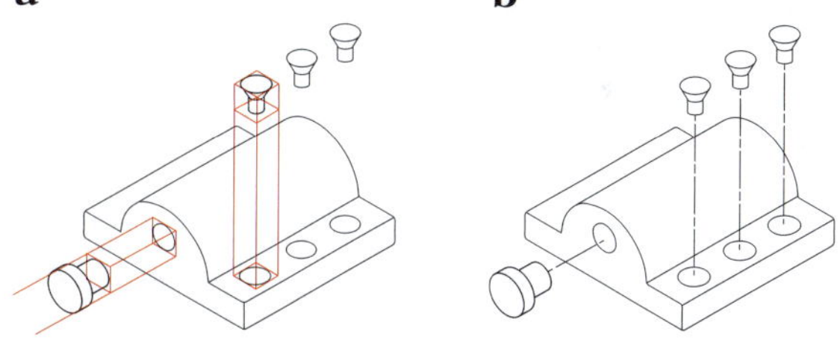

△ **Figure 23** Using crating to draw an exploded view

SKILLS ACTIVITY 8

Drawing isometric exploded views

Figure 24 is a pictorial drawing of a children's toy. The three shapes can be removed from the holes in the base. Also shown is the side elevation of the base of the toy. Draw an isometric exploded view of the toy with the shapes removed. Estimate all sizes.

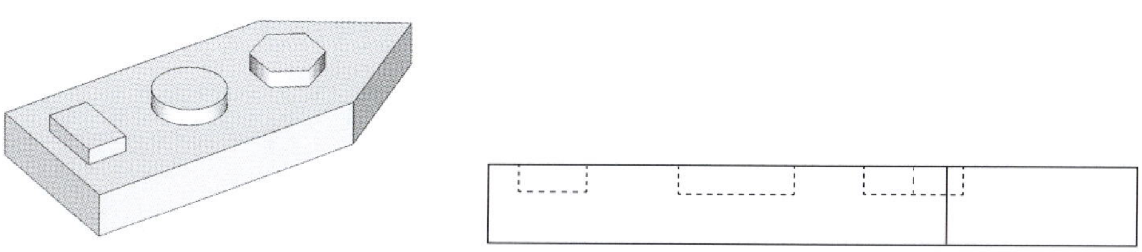

△ **Figure 24** A pictorial view of a children's toy

Parts list

A **parts list** often accompanies an exploded drawing. This shows all the parts and components needed to assemble the product. Compiling a parts list can help keep track of which components are needed for your product and are often used for calculating cost (Table 2).

Item	Quantity	Unit	Price/unit ($)	Total cost ($)
Red acrylic	1 sheet	3 mm sheet	6.63	6.63
Blue acrylic	1 sheet	3 mm sheet	6.63	6.63
Coated card	10 sheets	3 mm sheet	1.50	15.00
ABS	200 g	1 kg spool	20.00	4.00
Plastic rivets	10	100 pc	0.10	10.00
			Total	**42.26**

△ **Table 2** A parts list

Part drawings are individual component drawings from an assembly. These can be drawn separately using orthographic projection.

DESIGN IN ACTION

The ability to accurately represent three-dimensional objects is crucial for some careers, such as being a 3D artist (Figure 25). For example, creating 3D visuals for video games, virtual reality (VR) experiences and augmented reality (AR) relies heavily on the ability to accurately represent objects and environments in 3D space – a core skill taught by technical drawing.

Technical drawing provides a good foundation for a 3D artist by providing them with skills such as:

- *Precision and accuracy:* 3D artists need precise measurements and scale, emphasised in technical drawing, for accurate modelling of characters, buildings and other assets.
- *Understanding form:* Geometrical constructions provide a foundation for realistic and functional models, from vehicles that move correctly to characters with believable anatomy.
- *Visual communication:* 3D artists use visual communication skills, including sketches and technical drawings, to convey design ideas to clients and team members.

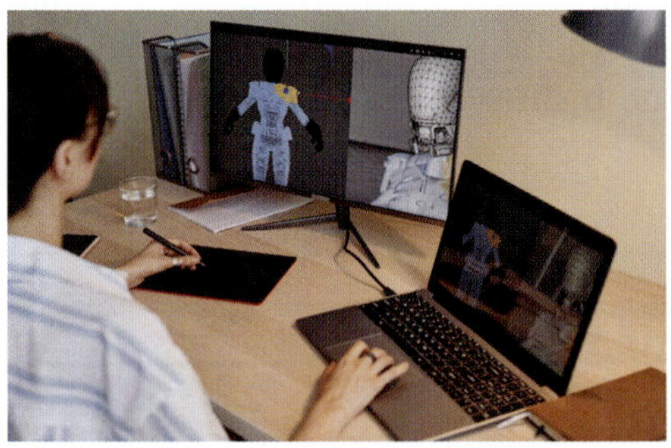

△ **Figure 25** A 3D artist at work

DEVELOPMENTS

To design your own packaging or 3D products you will need to understand developments (also called nets). This section shows you how to create flat patterns and temporary and permanent ways to join these patterns together to make 3D shapes.

Three-dimensional shapes

Three-dimensional shapes have length, width and height (Figure 26). This means they take up space and have volume, unlike 2D shapes which are flat. Look around you. There are 3D shapes everywhere: boxes, cans, balls and many more.

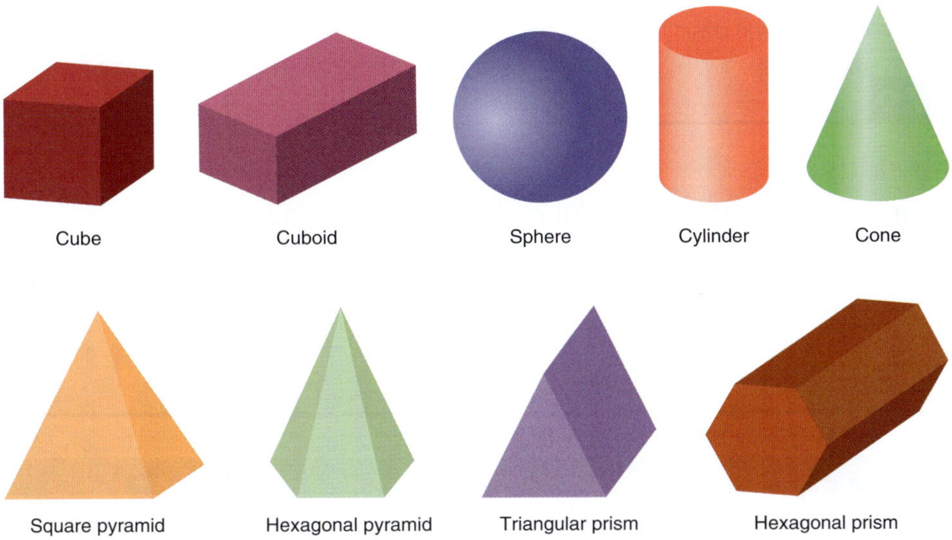

△ **Figure 26** There are many different three-dimensional shapes

Freehand drawing

While tools like rulers and protractors are useful, freehand drawing is all about *speed* and *energy*. It empowers designers to quickly visualise and share their vision, whether they are sketching out a new gadget or designing a whole building.

You can use the crating technique to draw various 3D shapes (Figure 27). Remember, crating involves drawing the shape within a lightly sketched cuboid frame to help maintain proportion and accuracy. For example, follow these steps to use crating to draw a cylinder:

1. Draw the cuboid: Begin by sketching a transparent isometric cuboid (lightly!) that will fully enclose the cylinder.
2. The height of the cuboid will be the height of the cylinder.
3. The base of the cuboid will be a square with sides equal to the diameter of the cylinder's circular ends.
4. Draw the ellipses: Sketch ellipses within the top and bottom faces of the cuboid. These ellipses represent the circular ends of the cylinder.

5. Important: In isometric drawings, remember that circles appear as elongated ellipses, not perfect circles.
6. Connect the ellipses: Finally, draw straight lines connecting the edges of the top and bottom ellipses. These lines form the sides of the cylinder.

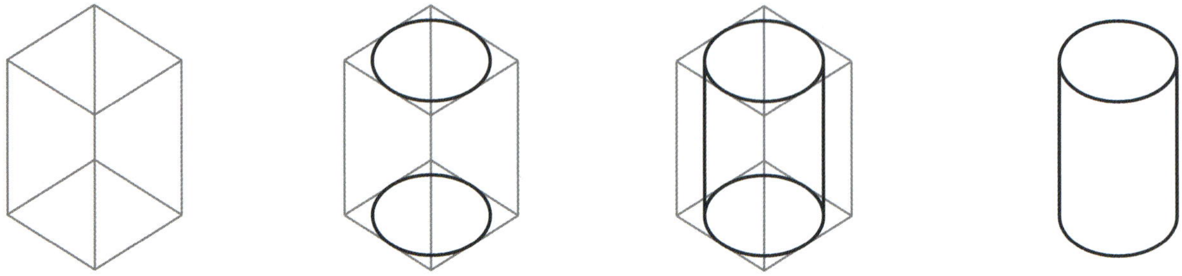

Δ **Figure 27** Steps for drawing a cylinder using crating

SKILLS ACTIVITY 9

Freehand drawing skills

Using freehand drawing and the crating technique, draw the following 3D shapes.

- Triangular prism
- Hexagonal prism
- Cone

TOP TIP

Mix it up! To communicate your designs effectively, practise selecting and using a range of different types of drawing for each idea (for example, isometric to show the whole product, sectional to show a part inside, exploded to show how components fit together, orthographic to give information on dimensions).

From three-dimensional shapes to developments

A development (or net) is a 3D shape flattened out to form a template. Designers need to visualise and draw developments accurately for efficient packaging design.

In design and manufacturing, CAD helps create great nets and **die cutters** can produce them quickly.

TOP TIP

The first step in producing a development from a pictorial (3D) view is to visualise unfolding the shape. In your head, begin with the side that is flat on the surface and unfold each side until it is flat. It helps to make a quick sketch of the development before you draw it accurately or to scale. Remember to consider how many sides the shape has and position the first face carefully on the paper so you can fit it all in.

SKILLS ACTIVITY 10

Sketching developments

Figure 28 shows pictorial views of three shapes. Sketch the development of each shape. Estimate all sizes.

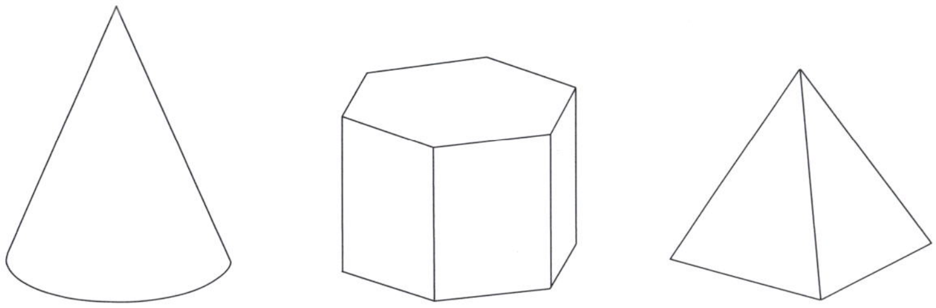

Δ **Figure 28** A pictorial view of three shapes

PACKAGING AND CONSTRUCTION DETAILS

To design packaging that works, you have not only got to be able to draw its development but also include all the crucial **construction details**, such as flaps and tabs. Dust flaps are guards against dirt, tuck flaps lock the lid in place, and glue tabs are what you use to stick the sides together (Figure 29). Remember that the dashed lines are your fold lines.

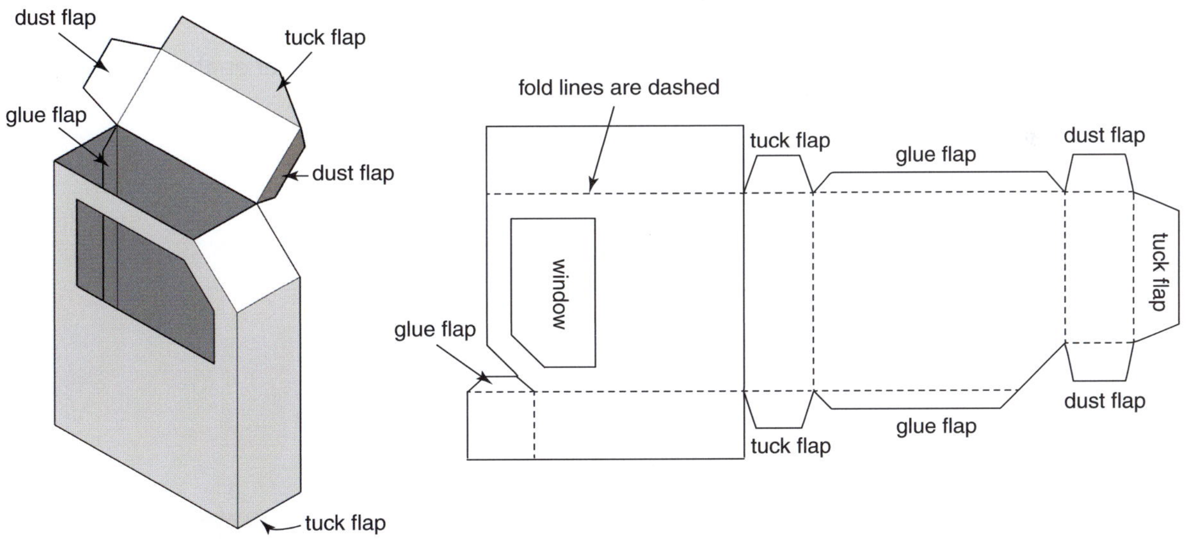

Δ **Figure 29** Packaging developments (nets) have flaps and tabs added to allow for easy assembly and security.

SKILLS ACTIVITY 11

Sketching developments with flaps and tabs

Using freehand drawing, sketch the developments of all pieces of packaging in Figure 30. Add any relevant flaps and tabs to ensure the packaging is secure and can be opened easily. Estimate all sizes.

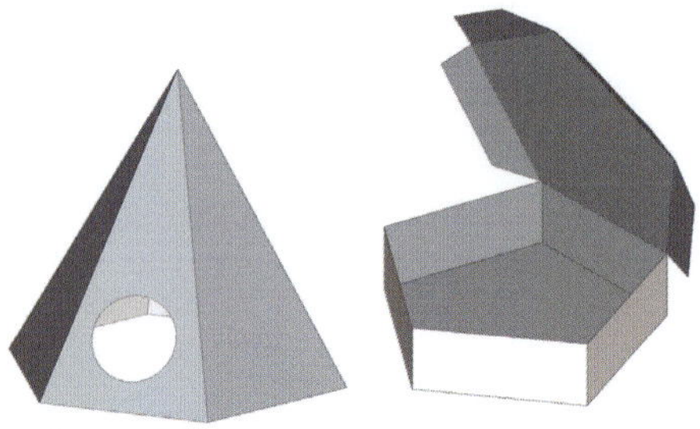

∆ **Figure 30** Pieces of packaging

REFLECTIVE LOG

Tetra Paks®, as you may have learned in unit 3.1.4, are composite wonders (Figure 31). But how does a flat net become a carton *in seconds*?

Your task is to uncover the secrets of automated Tetra Pak® assembly!

1. Research how the net design is designed for high-speed manufacturing.
2. Identify the critical construction details and explain how the manufacturer enables efficient, automated folding and sealing.

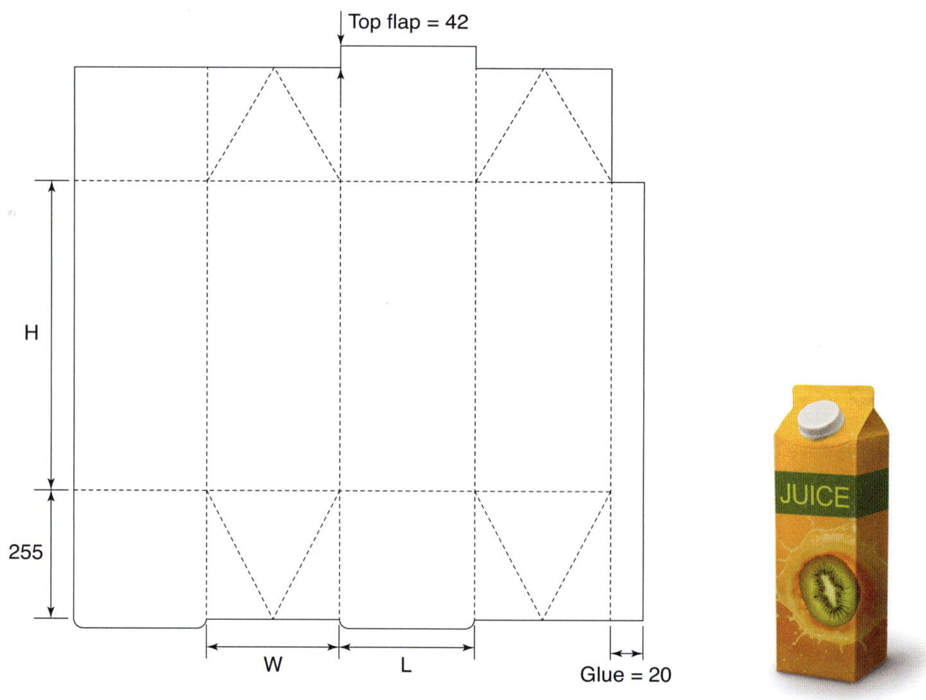

∆ **Figure 31** Tetra Paks® are designed to be assembled by automated manufacturing.

Methods of joining developments

So, you have gone from three-dimensional shapes to unfolded nets and looked at those crucial construction details. But what about those essential methods for joining developments? From quick fixes like tape, to more permanent solutions like glue and clever tab designs, there are multiple ways to create functional packaging from developments.

Adhesives are an example of permanent joining methods in packaging. Choose carefully – glue sticks are easy but not super strong, while hot glue is great for thicker card. Double-sided adhesive tape gives a tidy, tough bond if you apply it carefully. These methods make sure your packaging stays firmly together.

Tabs and flaps mean no glue is needed. Pizza boxes are an example of temporary joining methods. They are shipped flat and assembled fast by folding and slotting (Figure 32). The double fold of the front edge locks onto a side tab and into the base, creating a strong, stable box. Simple!

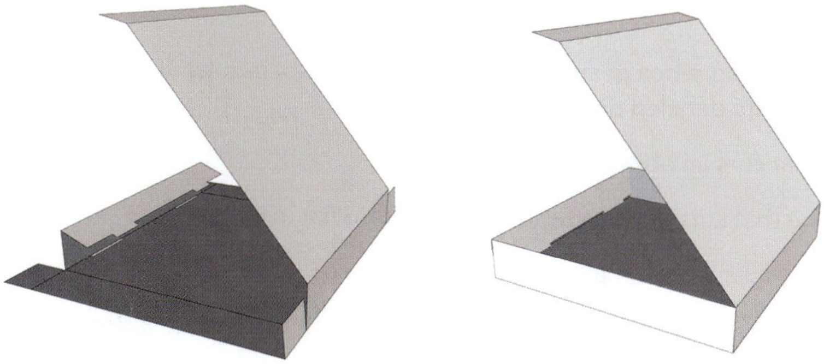

Δ **Figure 32** Pizza boxes use foldover locking flaps

TOP TIP

To go deeper into joining methods, look at unit 3.3.3 Joining.

SKILLS ACTIVITY 12

Investigating packaging

Find three items of packaging at home. Take them apart so they are flat and consider the following questions:

1. What materials are they made from? What properties make them suitable for this kind of packaging?
2. How is the packaging assembled? Are there any flaps or tabs? How do they each lock together as packages?
3. What adhesives have been used to hold the packages together?
4. Using freehand drawing, sketch the developments and label the construction details (folds, flaps and tabs).

KNOWLEDGE CHECK

1. Describe the difference between 'dimensioning' and 'scale' in technical drawing.
2. Identify **three** regular plane linear shapes.
3. Compare planometric and isometric drawing.
4. Sketch the symbols for first and third angle orthographic projection.
5. Explain what is meant by 'hidden detail'.
6. Explain how crating is used in isometric or planometric drawing.
7. Explain why construction details are necessary when designing a net for packaging.
8. Justify **one** reason why temporary joining methods are used for pizza boxes.

KEY TERMS

Bisection: Splitting a segment into two equal parts

British Standards: In technical drawing, British Standards are guidelines from the British Standards Institution that define how drawings should be created and presented

Construction details: Additional elements added to a net design to enable assembly, such as tabs, flaps and fold lines

Crating: Drawing a simple 3D shape first (e.g. a box or cylinder), or combination of regular 3D shapes, inside which you can draw a more detailed design.

Cutting plane: An imaginary slice that cuts an object

Die cutter: A manufacturing machine that cuts out the desired shapes from flat material

Ellipse: An oval shape like a flattened circle; it has a major axis and a minor axis

First angle projection: A method of laying out an orthographic drawing with the end elevation in the top left and the plan view below the front view

Hidden detail: Parts of an object that cannot be seen, shown by a dotted line on the drawing

Isometric drawing: A 3D drawing method using 30° angles to give a realistic sense of shape

One-point perspective: A method of making a realistic three-dimensional drawing using one vanishing point and a horizon line

Part drawings: Component parts from an assembly which are usually drawn using orthographic projection

Parts list: A table that itemises all the components required to assemble a product

Planometric drawing: A method of drawing a three-dimensional object at 45° angles, and with no distortion of the floor plan or base.

Regular plane linear shapes: Two-dimensional shapes with straight sides where all sides have equal length and all interior angles are equal

Tangent: A line that touches a circle or curve but does not intersect it

Tangential arc: An arc that touches a circle or curve but does not intersect it

Third angle projection: A method of laying out an orthographic drawing with the end elevation in the bottom right and the plan view and front elevation to the left

Two-point perspective: A method of making a realistic three-dimensional drawing using two vanishing points and a horizon line

3·2·2 Methods of communicating information

LEARNING AIMS

By the end of this unit, you should:

✓ Draw histograms, pie charts, bar charts and graphs from data provided
✓ Interpret histograms, pie charts, bar charts and graphs
✓ Draw flowcharts to describe processes, operations or assemblies

Graphic designers often need to present information in visual form. This could be anything from showing data to a client, explaining a design process to a team or creating an **infographic** for a magazine. They use different types of charts, graphs and diagrams to help to:

- present numerical data clearly (such as sales figures or website statistics)
- show how things are connected (such as the steps in a design project)
- make complex information easy to understand at a glance.

GRAPHS AND CHARTS

Graphs and charts are not just abstract diagrams; they are essential tools for graphic designers. They help you communicate information effectively, whether it is showcasing the success of a marketing campaign or outlining the steps in a design process.

Bar charts

Bar charts are used to compare data that falls into distinct categories:

- The ***x*-axis** shows the *categories* (for example, age groups).
- The ***y*-axis** shows the *quantity* for each category (for example, the number of students).

SKILLS ACTIVITY

Interpreting bar charts

Interpret the two-dimensional and three-dimensional bar charts in Figure 1 and state:

- the total number of students aged 14
- the total number of students aged below 13
- the total number of students altogether.

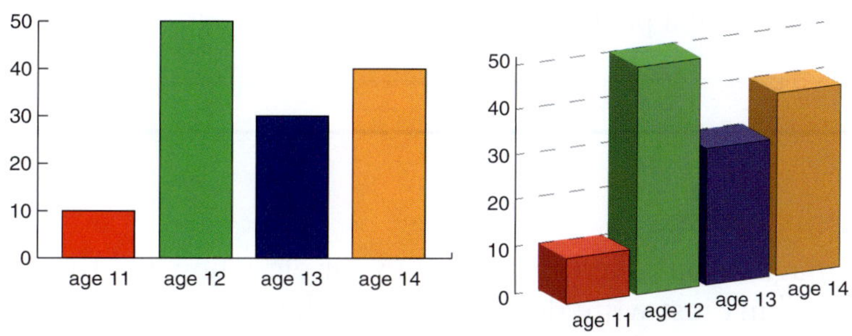

△ **Figure 1** Bar charts can be two-dimensional or three-dimensional.

TOP TIP

When drawing bar charts and line graphs, use a ruler or grid paper to measure out the equal distances between the data range on the *x*- and *y*-axes.

Line graphs

Line graphs often show changes over time.

- The *x*-axis is the *time scale* (for example, days of the week).
- The *y*-axis is what is being *measured* (for example, temperature).

In Figure 2, the line graph also shows the highest and lowest temperatures, represented by different lines. There is a **key** to explain what the lines on the graph mean.

SKILLS ACTIVITY

Interpreting a line graph

Interpret the line graph in Figure 2 and identify:

- the highest temperature on Wednesday
- the average temperature on Friday
- the coldest and warmest days.

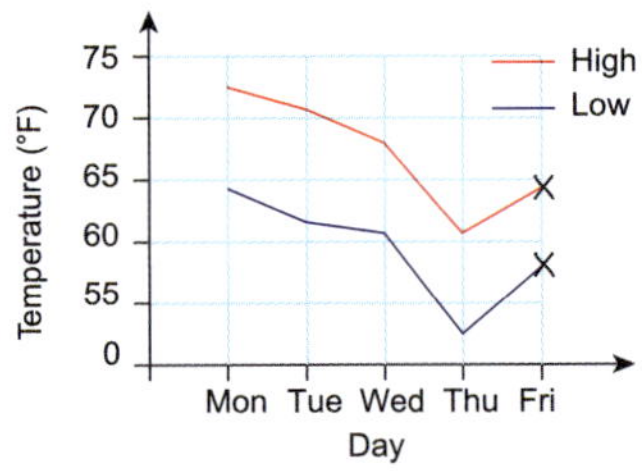

Δ **Figure 2** An example of a line graph

Pie charts

Pie charts can be used to compare percentages or parts of a whole. Again, a key is used to label the sections of the chart.

SKILLS ACTIVITY

Interpreting a pie chart

Interpret the pie chart in Figure 3 and identify:

- the most popular lunch option for students
- the least popular lunch option for students
- an estimate of the percentage of students who take a packed lunch to school.

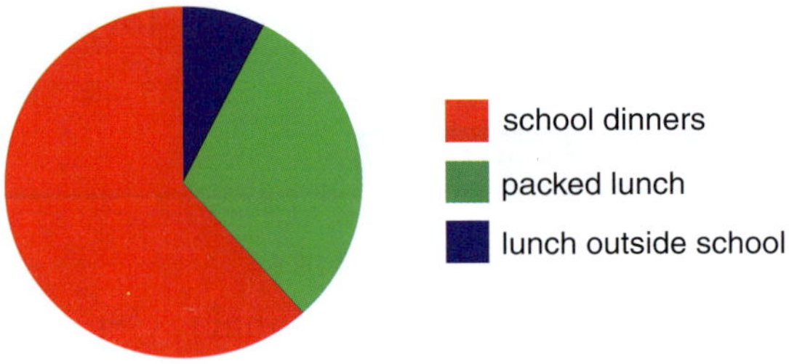

Δ **Figure 3** An example of a pie chart

Histograms

Imagine you asked everyone in your class how tall they are. You wouldn't just write down everyone's height in a list, right? That would be hard to understand quickly. A histogram is one way to organise that height information into groups.

Instead of each person's exact height, you could put people into height **bins** (for example, 140–150 cm, 150–160 cm). Then, you count how many people are in *each* height range.

- The x-axis shows the height bins.
- The y-axis shows how many people are in each range.

The *taller* the bar, the *more* people are in that height range.

SKILLS ACTIVITY

Interpreting a histogram

Interpret the histogram in Figure 4 and identify:

- the number of students in the 140–150 cm height bin
- the height bin with the highest number of students.

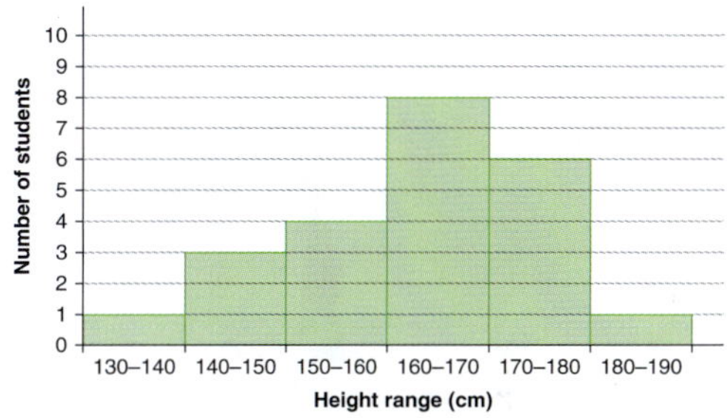

Δ **Figure 4** Histograms are useful for organising information into bins.

TOP TIP

Graphs and charts can be automatically generated from data using CAD or spreadsheet software.

SKILLS ACTIVITY

Drawing a graph or chart

Draw a suitable graph or chart to represent each of the following:

1. A school of 1150 students is organising a sports festival and has offered three sports options to students: 220 choose basketball, 570 choose baseball and 360 choose swimming.
2. A school wanted to record the change in the number of students who walk, cycle and take the bus to school over a three-year period between 2021 and 2023. Table 1 shows the data.

	2021	2022	2023
Walk	145	258	340
School bus	387	270	210
Cycle	38	42	20

Δ **Table 1** Students who walk, cycle or bus to school, 2021–2023

DESIGN IN ACTION

The power of visual information

Infographics are a great way to transform complex information into visually engaging formats (Figure 5). Designers use them to simplify, inform, persuade and engage. Infographics often have a variety of different types of charts and graphs on one graphic to communicate a range of data and information.

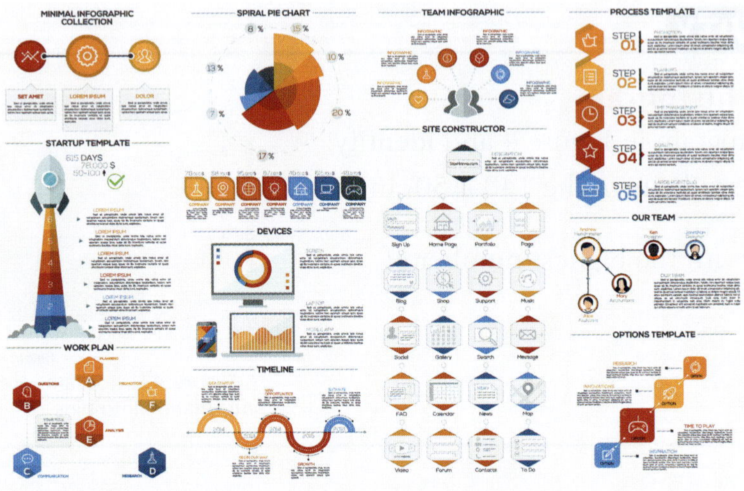

△ **Figure 5** Infographics are a visually appealing way to present complex data.

FLOWCHARTS

A flowchart shows a process in a sequential manner. It is often used in design to give information on how to make something. A flowchart always runs from top to bottom and consists of a series of shapes (Figures 6 and 7) with connector arrows. The shapes used to show different functions during the process are as follows:

- A rounded shape is called a terminator, and is used at the start and end of the process.
- A rectangle is used to show a stage in the process.
- A diamond shape is used for a decision or quality check. There should be two arrows leading from this box to other parts of the process. This is called a feedback loop.
- A parallelogram is used for input/output. This stage indicates something which is added or removed from the process.

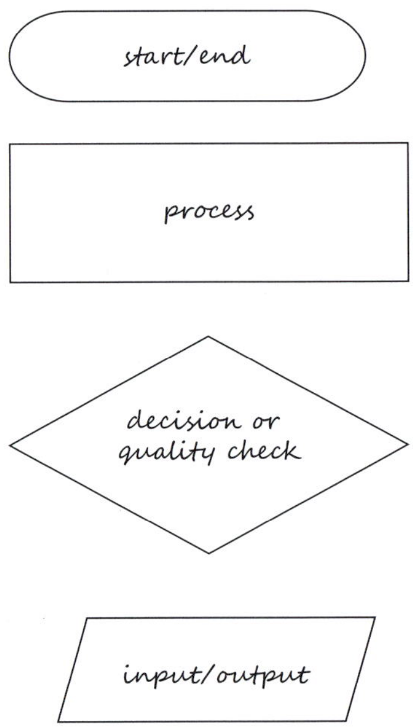

△ **Figure 6** Flowchart symbols

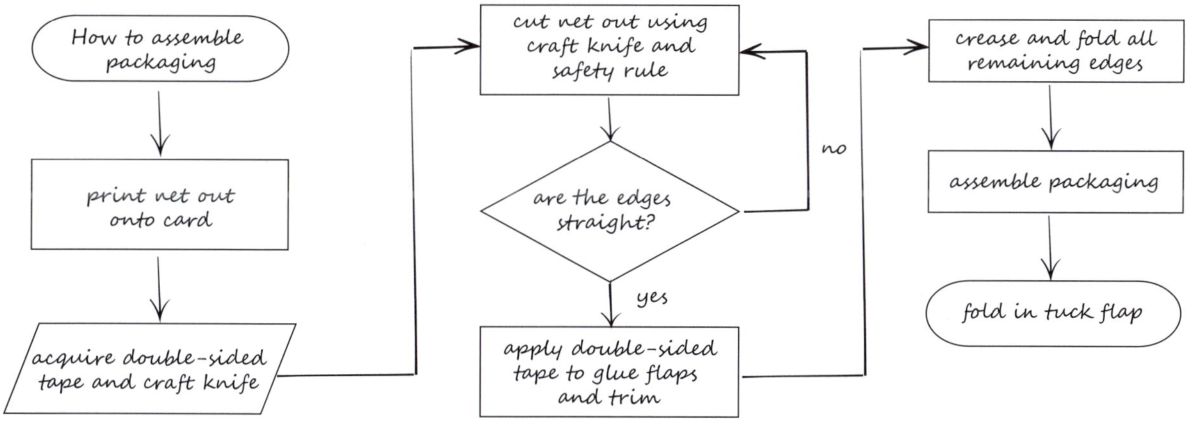

△ **Figure 7** Flowcharts always read top to bottom.

SKILLS ACTIVITY

Using flowcharts

Using a flowchart, explain how to draw an ellipse using the trammel method.

KNOWLEDGE CHECK

A manufacturer of stationery products requires some data analysis of who buys their products and which products are most popular. Answer the following questions:

1. State the graph or chart they should use to represent the increasing or declining popularity of pencil sharpeners over the period of five years. Justify your answer.
2. State the graph or chart they should use to represent the proportion of different age groups that purchase protractors. Justify your answer.
3. State the graph or chart they should use to compare the sales of five different stationery products. Justify your answer.
4. State the graph or chart they should use to display the amount of sales within different cost ranges.
5. Give an example of how you would use an input/output box in a flowchart.

KEY TERMS

Bin: A range of values on the *x*-axis that groups the data in a histogram

Infographic: A visual way to present information, data or knowledge in an easy-to-understand and engaging format

Key: A list of explanations for the different categories used on a chart or graph

***x*-axis:** The horizontal line of a graph

***y*-axis:** The vertical line of a graph

3·2·3 Presentation

LEARNING AIMS

By the end of this unit, you should:

✓ Use the thick and thin line technique to enhance a drawing
✓ Understand light source and its effect on light and shade
✓ Use rendering to emphasise three dimensions, textures and materials

So, how can you effectively sell your design concepts? Present them clearly and attractively. Enhance sketches with techniques such as varied line weights and shading, or use CAD software to create photorealistic visualisations that help clients and teams perfectly visualise your vision.

THICK AND THIN LINE TECHNIQUE

By using different line widths it is possible to give a three-dimensional drawing emphasis. You can use technical fine-line pens with different widths or different pencils to achieve this effect.

TOP TIP

Look at the isometric cube in Figure 1 and imagine a spider on the top face. Now imagine the spider crawling over one of the edges. Can you still see the spider? If so, then the line that the spider has crossed over is thin. If the spider disappears behind, inside or under the cube, then that line is thick.

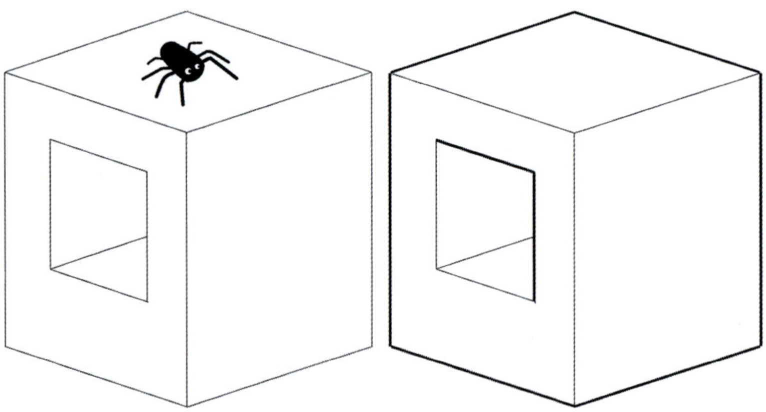

△ **Figure 1** Thick and thin lines on an isometric cube

SKILLS ACTIVITY

Using the thick and thin line technique

Sketch the shapes in Figure 2 in freehand. Use the thick and thin line technique to enhance your drawings.

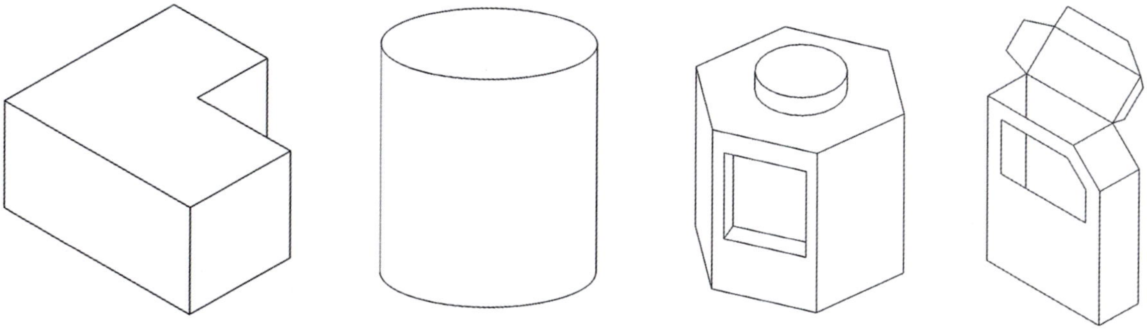

Δ **Figure 2** Three-dimensional shapes

LIGHT SOURCE AND RENDERING

Before rendering a drawing you will need to consider where the **light source** is coming from. The direction of the light source will affect what tone you need to apply to the object's faces (Figure 3). For cylindrical objects you should use a smooth gradient from dark to light to dark.

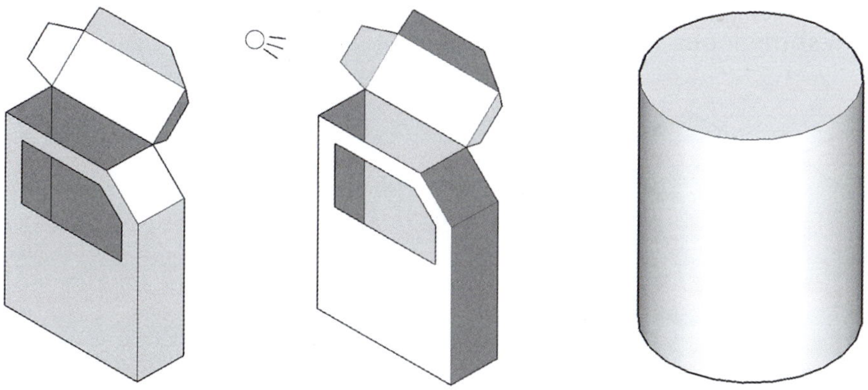

Δ **Figure 3** The direction of the light source affects the tones on an object.

TOP TIP

For a smoother finish, use a softer pencil such as a 2B. Turn the paper as you render so the pencil strokes are applied in different directions.

SKILLS ACTIVITY

Rendering shapes

Practise rendering by shading in the shapes you drew in the previous Skills Activity. Use a light source coming from the top left of the object.

RENDERING MATERIALS AND TEXTURES

By using coloured pencils and an eraser, you can achieve different textures to represent materials.

Polymers

Shade the faces taking into account the light source (Figure 4). Use an eraser to make streaks on the faces in the same direction to give a reflective look. Finally, lightly add in the back edges to give a transparent look.

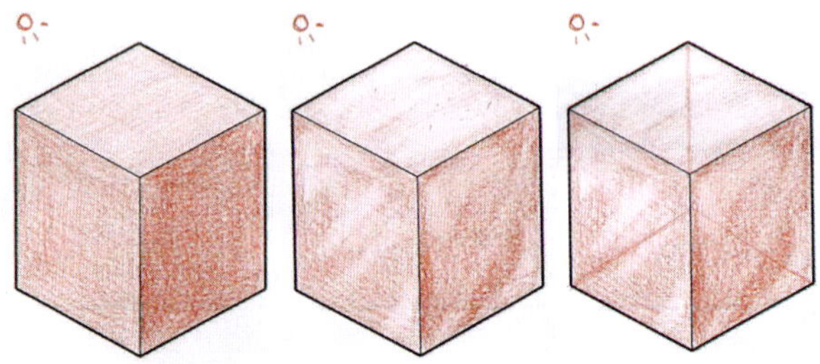

∆ **Figure 4** Polymer rendering showing a translucent cube with highlights

Metal

Use a grey coloured pencil to shade in the faces, taking the light source into account (Figure 5). Add some light blue tints. Use an eraser to remove highlights to give a shiny look.

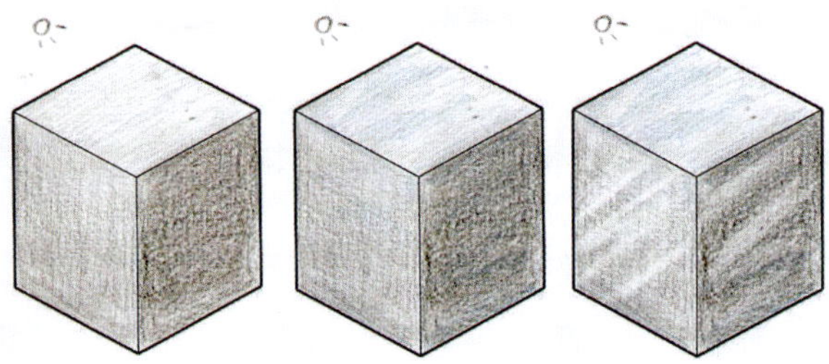

∆ **Figure 5** Use a grey and light blue pencil to give a metallic effect.

Timber

Use a brown, ochre and yellow pencil to roughly and unevenly shade the faces (Figure 6). Since wood does not have a smooth finish, aim to produce a rough look. Finally, add grain with the brown pencil, loosely following the correct angles on the face.

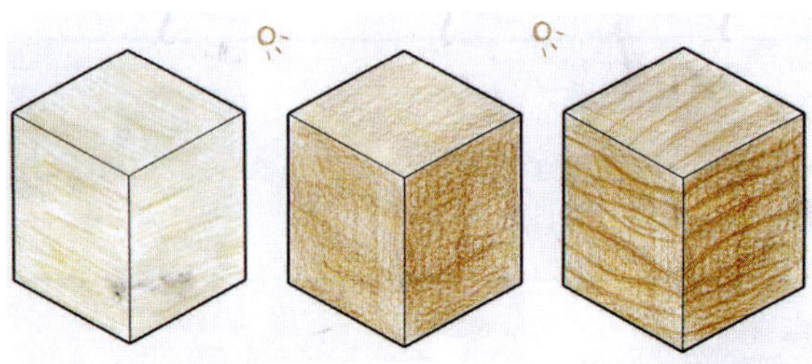

∆ **Figure 6** Grain can be shown using uneven lines.

Shadow

For further realism when rendering, add shadow on the surface your object is on. Shadows should be on the opposite side to your light source and be rendered as a gradient from dark to light. (Figure 7).

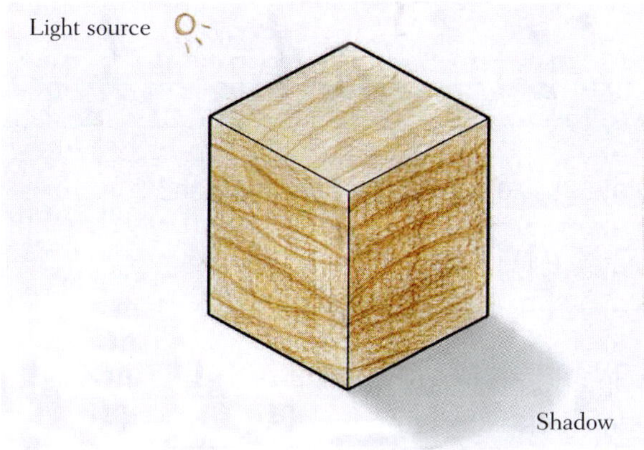

△ **Figure 7** Shadow can be added for further realism

SKILLS ACTIVITY

Rendering a toy train

Figure 8 is a pictorial (3D) view of a toy train. Draw the toy train and render it to give a realistic effect of the materials stated below. Use a light source from the top left to show different tones and finish using the thick and thin line technique.

- Render the cylindrical front part as a polymer (any colour).
- Render the wheels as metal.
- Render the body as timber.
- Add shadow.

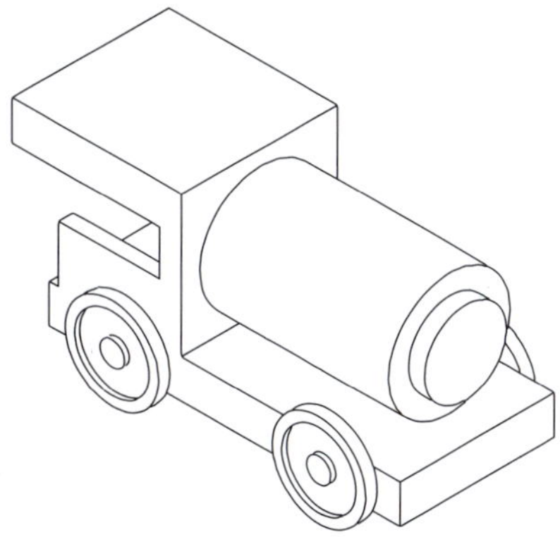

△ **Figure 8** A pictorial view of a toy train

KNOWLEDGE CHECK

1. Explain why presentation is important in design.
2. State **three** ways you can improve the presentation of your design ideas.
3. Identify a shape that would have a gradient applied.
4. Suggest a type of pencil for rendering.

KEY TERMS

Light source: The point or place from which the light is coming

3·3 Making processes

3·3·1 Measuring and marking out

LEARNING AIMS

By the end of this unit, you should:

✓ Measure and mark out materials accurately using appropriate hand tools and equipment

✓ Measure and mark out materials accurately using CAD

How do graphic designs look so crisp and perfectly put together? Whether it is a cool poster, sleek packaging or a sharp logo, getting things in *exactly* the right place is important. It is all about precision (Figure 1).

In graphic products, accuracy is very important. From using hand tools to diving into the digital world of CAD, mastering measuring and marking out is your first step towards creating seriously impressive designs and prototype models.

Δ **Figure 1** Accuracy is important whether you are using computers or marking out by hand.

USING HAND TOOLS AND EQUIPMENT

Ready to get hands-on? The tools in Figure 2 will help you get lines straight and measurements perfect.

Accuracy and good presentation are essential for communicating ideas to other designers, the client or the manufacturer. Having the ability to select the correct drawing aid is important.

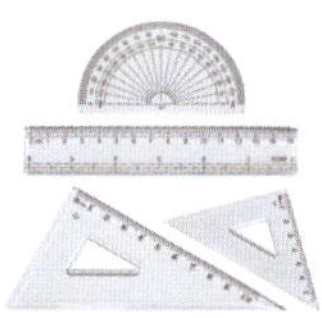

Measuring and drawing tools

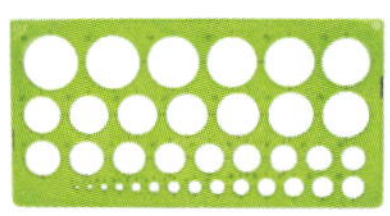

A circle stencil

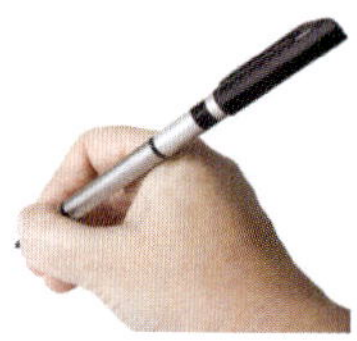

Drawing pens come in different thicknesses.

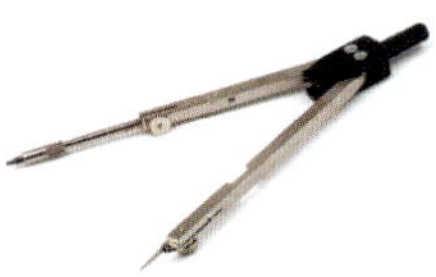

A set of compasses is essential in technical drawing.

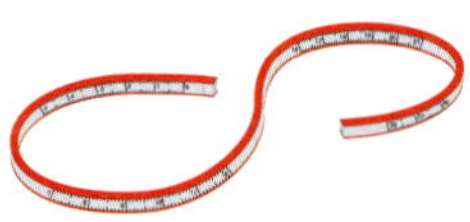

A flexicurve

Δ **Figure 2** Hand tools and drawing equipment

Rulers, protractors and set squares

Use a ruler to measure lines. Protractors are for drawing angles accurately. Set squares can be 30°/60° or 45°/45° and are used to draw these angles accurately.

Stencils

Stencils can be used to draw circles, ellipses and lettering.

Technical pens

Technical pens have a small nib. They come in different nib sizes in mm, and the correct pen should be selected to correspond with the thickness of the line you are drawing.

Compasses

A compass is essential for drawing circles; simply set the radius of the circle you want to draw. Compass cutters are also available for cutting circles from paper or vinyl.

Flexicurves

Flexicurves can be moulded to any given curve. They can be used as a curved ruler, to measure and draw curved lines.

Drawing board

A drawing board has a parallel motion rule which moves up and down on the board. This keeps lines horizontal. You can place set squares on this rule to draw lines in 30°/60°and 45°.

The datum edge

The **datum edge** is a clean, straight and reliable edge on your material from which all your measurements should originate. Think of it as your starting line for accuracy. Consistently measuring from the same datum edge prevents cumulative errors and ensures all your markings are correctly positioned relative to one another.

TOP TIP

You already have pre-cut datum edges on the material – use them! For example, if you need to cut a rectangle, you only need to mark out and cut two more edges from your material, not four. That is inaccurate and a waste of material (Figure 3).

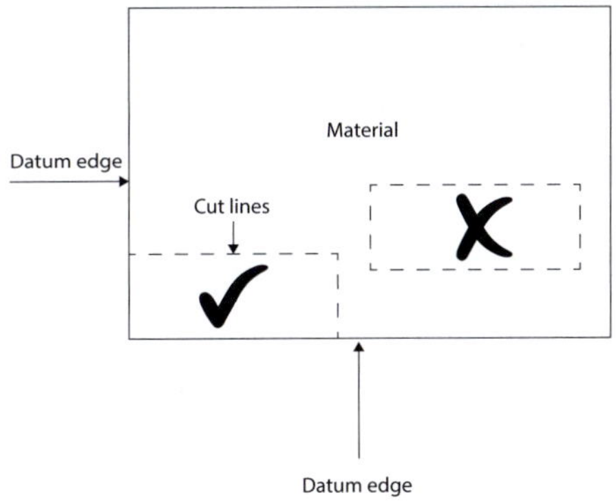

△ **Figure 3** Use a datum edge to measure from. Datum lines are also pre-cut edges for your shapes.

SKILLS ACTIVITY

Using a datum edge

Accurately cut out a rectangle, a hexagon and a triangle (Figure 4) from a piece of stock material, consistently using a datum edge for precise measurements and straight lines.

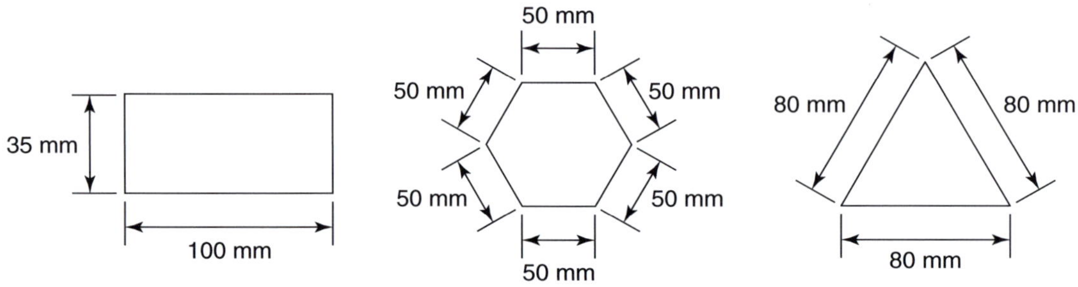

△ **Figure 4** A rectangle, a hexagon and a triangle

Using CAD tools

Using CAD tools, you can draw shapes to exact dimensions. You can align elements using grids, guides and the snap function, and organise drawings using layers. Editing and duplicating are quick and accurate with CAD, and outputting for CAM is an efficient method of manufacture.

Graphic designers use two main image types in CAD:

- **Vector** graphics (for example, logos) use mathematical equations, allowing for accurate shapes and scaling without loss of quality (Figure 5).
- **Bitmap** graphics are made of pixels. Their quality depends on resolution (dots per inch or dpi); use 300 dpi for print and 72 dpi for screens (Figure 6).

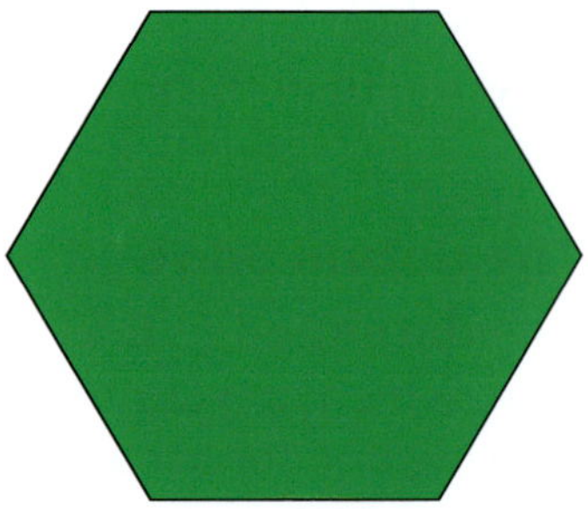

△ **Figure 5** Vector graphics use lines, curves and fills.

△ **Figure 6** A bitmap image of a dog at 20 dpi, 72 dpi and 300 dpi. Notice how the quality of the image changes with an increase in dpi.

TOP TIP

The Shift key on the keyboard is your best friend. Hold this key down to draw straight lines, equilateral shapes and 45° angles.

SKILLS ACTIVITY

Design and develop a logo

A confectionery manufacturer has asked you to design a new logo for a chocolate called 'Rush'. Using suitable vector graphics software, design and develop the logo.

KNOWLEDGE CHECK

1. State the purpose of a datum edge.
2. Describe **two** key characteristics of vector graphics.
3. Compare vector and bitmap graphics in terms of scalability.

KEY TERMS

Bitmap: Image composed of pixels, making its quality dependent on resolution (dpi)

Datum edge: A straight, reference edge on material used as the starting point for all measurements to ensure accuracy

Vector: Uses mathematical equations to create scalable images without loss of quality

3·3·2 Cutting, shaping and forming

LEARNING AIMS

By the end of this unit, you should:

- ✓ Describe appropriate methods for cutting, shaping and forming materials
- ✓ Explain the safe use of hand tools, power tools, machinery and CAD/CAM for cutting, shaping and forming
- ✓ Select and perform cutting, shaping and forming techniques to create accurate graphic products

From cool posters to funky packaging and pop-up cards, making graphic designs real always involves cutting, shaping and forming materials. While measuring and marking out prepares your design, cutting, shaping and forming gives it physical form and functionality.

Accuracy is vital! Wobbly cuts or wrong sizes can spoil a great design. Choosing the right tools and methods is crucial, whether you use hand tools, powerful machinery or computer-controlled equipment. In this unit, you will learn how to select and perform these essential techniques.

HAND TOOLS FOR CUTTING, SHAPING AND FORMING

Ready to get hands-on? Hand tools are often the first tools you will learn to use, and they are extremely versatile for cutting, shaping and forming lots of different materials used in graphic products, such as paper, card and foamboard (Table 1). They are essential skills for any designer.

Hand tool	Description	What it looks like
Scissors	Great for cutting curves and shapes, especially in paper or thin card. Choose sharp ones for clean cuts.	
Craft knife	This is a must-have tool for cutting straight lines and intricate shapes against a **safety rule**. They have sharp, replaceable blades.	
Safety rule	NOT a plastic ruler! A metal rule with a raised edge helps protect your fingers when using a craft knife. Always use one when cutting with a blade.	
Cutting mat	Protects the surface you are working on and keeps your blade sharper for longer. Never cut directly onto a desk.	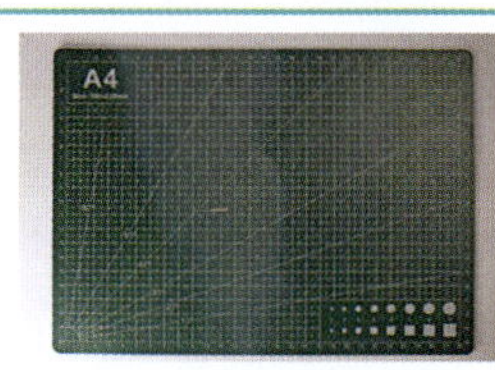

Hand tool	Description	What it looks like
Punches	Tools that can punch out specific shapes (such as circles or decorative edges) from paper or card.	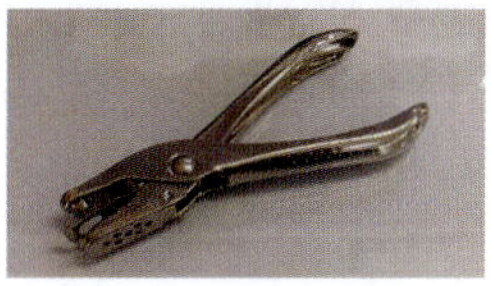
Creasing tools	These do not cut. However, they create a crisp fold line in card, which is essential for making things like boxes and cards.	
Paper trimmer	A paper trimmer allows you to trim card and paper accurately, safely and quickly.	

△ **Table 1** Important hand tools for cutting, shaping and forming graphic materials

For details about safe working practices when using hand tools, refer to unit 3.3.6.

TOP TIP

Always cut in several light passes with a craft knife rather than trying to cut all the way through in one go. This gives you more control and a cleaner, more accurate cut.

SKILLS ACTIVITY

Material vs cut

From Topic 3.1, you know that different materials have different properties. How do these properties affect how you cut them?

1. Choose a simple shape to cut (such as a 50 mm square or circle).
2. Select 3–4 different materials commonly used in graphic products (ask your teacher for small pieces if available), such as:
   - thin paper/card
   - thicker card
   - foamboard
3. Using a craft knife, safety rule (for straight lines) and cutting mat, carefully cut out the same shape from each material. Remember to follow all safety rules from unit 3.3.6.
4. Compare the shapes you cut from each material.
   a. Which material was easiest to cut? Which was most difficult?
   b. Look closely at the cut edge of each shape. How do they differ? Is one cleaner or rougher than another?
   c. Did you need to change your technique at all for different materials (for example, more passes, more pressure)?

DIGITAL PRECISION: CAD/CAM CUTTING, SHAPING AND FORMING

CAD allows you to design shapes on a computer and then use another machine (CAM), controlled by the computer, to cut those shapes perfectly. This is fantastic for accuracy, intricate details and making multiple identical items.

From screen to shape

The process usually involves:

1. Designing your shape using CAD software (such as the vector graphics drawing you learned about in unit 3.3.1).
2. Sending your design file to a CAM machine.
3. The CAM machine reads the design and uses a laser or blade to cut the material precisely as drawn.

CAM machines for graphics

Table 2 describes some CAM machines used for graphics.

CAM machine	Description	What it looks like
Laser cutter	Uses a computer-controlled laser beam to cut or engrave materials like paper, card, acrylic, wood and fabric. Great for precise, intricate shapes and sealing edges of synthetics.	
Plotter cutter (vinyl cutter)	Uses a tiny, computer-controlled blade to cut shapes from thin materials like self-adhesive vinyl, paper or card. Perfect for stickers, stencils and signs.	
3D printing	Can create 3D objects and components layer by layer.	

△ **Table 2** Laser cutters, plotter cutters and 3D printers offer incredible precision using CAD/CAM.

KNOWLEDGE CHECK

1. State **one** hand tool used for making a crisp fold line in card.
2. Compare a laser cutter and a plotter cutter in terms of the materials they typically cut.
3. Explain why vector graphics are commonly used for output to CAM.

KEY TERMS

Safety rule: A ruler, normally made of metal, which keeps your fingers away from the blade when cutting straight lines with a knife

3·3·3 Joining

LEARNING AIMS

By the end of this unit, you should:

- ✓ Select and describe appropriate methods for permanently or temporarily joining materials in graphic products
- ✓ Explain how different joining methods work
- ✓ Identify and describe appropriate use of adhesives, slots, arrow tabs and flaps, pre-manufactured components and fasteners for joining materials
- ✓ Apply joining techniques to create functional graphic products

Choosing the right joining method is important. In fact, it is just as important as selecting the right material or cutting it accurately. A strong joint will ensure a product holds together, while a temporary joining method might allow for assembly and disassembly. In this unit, you will explore various techniques for joining materials in graphic products, from simple folds and tabs, to **adhesives** and mechanical fasteners.

PERMANENT JOINING METHODS

So, how do we make graphic products hold together? Permanent joining methods are all about creating strong, lasting connections that are not meant to be easily undone. These are techniques for building graphic products that need to be tough and durable.

Adhesives

Adhesives are also known as glues and cements. These fantastic substances are essential for joining materials securely (Figure 1). In the world of graphic products, adhesives are everywhere, from holding together packaging, to binding your favourite books. The bond they create can be strong, but it all depends on picking the right adhesive for the job and the materials you are working with (Table 1).

Adhesive	Description
PVA (polyvinyl acetate) glue	The classic white glue you probably use at school. It is water-based, versatile for paper, card and other natural materials. Dries clear and forms a strong, permanent bond.
Spray adhesives	These come in cans and give you a quick, even layer. Brilliant for mounting posters or sticking down large sheets without wrinkles.
Contact adhesives	You put a layer on *both* surfaces, let them get a bit tacky, and then carefully press them together.
Hot-melt adhesives (glue gun)	These solid sticks melt in a glue gun and give you a hot, liquid adhesive that sets fast as it cools. Fantastic for quick assembly of prototypes or joining different materials.
Double-sided tape	Clean, quick and no mess. This tape has adhesive on both sides and is excellent for packaging tabs.

△ **Table 1** Different adhesives

△ **Figure 1** Application of adhesive to create a permanent bond between two components of a graphic product

TOP TIP

Always check the label for the best way to use the adhesive, what materials it is compliant with, how long it takes to dry and, importantly, how to use it safely.

TEMPORARY JOINING METHODS

Sometimes you do not want a joint that is forever. Temporary joining methods are fantastic for graphic products that need to be assembled for use and then perhaps taken apart. These methods allow for flexibility without damaging the materials when you separate them.

Can you think of any reasons why designers may choose temporary joining methods?

Slots, arrow tabs and flaps

Table 2 describes slots, tabs and flaps.

Temporary joint	Description
Slots	Cut lines or shapes that one piece of material can slide into.
Tabs and flaps	Extensions of a material that are designed to fit into slots or fold and tuck to create a joint.
Arrow tabs	A specific type of tab shaped like an arrow, designed to easily push through a slot and then expand slightly to hold in place.

△ **Table 2** Different temporary joints

In the packaging in Figure 2, a tuck flap tucks into the packaging to keep the lid down. There is a slot tab on the front of the box with slots into the lid to hold it in place. The dust flaps add extra reinforcement and prevent dust from entering. Two glue tabs hold the package together.

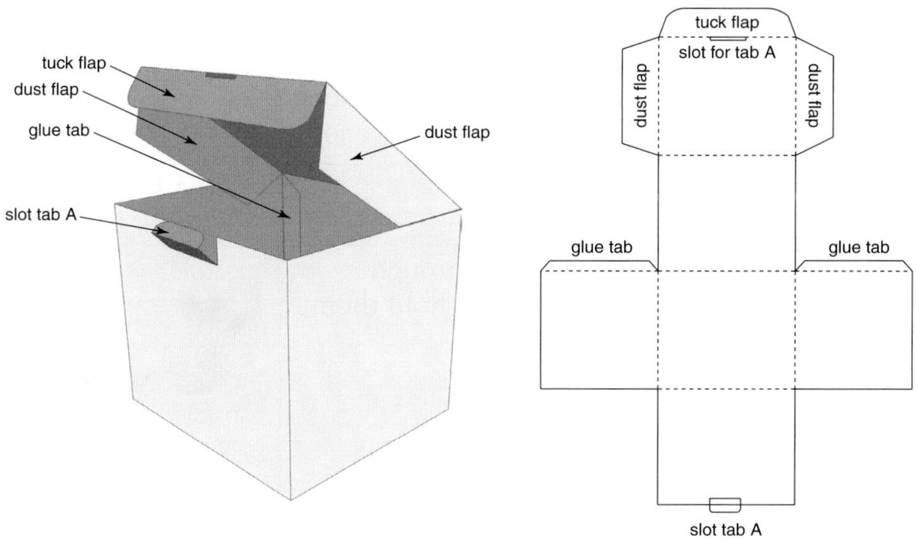

Δ **Figure 2** Tuck flaps and dust flaps are often added to packaging for security.

In the packaging in Figure 3, lock rudder flaps act as a base-locking mechanism. When they are assembled in the correct order, they can securely hold the base of the packaging together. A single glue tab connects the sides.

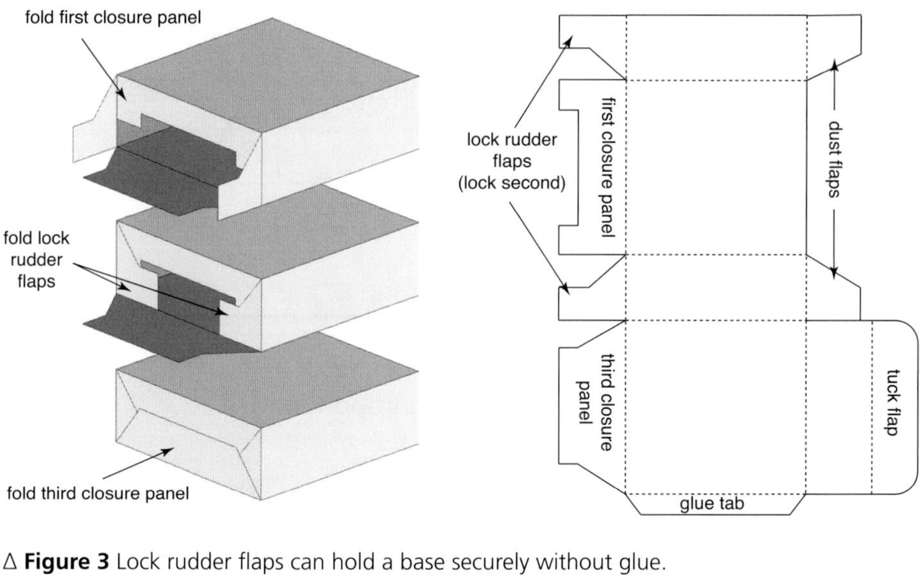

Δ **Figure 3** Lock rudder flaps can hold a base securely without glue.

Arrow tabs can slot in to hold two faces together (Figure 4).

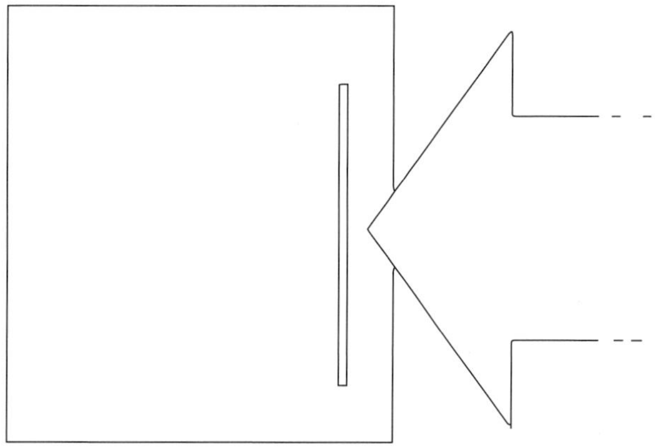

Δ **Figure 4** An arrow tab slides into a slot to hold two faces together.

Components and fasteners

Mechanical fasteners are physical objects used to join materials (Table 3). Unlike adhesives that rely on bonding substances, fasteners use mechanical force, friction or interlocking shapes to create a joint.

Component or fastener	Description	What it looks like
Staples	Small metal fasteners driven through paper or card and then bent to hold them together.	
Screws and bolts	Not typically used in graphic products. Why not experiment with them?	
Paper fasteners	Small metal fasteners with two legs that are pushed through holes and then bent flat to secure.	
Binding combs and wires	Used for binding multiple sheets of paper together (like in calendars). The comb or wire is threaded through punched holes.	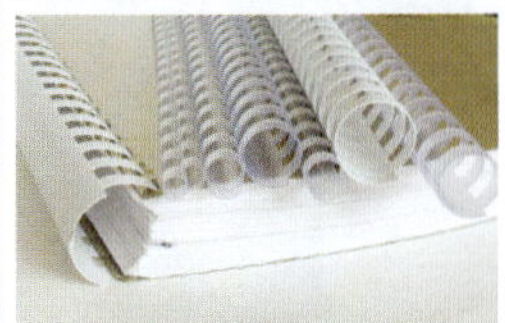

△ **Table 3** Mechanical fasteners are used in the assembly of graphic products.

SKILLS ACTIVITY

Which joint works best where?

Test different joining methods (adhesives, tabs, fasteners, components) on materials (paper, card, boards).

Join the samples. Observe the strength and look.

Which join works best where?

KNOWLEDGE CHECK

1. Explain the difference between permanent and temporary joining methods.
2. Give a graphic product example for each from question 1.
3. Identify **one** type of adhesive and **one** type of mechanical fastener used in graphic products.
4. Describe **one** advantage of using slots, arrow tabs or flaps for joining materials in graphic products.

KEY TERMS

Adhesive: A substance used to bond materials together

3·3·4 Printing

LEARNING AIMS

By the end of this unit, you should:

✓ Understand printing techniques used in the manufacture of graphic products

Printing turns digital artwork into physical objects you can see and touch. It is how graphic products, from packaging to posters, get their appearance. Different materials need different printing techniques. In this unit, you will explore how printing works, from school methods in a workshop to the large-scale techniques used in commercial production.

WORKSHOP PRINTING TECHNIQUES

Table 1 describes a few printing techniques you might use in school for creating graphic products.

Printing technique	Description	What it looks like
Laser printing	Uses a laser and toner powder fused with heat. Great for fast, sharp text and images on paper.	
Inkjet printing	Sprays tiny liquid ink droplets onto the surface. Versatile for colourful graphics and photos on various papers.	
Sublimation printing	Uses special inks that turn into a gas when heated, dyeing compatible materials such as polyester fabric for durable, full-colour prints.	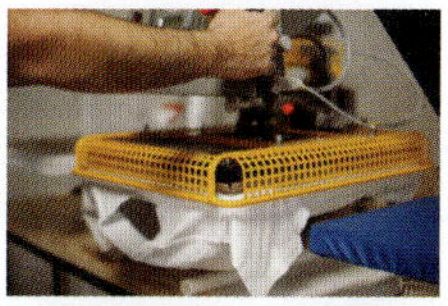
Screen printing	Pushes ink through a mesh screen with blocked areas. It is often used for printing designs onto textiles or thicker card.	

△ **Table 1** Examples of equipment and graphic products created using common workshop-based printing techniques

TOP TIP

When starting to construct a design using CAD, it is important that you consider the final medium in which it will be viewed. If your design will only be seen on a computer screen, such as a web page, make sure you set the resolution of your document to 72 dpi (dots per inch). If you are intending to print the graphic, you should set the resolution to 300 dpi for a good print quality.

COMMERCIAL PRINTING TECHNIQUES

While school-based methods are great for learning and smaller projects, producing graphic products on a large scale, such as millions of cereal boxes or newspapers, requires different technologies. Commercial printing techniques are high-speed, high-volume processes designed for efficiency and consistent quality across huge print runs (Figure 1).

△ **Figure 1** Commercial printing techniques use complex machinery for high-volume production of graphic products on various materials.

Table 2 describes some of the main commercial printing methods.

Printing technique	Description
Offset lithography	Uses a rubber blanket to transfer ink onto a **substrate**. This technique is widely used for books, magazines and packaging on paper/card.
Gravure	Uses an etched **printing plate** which deposits the colour as small dots. This technique is known for its detail and high quality.
Flexography	Uses flexible printing plates. It is fast and versatile for packaging films and labels.

△ **Table 2** Commercial printing techniques

SKILLS ACTIVITY

Exploring types of printing

Look at some printed items around you. These could be forms of packaging, books, clothing, wrappers or posters. There are examples everywhere. Consider the quality of the print, how many would have been printed and the material that has been printed on.

What type of printing do you think was used for these products? Explain your answer.

KNOWLEDGE CHECK

Identify the best printing method to print the following items:

1. A foil bag of snacks.
2. A newspaper of 200 000 copies.
3. One T-shirt in a school workshop.
4. Postage stamps.

KEY TERMS

Printing plate: A sheet which is wrapped round a roller and used to transfer the image to the substrate

Substrate: The material that something is printed on

3·3·5 Finishing

LEARNING AIMS

By the end of this unit, you should:

✓ Select and use appropriate decorative and protective finishes for graphic products

✓ Show an understanding of self-finishing materials used in graphic products

So, you have designed and made your graphic product, but is it complete? In this unit, you will explore different ways graphic products are finished, from applying decorative and protective coatings to using materials that already have their finish built-in.

APPLIED FINISHES: DECORATIVE AND PROTECTIVE

Finishes are materials or processes added to the surface of a graphic product to improve its look, feel or performance.

Decorative finishes

Decorative finishes allow the product to look appealing and stand out. They add visual flair or interesting textures (Table 1).

Decorative finish	How it works	Effects
Varnishing	Applies a clear/tinted liquid. **Spot UV varnishing** highlights specific areas.	Adds shine, depth or a matte effect.
Lamination	Bonds a thin layer onto the surface. Uses heat or pressure.	Creates a smooth finish.
Foil blocking	Applies a thin metallic film to the surface. Uses heat or pressure.	Creates a shiny effect.
Embossing/ Debossing	Creates raised (embossed) or recessed (debossed) patterns or text. Uses dyes and pressure.	Adds a tactile, as well as a visual element.

△ **Table 1** Decorative finishes

Protective finishes

Protective finishes are applied to shield the graphic product from damage, wear, moisture or UV light, helping it last longer and stay in good condition (Table 2).

Protective finish	Application
Varnishing and lamination	These can also provide protection, making the surface more durable, water-resistant and resistant to scuffs or tears.
Protective coatings	Special coatings can be applied to provide specific protection, such as UV resistance for outdoor signs or food-safe barriers for packaging.

△ **Table 2** Protective finishes

SKILLS ACTIVITY

What type of finish?

Look at the finished graphic products in Figures 1 and 2. For each, identify the finish and its purpose. Is it decorative or protective?

△ **Figure 1** One finished graphics product. Look at the finish.

△ **Figure 2** Another finished graphics product. Look at the finish.

TOP TIP

You can replicate spot UV varnish and foil-blocking finishes in the school workshop using clear vinyl (for spot UV effect) and metallic vinyl (for foil-blocking effect).

You can use a vinyl cutter to cut out precise shapes, but you need to apply them carefully to the graphic product surface. Why not experiment and see if you can replicate these processes in your own designs?

SELF-FINISHING MATERIALS

Not all graphic products need extra finishes applied to their surface. Some materials already have the desired look and feel built into them when they are made. These are called **self-finishing materials**.

Self-finishing materials save time and cost in manufacturing because they do not need additional processes after being cut or shaped. Table 3 describes some examples of self-finishing materials.

Self-finishing material	Description	What it looks like
Plastics	Coloured or textured plastics. The colour and surface finish are added during the plastic's manufacture.	
Pre-coated boards	Card or board that has already been coated with a smooth layer, ready for printing.	

△ **Table 3** Self-finishing materials

KNOWLEDGE CHECK

1. Identify **two** different applied finishes and give an example of a graphic product where each is used.
2. Suggest a suitable protective finish for a graphic product that needs to be very durable and resistant to scratches.
3. Explain why a designer might choose a self-finishing material for a product instead of applying a finish.

KEY TERMS

Debossing: Creating a recessed (sunk in) pattern or design on a material using pressure

Embossing: Creating a raised pattern or design on a material using pressure

Foil blocking: Applying a thin metallic or coloured foil onto a surface using heat and pressure to create a shiny design

Lamination: Bonding a thin plastic film onto a surface using heat and pressure, often for protection

Self-finishing materials: Materials that have their desired finish built in during manufacture and do not need additional finishing processes

Spot UV varnishing: Applying a shiny, clear varnish to specific areas of a printed surface for decorative effect

3·3·6 Safe working practices

LEARNING AIMS

By the end of this unit, you should:

✓ Demonstrate safe use of hand tools, power tools, machinery and/or computer-aided manufacture (CAM) equipment relevant to your workshop

✓ Select and use appropriate Personal Protective Equipment (PPE) when working practically

Every tool and machine have the potential to cause harm if you do not use them correctly or if you do not take proper safety precautions. Understanding the risks associated with different pieces of equipment in a Design and Technology workshop is an important part of working safely.

TOP TIP

Always pay full attention when your teacher is demonstrating how to use tools or machinery. They are showing you the safest way to work. If you are ever unsure about how to use something, stop and ask for help before you continue.

UNDERSTANDING AND MANAGING RISKS

A hazard is anything that has the potential to cause harm. For example, a sharp craft knife is a hazard.

Risk is the likelihood that a hazard will cause harm and how severe that harm could be. The risk depends on how carefully you use a tool and whether you follow safety measures (such as cutting away from your body). Using a craft knife incorrectly increases the risk of a cut.

SKILLS ACTIVITY

Identifying hazards and associated risks

Look around your Design and Technology workshop. Identify and list at least five different potential hazards. For each hazard you identify, describe the risk associated with it. What type of harm could it potentially cause and under what circumstances might that harm occur?

For example:

Hazard: A sharp craft knife blade.

Risk: The risk is getting a deep cut. This risk increases if you cut towards your hands, if the blade is not sharp (as you might apply too much pressure) or if you do not use a cutting mat.

PERSONAL PROTECTIVE EQUIPMENT (PPE)

PPE is crucial for safety in the workshop, minimising injury risk from specific hazards. Your teacher will guide you on what PPE to use and when.

Common PPE includes:

- Safety glasses/goggles to protect eyes from hazards.
- Hearing protection to shield ears from loud noises.
- Dust mask/respirator to prevent inhalation of dust or fumes.
- Protective gloves to guard hands from various hazards.
- Apron/workshop coat to protect clothing and skin.
- Sturdy footwear for foot protection.

△ **Figure 1** Common PPE

SKILLS ACTIVITY

Designing a safety sign

Choose one specific hand tool, power tool, machine or piece of CAM equipment that is used a lot in your workshop.

Your task is to design a clear and informative safety sign for this equipment. You sign must communicate:

1. Hazards: What is the main potential danger?
2. Risks: What kind of harm could it cause?
3. PPE: What specific PPE must be worn?

Design signs for quick understanding (Figure 2). Use minimal words and consider colour carefully.

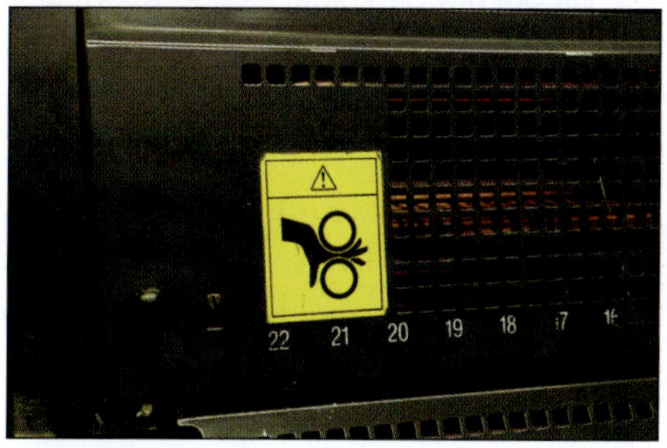

△ **Figure 2** A safety sign

REFLECTIVE LOG

Think over the practical activities you have completed in previous units 3.3.1–3.3.5. Write down the tools, equipment and processes you used.

- For each unit, can you identify any potential hazards that existed during the practical work?
- What safety precautions did you take, or were you instructed to take, when using hand tools, power tools, machinery or CAM equipment in those units?
- What types of PPE did you use, or should you have used, for specific tasks in those units? Why was that PPE necessary?
- Was there anything you did in a previous practical activity that you would do differently now, based on what you are learning about safe working practices?
- How can thinking about safety *before* you start a practical task help you avoid accidents?

KNOWLEDGE CHECK

1. State *three* general safety principles that you should always follow in a Design and Technology workshop.
2. Explain the difference between a hazard and a risk in the workshop, giving an example for each.
3. Suggest the appropriate PPE you should wear when using machinery that creates a lot of dust and is very noisy.

3·4 Product analysis

3·4·1 Understanding product analysis

LEARNING AIMS

By the end of this unit, you should:

✓ Understand how to analyse real-world graphic products
✓ Understand the main scales of production
✓ Understand the importance of quality control and quality assurance
✓ Understand the different stages of a graphic product's life
✓ Understand the concepts of planned and unplanned obsolescence and their impact on sustainability

So, what is product analysis? It involves looking closely at a product to understand how it was designed, made and what will happen to it at the end of its life. It helps us understand why products are the way they are and the impact they have.

ANALYSING REAL-WORLD GRAPHIC PRODUCTS

To *really* understand graphic products, there is no substitute for getting hands-on. Instead of just searching online, a deep dive into a real-world product can teach you so much about the design, materials and how things are made.

Follow these steps for analysing a graphic product.

1 **Observe** — What is its main purpose of the product? Who is it for (the user)? What does it look like – its aesthetics, colours, typography, layout? How does it function?

2 **Materials** — Can you identify the types of paper, card, board, plastic, foam or composite used? Think back to what you learned about their properties and stock forms. Why do you think these materials were chosen?

3 **Joining** — How are different parts of the product put together? Are they folded, glued, stapled, taped or joined using tabs and flaps? Are the joining methods temporary or permanent?

4 **Printing and finishes** — Can you identify the printing technique used? Are there any finishes applied, such as varnish, lamination or foil blocking? Are the finishes decorative or protective?

5 **Making** — Based on your observations of materials, construction and printing, what making processes (cutting, shaping, joining, printing, finishing) do you think were used to create this product?

SKILLS ACTIVITY

Hands-on graphic product analysis

Find a real-world graphic product to analyse (for example, a piece of food packaging, a book cover, a greetings card, a promotional leaflet). Use the steps for analysing real-world graphic products to conduct a detailed, hands-on analysis.

SCALES OF PRODUCTION

When you look at a graphic product, it is interesting to think about how many copies were made. Was it just one, a few hundred or millions? The number of items produced affects the methods of manufacturing, cost and time involved. This is known as the **scale of production**.

Different scales are suitable for different graphic products (Table 1).

Scale of production	Description
Prototype or one-off production	Making just one item. Highest cost per item, often needs skilled craftspeople. Used for unique items or testing a design before mass production.
Batch production	Making a limited number of identical items in groups (batches). More cost-effective than one-off for medium quantities, allows for changes between batches. Used for products needed in moderate amounts.
Mass production	Making huge quantities of identical items, often millions. Requires expensive machines and automation, but results in a very low cost per item. Efficient for products needed in vast numbers.
Continuous production	Making identical items non-stop, 24/7, for extremely high demand. Highly automated and integrated. Often used for producing raw materials like paper rolls or plastic film, which are then used for graphic products.

△ **Table 1** Different scales of production

Understanding the scale of production helps explain why graphic products are made in certain ways and their cost.

QUALITY CONTROL AND QUALITY ASSURANCE

Making sure graphic products are made correctly is vital. This is done through **quality control (QC)** and **quality assurance (QA)**. QC is checking products during manufacture to find any faults, while QA is the system put in place to prevent mistakes and ensure the whole process meets quality standards.

QC and QA are important to make sure products look good, work properly, meet customer needs and reduce waste. What might the impact be of poorly made or faulty products?

Here are some QC checks made during graphic product manufacture:

- *Materials checked*: Is the paper the correct weight (gsm)? Is the plastic film the correct thickness?
- *Printing checked*: Are the colours correct? Is the text sharp? No smudges or errors?
- *Cutting, shaping and forming checked*: Are sizes accurate? Are folds in the right place? Are edges clean?
- *Joining checked*: Are seams strong? Are parts aligned correctly?
- *Finishing checked*: Is the finish applied evenly? Is lamination smooth? Is foil blocking clear?

DESIGN IN ACTION

Printer's marks

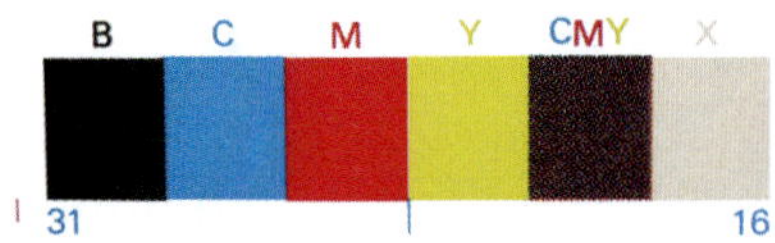

When an image comes off the printing press, it does not look like the finished article. There are a series of symbols surrounding the image.

These are called printer's marks and are used to check the quality of the colour and the alignment of the image.

If hundreds of thousands of copies are being made of a newspaper or leaflet, one small mistake could be very costly for the printer. This is why the prints need to be checked thoroughly for any problems.

THE STAGES OF A GRAPHIC PRODUCT'S LIFE

Graphic products do not just appear; they go through several stages after the initial idea. Thinking about these stages helps designers make better choices.

1	**Designed**	Designers decide the product's purpose, who will use it, what it will look like (aesthetics, layout, colours), what materials are best and how it will be made. Importantly, thinking about what happens at the end of the product's life should also start here.

2	**Manufactured**	The design becomes a reality. This stage involves all the making processes you have learned about, such as selecting materials, cutting, shaping and forming, joining parts together, applying printing techniques and adding finishes.
3	**Used**	Some graphic products are used only once or for a short time (such as packaging or tickets), while others are used for years (such as books, signs or durable display items). What happens at the end of the product's life? Can it be reused, recycled or disposed of sustainably?

Designers need to consider all these stages when creating a graphic product to minimise its negative impact and make it as sustainable as possible.

SKILLS ACTIVITY

Designing with the product's life in mind

Choose one of the following graphic products to design:

- a promotional flyer for a school event
- a small folded box for a small item
- a sign for a classroom.

As you develop your design ideas, think critically about what will happen to your product throughout its journey – use the 'stages of a graphic product's life' to guide your thinking.

Present your design ideas along with annotations or a short explanation highlighting how you considered each stage of the product's life in your design decisions.

OBSOLESCENCE AND SUSTAINABILITY

Obsolescence means a graphic product becomes unusable or outdated. This impacts sustainability. There are two types of obsolescence: **planned obsolescence** and **unplanned obsolescence**.

Planned obsolescence

Products are deliberately designed not to last long, or to go out of fashion. For example, single-use packaging which is hard to recycle (such as laminated pouches), magazines and brochures for short events, trend-driven graphics.

Unplanned obsolescence

Products failing unexpectedly due to faults or degradation. For example, ink fading, paper turning brittle, seams failing on boxes or poor-quality signs fading.

Obsolescence creates waste. More products mean more raw materials, energy for making and transport, and waste, especially from mixed graphic materials. Sustainable design aims for longer life or easier recycling/reuse.

TOP TIP

You can combat obsolescence by designing for disassembly. This makes products easy to repair or recycle.

KNOWLEDGE CHECK

1. State **one** difference between quality control and quality assurance.
2. Give **one** example of a graphic product typically made using batch production.
3. Describe **one** thing that happens during the 'manufactured' stage of a graphic product's life.
4. Explain why planned obsolescence might be used for some graphic products.
5. Identify the type of obsolescence that happens when a product breaks due to a manufacturing defect.
6. Suggest **one** way a designer could make paper packaging easier to recycle at the end of its life.
7. Compare mass production and batch production in terms of the cost per item for graphic products.
8. Analyse how using a composite material might affect the end-of-life options for a graphic product.

KEY TERMS

Quality assurance (QA): The system put in place to prevent errors and ensure quality throughout manufacturing

Quality control (QC): Checking products at stages during manufacture to find faults

Scale of production: The number of identical products made – one-off/prototype, batch, mass, continuous

Unplanned obsolescence: A product breaks down unexpectedly

3.5 Use of technology

3·5·1 Understanding the use of technology

LEARNING AIMS

By the end of this unit, you should:

✓ Understand the advantages and disadvantages of using text, emails and social media platforms in communicating design proposals
✓ Understand the advantages and disadvantages of using collaborative and remote working software in communicating design proposals
✓ Show knowledge of the use of digital tools and software in graphic design
✓ Understand the advantages and disadvantages of using computer-aided design (CAD) to design products
✓ Understand the benefits and risks of using artificial intelligence (AI)
✓ Understand the advantages and disadvantages of using computer-aided manufacture (CAM) to make graphic products

Technology is everywhere you look – and it is a vital, ever-evolving force for graphic designers and manufacturers. From creating cool designs on a tablet or phone, to controlling amazing digital printers and sharing ideas instantly across the globe, digital tools are now essential in graphic products. But, like any powerful tool, they come with their own set of benefits and things to watch out for.

TECHNOLOGY IN COMMUNICATION

In the fast-paced world of design, being able to collaborate and share your ideas quickly is important. Technology changes how designers talk to each other, clients and manufacturers.

Communication channels

Think about how you share things with friends. Designers use similar tools, but for professional reasons, including:

- text messages
- emails
- social media.

Collaboration and remote working

Working with others on design projects often means collaborating remotely or from different locations. Digital tools are used to enable real-time teamwork online (Figure 1). They include:

- video calls
- screen sharing
- shared online documents and design files (often using **cloud** storage)
- project management platforms.

∆ **Figure 1** Digital tools enable designers to communicate and collaborate remotely.

REFLECTIVE LOG

Which tools have you used to communicate and collaborate with others online? What are the advantages and disadvantages of using these tools for communication, teamwork and sharing ideas?

TECHNOLOGY IN DESIGNING

Graphic design today relies heavily on computers and software, from simple apps on phones and tablets to powerful professional software on computers for creating detailed illustrations, editing photos, or designing complex layouts for books, websites or animation.

Computer-aided design (CAD)

While hand sketching is great for quick ideas, most finished graphic design uses computer-aided design (CAD) software (Figure 2). CAD lets designers create graphics digitally, such as:

- working drawings
- logos
- layouts
- packaging
- assets for games, websites and apps
- posters

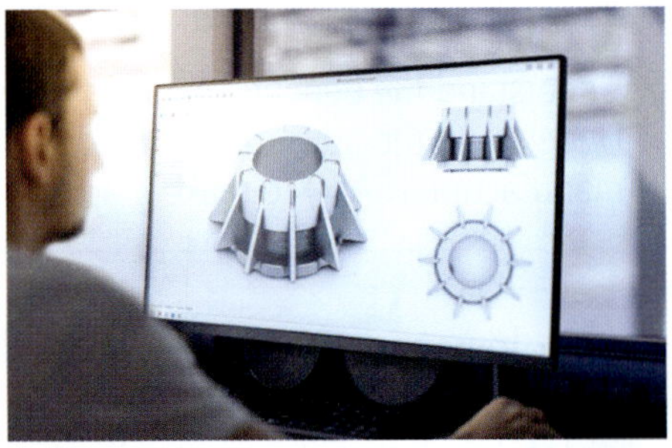

△ **Figure 2** Using CAD can enable designers to visualise and share ideas and to create prototypes quickly.

REFLECTIVE LOG

Thinking about how CAD is used, what advantages and disadvantages might it have for graphic designers compared to hand drawing?

SKILLS ACTIVITY

Collaboration

Find another student in your class who is part of the same community at school. This could be a sports team, music group, school event or club.

One of you should design a logo for the community, the other a poster. You will need to communicate, collaborate and share ideas to be successful. For example, the poster will need to have the logo on it, while the text style and colours of the logo and poster will need to be similar.

You could use technology and digital tools if you have access to them.

Reflect on how well the collaboration went:

1. What challenges did you face, and how did you overcome them?
2. How well do you think your logo and poster work together visually?
3. What tools did you use to collaborate, communicate and share ideas?

Artificial intelligence (AI)

Artificial intelligence (AI) helps graphic designers in interesting ways, such as to help brainstorm initial ideas.

AI is used in **generative design**, where algorithms can help to:

- generate quick photorealistic variations of a design
- create design assets
- assist with tasks including animation, video and image editing.

The list is growing daily. But as technology advances, designers must critically evaluate the risks and benefits of using AI in design.

TOP TIP

If you use AI tools in your design work, it is important to acknowledge its use. Just like citing sources for research, being transparent about using AI is part of academic honesty and good practice in design. Check with your teacher for specific guidelines. Generally, however, you should mention which AI tool you used, how you used it and the prompts used.

SKILLS ACTIVITY

Automated design

Choose **one** of the following options.

Option 1: Use AI. With your teacher's permission and guidance, use an accessible AI tool for a small graphic design task (for example, generate ideas or inspiration, create a rendered model from a sketch or an animation). Compare its reliability, speed, accuracy, originality and quality with the same task completed by a human. Remember to cite how you used it.

Option 2: Research AI. Research examples of AI in graphic design (showing outputs). Compare the AI tools/outputs based on reliability, speed, accuracy, originality and quality with the same task completed by a human.

Write a short evaluation (150–200 words) discussing benefits, risks and AI's future role in graphic design, based on your experience or research.

DESIGN IN ACTION

Lucy leverages technology to create illustrations, showcase her portfolio and connect with fellow digital artists and potential clients through engaging posts and videos (Figure 3). For commissioned work, she begins by using AI tools to generate inspiration and ideas. She then brings her concepts to life on a digital tablet. To streamline collaboration and communication, Lucy relies on social media platforms, making her creative process more efficient and accessible.

△ **Figure 3** Lucy uses technology to generate inspiration, collaborate, share her ideas, connect to others and get feedback on her work.

TECHNOLOGY IN MAKING

After designing your graphic product, technology steps in to make it a physical reality. Computer-controlled systems are essential in manufacturing today, ensuring precision, speed and consistency as designs come to life.

Computer-aided manufacture (CAM)

After designing (often with CAD), computer-aided manufacture (CAM) is used. CAM means using computer-controlled machines to turn digital designs into physical graphic products, precisely and efficiently (Figure 4). For details on the different types of CAM processes used in graphic products and how they work, refer to unit 3.3.2.

Δ **Figure 4** CAM machines efficiently turn digital designs into precise, physical graphic products.

REFLECTIVE LOG

What do you think are the advantages and disadvantages for making graphic products using CAM rather than by hand?

SKILLS ACTIVITY

Hand vs technology challenge

Challenge a classmate or group of classmates to a competition. One team creates a simple box by hand, the other team uses CAD and CAM.

1. Which is faster, more efficient and more accurate?
2. Which is more expensive (consider cost of tools and machinery)?
3. What if you had to make 100 boxes instead of one?

Remember: Safety first!

KNOWLEDGE CHECK

1. State **one** advantage of using email for communicating a design proposal compared to text messages.
2. Give **two** examples of how digital tools and software are used in the graphic design process.
3. Explain **one** potential risk associated with using artificial intelligence (AI) in graphic design.
4. Identify **one** advantage of using computer-aided manufacture (CAM) for making graphic products.
5. Describe **one** way that collaborative working software helps graphic designers work together remotely.

KEY TERMS

Artificial intelligence (AI): Computer systems that can perform tasks usually needing human intelligence, such as learning or problem-solving

Cloud: Storing and accessing digital files, software and services over the internet, rather than directly on your local computer or device

Generative design: A process where AI algorithms quickly create many design variations based on rules or parameters set by the designer

Practice questions

Question 1

A garden sculpture is designed using a combination of shapes: a circle, a regular hexagon and tangential arcs.

a) Using the following information, draw a 2D geometric design of the sculpture to a scale of 1:10 using the measurements stated:

- The circle has a diameter of 80 mm and is positioned at the centre of the design.
- A regular hexagon is inside the circle with the points of the hexagon touching the circle.
- Tangential arcs (radius: 40 mm) are drawn from each point of the hexagon to extend outward from the circle.

Ensure that your drawing:

- Uses correct geometric construction methods.
- Include accurate dimensioning. (9)

b) A prototype model of the garden sculpture will be made from foamboard and self-adhesive vinyl.

i) State **one** property of foamboard that makes it suitable for the prototype model. (1)

ii) Describe the process of applying the self-adhesive vinyl to the foamboard prototype model. (2)

iii) State **one** protective and **one** decorative benefit of using self-adhesive vinyl as a finish for the sculpture. (2)

Question 2

A promotional display is being designed for a technology trade show to advertise a new range of wireless headphones called 'SoundWave'.

a) The display will feature a printed header card made from solid white board. Sketch a design for the header card.

Your sketch should include the product name 'SoundWave' to attract attention. (2)

b) Figures 2.1 and 2.2 show isometric and front views of the promotional display with a triangular prism base for stability.

Suggest a suitable block material for the base. Give a reason for your choice of material. (2)

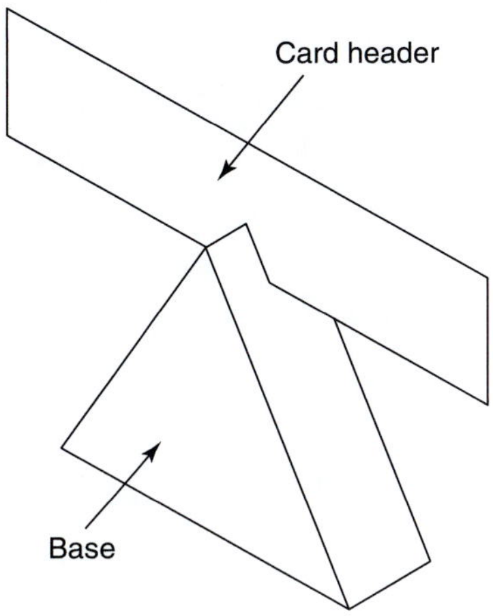

Δ **Figure 2.1**

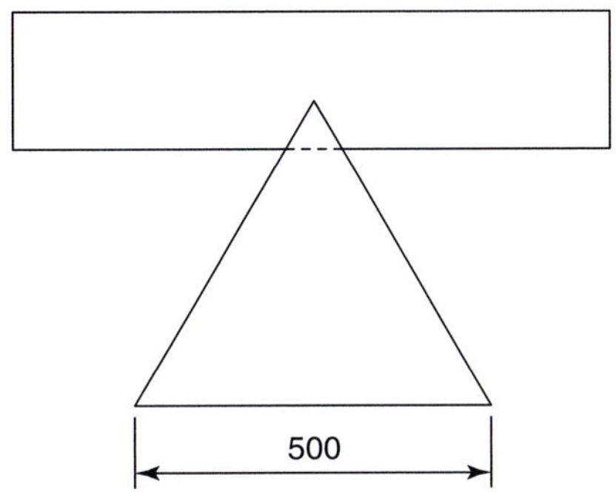

Δ **Figure 2.2**

c) Using a scale of 1:10 complete an exploded view of the promotional display in Figure 2.1, showing the card header separate from the base. Do not add your design from 2(a). (3)

d) Figure 2.3 shows an existing logo for 'SoundWave'.

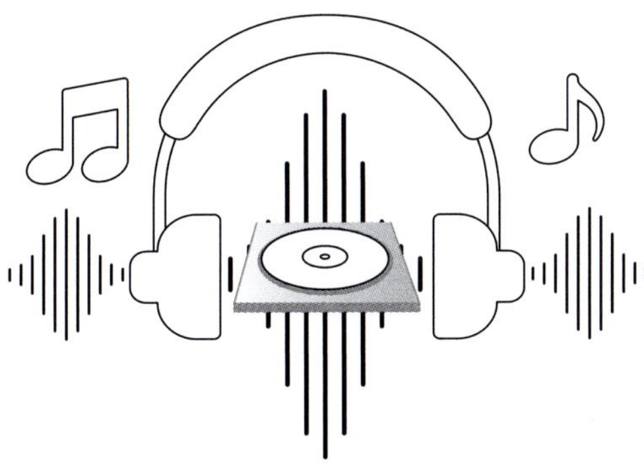

Δ **Figure 2.3**

i) Describe **one** printing technique that could be used to apply the logo to the display header. (2)

ii) The company would like to cut the logo using computer-aided manufacturing (CAM). Sketch a redesign of the logo so it can easily be cut using CAM. (2)

Question 3

A packaging design is needed for the SoundWave wireless headphones. The packaging will be made from 2 mm corrugated card and will feature a foldable box with a secure lid and a transparent window.

The packaging is shown in Figure 3.1.

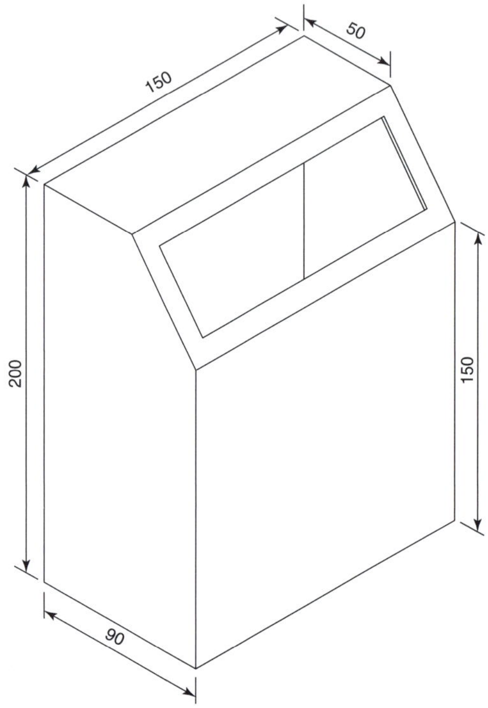

∆ **Figure 3.1**

a) Draw the orthographic views of the packaging design to a scale of 1:2. Use third angle projection and estimate any sizes not given. Do not show hidden detail. (12)

b)i) Explain the scale of production that would be used to produce the packaging for the headphones for the trade show. (3)

The packaging is to be used at a trade show, so not many would be required and would be made using batch production, ✓ (1) *a limited amount made* ✓ (1) *for display purposes. The packaging could be made for specific headphone models* ✓ (1) *to be shown at the trade show.*

ii) The company wants the packaging to be fully biodegradable. Name a biopolymer that could be used for the transparent window. (1)

COMMENTS

3) b) i) The sample answer correctly identifies that the product would be shown at a trade fair and therefore the scale of production would be batch production (limited number). The response also goes into further depth by correctly explaining that the packaging could be made for specific headphone models (customised).

c) Draw the development (net) of the packaging to a scale of 1:5. (6)

d) Explain how the packaging can be designed to minimise the environmental impact at the end of the product's life. (3)

Most people choose Design and Technology because they like designing and making things! Project work is often the most enjoyable, exciting and rewarding part of this course. It gives you the opportunity to demonstrate your understanding of real-world challenges, user needs and sustainability, and your skills through the use of a range of materials, media, tools and equipment.

Your project work has two elements: the portfolio and the product you make. It is important that you put evidence of your work into the design portfolio, so do not throw anything away. You will also need to provide good-quality, clear photographs of your design process and the final outcome, to demonstrate your skill and the effectiveness of your prototype.

Project work in Design and Technology is an iterative design process – this means developing your ideas step-by-step, improving them as you go. Your design portfolio and final product should clearly show how you have worked through each stage of the iterative design process.

This section will help you plan your work. You will see examples of portfolio sheets. These are just guides, however, and it is important that you follow the instructions given to you by your teacher.

Work hard and you will make a product to be proud of for a long time. A good project and portfolio can also be useful when talking to prospective employers or applying to universities, as it will demonstrate that you have a wide range of skills, knowledge and understanding. Good luck and enjoy the creative process!

STARTING POINTS

- What evidence or technique is the best choice for your project? Consider the following design stages: identifying, defining, proposing, developing, planning and testing/evaluating.
- What knowledge or skills will you need to develop?
- How much of the evidence will naturally occur during the designing and making of your project?
- Which presentation techniques will help you clearly show your thoughts and ideas? This could include digital tools such as graphs, charts, infographics, 2D and 3D CAD designs, simulations and photographs or screenshots of CAM processes.

SECTION CONTENTS

4 The Project

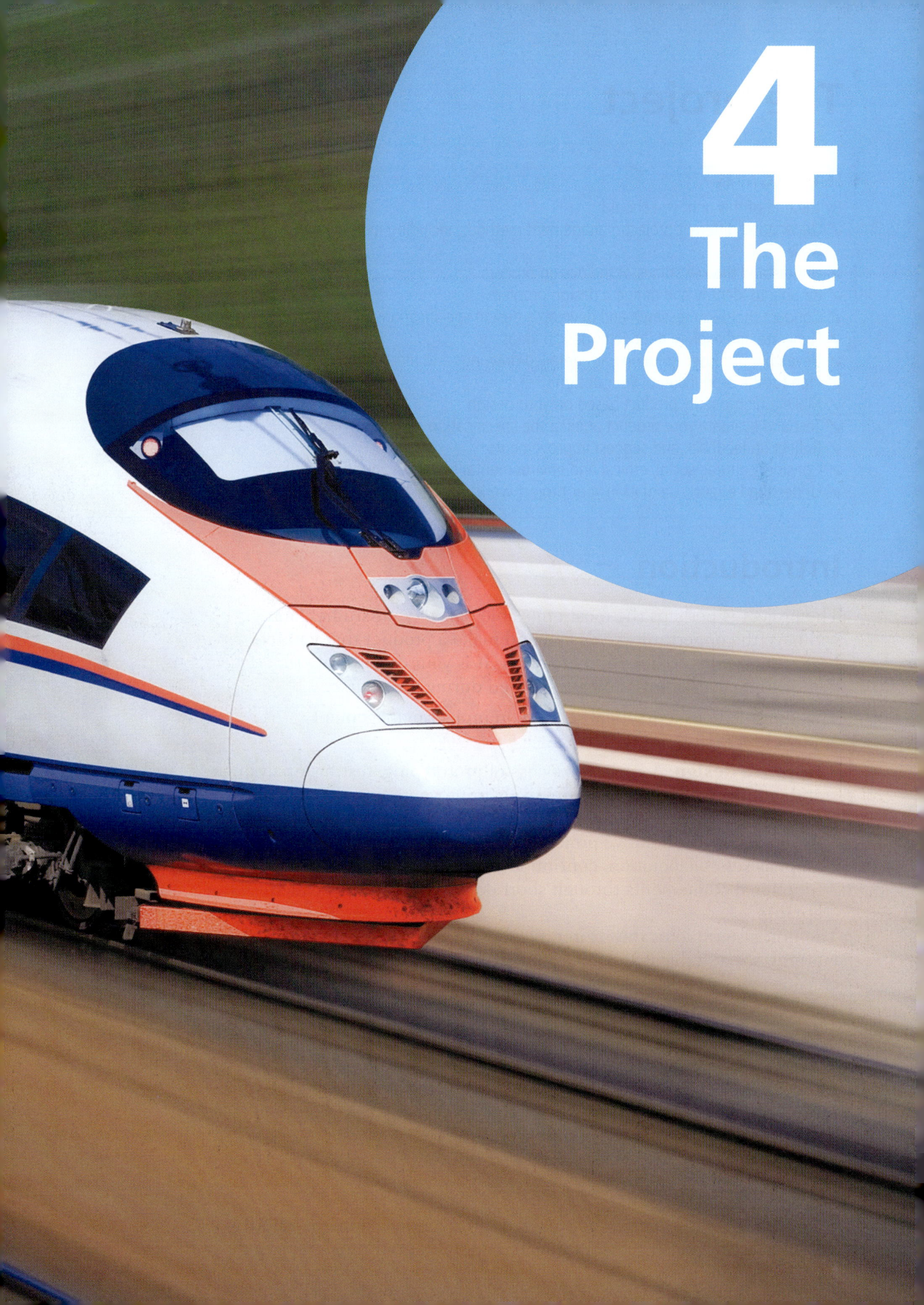

The project

LEARNING AIMS

By the end of this unit, you should:

✓ Understand different project management methods, including iterative design and Agile
✓ Understand the key stages of the design process
✓ Be able to identify and define a design problem
✓ Conduct thorough research and develop a design specification
✓ Generate and explore a range of design ideas
✓ Develop a proposed solution with detailed drawings and models
✓ Plan for the production of your design
✓ Make a high-quality product based on your design
✓ Test and evaluate your product against the specification
✓ Reflect on feedback and suggest improvements
✓ Consider cultural, social, ethical and environmental factors in your project work
✓ Understand ethical use of AI in your project work

Introduction

The project is perhaps the most enjoyable part of your studies. You will have the opportunity to design and make a product that you feel best reflects your abilities and creativity. It is your opportunity to demonstrate everything you have learned during the course.

This unit includes a practical section on project management approaches, including:

- **Iterative design**: A cyclical process of prototyping, testing, analysing and refining a product to progressively improve its functionality and user experience based on continuous feedback.
- **Agile**: A flexible, iterative project management approach that emphasises collaboration, continuous feedback and rapid delivery of functional components through short development cycles called **sprints**.

The unit also explores the six iterative designing principles, as well as cultural, social, ethical and environmental factors that you should consider, and strategies for addressing them in your project work.

Project management

Project management is about planning, organising and completing your project efficiently and effectively. It helps you stay on track, meet deadlines and produce high-quality work.

ITERATIVE DESIGN

Iterative design is a cyclical approach to product development where a design is continuously tested, evaluated and refined through repeated cycles of prototyping and feedback. In iterative design processes, the designer moves back and forth between design activities, rather than following steps in a linear fashion (Figure 1).

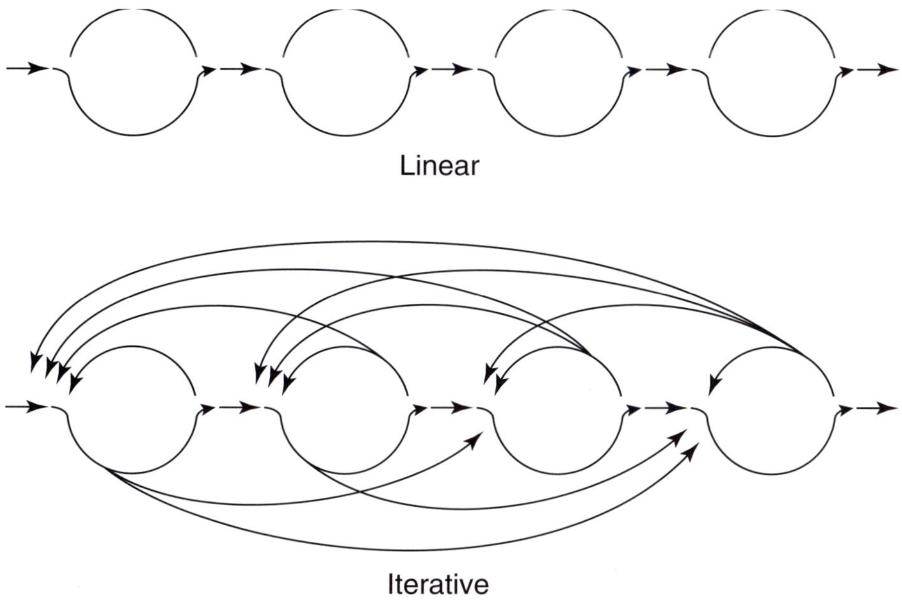

△ **Figure 1** Linear vs iterative design processes

This mirrors how designers and engineers work in the real world, where new information and ideas are discovered through a design project, requiring them to revisit and refine (or change) earlier work. It involves the following steps:

1	**Plan and prototype**	Begin with a basic version of your design. For example, create an exploratory model or sketch of your product idea.
2	**Test and gather feedback**	Evaluate the model with users or stakeholders. For example, ask classmates or teachers to test your model and provide suggestions.
3	**Refine and improve**	Make changes based on feedback and test again. For example, adjust dimensions, materials or features to better meet user needs.
4	**Repeat the cycle**	Continue refining until the design meets the specification and user expectations. For example, go through several versions of your design before finalising the prototype model.

AGILE APPROACHES

The Agile approach is a flexible and iterative method that focuses on delivering small, incremental improvements through sprints. It promotes collaboration, adaptability and continuous feedback (Figure 2).

△ **Figure 2** The Agile project management cycle

Agile methods are highly recommended for projects due to their flexibility, adaptability and focus on continuous improvement. Scrum is an Agile approach developed for software and other industries, and can even be used in education settings. In the context of your Design and Technology course, you can use the Agile method to help you manage your time, stay organised and improve your final product through regular reflection and adaptation. The following explains how you can apply it.

1. Understand the basics

Scrum is a framework within Agile that breaks work into manageable chunks called 'sprints' (typically 1–2 weeks). It includes roles, events and tools that help teams (or individuals) stay on track.

Key concepts:

- A *sprint* is a short, focused period to complete a set of tasks.
- A *backlog* is a list of all the tasks or features you want to include in your project.
- A *weekly stand-up* is a quick check-in (even if just with yourself) to review progress and plan the day.
- Hold a *sprint review* at the end of each sprint. Review what you have achieved and what needs improvement.
- Hold a *sprint retrospective* to reflect on how you worked and how you can improve your process.

2. Create a project task list

Start by listing everything you need to do for your project. This includes research, sketches, prototypes, testing, evaluations and final presentation. The backlog tasks are not completed sequentially, but some will overlap and/or run throughout the project (Table 1).

Task	Priority	Notes
Research/define problem	High	Use observation, interviews, internet and books (ongoing during project)
Sketch initial ideas	High	Use ideation strategies/approaches to generate a range of ideas
Write a design specification	Medium	List the desirable and essential requirements based on research
Model and test ideas	Medium	Use cardboard or foam to make quick models to mock-up ideas
Develop design ideas	High	Annotated and production drawings, systems and exploded diagrams
Build prototype	High	Plan and construct a functional prototype

Task	Priority	Notes
Test prototype	Medium	Ask classmates or users for feedback on the function of the prototype
Final evaluation	High	Evaluate against the specification, and include user feedback

Δ **Table 1** An example of a project backlog

3. Plan your project in steps

Break your project into small chunks of time (called sprints) that last 1 or 2 weeks. In each sprint, focus on a few tasks from your to-do list. For example:

Sprint 1 (Week 1–2):

- Find out what the problem is.
- Draw some rough ideas.
- Try out and test your ideas.

Sprint 2 (Week 7–8):

- Write down what your design needs to do.
- Keep testing your ideas.
- Start building your design.

Sprint 3 (Week 15–16):

- Test your final model.
- Make it better.
- Get ready to show your work.

4. Use a scrum board

A **scrum board** helps you visualise your progress (Figure 3). You can use sticky notes on a wall or whiteboard, a notebook or a digital tool like Trello. This helps you stay focused and motivated as you move tasks across the board.

Δ **Figure 3** Example scrum board

Columns:

- 'To do' are the tasks that you have not yet started.
- 'In progress' or 'Work' are the tasks you are working on.
- 'Done' are the completed tasks.

5. Hold regular check-ins

Even if you are working alone, take 5 minutes each week or every few weeks to reflect on:

- What did I do last week?
- What will I do today?
- What is blocking me?

If you are working in a group, do this together and keep your teacher in the loop. It keeps everyone aligned and accountable.

6. Review and reflect

At the end of each sprint:

- Review what you have completed.
- Ask for feedback from your teacher or classmates.
- Reflect on what went well and what could be improved.

Use this to adjust your next sprint. Maybe you need to change an aspect of a backlog item, add more time for testing or simplify your design.

7. Adapt and improve

Agile is all about flexibility. If something is not working – change it! Maybe your early ideas or prototype model did not work as expected. That's okay. Use what you learned to make it better in the next sprint.

Tools you can use:

- Online platforms for digital scrum boards, such as Trello or Notion.
- Office suites for collaborative planning and documentation, such as Microsoft Office or Google Docs.
- Timer or Pomodoro apps to stay focused during lessons.
- Sketchbooks and journals and/or digital devices for recording ideas and reflections.

Project designing principles

You should be able to demonstrate that you have been through all of the following designing principles in your project work (Figure 4), as part of an iterative design process, but not necessarily in the order presented here:

1. Identifying
2. Defining
3. Proposing
4. Developing
5. Planning
6. Testing and evaluating

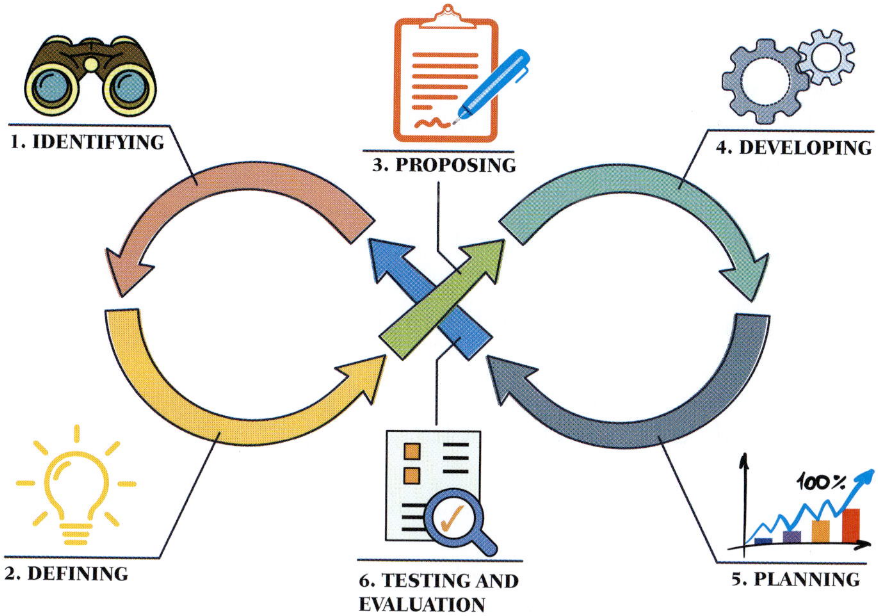

Δ **Figure 4** Designing principles

IDENTIFYING

Finding a suitable problem can sometimes be a challenging task. If it is too simple, then you may find it hard to demonstrate and use all the skills you have learned. If it is too complex, then you may not address the problem sufficiently or even manage to complete the task. Remember that you will be spending many months on your project, so finding a problem that you are interested in is extremely important too (Figure 5).

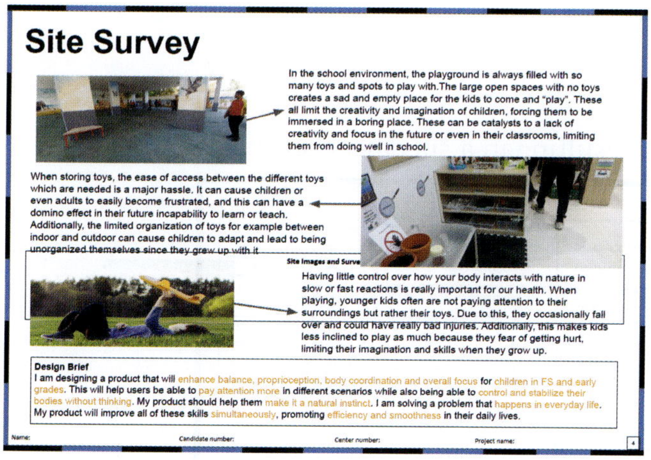

Δ **Figure 5** Identifying a need and establishing a design brief

Some things to consider when choosing your project include:

- Is there a product that could be improved for a hobby or interest you have?

- Ask your friends and relatives – they may have a few suggestions or ideas about design problems you can solve for them.
- Is there an item that you use every day that could be improved?
- Is there an item that could be developed for people with disabilities, young children or the elderly, or another exclusive group?

When you have identified your design need, problem or opportunity, you will need to write a problem description. It is a good idea to state the following:

- What is the problem? Also add photographs or sketches of the problem.
- Where is the problem? Add photos or sketches.
- Why has this problem been identified? Give details of the circumstances for choosing the project.
- Who is the user of the intended product? Present details of your target market or customer profile.
- What is the intended finished product? Give details of what you are intending to make.

Then, to get started you may consider:

- Identifying trends using Google trends, product analysis for redesign opportunities, market research or perceptual mapping (designing for markets).
- Conducting interviews, observations, task step analysis, empathy maps (designing for users).
- Researching school, local or global environmental issues or site visits (designing for the environment).
- Researching accidents or safety issues, experiencing cultural events and products, or conducting surveys of members of organisations or events (designing for society).

DEFINING

Research into the design brief, resulting in a specification (Figure 6).

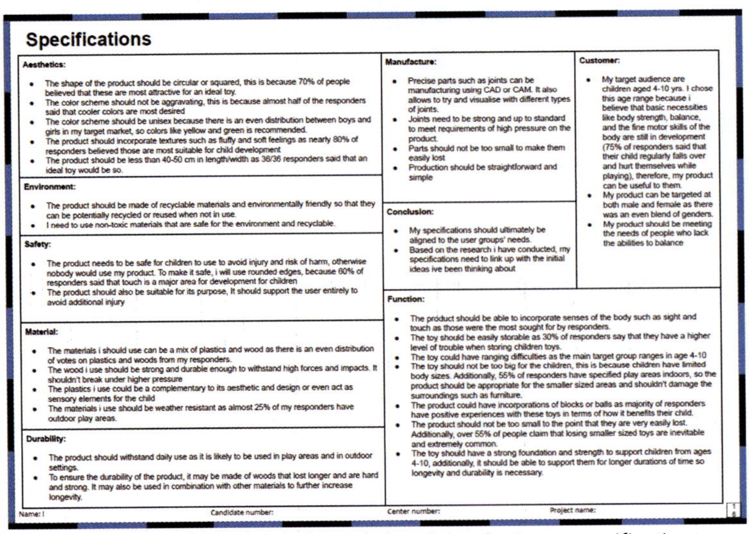

Specifications

Aesthetics:

- The shape of the product should be circular or squared, this is because 70% of people believed that these are most attractive for an ideal toy.
- The color scheme should not be aggravating, this is because almost half of the responders said that cooler colors are most desired
- The color scheme should be unisex because there is an even distribution between boys and girls in my target market, so colors like yellow and green is recommended.
- The product should incorporate textures such as fluffy and soft feelings as nearly 80% of responders believed those are most suitable for child development
- The product should be less than 40-50 cm in length/width as 36/36 responders said that an ideal toy would be so.

Environment:

- The product should be made of recyclable materials and environmentally friendly so that they can be potentially recycled or reused when not in use.
- I need to use non-toxic materials that are safe for the environment and recyclable.

Safety:

- The product needs to be safe for children to use to avoid injury and risk of harm, otherwise nobody would use my product. To make it safe, i will use rounded edges, because 60% of responders said that touch is a major area for development for children
- The product should also be suitable for its purpose, It should support the user entirely to avoid additional injury

Material:

- The materials i should use can be a mix of plastics and wood as there is an even distribution of votes on plastics and woods from my responders.
- The wood i use should be strong and durable enough to withstand high forces and impacts. It shouldn't break under higher pressure
- The plastics i use could be a complementary to its aesthetic and design or even act as sensory elements for the child
- The materials i use should be weather resistant as almost 25% of my responders have outdoor play areas.

Durability:

- The product should withstand daily use as it is likely to be used in play areas and in outdoor settings.
- To ensure the durability of the product, it may be made of woods that lost longer and are hard and strong. It may also be used in combination with other materials to further increase longevity.

Manufacture:

- Precise parts such as joints can be manufacturing using CAD or CAM. It also allows to try and visualise with different types of joints.
- Joints need to be strong and up to standard to meet requirements of high pressure on the product.
- Parts should not be too small to make them easily lost
- Production should be straightforward and simple

Conclusion:

- My specifications should ultimately be aligned to the user groups' needs.
- Based on the research i have conducted, my specifications need to link up with the initial ideas ive been thinking about

Customer:

- My target audience are children aged 4-10 yrs. I chose this age range because i believe that basic necessities like body strength, balance, and the fine motor skills of the body are still in development (75% of responders said that their child regularly falls over and hurt themselves while playing), therefore, my product can be useful to them.
- My product can be targeted at both male and female as there was an even blend of genders.
- My product should be meeting the needs of people who lack the abilities to balance

Function:

- The product should be able to incorporate senses of the body such as sight and touch as those were the most sought for by responders.
- The toy should be easily storable as 30% of responders say that they have a higher level of trouble when storing children toys.
- The toy could have ranging difficulties as the main target group ranges in age 4-10
- The toy should not be too big for the children, this is because children have limited body sizes. Additionally, 55% of responders have specified play areas indoors, so the product should be appropriate for the smaller sized areas and shouldn't damage the surroundings such as furniture.
- The product could have incorporations of blocks or balls as majority of responders have positive experiences with these toys in terms of how it benefits their child.
- The product should not be too small to the point that they are very easily lost. Additionally, over 55% of people claim that losing smaller sized toys are inevitable and extremely common.
- The toy should have a strong foundation and strength to support children from ages 4-10, additionally, it should be able to support them for longer durations of time so longevity and durability is necessary.

Name: I Candidate number: Center number: Project name: 16

△ **Figure 6** Researching the design brief and developing a specification

Once you have a clear design brief, you will need to analyse it. At this stage of the process, it is a good idea to gather as much information as you can about the problem and situation. Ask lots of questions and record them. One initial technique is to highlight the key words from the design brief statement and analyse them.

Other research may include interviews, observations, surveys and disassembly and analysis of similar products. When you have completed your research, it needs to be gathered, ordered, analysed and presented. Make sure the research is useful to your theme/brief and consists of a good mix of primary and secondary research. Ensure your brief meets the requirements of the user and discard any irrelevant information.

The specification is a list of design considerations your product will follow. Design considerations should also address relevant cultural, social, ethical, and environmental factors. If your research is thorough and detailed, the specification should be easy to write as your conclusions for each aspect of the research should help you. Specifications are usually bullet point lists of statements. Keep these short and clear and make sure each one is measurable.

PROPOSING

Generation and exploration of design ideas (Figure 7).

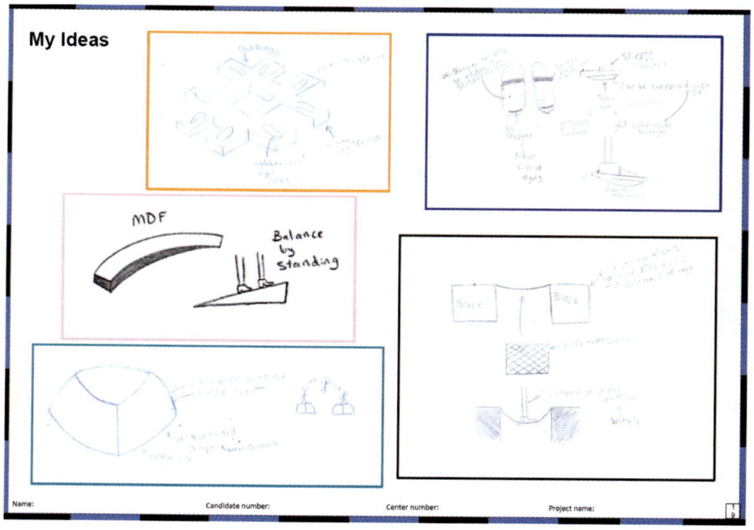

◁ **Figure 7** Generating and exploring design ideas

This is the really fun and creative aspect of the design process. Try to use a range of presentation techniques, whichever area you are specialising in, including:

- Quick sketches and design ideation activities using pencil, pen or digital tools (note: using pen forces you to keep every idea and move on quickly to the next).
- Sketch modelling to rapidly test early ideas in 3D.
- Annotation using written notes and labels, or audio/audiovisual recordings, to evaluate and critique ideas.

- Techniques: thick and thin line drawing, marker or colour pencil renderings, and use of shade and tone, 3D isometric and perspective drawing, 2D line drawings, CAD drawings (2D and 3D).

When designing, you should try to demonstrate a wide range of solutions with developments, no matter how impractical they are. This stage is all about ideas, creativity and innovation. You need to create an idea and develop it. Try to make each idea conceptually different. This is where the real thinking takes place.

It is a good idea to annotate your drawings so that they relate directly to the specification. You should try to include construction and minor details, decoration and any images or notes that have helped develop your ideas. Label and identify key aspects of your design – for example, how parts are joined, which materials are used, measurements and sizes. This could also include cultural, social, ethical and environmental factors. Make the annotation clear and relevant to your specification to help you justify your decision later on when you have to choose a specific idea to continue with and develop thoroughly. Refer to unit 1.3.1 for more detail.

DEVELOPING

Development of proposed solution (Figure 8).

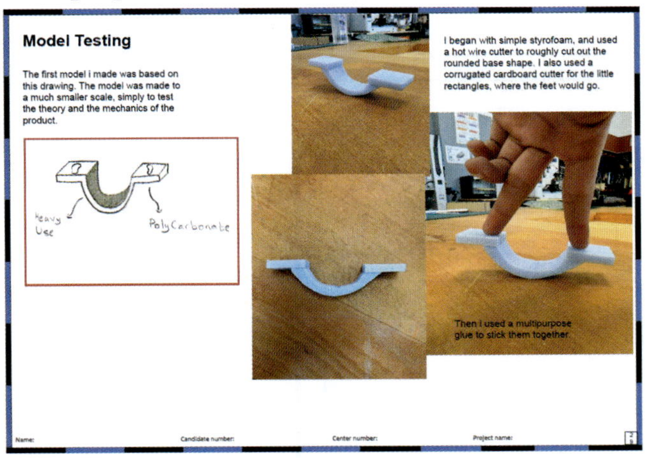

△ **Figure 8** Developing a proposed solution

In this stage of the project, you will need to bring together the best and most suitable ideas from the previous stages and make decisions about form, materials, construction, production methods and finishes. You should develop your concept through drawing, sketching, and testing models. This could include using 2D mock-ups, 3D models (physical or CAD), or a combination. Make sure to document the refinement process and the testing results and include any user feedback to justify your chosen solution.

You could explore:

- Testing material properties and finishes
- Construction techniques
- Structural elements

- Moving and mechanical parts
- Electronics subsystems
- Exploratory and prototype models for testing
- Manufacturing methods

It is advisable at this stage to demonstrate that you have carried out appropriate and specific testing with regard to all of the points covered in your specification. For example, if you are designing an electronic system, have you tested a range of circuits for suitability and shown the changes you have made to get a working solution?

Following your development, you should present your final design proposal using hand-drawing methods (Figure 9) or CAD. Annotate all relevant dimensions, materials and construction techniques.

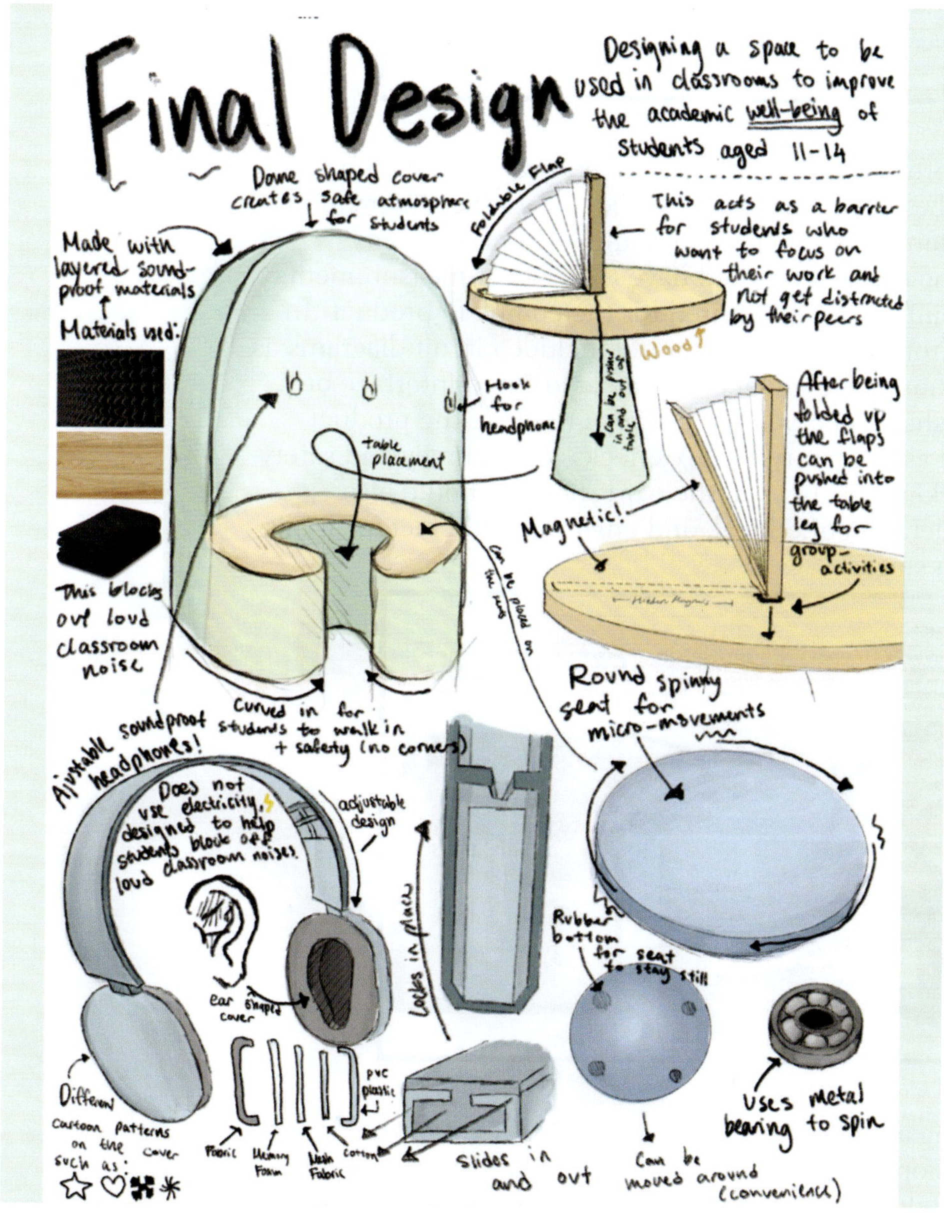

△ **Figure 9** A final design proposal

PLANNING

Planning for production (Figure 10).

Production Plan

Part 2: Base layer				Material: Plywood		
Task type	**Task detail**	**Tools**	**Quality checks**	**Safety**	**Time**	**Comments**
Measuring & marking	I will mark out the material to the intended size	Combination square, pencil, compass	Make sure lines are straight and perpendicular to edges		5 mins	
Cutting	I will cut down the piece into the parts i need.	Bandsaw, tenon saw, scroll saw	Make sure cuts are straight and neat. Ensure that there are no wood chips	Safety glasses, pistol grip on tenon saw	15 mins	Dont go directly over marking lines, give some space to prevent error
sanding	I will sand down the piece for a cleaner edge	Sandpaper, files	Ensure that the sides are smooth and have no bumps		15 mins	Use a vice to hold piece securely during filing and sanding
glueing	Apply wood glue between the cut off piece from top layer and backside of base layer, put them together and clamp them down	Wood glue, clamp	Ensure the pieces are properly aligned, tighten clamps thoroughly	Gloves	2 hrs 30 mins	Use a paper/cardboard underneath to minimize mess.
Drilling	Drill 8 light holes using a forstner bit. Drill 2 more on the other side	Drill press	Ensure the diameter of the hole is greater than the diameter of the insert	Safety glasses	25 mins	
Drilling	Drill 8 clean holes in the base layer that don't go all the way through. Drill 2 more on the other side	Drill press	Visual check for any wood chips and overall quality of hole, Make sure the depth of hole matches the size of insert	Safety glasses	30 mins	Ensure that the piece is secure on the drill bed. (try to limit movement of piece)
Finish	Apply layers of polycrylic to the wood for a nice finish	brush	Use reflection of sun to ensure all parts are covered with polycrylic	gloves	1 hr	Place paper / cardboard underneath to reduce mess
Glueing	Attach the straps onto the side of the base layer	Hole punch, hammer, soldering iron	Visual check - ensure the sides don't have rough burr	Cautious of the soldering iron's intense heat, safety glasses	15 mins	

Name: Candidate number: Center number: Project name:

Δ **Figure 10** Planning for production

At this stage, your project folder should have enough information in it for a third-party to be able to make your project from the information given: a plan of making, working drawings and a list of materials required. All working drawings should have the correct measurements and provide all the information required for the complete product. In the case of an electronic product, this could include circuit diagrams as well as the case to house the project and the associated interface or controls. The plan should include all the steps to make the product (Figure 11), as well as necessary quality checks for accuracy and safety checks for safe working practices in the workshop. It should also demonstrate consideration of ethical, and environmental factors at all relevant production stages.

7 - Fixing the inserts

Now it was time to put the shaved inserts inside the base piece. So i first started by attaching a full sized insert to an allen key, and driving it into my drilled hole to create my own threads inside the whole. This made it so that it would be easier to insert later on. After creating my own threads, i started to drive in the shaved down inserts using the allen key to start off, and there was little remaining, i finished it off using a socket bit in a drill. The same process was done to the bottom side, for the changeable soles.

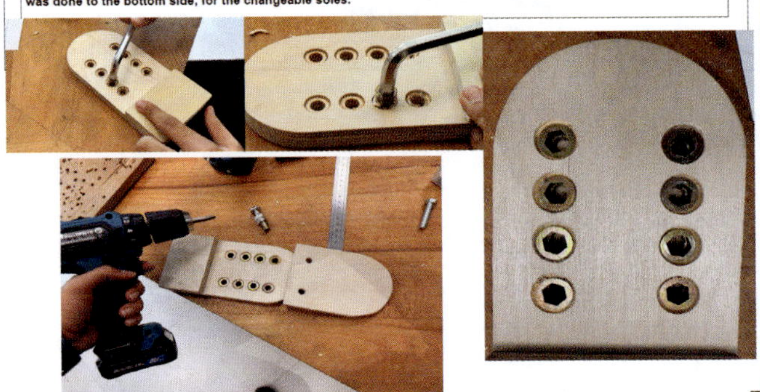

Name: Candidate number: Center number: Project name:

Δ **Figure 11** Making a product

Realising, or making a product is, for many, the highlight of the design process. Here is an opportunity for you to manipulate a range of materials and to produce usable, high-quality products for the target user, as set out in your design brief. Your final product should be based on your design drawings from the previous stages, but modifications can be made as the making process progresses. Designs often have to be modified at this stage as it is easy to overlook potential problems and constraints in the design stages. Do not be afraid of this and avoid thinking you are getting it wrong. However, make notes of any changes or modifications and refer to these in the evaluation stage of the designing process. It is often useful to use a range of construction techniques and different materials in order to demonstrate your abilities.

Include annotated photographs to record your making process and any changes made to the product. This should evidence your technical skill, safe working practice and quality assurance.

TESTING AND EVALUATING

It is a good idea to carry out testing to ensure it is safe and does what it is supposed to do at every stage of the design process (Figure 12). Consider the following:

- Has the product been tested in the physical environment proposed in the brief?
- Has the product been tested with the intended user group?
- Has the product been evaluated against the design specification?

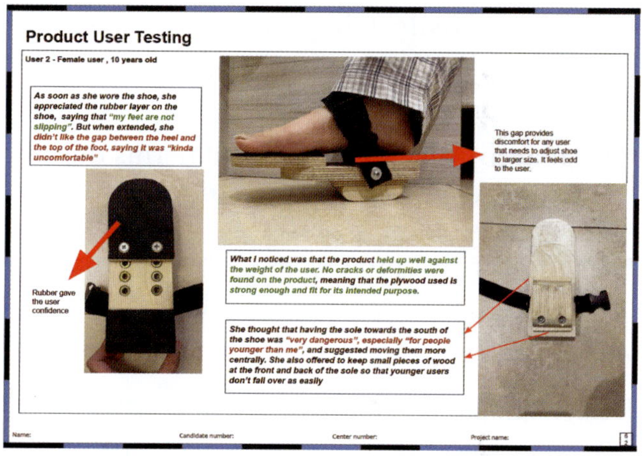

△ **Figure 12** Testing and evaluation

Use your design specification to plan your testing. You can then reference your brief and specification points in your testing and make judgements on whether each point has been met.

When writing up this section, you can use photographs, text and diagrams to illustrate your findings. Include feedback from people who have helped you test your product. Yours and others' opinions are extremely valuable and useful here.

Finally, make proposals for further modifications and development where the design does not meet the design specification or customer requirements. You can do this in text format, but drawing out your modifications is also very useful. Include comments about the strengths and weaknesses of the product and an overall evaluation of your work on the project.

TOP TIP

Remember to take photographs of all of your testing. This provides real evidence that the testing actually took place! You can also keep a design journal or digital log to track what decisions and actions you made over time.

CULTURAL, SOCIAL, ETHICAL AND ENVIRONMENTAL FACTORS IN YOUR PROJECT WORK

Designers must consider a wide range of influences beyond aesthetics and function. Cultural, social, ethical and environmental factors shape how products are perceived, used and valued. Ignoring these can lead to designs that are unsuitable, insensitive or unsustainable. Below are examples of each factor and strategies for addressing them in your projects.

Cultural factors

Products often carry meanings that vary across cultures. For example:

- **Colours:** white may symbolise purity in Western cultures but mourning in some Asian traditions.
- **Eating utensils:** Chopsticks, forks or hands are used in different regions.

You can address this by:

- **Research:** Investigate cultural norms during the design brief stage.
- **Iterate:** Adapt colours, patterns and instructions to respect cultural differences.
- **Evaluate:** Test prototypes with users from diverse backgrounds.

Social factors

Design should be inclusive and accessible for all users. For example:

- **Accessibility:** Products for people with limited hand strength or mobility.
- **Ergonomics:** Designs that suit different ages, sizes and abilities.

You can address this by:

- **Inclusive design:** Apply ergonomics and anthropometrics (design for 5th–95th percentile).
- **User-centred design:** Include adjustable features and intuitive controls.
- **Participative design:** Gather feedback through iterative design and user testing.

Ethical factors

Ethical design respects people and intellectual property. For example:

- **Ethical practices:** Fair labour practices and safe working conditions.
- **Ethical sourcing:** Avoiding exploitation in supply chains.
- Respecting intellectual property.

You can address this by:

- **Sourcing:** Source materials responsibly (e.g., Fairtrade-certified).
- **Compliance:** Ensure compliance with safety standards (CE mark, local regulations).
- **Protection:** Respect originality through patents, trademarks and copyright and do not use the work of others.
- Use Artificial Intelligence (AI) responsibly. Be transparent if you have used AI in your design development.

Environmental factors

Every product impacts the planet throughout its life cycle. For example:

- **End of life cycle:** Non-recyclable plastics contributing to landfill waste.
- **Embodied energy:** High energy consumption during production.

You can address this by:

- **Sustainable practice:** Apply the environmental sustainability tools such as the 6Rs: Reduce, Reuse, Recycle, Rethink, Repair, Refuse (see Unit 1.1.3 for more on this).
- **Material selection:** Choose sustainable materials (biopolymers, FSC timber).
- **Circular economy:** Design for disassembly and circular economy principles.
- **Transportation:** Minimise transport distances and energy use in manufacturing. Investigate local suppliers.

Integrating these factors into your project work

- **Investigating** Investigate cultural, social and environmental contexts early.
- Set measurable design criteria related to a wide range of factors, including cultural, social, ethical and environmental alongside functionality and aesthetics.
- **Designing:** Annotate sketches to show inclusivity and sustainability.
- **Making:** Select sustainable materials and plan for minimal or zero-waste techniques.
- **Testing and evaluating:** Test prototypes for usability, safety and environmental impact using tools like RAG rating or a design matrix.

ETHICAL USE OF AI IN YOUR PROJECT WORK

Artificial Intelligence (AI) tools can support research, ideation, and documentation, but must be used ethically and transparently. There are a wide range of AI tools to support with written/information-based activities and visualisation/ideation. Ethical use of AI demonstrates integrity, critical thinking, and respect for intellectual property. You should:

- Clearly acknowledge and reference any AI-generated content, including the prompts you used.
- Verify the accuracy and reliability of AI-sourced information.
- Address biases inherent to AI-based work, such as ideas that fixate on existing products or cultural norms/expectations.
- Avoid using AI to generate final design ideas or solutions, which must be your own work.
- Show that you are critically evaluating and improving AI-generated content, showing how human–AI collaboration is enhancing your design process.
- Use AI to expand and enhance your thinking, not replace it.
- Follow Cambridge International's guidance on the use of generative AI in coursework: www.cambridgeinternational.org/generative-ai-in-coursework

KEY TERMS

Agile: A flexible, iterative project management approach that emphasises collaboration, continuous feedback and rapid delivery of functional components through short development cycles called sprints, weekly stand-ups, reviews and retrospectives

Iterative design: A way of designing where you test, improve and repeat changes based on feedback

Scrum board: Visualisation of a progress using sticky notes on a wall or whiteboard, a notebook, or a digital tool such as Padlet or Trello

Sprint: A short, focused period to complete a set of tasks

Glossary

Actuator A device that converts electrical energy into mechanical energy (motion)

Addition When material is added to build or make a product

Adhesive A substance used to bond materials together

Aesthetics The visual and tactile appeal of a product, including how it looks and feels to the user

Agile A flexible, iterative project management approach that emphasises collaboration, continuous feedback and rapid delivery of functional components through short development cycles called sprints, weekly stand-ups, reviews and retrospectives

Alloy A mixture of two or more metals

Alternative materials Used as substitutes for common materials, often chosen for benefits like sustainability, cost, or performance

Amplifier An electronic device that increases the power of a signal

Annotate Written explanation of a features or design decisions – more than a label

Anthropometrics The study of measurements and data of the human body that is used in designing products and systems

Artificial intelligence (AI) Computer systems that can perform tasks usually needing human intelligence, such as learning or problem-solving

Barrier properties The ability of a material to block things like light, oxygen, or moisture

Base current The current that flows into the base terminal of a transistor to activate it

Beam A member which spans gaps and supports the loads acting on it

Bearing A mechanical device that reduces friction between moving parts, enhancing efficiency and longevity

Belt drive A system that transmits power using an endless belt wrapped over two pulleys

Bending A force that causes an object to bend

Bin A range of values on the x-axis that groups the data in a histogram

Bio-based materials Materials made from renewable biological sources, such as plants or natural fibres

Biodegradable Breaks down naturally in the environment

Biomimicry An approach to design that takes inspiration from how nature solves problems

Biopolymer A polymer derived from renewable biomass sources

Bisection Splitting a segment into two equal parts

Bitmap Image composed of pixels, making its quality dependent on resolution (dpi)

Brief A short, clear statement outlining what the design needs to achieve

British Standards In technical drawing, British Standards are guidelines from the British Standards Institution that define how drawings should be created and presented

Buckling Failure mode where a component bends out of shape due to excessive compressive force or heat

Cam A specially shaped part attached to a rotating shaft that imparts linear motion to a cam follower

Capacitor A component that stores and releases electrical energy in an electric field

Carbon footprint The total greenhouse gases produced during the life of a product or activity, usually measured in carbon dioxide equivalents

Circular economy A system where products are designed to last, be repaired, reused or recycled, keeping resources in use for as long as possible

Client The person who has asked for the product or is paying for it. Sometimes the user and the client are the same, but not always

Closed loop system A system that incorporates feedback to continuously regulate and adjust its operation, ensuring the desired output is achieved

Cloud Storing and accessing digital files, software and services over the internet, rather than directly on your local computer or device

Column A vertical support that carries the weight of a structure

Commercial manufacturing Manufacturing method used to produce products in quantity

Composite A material made by combining two or more different materials to create a new material that has improved properties

Compression A squashing force

Computer-aided design (CAD) Using specialist computer programs to help create or test designs

Computer-aided manufacture (CAM) Using machines like 3D printers or computer numerical control (CNC) routers to make models

Concept A vision that defines the essential character, purpose, and approach of a design solution

Construction details Additional elements added to a net design to enable assembly, such as tabs, flaps and fold lines

Control of substances hazardous to health (COSHH) A set of regulations designed to ensure the safe use of hazardous substances

Conversion of motion When one type of movement or motion changes into another

Corrugation A surface that has ridges and grooves

Crank and slider A mechanism used to change rotary motion to linear motion, or vice versa

Crating Drawing a simple 3D shape first (e.g. a box or cylinder), or combination of regular 3D shapes, inside which you can draw a more detailed design

Cross-brace A diagonal support forming an 'X' shape to strengthen and stabilise a structure

Cure The chemical process of allowing a substance, such as a polymer resin used within a composite, to harden and set

Current (electrical) The flow of electricity through a circuit or a measure of the rate of this flow – unit of measurement:amp (A)

Cutting plane An imaginary slice that cuts an object

Datum A reference line or point for all measurements when marking out material

Datum edge A straight, reference edge on material used as the starting point for all measurements to ensure accuracy

Debossing Creating a recessed (sunk in) pattern or design on a material using pressure

Deforming When a material is shaped without adding or removing material

Design brief A written summary of the problem to solve and the client's needs

Design for disassembly Designing products so they can be taken apart easily for recycling or repair

Design proposal Suggestion(s) for a design of a product that is developed using the criteria and needs given

Design solution A design idea or development of an idea that meets the required needs. This can be a drawn design, a prototype or an existing product

Development/Net A 2D shape that folds into a 3D object

Die cutter A manufacturing machine that cuts out the desired shapes from flat material

Digital design Uses computers, graphics tablets, and various electronic devices to design and create products in a digital format

Dimensions The measurements of an object

Diode An electronic component which allows current to flow predominantly in one direction only

Driven gear The gear that receives motion from the driver gear

Driver gear Is the main gear in a system that makes other gears move; it turns first and transfers motion to the driven gear, controlling speed and direction

Dynamic load A changing force caused by movement, impact, or varying pressure over time

Eccentric A disc with the centre of rotation moved away from the centre of the circle

Efficiency The ratio of useful output work or power to the actual input work or power, expressed as a percentage

Effort The force applied to the input side of a mechanism to produce movement or work

Elastic state The condition of a thermo polymer when heated; it can be shaped, but will return to its original form

Ellipse An oval shape like a flattened circle; it has a major axis and a minor axis

Embodied energy The total energy required to extract, process, manufacture, transport, and install a material or product — from raw resource to final use

Embossing Creating a raised pattern or design on a material using pressure

Environmental conditions Physical factors (such as temperature, light, moisture)

Ergonomics The study of how people interact with products and systems

Ethical consumerism Choosing to buy products that are made responsibly, considering environmental and social impacts

Ethical sourcing Ensuring materials and labour are obtained in a responsible way

Evaluate Judging how well a design meets its specification and wider goals

E-waste Discarded electrical or electronic devices, often containing harmful substances if not recycled properly

Exploded drawing A drawing that separates parts to show how they fit together

Exploratory modelling A physical or virtual representation of a design idea, used to test initial concepts, explore different forms and basic proportions

Fairtrade A certification that ensures producers in developing countries are paid fairly and work in safe conditions

Fast fashion The rapid production of inexpensive clothing that follows current fashion trends but often results in poor-quality items and high environmental waste

Fastener A component that mechanically joins two or more objects together

Feedback A key feature of a closed loop system that monitors the output and sends a signal back to the input, enabling adjustments to maintain the desired performance

Ferrous metal A metal that contains iron

Finite Having a limit or an end; a finite resource will eventually run out

First angle projection A method of laying out an orthographic drawing with the end elevation in the top left and the plan view below the front view

Fixed resistor A resistor with a constant resistance value

Flexural strength A material's ability to resist bending before deforming or breaking under load

Flowchart A diagram showing a process or decision path

Fluting The zigzag wavy layer in corrugated card

Foamboard Lightweight, rigid 'sandwich' of foam core between stiff outer layers available in sheets

Foil blocking Applying a thin metallic or coloured foil onto a surface using heat and pressure to create a shiny design

Foil-based composite A composite containing a thin layer of metal foil, usually aluminium

Force Push or pull that can change the shape of a material; there are five main types of force that can act on materials: compression, tension, torsion, shear and bending

Forest Stewardship Council (FSC) A logo showing the paper comes from well-managed forests

Form The three-dimensional structure of a product, including volume and depth

Forward bias The main direction of current flow through a diode

Frame structure A structure made of connected parts, forming a strong framework (for example, bridges, towers)

Freehand sketch A quick drawing to visualise an idea

Friction A force that resists movement between two surfaces touching each other, slowing things down

Fulcrum The pivot point around which a lever rotates

Gantt chart A chart that shows a project schedule, showing the start dates and durations of different tasks in the project

Gear A circular mechanical part with teeth that mesh with another gear to transmit motion or force

Gear system (gear train) A system of interlocking gears used to transmit motion and torque between rotating shafts

Generative design A process where AI algorithms quickly create many design variations based on rules or parameters set by the designer

Grain The pattern you see in wood created by how the tree grew. The grain can be straight, wavy, spiral, or irregular

Grain direction The way the fibres line up in paper

gsm (grams per square metre) A measure for the weight of paper; the higher the gsm, the heavier or thicker the paper

Gusset plate A flat metal plate at structural joints connecting beams, columns, and trusses for reinforcement

Hardwood Wood that comes from broad-leaved trees, such as oak, beech and ash

Hazard A potential source of harm or damage

Hazardous chemical A substance or mixture that can cause harm to humans and the environment

HDPE High-density polyethylene – a thermo polymer with good chemical resistance

Hidden detail Parts of an object that cannot be seen, shown by a dotted line on the drawing

Hot wire cutter Tool with a heated wire for smooth cuts to a foam material

Impact resistance Material's ability to withstand shock without damage

Inclusivity Producing designs, or modified designs, that are suitable for all users

Infographic A visual way to present information, data or knowledge in an easy-to-understand and engaging format

Infringement When someone uses or copies protected work, designs or inventions without permission

Innovation The use of new methods or ideas to generate or develop design proposal

Intellectual property (IP) Creations of the mind – including inventions, designs and creative work – that can be legally protected

Isometric drawing A 3D drawing method using 30° angles to give a realistic sense of shape

Iteration A new version of your idea after making changes or improvements

Iterative design A cyclic process of prototyping, testing, analysing, and refining a product or process, where each version is improved based on feedback and evaluation

Jig Holds something in place for the same task to be performed repeatedly or more accurately – for example, drilling a hole

Key A list of explanations for the different categories used on a chart or graph

Key findings Important information or conclusions discovered during research that help guide your design decisions.

Knock-down (KD) fitting Pre-manufactured components used to join materials together, either temporarily or permanently

Lamination Bonding a thin plastic film onto a surface using heat and pressure, often for protection

LDPE Low-density polyethylene – a thermo polymer with good chemical resistance

Lever A rigid bar that rotates around a fulcrum, used to move loads with mechanical advantage

Life cycle The journey of a product from raw material to disposal or recycling

Light source The point or place from which the light is coming

Light-dependent resistor (LDR) A resistor whose resistance changes with light intensity

Light-emitting diode (LED) A type of diode which emits light when operating

Linear motion Motion that follows a straight line

Linkage A system of rigid components connecting two or more parts of a mechanism, with each link having at least two attachment points

Load The force that a mechanism supports or moves during operation

Lubrication The application of oil, grease or other substances to minimise friction between moving components

Manufactured board Sheet material made from wood particles, fibres, or veneers bonded with adhesive

Marking out The process of transferring measurements in the form of lines or shapes onto a material in advance of cutting, shaping, bending or forming

Mass production Manufacturing large quantities of identical products using mechanised processes efficiently

Mass structure A structure built by piling materials like stone or concrete, relying on its weight for strength (for example, dams, pyramids)

Matrix The material in a composite that performs the binding function

Mechanical advantage The ratio of output force to input force in a mechanism, indicating how much a tool or machine amplifies force

Mechanism A system of moving parts designed to transform motion and force into a desired outcome

Memory The property by which a material returns to its original shape under environmental conditions such as heat

Microcontroller A compact integrated circuit designed to govern a specific operation in an embedded system

Micron Tiny unit to measure thickness (often for boards)

Microplastics Tiny plastic particles that pollute the environment

Modern materials Recently developed substances engineered to have special properties and improved performance over traditional materials

Modular design A design approach that allows individual parts of a product to be replaced or upgraded without discarding the whole item

Nanoparticles Very tiny particles. Materials made with nanoparticles have special properties

Natural structure A structure formed in nature, created by animals, plants or geology (for example, nests, caves, coral reefs)

Nesting Arranging shapes or parts on a material sheet in the most efficient way to minimise waste

Newton The unit of force (which has the symbol N)

Non-ferrous metal A metal that does not contain iron

NPN transistor A component used for switching or amplifying electronic signals; constructed from negative-positive-negative layers of semiconductive materials

Observation Watching people use things in real life

One-point perspective A method of making a realistic three-dimensional drawing using one vanishing point and a horizon line

Opacity How much you can (or cannot) see through paper

Open loop system A system that operates without feedback, meaning its output does not affect its input during operation

Opportunity A chance to solve a problem with design

Orthographic drawing A set of 2D views used to show accurate dimensions and layout

Oscillating motion Repetitive movement that swings back and forth along a curved path

Parallel circuit A circuit in which components are connected along parallel paths

Part drawings Component parts from an assembly which are usually drawn using orthographic projection

Particle-based composite A composite where small particles of one material are mixed into a matrix material

Parts list A table that itemises all the components required to assemble a product

Permanent joining A join that is not required to be separated and cannot be taken apart

Photochromic Changes colour with light

Physical modelling Creating a physical representation of a design to test or communicate ideas

Physical property An observable or measurable characteristic of a material, for instance strength

Pitch The distance between consecutive tops (or crests) of a screw thread

PLA Polylactic acid (polylactide) – a biopolymer made from natural materials such as corn starch

Planned obsolescence Deliberately designing the life cycle of a product to be short, forcing the user to update their products quickly

Planometric drawing A method of drawing a three-dimensional object at 45° angles, and with no distortion of the floor plan or base

Plastic state The condition of a thermo polymer when heated to a higher temperature than its elastic state; it will not return to its original form

Polymer A large molecule built from smaller molecules, called 'monomers'

Polymorph A polymer that can be easily shaped when heated

Potential difference The difference in voltage between two points in a circuit – unit of measurement: volt (V)

Potential divider Two resistors in series splitting the voltage directly proportional to their resistance

PP Polypropylene – a very common thermo polymer found in food packaging

PPE Personal protective equipment (PPE) such as eye protection, gloves and face masks

Pre-manufactured components Parts or components that are manufactured elsewhere and bought in to produce products

Preparation The process of making the surface of the material ready before applying a finish

Primary research New information collected directly from users or tests

Printed circuit board (PCB) A thin, insulated board with copper tracks etched onto its surface, used to mount and connect electronic components, forming a functional electrical or electronic circuit

Printing plate A sheet which is wrapped round a roller and used to transfer the image to the substrate

Product analysis Studying how existing products work (and what could be better)

Production plan A step-by-step guide for how a product will be made

Program/Programming The process of designing and building an executable computer program to accomplish a specific task

Proportion The relationship between different parts of a product in terms of size and scale

Prototype An early model or sample of a product used to test a concept

Prototype board Also known as a breadboard or stripboard; it is a thin, insulated board with a grid of electrically connected holes for prototyping circuits without soldering; used for temporary circuit development

Pulley A wheel with a groove that helps lift or move loads using a rope or belt

Pulley A wheel with a grooved rim that guides a belt, rope or chain to transmit motion or lift loads

Qualitative data Descriptive information based on opinions or observations.

Quality assurance The system put in place to prevent errors and ensure quality throughout manufacturing

Quantitative data Measurable information such as numbers or percentages.

RAG rating A simple colour-coded system (Red, Amber, Green) used to evaluate how well something meets certain criteria

Raw material Unprocessed material; it has not yet been manufactured

Rechargeable battery An electrical battery that can be charged, discharge and recharged multiple times

Reciprocating motion Repetitive straight-line movement back and forth along a linear path

Recycling code A numerical symbol used to identify the type of polymer for recycling classification

Reforming When a shaped material is shaped again without adding or removing material

Regular plane linear shapes Two-dimensional shapes with straight sides where all sides have equal length and all interior angles are equal

Reinforcement The material in a composite that adds tensile strength and toughness

Relay An electrically operated switch that uses an electromagnet to mechanically operate a switch

Rendering The process of shading a drawing using light and dark tones

Renewable energy Using power from natural sources, such as sunlight, wind and water

Research plan A document detailing what you need to find out, how you will do it and where you will get your information

Resistance The extent to which a component or material reduces the flow of current through that part of a circuit – unit of measurement: ohm (Ω or R)

Resistor A component that limits the flow of electrical current in a circuit

Reverse bias The direction where there is no current flow until the diode breaks down

Risk How likely it is that harm will happen from a hazard, and how serious the harm could be

Risk assessment Process of identifying hazards and evaluating risks to ensure safe working practices

Rotary motion Motion in a circular path

Safety rule A ruler, normally made of metal, which keeps your fingers away from the blade when cutting straight lines with a knife

Safety standards Legal rules that make sure products do not harm users and are safe to use

Scale of production The number of identical products made – one-off/prototype, batch, mass, continuous

Screw jack A device designed to lift a load, operated by turning a leadscrew

Scrum board Visualisation of a progress using sticky notes on a wall or whiteboard, a notebook, or a digital tool such as Padlet or Trello

Seasoning The process of drying out timber so that it becomes strong and stable to use

Secondary research Existing information from books, websites, reports or studies

Sectional view A view of a face of an object as if it has been cut through

Self-finishing materials Materials that have their desired finish built in during manufacture and do not need additional finishing processes

Sensor A device that detects physical changes and converts them into electrical signals

Series circuit A circuit in which components are connected along the same path

Shape memory polymer A polymer that returns to its original shape when heated

Shear A cutting or slicing force

Shell structure A thin, curved structure enclosing space while staying strong (for example, domes, car bodies, tents)

Simulation A virtual test, such as stress or airflow analysis, used in digital modelling

Six Rs Six things a designer must consider when designing a product for sustainability: reduce, reuse, recycle, rethink, repair, refuse

Slide and the follower A mechanism where one-part slides in a straight line while another part follows its motion, often used to convert rotary motion into linear motion

Smart materials Materials that change their properties in response to external conditions like heat, light, pressure, or electricity.

Social impact The effect a design or product has on communities and people's day-to-day lives

Softwood Wood from coniferous trees (trees with needles and cones), like pine, spruce, or fir

Solder (electrical) An alloy, typically made of tin and lead (or lead-free alternatives), with a low melting point used to create secure electrical connections

Soldering Bonding components or wires by melting and solidifying, ensuring conductivity and mechanical strength in circuits

Specification A detailed list of the functions and features that a design must have

Spot UV varnishing Applying a shiny, clear varnish to specific areas of a printed surface for decorative effect

Sprint A short, focused period to complete a set of tasks

Sprocket A toothed wheel designed to mesh with a chain; used to transmit rotary motion in a chain drive system

Sprocket and chain A system that uses toothed wheels (sprockets) and a chain to transfer motion

Standard component A pre-prepared part that is used in the production of many products

Static equilibrium An object is at rest, with no linear or rotational motion

Static load A constant, unmoving force applied to a structure, like a resting weight which never increases or moves

Stiffness Resistance to deformation under any applied force

Stock forms The standard shapes, sizes and forms that a material can be bought in

Stress or strain A force created by pressure on an object or material, that has the potential to damage it by changing its shape

Stress-strain graph A graph showing how a material deforms under stress

Structural member A single component of a structure

Strut A member designed to resist compressive forces

Styrofoam Extruded polystyrene foam available in blocks

Substrate The material that something is printed on

Sustainability The use of resources and energy in a way that meets the need of the present generation without compromising the ability of future generations to meet their own needs

Sustainable design Creating products that solve real problems while considering long-term impacts on people and the planet

Switch A device used to start or stop the flow of electricity in a circuit

System A collection of interconnected components or processes that interact to perform a specific function or achieve a desired outcome

System or block diagram A visual representation that outlines the main components, processes or functions of a system, typically using blocks and arrows to show inputs, operations and outputs

Tangent A line that touches a circle or curve but does not intersect it

Tangential arc An arc that touches a circle or curve but does not intersect it

Temporary joining A join designed so that it can be easily taken apart

Tension A pulling force that stretches a material, trying to make it longer or break it apart

Testing Carrying out experiments or trials to check if something works

Tetra Pak® Brand name that refers to both a multinational food packaging and processing company and the multi-layered carton containers it produces for liquid food products

Thermistor A component whose resistance changes with temperature

Thermo polymer A polymer that softens when heated and can be repeatedly reshaped upon cooling

Thermochromic Changes colour with temperature

Thermosetting polymer A polymer material that can't be remoulded or reshaped by heating or melting

Third angle projection A method of laying out an orthographic drawing with the end elevation in the bottom right and the plan view and front elevation to the left

Tie A member designed to resist tension forces

Timber Wood that has been processed and turned into a form that can be easily used, often planks

To scale A ratio that shows the relationship between the size of a drawing and the actual size of the object

Tolerance The amount of variation in a physical dimension or measurement that is allowed in a part or component

Torque A force that causes something to turn or rotate

Torsion The result of a turning or twisting force

Transistor A semiconductor device that can amplify or switch electronic signals and electrical power

Trend A general direction in which something is developing or changing, especially in fashion, technology or culture

Triangulation Using triangular shapes to enhance structural stability

Truss A triangulated framework that supports loads, commonly used in roofs and bridges

Two-point perspective A method of making a realistic three-dimensional drawing using two vanishing points and a horizon line

Unplanned obsolescence A product breaks down unexpectedly

Upcycling Transforming old or unwanted materials or artefacts into more desirable products

User experience (UX) Designing products that provide meaningful and relevant experiences to users

User interface (UI) Visual and interactive elements of the product, such as colour, typography and layout

Variable resistor A resistor whose resistance can be adjusted; also known as a potentiometer

Vector Uses mathematical equations to create scalable images without loss of quality

Velocity ratio (gear ratio) The ratio of the distances moved by the effort and the load at the same time, influencing speed and force transmission

Veneer A thin layer of wood that is glued on top of another material (like plywood or MDF) to make it look like solid wood

Virtual modelling Using software to visualise, test or simulate a product digitally

Volatile organic compound (VOC) An organic chemical that, at room temperature, releases fumes into the air. Many synthetic resins, including polyester resin and epoxy resin, release VOCs during curing or processing

Voltage A measure of electrical potential difference – unit of measurement: volt (V)

Wants The things people would like to have

Wastage The process of cutting away material to leave the shape you want

Wheel and axle A simple machine part that consists of a wheel attached to an axle

Working drawing A detailed drawing that shows dimensions, views and notes for making a product

Working property How a material behaves when it is being shaped

***x*-axis** The horizontal line of a graph

***y*-axis** The vertical line of a graph

Index

Q

R

S

T

U

V

W

X

Y

Acknowledgements

The publishers wish to thank the following for permission to reproduce photographs. Every effort has been made to trace copyright holders and to obtain their permission for the use of copyright materials. The publishers will gladly receive any information enabling them to rectify any error or omission at the first opportunity.

(t = top, c = centre, c1/2/3 = 1st/2nd/3rd centre image, b = bottom, r = right, l = left)

Thanks to the students of Al Salam School, Dubai, United Arab Emirates, for contributing examples of coursework on p347–350 and p352–353.

Thanks to the students of Jerudong International School, Brunei, for contributing examples of coursework on p28 and p82t.

Thanks to Terry Bream for his photograph on p155.

Thanks to Gary England for the image on p62.

Thanks to Matt McLain for images on p138t and p143.

Thanks to Stewart Ross for the images on p239, p240, p241t, p334 and p351.

p6–7 sayhmog/ Shutterstock, p11 Lewis Tse/ Shutterstock, p12 zhukovvvlad/ Shutterstock, p13 Jo Panuwat D/ Shutterstock, p18t Tatevik Bagdasaryan/ Shutterstock, p18b Dusan Petkovic/ Shutterstock, p19 sweeann/ Shutterstock, p20b FAMILY STOCK/ Shutterstock, p22tl Addictive Creative/ Shutterstock, p22tc Ann Haritonenko/ Shutterstock, p22tr Santhosh Varghese/ Shutterstock, p22b ricochet64/ Shutterstock, p24 Rudmer Zwerver/ Shutterstock, p25t Bilanol/ Shutterstock, p25c fokke baarssen/ Shutterstock, p25b Evgeny_V/ Shutterstock, p29t witsarut sakorn/ Shutterstock, p29c Photographee.eu/ Shutterstock, p29b NEGOVURA// Shutterstock, p30 Dawid K Photography/ Shutterstock, p34t Bankrx/ Shutterstock, p34c Gorodenkoff/ Shutterstock, p34b Tinxi/ Shutterstock, p35t INTHEBLVCK/ Shutterstock, p35b Towfiqu ahamed barbhuiya/ Shutterstock, p36t Anwarul Kabir Photo/ Shutterstock, p36b DAMRONG RATTANAPONG/ Shutterstock, p38 Dabarti CGI/ Shutterstock, p45 THICHA SATAPITANON/ Shutterstock, p46 IMG visuals icons/ Shutterstock, p51tl EcoPrint/ Shutterstock, p51tl EcoPrint/ Shutterstock, p51tr Thomas Cockrem/ Alamy, p51bl Yuriy Balagula/ Shutterstock, p51br May_Chanikran/ Shutterstock, p53 Nicholas Ahonen/ Shutterstock, p57l kazoka/ Shutterstock, p57r Media_Photos/ Shutterstock, p59t KYNA STUDIO/ Shutterstock, p59b DC Studio/ Shutterstock, p60t SofikoS/ Shutterstock, p60b grafvision/ Shutterstock, p61 NONGASIMO/ Shutterstock, p64 Miha Creative/ Shutterstock, p71 Nicole Kwiatkowski/ Shutterstock, p75b Audrius Merfeldas/ Shutterstock, p81 Gorodenkoff/ Shutterstock, p82b Frame Stock Footage/ Shutterstock, p83 Vladimir Tretyakov/ Shutterstock, p87c takepicsforfun/ Shutterstock, p87b Axtem/ Shutterstock, p88 Michael Dechev/ Shutterstock, p89tl Ground Picture/ Shutterstock, p89tr MaRoDee Photography/ Alamy, p89b discpicture/ Alamy, p95bl Preto Perola/ Shutterstock, p95br crbellette/ Shutterstock, p96 Ramon Cliff/ Shutterstock, p97tl Pit Stock/ Shutterstock, p97tc Jaromir Chalabala/ Shutterstock, p97tr mr_bom/ Shutterstock, p97b OSTILL is Franck Camhi/ Shutterstock, p98tl cowardlion/ Shutterstock, p98tr leungchopan/ Shutterstock, p98b IM Imagery/ Shutterstock, p100 Wirestock Creators/ Shutterstock, p105 Me.Karim1983/ Shutterstock, p109 Jin Odin/ Shutterstock, p110r Maksim Pasko/ Shutterstock, p114 Mikola Tsimbaluk/ Shutterstock, p133tl Achira22/ Shutterstock, p133tr Timothy Hodgkinson/ Shutterstock, p134 Viktorija Reuta/ Shutterstock, p136tl Tsekhmister/ Shutterstock, p138bl vlabo/ Shutterstock, p138bc Nunng/ Shutterstock, p138br Nafadh/ Shutterstock, p145 Hsyn20/ Shutterstock, p146l Oleg1824/ Shutterstock, p146r Engin Subasi/ Shutterstock, p152 Ziga Cetrtic/ Shutterstock, p154 Wasana Kunpol/ Shutterstock, p158 Runrun2/ Shutterstock, p162–163 VLADGRIN/ Shutterstock, p166t photo_korobko_olya/ Shutterstock, p166c1 OttoPles/ Shutterstock, p166c2 MIGUEL G. SAAVEDRA/ Shutterstock, p166c3 Azura Yeray/ Shutterstock, p166b Daniele RUSSO/ Shutterstock, p167t Sawangkaew/ Shutterstock, p167c1 MikeDotta/ Shutterstock, p167c2 Alex Yeung/ Shutterstock, p167c3 Evawae/ Shutterstock, p167c4 Rhys Leonard/ Shutterstock, p167b StudioIlanP/ Shutterstock, p168 EveVectors/ Shutterstock, p170l Zmaj88/ Shutterstock, p170r Matt Watdle/ Shutterstock, p172t James Marvin Phelps/ Shutterstock, p172c1 theeraphatt uamduang/ Shutterstock, p172c2 Artur Makarov/ Shutterstock, p172c3 Zachary VanHoy/ Shutterstock, p172b tolobalaguer.com/ Shutterstock, p173t sae jun oh/ Shutterstock, p173c1 zhang sheng/

Shutterstock, p173c2 Hanif Sparkle Of Lens/ Shutterstock, p173c3 yas_creative/ Shutterstock, p173b Nattika/ Shutterstock, p174t Pavel Hlystov/ Shutterstock, p174c eyal granith/ Shutterstock, p174b Stock image/ Shutterstock, p175 prapann/ Shutterstock, p176t sockagphoto/ Shutterstock, p176c Cliff Day/ Shutterstock, p176b PARALAXIS/ Shutterstock, p178 Aumm graphixphoto/ Shutterstock, p180t OLGA DANA/ Shutterstock, p180c1 T.Krit/ Shutterstock, p180c2 evkaz/ Shutterstock, p180c3 Nurul Akmal/ Shutterstock, p180b Funtay/ Shutterstock, p181t KimTieng Tow/ Shutterstock, p181c1 gresei/ Shutterstock, p181c2 Chumphon_TH/ Shutterstock, p181c3 ALEXANDER KOLIKOV/ Shutterstock, p181b Mouse family/ Shutterstock, p182t InWay/ Shutterstock, p182c ancient-image/ Shutterstock, p182b Parilov/ Shutterstock, p183 jirayu0036/ Shutterstock, p184 Valeriy Lebedev/ Shutterstock, p185 ArtSvetlana/ Shutterstock, p187 Parilov/ Shutterstock, p188t TASER/ Shutterstock, p188c Luciavonu/ Shutterstock, p188b ZRyzner/ Shutterstock, p189t Elder Vieira Salles/ Shutterstock, p189c Pablo77/ Shutterstock, p189b PK-Donovan/ Shutterstock, p190 Real Sports Photos/ Shutterstock, p191l Istomina Olena/ Shutterstock, p191r Daniel Krason/ Shutterstock, p194t Teerapong mahawan/ Shutterstock, p194b Photo Oz/ Shutterstock, p197t Igor Pshenin/ Shutterstock, p197c2 Alexander-2020/ Shutterstock, p197c3 Trong Nguyen/ Shutterstock, p197c4 Bill McKelvie/ Shutterstock, p197c5 Tarzhanova/ Shutterstock, p197c6 ONI SAHRONI/ Shutterstock, p197b Opilian/ Shutterstock, p198t Chongsiri Chaitongngam/ Shutterstock, p198c1 Nafadh/ Shutterstock, p198c2 ZhakYaroslav/ Shutterstock, p198b Manuel Trinidad Mesa/ Shutterstock, p199 NASA/JPL/Corby Waste/ Wikimedia Commons, p200l wabeno/ Shutterstock, p200c graalz/ Shutterstock, p200r Sergey Ryzhov/ Shutterstock, p201t Lotus_studio/ Shutterstock, p201c1 RedDaxLuma/ Shutterstock, p201c2 Artography/ Shutterstock, p201c3 Flas100/ Shutterstock, p201c4 rawf8/ Shutterstock, p201b Martin Haas/ Shutterstock, p202t Sergiy Kuzmin/ Shutterstock, p202c1 Ana Hollan/ Shutterstock, p202c2 Ariyaporn chumkong/ Shutterstock, p202c3 Sean van Tonder/ Shutterstock, p202c4 Matveev Aleksandr/ Shutterstock, p202b Anton Starikov/ Shutterstock, p204t BaudaLab/ Shutterstock, p204c1 laurello/ Shutterstock, p204c2 ZhakYaroslav/ Shutterstock, p204c3 leungchopan/ Shutterstock, p204b Zyabich family/ Shutterstock, p205t Zyabich family/ Shutterstock, p205c1 Chelmicky/ Shutterstock, p205c2 Sergey Ryzhov/ Shutterstock, p205b Mr.1/ Shutterstock, p206 Around the World Photos/ Shutterstock, p207t Igor Pshenin/ Shutterstock, p207c pinkfloyd yilmaz uslu/ Shutterstock, p207b MDV Edwards/ Shutterstock, p208t KingSaxlingham/ Shutterstock, p208c1 Ors Mate/ Shutterstock, p208c2 Mr Bag/ Shutterstock, p208b kikujungboy CC/ Shutterstock, p209 Huseyin Eren Obuz/ Shutterstock, p210 Nafadh/ Shutterstock, p211 Stephen B. Goodwin/ Shutterstock, p214t New Africa/ Shutterstock, p214b Prabhjit S. Kalsi/ Shutterstock, p215t Steve Cordory/ Shutterstock, p215c AdrianFinlay/ Shutterstock, p215bl PhotoRelax/ Shutterstock, p215br Voyagerix/ Shutterstock, p216t xiaorui/ Shutterstock, p216b Zoltan Fabian/ Shutterstock, p218t Cliff Day/ Shutterstock, p218c NataVilman/ Shutterstock, p218b Sve_M/ Shutterstock, p219t SmarterMedium/ Shutterstock, p219c1 Brian A Jackson/ Shutterstock, p219c2 Ezalo/ Shutterstock, p219c3 pondpony/ Shutterstock, p219b trezordia/ Shutterstock, p220t Ammit Jack/ Shutterstock, p220c1 TunedIn by Westend61/ Shutterstock, p220c2 Vladimir Kramin/ Shutterstock, p220c3 Spok83/ Shutterstock, p220c4 SURAKIT SAWANGCHIT/ Shutterstock, p220c5 Jong42/ Shutterstock, p220c6 ANDRANIK HAKOBYAN/ Shutterstock, p220b FabrikaSimf/ Shutterstock, p221t sueperjoe1/ Shutterstock, p221c Aek Foto/ Shutterstock, p221b chemical industry/ Shutterstock, p223t Giruba_86/ Shutterstock, p223c Apurnomo/ Shutterstock, p223b ADS-DESIGN/ Shutterstock, p224l STRINGER Image/ Shutterstock, p224r Michael Leslie/ Shutterstock, p225t Technicsorn Stocker/ Shutterstock, p225c1 stuar/ Shutterstock, p225c2 Jeffrey B. Banke/ Shutterstock, p225c3 Nomad_Soul/ Shutterstock, p225b kasarp studio/ Shutterstock, p226t alan payne/ Shutterstock, p226b Sergey Ryzhov/ Shutterstock, p227 Aleksandr Kondratov/ Shutterstock, p229tl Pixel B/ Shutterstock, p229tc Soon_Sound/ Shutterstock, p229tr Pixel B/ Shutterstock, p229b Denis Morin/ Shutterstock, p230t ZhakYaroslav/ Shutterstock, p230c Roman Zaiets/ Shutterstock, p230bl nimito/ Shutterstock, p230bc Surasak_Photo/ Shutterstock, p230br oYOo/ Shutterstock, p231l koosen/ Shutterstock, p231r StevanZZ/ Shutterstock, p232t genkur/ Shutterstock, p232c Lazy_Bear/ Shutterstock, p232b Phonlamai Photo/ Shutterstock, p233t Jenson/ Shutterstock, p233bl MNBB Studio/ Shutterstock, p233bc FUN FUN PHOTO/ Shutterstock, p233br BigBlueStudio/ Shutterstock, p235 Kryuchka Yaroslav/ Shutterstock, p236t Nordroden/ Shutterstock, p236c i viewfinder/ Shutterstock, p236b noomcpk/ Shutterstock, p237 Biehler Michael/ Shutterstock, p238 Zsolt Biczo/ Shutterstock, p241bl H_Ko/ Shutterstock, p241br matka_Wariatka/ Shutterstock, p245 PeopleImages/ Shutterstock, p248 Ole.CNX/ Shutterstock, p249 Kateryna Muzhevska/ Shutterstock, p250t Kornienko Alexandr/ Shutterstock, p250b Rohane Hamilton/ Shutterstock, p252t HungryCat/ Shutterstock, p252c grey_and/ Shutterstock, p252b Byjeng/ Shutterstock, p254–255 millann/ Shutterstock, p256 Chaosamran_Studio/ Shutterstock, p257l valiantsin suprunovich/ Shutterstock, p257r arigato/ Shutterstock, p258 oleschwander/ Shutterstock, p264t sasirin pamai/ Shutterstock, p264c1 Maha Heang 245789/ Shutterstock, p264c2 Patrick Hatt/ Shutterstock, p264b HelgaQ/ Shutterstock, p265t Stokkete/ Shutterstock, p265c1 Andika Nur/ Shutterstock, p265c2 asharkyu/ Shutterstock, p265c3 Svetliy/ Shutterstock, p265b MarinaGrigorivna/ Shutterstock, p266 Me dia/ Shutterstock, p268 DC Studio/ Shutterstock, p269t vladgphoto/ Shutterstock, p269b Photology1971/ Shutterstock, p273t Dragan drmr_foto/ Shutterstock, p273bl Lemonsoup14/ Shutterstock, p273br BigTunaOnline/ Shutterstock, p274 Mr_Mrs_Marcha/ Shutterstock, p276 Lemonsoup14/ Shutterstock, p277t Vandy Apeldo/ Shutterstock, p277c AlvaroMP/ Shutterstock, p277b Kononov Oleh/ Shutterstock, p292 SeventyFour/ Shutterstock, p296 posteriori/ Shutterstock, p302 Andrew Krasovitckii/ Shutterstock, p308t Woodpond/ Shutterstock, p308cl Odua Images/ Shutterstock, p308c Taigi/ Shutterstock, p308cr joingate/ Shutterstock, p308bl Ilja Generalov/ Shutterstock, p308br Lichtmeister/ Shutterstock, p310 Pixaby/ Shutterstock, p312t S. Kawita/ Shutterstock, p312c1 Hasim Ramle/ Shutterstock, p312c2 DashaStarr/ Shutterstock, p312b Mieayamjogja/ Shutterstock, p313t Sakurai. do/ Shutterstock, p313c Early Spring/ Shutterstock, p313b Elena Chevalier/ Shutterstock, p313c Vladyslav Lehir/ Shutterstock, p313b MarinaGrigorivna/ Shutterstock, p314t vallefrias/ Shutterstock, p314c Vladyslav Lehir/ Shutterstock, p314b MarinaGrigorivna/ Shutterstock, p316 EvgeniiAnd/ Shutterstock, p318t Suthida Sririttha/ Shutterstock, p318c1 sema srinouljan/ Shutterstock, p318c2 AnnJane/ Shutterstock, p318b vvetc1/ Shutterstock, p319t FabrikaSimf/ Shutterstock, p319c1 Aleksey Mnogosmyslov/ Shutterstock, p319c2 guruXOX/ Shutterstock, p319b photo_gonzo/ Shutterstock, p320 stoimilov/ Shutterstock, p322l Mateusz Atroszko/ Shutterstock, p322r kobitler/ Shutterstock, p323t Cat Us/ Shutterstock, p323b VGV MEDIA/ Shutterstock, p325t rawf8/ Shutterstock, p325b gene emrah/ Shutterstock, p326t r2dpr/ Shutterstock, p326c1 Gilbert - Illustration/ Shutterstock, p326c2 Ulifah Anna/ Shutterstock, p326c3 Shams Suleymanova/ Shutterstock, p326b designers circle/ Shutterstock, p331 metamorworks/ Shutterstock, p332 guteksk7/ Shutterstock, p335 socrates471/ Shutterstock, p340–341 Sailorr/ Shutterstock, p345 Pixel-Shot/ Shutterstock

Authors

Professor Dawne Irving-Bell, PhD, is a Head of Scholarship of Teaching and Learning at Arden University, UK, and Deputy Chair of AdvanceHE's National CATE Committee.
With extensive experience working across secondary, further, and Higher Education, as a teacher, Dawne is passionate about creating opportunities for others. Dedicated to raising the profile of scholarship, she established the award-winning National Teaching Repository, an Open Educational Resource with proven global reach and impact. Dawne enjoys lecturing on visual thinking and advocates for technology education, for which she received a National Award sponsored by The Royal Academy of Engineering in recognition of her outstanding contribution to teacher education. Dawne is a National Teaching Fellow, Principal Fellow of the Higher Education Academy and holds a Collaborative Award for Teaching Excellence.

Gary England is Head of Design & Technology at Jerudong International School, Brunei, having previously led D&T departments for over 10 years across several schools in Wiltshire, UK. He has supported school improvement in D&T and Art & Design and overseen STEM development across a multi-academy trust. Gary has led large-scale STEAM and sustainability initiatives across year groups and schools, inspiring students to address real-world challenges through creative and sustainable design. He is passionate about equipping young people with the skills and mindset needed to design innovative solutions for a more sustainable future.

Sarah Finnigan is an inspiring educator, leader, and lecturer in D&T at Liverpool John Moores University. With over a decade of experience across UK and international schools, she brings passion, creativity, and authenticity to D&T teacher education. Currently completing her Doctorate in Educational Leadership, Sarah's work focuses on teacher wellbeing, mentoring, and fostering positive professional relationships, all while supporting the continuous development of educators in the field. Dedicated to shaping future educators, she emphasises purpose, empathy, and innovation in teaching. A passionate advocate for D&T teacher development and student success, Sarah integrates evidence-based practice, leadership research, and a growth mindset philosophy, believing that effort transforms ability into accomplishment.

Dr Matt McLain is an academic at Liverpool John Moores University and a leading scholar and researcher in D&T education. With over three decades of experience as a teacher, teacher educator, and researcher, Matt has influenced national curriculum and qualification reforms in England and contributed to international policy discussions. He co-edited the Bloomsbury Handbook of Technology Education and serves as Associate Editor for two leading D&T journals. A former Advanced Skills Teacher and recipient of the D&T Association Excellence Award, Matt is passionate about supporting teachers and students to engage with creative, evidence-informed approaches to design and innovation.

Stewart Ross is a highly experienced design educator and curriculum specialist with 18 years of experience teaching in London and as Head of Design at schools in Hong Kong. Currently serving as a teacher and BTEC Coordinator at International College Hong Kong, Stewart is deeply passionate about maker education, design thinking, and human-centred design. His expertise extends to international curriculum development and assessment. A frequent speaker at international education conferences, Stewart also enjoys connecting his professional passion for design education with the outdoors through his interest in trail design.

Professor David Wooff is Director of Apprenticeship Quality and Regulation at BPP Education Group (UK) and a leading voice in D&T education. With more than 30 years of experience across schools, universities, and national bodies, he has shaped curriculum, quality assurance, and teacher development in the UK and globally. Co-editor of the Bloomsbury Handbook of Technology Education, he has contributed to both UN and ISSOTL initiatives. A Fellow of the Chartered College of Teaching, Society for Education and Training, and Senior Fellow of the HEA, he is also Vice-Chair of the Frank Field Education Trust, and he champions inclusive, evidence-informed education.

Notes